"The story of Christian creeds and confessions is fascinating, and Fairbairn and Reeves are spectacular at exploring the story of Spirit-led, faithful wisdom throughout the centuries. Tracing the development of the Christian faith informs our own engagement with Scripture today."

—**Justin S. Holcomb**, Reformed Theological Seminary and Gordon-Conwell Theological Seminary; author of *Know the Creeds and Councils* and *Know the Heretics*

"This volume provides a wonderful introduction to the creeds and confessions of the Christian church. It attends carefully to the various historical contexts within which these diverse texts were written and deployed and offers insightful comment on the theological claims that they advance. The result is a work that spurs the reader to greater appreciation and deeper understanding of the tradition of the church and the way in which its official texts have served at different points to express unity, continuity, and disruption. Above all, Fairbairn and Reeves witness to the desirability of taking these documents seriously not only as historical artifacts but also as ongoing witnesses, insisting that what binds Christians together is of much greater significance than what separates them."

—**Paul T. Nimmo**, University of Aberdeen

"A fine guide to creeds and confessions and an engaging narrative of church history from the perspective of doctrinal development. Of special note is the material on the early church, which will help fuel and inform current Protestant interest in the patristic discussions of the doctrines of God and Christ."

—**Carl R. Trueman**, Grove City College

"Fairbairn and Reeves trace in readable fashion the entire history of the church's creeds and confessions. Animating this development, maintain Fairbairn and Reeves, is neither morals nor doctrine per se. Instead, it is the name of the triune God that led Christians through the centuries to articulate their faith in creeds and confessions. Uniting Protestant convictions, ecumenical sensitivity, and scholarly acumen, this book is a solid introduction to the common heritage of the church."

—**Hans Boersma**, Nashotah House, Wisconsin

"Many churches and individual Christians who were once guided by but have forgotten about their rich heritage of creeds and confessions are beginning to 'remember.' And many others who were never consciously attentive to this heritage are discovering the knowledge and wisdom to be found in the creeds and confessions. Fairbairn and Reeves have provided all of these seekers with a valuable resource. They clearly and thoughtfully tell the story of the form, substance, and significance of Christian belief as this has been set forth in creeds and   ʒuidebook."

. **David Buschart**, Denver Seminary

T0385440

The Story of Creeds and Confessions

The Story of Creeds and Confessions

Tracing the Development of the Christian Faith

Donald Fairbairn and Ryan M. Reeves

Baker Academic

a division of Baker Publishing Group
Grand Rapids, Michigan

© 2019 by Donald Fairbairn and Ryan M. Reeves

Published by Baker Academic
a division of Baker Publishing Group
PO Box 6287, Grand Rapids, MI 49516-6287
www.bakeracademic.com

Printed in the United States of America

Library of Congress Cataloging-in-Publication Data
Names: Fairbairn, Donald, author.
Title: The story of creeds and confessions : tracing the development of the Christian faith / Donald
    Fairbairn and Ryan M. Reeves.
Description: Grand Rapids : Baker Academic, a division of Baker Publishing Group, 2019. |
    Includes bibliographical references and index.
Identifiers: LCCN 2018054492 | ISBN 9780801098161 (pbk.)
Subjects: LCSH: Creeds—History. | Church history.
Classification: LCC BT990 .F345 2019 | DDC 238.09—dc23
LC record available at https://lccn.loc.gov/2018054492

ISBN 978-1-5409-6219-5 (casebound)

Baker Publishing Group publications use paper produced from sustainable forestry practices and post-consumer waste whenever possible.

Donald Fairbairn dedicates this book
to the memory of Lionel R. Wickham,
his Doktorvater and friend,
whose passing on December 17, 2017,
came as the text of this book was being finalized.

Ryan Reeves dedicates this book
to Zoë, Owen, and Dexter

Contents

Part 4 The Reformation and Confessionalism (1500–1650)

Part 5 Confessions in the Modern World (1650–Present)

Preface

In one sense, the origins of this book lie at the University of Cambridge, where both of us did our doctoral studies (Fairbairn in the late 1990s in patristics, and Reeves in the late 2000s in early modern Christianity). It was there that we developed our love for our respective periods of Christian history and the perspectives that we present here. In another sense, this book's genesis lies with Gordon-Conwell Theological Seminary, which brought us together in friendship. We both joined the faculty of Gordon-Conwell in 2010, even interviewing on the same day, and the years since that time have given us opportunities for collaboration in the teaching of church history and theology. It was through our teaching at Gordon-Conwell that we honed the specific ideas that dominate this book.

We believe that the story of creeds and confessions is a single story, in which the latter developments built on earlier ones, and we have tried in this book to allow the consistency of that story to shine through in the midst of the many tensions between East and West, between Roman Catholic, Orthodox, and Protestant Christianity, and between different Protestant traditions. Accordingly, we have sought to write with a single voice throughout the book. At the same time, it should come as no surprise that each of us has taken the lead in the area of his specialty. Chapter 1 and the conclusion to the book are the work of both of us. Chapters 2 through 10 are largely Fairbairn's work, and chapters 11 through 18 are mainly Reeves's.

Along the way, we have benefited from the help of many people. Special thanks are due to Robert Hosack at Baker Academic, who graciously agreed to allow Reeves to bring Fairbairn into this project, even though a contract had already been issued with Reeves as sole author. Thanks go to Aldo Mondin and Kate Hendrickson for their help reading early drafts of several chapters, and Aldo must also be thanked for his help in selecting images, maps, and other important additions to the book.

At this point, it is appropriate to write a word about where one may find the many creeds and confessions we cite in this book, because Christian creeds and confessions have been collected and printed in many different places. Throughout this book, we cite the documents from modern editions or translations, often in standard series but occasionally in less well-known places. But students and interested laypeople are likely to want a one-stop shop, a single place where they can find many of these documents. For much of the twentieth century, the best such one-stop shop (still readily available and useful) was Philip Schaff's *The Creeds of Christendom*. A convenient and inexpensive one-volume edition is John H. Leith's *Creeds of the Churches*. The new library standard is the monumental work of scholarship by Jaroslav Pelikan and Valerie Hotchkiss, *Creeds and Confessions of Faith in the Christian Tradition* (*CCFCT*). In our footnotes, we include not only the citations of the works from which we are quoting but also references to the volume and page numbers of *CCFCT* where the documents may be found. Of course, many creeds and confessions are also readily available online.

D. F. and R. M. R.
Gordon-Conwell Theological Seminary
Charlotte and Jacksonville
March 2018

Abbreviations

ACW Ancient Christian Writers
CCFCT *Creeds and Confessions of Faith in the Christian Tradition.* Edited by Jaroslav Pelikan and Valerie Hotchkiss. 4 vols. New Haven: Yale University Press, 2003.
FC Fathers of the Church
NPNF¹ *Nicene and Post-Nicene Fathers*, Series 1. Edited by Philip Schaff. 1886–89. 14 vols. Reprint, Peabody, MA: Hendrickson, 1994.
NPNF² *Nicene and Post-Nicene Fathers*, Series 2. Edited by Philip Schaff and Henry Wace. 1890–1900. 14 vols. Reprint, Peabody, MA: Hendrickson, 1994.
PL Patrologia Latina [= *Patrologiae Cursus Completus.* Series Latina]. Edited by Jacques-Paul Migne. 217 vols. Paris, 1844–64.
PPS Popular Patristics Series

1

Beginning the Story

At the very heart of the Christian faith lies not an ethical system (as important as that is), nor a set of commandments (although there are many of those), nor even a set of doctrines (although they, too, are very important), but a *name*. Peter tells the Jewish leaders, "There is no other name under heaven given among men by which we must be saved" (Acts 4:12). Following Jesus's command, new Christians are baptized "in the name of the Father and of the Son and of the Holy Spirit" (Matt. 28:19). Indeed, by calling ourselves Christians, we are naming ourselves after Christ, our Lord. The most important thing about us is not what we do, or even what we believe per se, but to whom we belong as shown by the one whose name we bear.

Furthermore, the one to whom we belong is also the one *in whom we believe*. Paul writes to the Romans, "If you confess with your mouth that Jesus is Lord and believe in your heart that God raised him from the dead, you will be saved" (Rom. 10:9). This simple statement includes a fact that we believe—God raised Jesus from the dead—but even more fundamental is its confession of who this Jesus whom God raised from the dead was. He was and is the Lord. Therefore, at the most basic level, being Christian involves confessing who Jesus Christ is in relation to God, affirming that we belong to him because we bear his name, and believing the fundamental truths of his history—his incarnation, life, death, and resurrection. What we do grows out of what we confess, which grows out of the one to whom we belong and in whom we believe, the one by whose name we are called. As a result, throughout Christian history, believers have sought to articulate in summary

1

statements—creeds and confessions—the one in whom we believe, what we believe about him and ourselves, and what the implications of our faith in him are. The story of creeds and confessions is an account of these efforts on the part of Christians. As such, this story is an integral part of the story of Christianity more generally.

Why Should We Care about Creeds and Confessions from the Past?

Before we even begin such a story, however, we as twenty-first-century Christians in the West need to acknowledge that we have a problem. Creeds and confessions contain language that doesn't come from the Bible. Many of us proudly—and correctly—affirm our allegiance to Scripture alone as the ultimate authority for our faith. Why then should we use any language other than the Bible's own words to describe that faith? And not only do creeds and confessions come from elsewhere than the Bible, but they also are other people's articulations of our faith. Why would we want to dredge up dusty language from the distant past rather than speak of Jesus ourselves, in our own way?

These are good questions, and taken together they drive stakes into the ground to delineate two major features of Western (especially American) Protestant Christianity: biblicism and individualism. "I have no creed but the Bible," we often say. This statement carries with it good intentions to stick to the Bible and avoid the blind adoption of merely human ideas. We have elevated to iconic status the rugged individual who questions authority wherever he or she finds it. An ideal man or woman of faith, we insist, is a critical thinker, an unsubmissive student, who questions the ideas of the past and engages directly (and perhaps exclusively) with the Bible in order to deepen his or her faith. Our romantic model is the frontier woman or man reading the Bible alone—one person reading only one book—grasping its truth and speaking of Jesus using the words of Scripture. With such a model before us, what need do we have of creeds or confessions—or of a book that tells their story?

To address this issue, we need to go back to the assertion with which we began this chapter. Christianity is about a name. As Christians, we proclaim the name of the person to whom we belong, in whom we believe. Our life revolves around the joyous task of knowing this person whom we name and of speaking about him. Indeed, knowing and speaking are closely related. We have to *get to know* someone in order to *know* that person. We have to *learn to speak* in order to *talk*. When we first come to know Jesus, we know

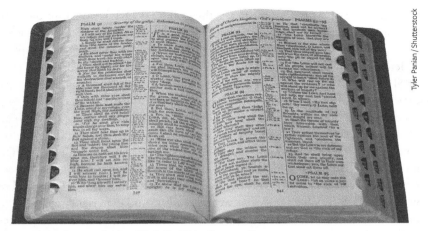

Do we need creeds or confessions? Or is the Bible all we need?

something about him, and we can say something. We may be prone to misplace our words, to speak haltingly or without confidence, or to speak too confidently without balance or accuracy. But we can speak of him—there is no Christian who has nothing to say about Jesus. However, to speak *well* of Jesus, we have to get to know him—through his Word, through prayer, through fellowship with other believers.

Getting to know Christ is akin to getting to know one's husband or wife. Any who have married can confess that they did not marry the person they thought they did. The ecstasy of the honeymoon doesn't change the fact that you wake up with a virtual stranger. You may be one flesh, but you are hardly one heart, one mind—at least not yet. And now that stranger is never going away! Our faith follows a similar path. We accept the embrace of Christ and the covenant in his blood; we are washed, anointed, and brimming with the joy of his peace. But we hardly know him—how could we? We were just recently rebels, far off, forsaking his gospel and forging our own way in this world. How can we really know him at the very beginning of Christian life? Over time, though, we get to know him as we get to know a spouse, and we can speak of him with an intimacy similar to the way we might speak of a spouse after many years of marriage.

In order to speak well, however, we need more than intimacy, more than "getting to know." We also need what could be called a grammar. Children must pick up the grammar of their native language, and before they do so, their expressions of love and relationship are clumsy and their words to describe love even clumsier (however charming!). So, too, Christians must learn the grammar of Christian intimacy, the grammar of relationships described through a Christian lens, the grammar of living in light of the one whose name we bear. We learn this grammar, first and foremost, from Scripture. But to learn it only from Scripture is akin to being handed the complete works of Shakespeare and being asked to describe the English language therefrom. Everything is in that massive volume—all the beautiful turns of phrase, the precision, balance, and elegance of which the language is capable in the hands of perhaps its greatest writer. But most of us could use a guide to help us navigate—let alone explain—the riches of Shakespeare's English. Similarly, most of us could use a guide to navigate the riches of Scripture—not as a replacement for Scripture, but as a brief summary that can help us find our way around and talk about what we are reading and experiencing. We affirm that the Bible stands alone as our ultimate authority, but if we are honest, we'll likely admit that we need some help with the Bible, in much the same way that we need some help with Shakespeare. Creeds and confessions—the grammar of the Christian faith provided for us by the church of the past—can help us to speak well of Jesus, whose name we bear.

There is yet another reason why many of us may object to the use of creeds and confessions. In contemporary English, the word "creed" often refers to a political allegiance or a general worldview. It usually has negative connotations, as if the act of holding to a creed makes one intolerant, in contrast to those who accept everyone regardless of race, gender, or creed. Well-meaning Christians, thinking of "creed" in this sense, proudly claim no creed but Jesus. And the word "confession" sounds even worse to contemporary ears, with connotations that we need to apologize for what we confess, or that we confess only when we have been placed in a situation where we have no choice.[1]

A look at the original sense of the word "creed" can help us overcome these negative connotations and see the value of giving attention to creeds and confessions. The Greek word used in the early church for a creed was *symbolon*, from which we get the English word "symbol." A *symbolon*, in the most basic use of the word, was a combination of two pieces placed side by side, allowing a person to verify one piece because it matched the second piece.[2] Think of a painting or tapestry, cut into two pieces, which are then verified by placing them back together again to show that they line up. We know that one piece is authentic because it matches the second. Nothing

---

1. For a discussion of several related reasons for an anticreedal bias in much contemporary Protestantism, see Carl R. Trueman, *The Creedal Imperative* (Wheaton: Crossway, 2012), 21–49.

2. Henry G. Liddell and Robert Scott, *A Greek-English Lexicon*, revised and augmented by H. S. Jones and R. McKenzie (Oxford: Clarendon, 1843 [9th ed. 1940, supplement added 1996]), 1676.

better describes the relationship between personal faith and ancient creeds: we have faith in Christ, but we must verify that we have not invented Christ according to our own fantasies. It is as if the authors of creeds and confessions are saying to us, "Come and lay your faith down next to this pattern and see whether the images match, or whether they reveal a fundamental difference between your impressions and the faith of our fathers. Should these images differ, then reflect, struggle against the parameters of the faith to see whether there is something to be learned."

The writers of creeds and confessions did not envision that we could quickly grasp every facet of the creed in one reading—as if the faith could be swallowed in one gulp and the bones of heresy spat out. Instead, creeds are, to recast a romantic phrase, *living documents*—not because they adapt to fit our changing attitudes, but because our attitudes must always be checked against their original design. Creeds, as symbols, instruct us in the design of our theological house; they are like blueprints. Imagine us, as contemporary builders, laying a foundation for rooms that, once built, will make the house unlivable because we proudly proclaim that we have no need of blueprints!

Creeds and confessions were not meant to be comprehensive, at least not comprehensive in the sense that all subsequent discussion became moot.[3] Christians over the centuries never shared our modern desire to explain everything all at once, even in the context of a lengthy confession. Their intention was to give Christians a guide, a blueprint—the second half of the *symbolon*—so that we might avoid the many pitfalls of those who too hastily attempted to explain Christ in their own words. And so creeds and confessions were pressed into service against a staggering variety of theological problems. The impulse of the church to write down its grammar sprang partly from the fact that some Christians, in their zeal to emphasize a certain facet of theology, had adopted views of God or Christ that were closer to their own imaginations than to the Scriptures. Far from being a means to depart from the Bible, creeds and confessions served to warn of the danger of straying from Scripture.

But the original design of a creed or confession, even if clear, still needs interpretation and explanation today. Creeds are composed of words used to encapsulate the biblical drama, just as we do when we choose to boil the essence of the gospel message down to a single concept such as grace, kingdom, evangel, salvation. There is nothing wrong with doing this, but such words demand an explanation. Imagine a pastor, in answering questions

---

3. As we will see in part 4, confessions often were not designed to cover each topic, and even if they did treat most topics, they did not cover them exhaustively.

about the faith, simply placing a Bible in our hands and saying, "This is our faith." There is nothing wrong with the pastor's motives—the Scriptures are the source of our faith, and we will do wonders for our faith if we begin a lifetime of exploration in the Old and New Testaments. But it would be a dereliction of duty if the pastor *never* helped us understand anything other than the individual passages of Scripture. He or she would have no justification either for preaching, counseling, teaching, exhorting, and so on—all of which require a pastor to gather and to apply the biblical faith rather than simply to read and preach the Bible passage by passage.

We gather our faith so as to explain it in shorthand all the time, and so do the creeds and confessions. We use language for our faith that is not found in the Bible, and so do the creeds. Like the writers of creeds, we understand that the Scriptures are meant to shape our language about Christ and his kingdom, how they relate to the covenant of the Old Testament, and how we serve the Lord from the cross until the final resurrection. Creeds and confessions can thus be an indispensable aid in helping us draw near to the Scriptures, draw near to the Jesus of the Scriptures whose name we bear, and speak well of him. They are worthy of our attention.

The Chronology of Creeds and Confessions

While the effort to confess in whom and what we believe has gone on throughout the entire two millennia of Christian history, that effort has been concentrated in two major time periods. The first is what we call the patristic period, the several hundred years after the end of the New Testament. The word "patristic" comes from the Latin word for "father," and the great Christian thinkers who articulated and reflected on the Christian faith in the centuries after Christ are collectively known as the church fathers. The patristic period began about AD 100, and scholars give varying dates for its close. For purposes of this book, we consider the patristic period—what we call the era of the creeds—to have extended until about 500, by which time all the ancient creeds were either in or near their final form.

The second period of intense confessional activity was the time of the Reformation. This period began in the early sixteenth century, and Martin Luther's alleged nailing of his Ninety-Five Theses to the door of the Schlosskirche in Wittenberg on October 31, 1517, serves as a nice symbolic starting point.[4] A convenient ending date for the Reformation is 1647, after

---

4. We write "alleged" because there is some dispute about whether and how this event actually happened. See our discussion in chap. 13.

the last of the great Reformation-era confessions, the Westminster Confession of Faith, was ratified. Using round numbers, we consider the Reformation period to extend from around 1500 to 1650.

As a result, the chronological arrangement of this book is as follows: Part 1 deals with the ancient creeds and covers approximately the years 100–500. Part 2 deals with the way both the East and the West explored the theology of the creeds, as well as the role of creeds in the split between East and West. It thus covers the period of roughly 500–900. Part 3 turns to medieval Europe and concerns the movement from creedal to confessional theology in the period 900–1500. Part 4 considers the Reformation from 1500 to 1650, and the writing of the great confessions by Protestants, as well as the reactions from Roman Catholics and Eastern Orthodox. Finally, part 5 deals with confession writing in the modern world, from 1650 to the present but especially in the nineteenth and twentieth centuries, again dealing with all three branches of the church. Because creed writing was concentrated in the patristic period, and confession writing occurred principally at the time of the Reformation, parts 1 and 4 are by far the longest.

Creeds versus Confessions: What's the Difference?

At this point one may well ask what the difference is between a creed and a confession, if both of them aim to articulate the Christian faith in summary form. The simple answer to this question, an answer that is by no means wrong, is that a creed is a summary statement written early in Christian history, and a confession is a summary statement written later in Christian history. Hence we have patristic creeds but Reformation-era confessions (or, for that matter, medieval or modern confessions). Beneath this obvious difference, though, is a much more fundamental one. Creeds are short statements (rarely composed of more than a couple dozen lines), they always focus on the Trinity, and they are designed with fixed wording so that they can be used in a liturgical context.[5] In contrast, confessions are almost always longer (usually several dozen paragraphs in length, and sometimes much longer than that), and while they reaffirm the great trinitarian statements of the creeds, they usually expend most of their ink on issues that *derive* from our faith in the Trinity. For example, the church and the sacraments get a lot of press in the

5. Recent scholarship has shown that the main difference between a creed and a rule of faith in the early church was that the former was meant to be used liturgically. See Liuwe H. Westra, *The Apostles' Creed: Origin, History, and Some Early Commentaries*, Instrumenta patristica et medievalia 43 (Turnhout: Brepols, 2002), 37–39.

Protestant confessions, even though those issues receive only brief mention in the creeds, which are dominated by the Trinity.

When we look at creeds and confessions this way, we can understand why the creeds were produced during the patristic period and the confessions only later. We have already seen that the most fundamental aspect of Christian faith is the name of the one to whom we belong. Since that is the case, the first task for the great Christian thinkers who articulated our faith was to summarize and explain the name of the Father and of the Son and of the Holy Spirit. Statements organized around and focused on the three persons thus arose very early in Christian history. These statements then became the basis for longer statements treating other aspects of the faith that derive from the name. Thus, short summaries of the one in whom we believe naturally preceded and led to longer statements about what we believe. Creeds came first, and confessions built on them.[6] This fact not only explains the chronological distinction between creeds and confessions; it also provides the rationale for linking them in a single book such as this one.

There is another distinction between creeds and confessions that is closely related: the distinction between local and universal statements. At one level, all theological statements are local. That is, all such statements are influenced by the particular situation in which they arise and the particular problems they address. This is true of the biblical writings themselves, which is why we insist on "context, context, context" as we interpret the texts. It is also true of every other writing produced in human history. The specific context affects the way the ideas are presented. Thus, even the early creeds were local and contextual. There were particular purposes (such as baptism) for which the creeds were written, and there were specific problems or mistakes (heresies, if you will) against which the creeds tried to guard. A creed might be written in, say, Antioch, without any direct attention to what another creed from Rome said. But as we will see, over time creeds became standardized, and the very fact that they all focused on the Trinity meant that they *could be* standardized and gain a high degree of similarity. In addition to this "accidental" commonality, the fourth century saw a deliberate movement toward standardizing and universalizing the creeds. As a result, the creeds that we are familiar with today have been agreed on by a wide swath of the Christian church. They are univer-

6. This does not mean that the church fathers never made confession-like statements. They did indicate what they believed about the Bible, the church, and so on in their theological writings. But when it came time to confess their faith communally and succinctly, they did so by focusing on the persons of the Trinity, in whom they believed, not by writing longer works focused on what they believed—akin to later confessions.

sal in character, even though we should not forget their local, contextual origins.

In contrast, confessions were local through and through. They were obviously prompted by and speaking to particular situations. Their organizational arrangement tended to follow the issues of their day and place, and the allocation of space was dominated by the issues that were most controversial, not by the issues that were and are most fundamental (which often were largely assumed). As a result, rarely did a given confession gain recognition and acceptance by a wider swath of Christendom than by the group that gave birth to it. There are Anglican confessions, Reformed confessions, Methodist confessions, even Baptist confessions, although many Baptists today tend to shy away from nonbiblical documents such as creeds or confessions. For that matter, there are Catholic confessions and Eastern Orthodox confessions. And while Christians might profit a great deal from reading confessions from a group different from their own, rarely has a group besides the one that wrote the confession endorsed it or affirmed it completely.[7]

Simply put: Creeds proclaim the common faith of the entire church throughout history, a faith in the Father, Son, and Spirit. Confessions explain the implications of that faith as understood by smaller groups within the church. Creeds precede confessions. Creeds (based on Scripture, of course) serve as the basis for confessions. Creeds are more universal than local (although they never lose their local component altogether); confessions are overtly local and contextual. With this distinction in mind, we are ready for a preliminary look at the content of this book—first the major creeds of the patristic period, and then the relation between creeds and confessions as Orthodoxy, Catholicism, and later Protestantism formed their distinct identities.

The Major Creeds

Many Christians in the West are familiar with only one creed, the Apostles' Creed. Others are familiar with two others, the Athanasian and Nicene Creeds. A few may have heard of the "Chalcedonian Creed," a misnomer because that document is not a creed but a "definition" explaining the Nicene Creed. Thus most Western Christians may be surprised to discover that neither the Apostles' Creed nor the Athanasian Creed has ever been formally approved by the whole church. As we orient ourselves to the creeds, a brief explanation of this strange fact is in order.

7. For a complementary explanation of the differences between creeds and confessions, see Justin S. Holcomb, *Know the Creeds and Councils* (Grand Rapids: Zondervan, 2014), 10–15.

The Apostles' Creed was not written by the apostles but grew out of what we call a baptismal symbol, an affirmation that baptismal candidates recited as they prepared to enter the water. There were various baptismal symbols (similar, but rarely identical) in use throughout the Christian world in the early centuries, and these baptismal symbols spawned a variety of creeds (this is the story of chap. 2). The baptismal symbol of Rome (often called the Old Roman Creed) emerged in Latin in the second century, and it gradually began to be used in other parts of the Western Christian world as the influence and prestige of the Roman episcopal see (later called the papacy) grew. The Old Roman Creed was first dubbed the Apostles' Creed in about the year 390, and it continued to evolve over time—most notably, through the addition of the famous clause "he descended into hell." It was basically complete by 500 but did not reach its final form until the early eighth century. We consider the Old Roman Creed in chapter 2 and the Apostles' Creed itself in chapter 6.

The Athanasian Creed was not written by the famous fourth-century Egyptian theologian Athanasius but by a Westerner sometime in the fifth or early sixth century. It was written in Latin (a strong reason not to attribute it to Athanasius, who wrote in Greek!), and it began to be used in Western churches in the early sixth century. From the beginning of its use, it was associated incorrectly with Athanasius in the Western world. We discuss the Athanasian Creed in chapter 7.

So these two Western creeds, the Apostles' and the Athanasian, were produced in very different ways, but what they have in common is that their eventual authority was a product of their widespread use in the Latin-speaking churches. The churches outside the Latin world, however, never officially approved them. So one could say that they hold traditional authority in one region (the West) of the church, but not "conciliar" authority, which comes only with official approval by the entire church.

In sharp contrast, the other great creed—the Nicene—emerged as the result of two major meetings of Christian leaders in the fourth century. The first meeting was held at Nicaea (a resort town just across the Bosporus from Constantinople, in what is today Iznik, on the Asian side of Istanbul) in 325 and the second at the imperial capital of Constantinople (corresponding to the "old town" on the European side of modern Istanbul) in 381. Because the results of these meetings were so widely approved in the churches, today they are referred to as the First and Second Ecumenical Councils. We dedicate chapter 3 to the conversion of the Roman Empire to Christianity, setting the stage for these great ecumenical councils. In chapter 4 we consider the story of the first two ecumenical councils in the fourth century, and thus of the Nicene Creed.

Public Domain / Wikimedia Commons

The Council of Nicaea

The delegates to the Second Ecumenical Council formally ratified the Nicene Creed, and the major groups of the Christian church that did not send delegates to that council later formally approved it as well. Today every organized Christian group that values any creeds at all accepts the Nicene Creed, and no other creed has anything like that degree of acceptance. J. N. D. Kelly, the great English historian of the creeds, famously claims, "Of all existing creeds it is the only one for which ecumenicity, or universal acceptance, can be plausibly claimed. . . . It is thus one of the few threads by which the tattered fragments of the divided robe of Christendom are held together."[8] It is thus fair to say that the Nicene Creed is *the* creed of the Christian church. Of course, this does not put the Nicene Creed on a par with Scripture, but it is a statement that Christians of all stripes and in all time periods have agreed on, and thus it deserves to be taken very seriously as a faithful summary of scriptural teaching.

Closely associated with the Nicene Creed is the Chalcedonian Definition, produced as a result of two other major meetings, later approved by most of the church. These meetings are called the Third Ecumenical Council (held in Ephesus, near modern-day Selçuk on the west coast of Turkey) in 431 and the Fourth Ecumenical Council (held in Chalcedon, near Nicaea on what is today the Asian side of Istanbul) in 451. The Chalcedonian Definition is an explanation of the Nicene Creed, giving greater specificity to the creed's statement about Christ. We discuss the road to the Chalcedonian Definition in chapter 5.

8. J. N. D. Kelly, *Early Christian Creeds*, 3rd ed. (London: Longmans, 1972), 296.

This definition is accepted today by most major groups of the church—specifically, the Eastern Orthodox, Roman Catholic, and Protestant churches. At the time, though, it was the source of intense division in the Eastern Christian world, and eventually two other groups emerged that were and are separate from what we today call the Eastern Orthodox Church. These are the Church of the East and the Oriental Orthodox churches, and this book addresses these groups and the reasons for their rejection of the Chalcedonian Definition as part of the story of chapter 5.

Even though all Christian churches affirmed the Nicene Creed, and most affirmed the Chalcedonian Definition, the Eastern and Western Christian thought worlds were somewhat different, and as these regions sought to explain and elaborate on their common creedal affirmations, their theologies began to move in different directions. Chapter 8 considers Eastern developments after Chalcedon, especially further debates about Christ that led to three more ecumenical councils. Chapter 9 then deals with the direction of Western theology after Chalcedon.

Eventually, divergent theology and, much more important, divergent ecclesiastical practices led to a schism between East and West into what we today call Eastern Orthodoxy and Roman Catholicism. While this schism was not directly related to the creeds, a difference of opinion about the Nicene Creed played a role in the split, and we consider the events related to that schism in chapter 10.

Confessional Identity in Relation to the Creeds

As we indicated above, this book explores the full scope of Christian confessions, not merely those of Protestant communities. We begin by looking at the decrees of the medieval church, treating them as Catholic *confessions*. There are two reasons for designating the decrees thus. First, the medieval church in the West issued many decrees on doctrine and practice, at times through councils, at times by the pope.[9] None of the medieval doctrines, however, dealt with the subject of God or the person of Christ, and so they did not touch on the main subjects of the creeds. Thus, they were more like confessions than like creeds per se. Second, and more important, these medieval decrees held normative force for Catholics, but because they were never accepted by

9. It is important to note that any decision by a Western council must be ratified by the pope. A council's decrees are neither binding on the pope, nor mandatory for Christians, unless the pope agrees. On this, see Walter Ullmann, *The Growth of Papal Government in the Middle Ages: A Study in the Ideological Relation of Clerical to Lay Power* (London: Methuen, 1970).

Orthodox or later Protestants, they cannot legitimately be seen as ecumenical. Catholic decrees, therefore, functioned and function as confessions for Catholics alone.

Of course, the medieval church came to see these decrees as having the same authority as the creeds; indeed, the Fourth Lateran Council in 1215 even created what could be called a creed in the sense that after that year it was impossible to be a Catholic without affirming the doctrine of transubstantiation.[10] But papal decrees were not universal in the same way as creeds, since they were not embraced by Orthodox or Protestant churches. Thus, even though Catholics treat their own medieval and modern decrees as necessary for Christian faith, those decrees in fact function as *local* confessions. Indeed, the doctrine of papal authority itself is a confessional boundary, since it is embraced only by Catholics and forms part of their confessional distinctiveness.

The same can be said for developments in the Eastern Orthodox churches. After the Seventh Ecumenical Council in 787, the East never issued anything else that could remotely be called a creed. Still, there were interpretations of creeds that functioned as confessions. For example, a generation after the Reformation, the patriarch of Constantinople, Jeremiah II, issued a verdict on the teachings of Lutheranism. His confession, as we call it today, was not entirely negative, although Jeremiah refused to see Lutheranism as fully consistent with orthodoxy. The local character of his judgment—it was a reaction to a recent phenomenon in the Western church—obviously marks it out as a confession, not a creed.

Paying attention to the local nature of confessions will help us in our exploration of Protestant confessions. Nearly all Protestant confessions state their positions as timeless and universal, but as we have already seen, each confession is actually normative only for its own specific community. Lutherans confess the physical presence of Christ in the Eucharist, but they know that such a confession can never bind Zwinglian or Anglican churches. In fact, Protestant confessions frequently state their opposition to other Protestant communities. Reformed and Lutheran confessions often explicitly oppose Anabaptist teachings, and Reformed churches stress their view of the Lord's Supper in direct opposition to Lutheranism. In each of these cases, the confession is used to define a Protestant community or tradition over against other Protestant churches.

Noting the give-and-take between confessions by different groups of Christians will help us in our last chapter, where we explore the nature of modern confessions. It would be tempting to see the period of confessionalism ending

10. See our discussion in chap. 12.

in the seventeenth century, but only if one's definition were too narrow, seeing a confession as a precise statement on theology. The broader definition that we have adopted shows how confessions—as expressions of specific communities that define important issues—continue into the modern world. Although the Barmen Declaration (1934) might focus on a smaller set of issues than confessions from the sixteenth century, it functions the same way as early Protestant confessions.

The initial surge of Protestant confessions (1517–60) are the focus of chapters 14 through 16. These chapters are vital to our appreciating the changes in later Protestant history between 1560 and 1650, changes to be discussed in chapter 17. The opening years of the Reformation were marked by an immediate fracturing of the various Protestant churches—not on the core issues of salvation but on issues of worship, the sacraments, and politics. After the Marburg Colloquy in 1529, at which Luther and Huldrych Zwingli failed to unite on the presence of Christ in the Eucharist, both Lutheran and Reformed confessions began to focus on that issue. Anabaptist confessions, likewise, focused on their theological distinctives, especially their aversion to the church's involvement in politics, an aversion that set them over against the magisterial Reformers.[11] So influential were these confessions that attempts to bridge the divide and thus create a wider Protestant unity always failed. Thus, between 1517 and 1560 nearly every confession focused mainly on issues of controversy.

From 1560 to 1650, however, Protestant confessions shifted their emphasis in two ways. First, the shorter confessions of the early Reformation gave way to longer confessions, with more detail on issues that pertained to each community. Reformed and Lutheran confessions, for example, offered more nuanced language on their own doctrinal standards, focusing more on explaining their position to their own churches. Second, for most Protestant confessions of this period, there was an increased need to deal with *internal* controversy. For example, the three most influential confessions from this period—the Book of Concord, the Canons of Dordt, and the Standards of Westminster— each dealt with controversies within a tradition. For this reason, these later confessions rarely said much on matters related to other Protestant traditions. By this point in the Reformation, their divisions were well established and seemingly permanent.

After the time of the Reformation, confessional development continued largely through the widening scope of confessional language. Not only did

---

11. Historians refer to non-Anabaptist reform movements as *magisterial* for this very reason—they were in league with the magistrate, or political government.

new denominations and traditions, such as the Methodists or Assemblies of God, create their own confessions, but existing traditions also created new confessions to address new issues—for example, the Barmen Declaration, occasioned by the rise of Nazism in the early twentieth century. This period was also when confessions went increasingly global, as new communities around the world began to shape their own identity. We consider these developments in chapter 18.

Thus, in contrast to the story of creeds focusing on the universal Christian faith in Father, Son, and Spirit, the story of confessions is one of immense variety, as a changing set of specific issues rises to the fore. Creeds have a standard shape, but confessions come in all shapes and sizes. We now turn to the story of creeds and confessions.

PART 1

The Era of the Creeds

(100–500)

2

The Creedal Impulse in Scripture and the Early Church

In about the year 404, an Italian Christian author/translator living in Aquileia by the name of Tyrannius Rufinus recounted the well-known story that after the tongues of fire fell on the apostles in Acts 2, the Lord commanded the Twelve to split up and take the gospel to different countries. Rufinus continues this traditional account with a surprising twist:

> When they were on the point of taking leave of each other, they first settled on a common form for their future preaching, so that they might not find themselves, widely dispersed as they would be, delivering divergent messages to the people they were persuading to believe in Christ. So they all assembled in one spot and, being filled with the Holy Spirit, drafted this short summary, as I have explained, of their future preaching, each contributing the clause he judged fitting: and they decreed that it should be handed out as the standard teaching to converts.[1]

Thus, Rufinus would have us believe that twelve men chosen by the Lord went to the whole known world with a single message, summarized in a single creed or symbol, to which each apostle contributed one clause. It is a striking story that has had a long and persistent hold on the imagination of Western Christians.[2]

---

1. Rufinus, *A Commentary on the Apostles' Creed* 2, trans. J. N. D. Kelly, ACW 20 (New York: Newman, 1955), 29–30.
2. By about the eighth century, the story had grown to include a list of which phrases each apostle allegedly contributed to the creed. See a sermon of Pseudo-Augustine translated in J. N. D. Kelly, *Early Christian Creeds*, 3rd ed. (London: Longmans, 1972), 3.

And while it certainly is true that the apostles personally took the gospel far and wide in the ancient world, it cannot possibly be true that they devised the Apostles' Creed in one meeting before they left on their missionary travels.

Why not? Well, if we leave aside the question of whether this story is inherently improbable and focus our attention on unassailable facts, we find that the creed Rufinus quotes and comments on is by no means identical to the later document that we call the Apostles' Creed. There are some trivial differences: Rufinus's creed affirms faith "in Christ Jesus," rather than "in Jesus Christ." Rufinus's creed speaks of Christ's crucifixion and burial, but not of his death as in the later creed. Rufinus's creed speaks of "resurrection of this flesh" instead of the later "resurrection of the body." There are also some fairly significant differences. Rufinus's creed says of Christ, "who was born by the Holy Spirit from the Virgin Mary," whereas the later creed is more specific: "who was conceived by the Holy Spirit, born of the Virgin Mary." Rufinus's creed has Christ sitting at the right hand of the Father, rather than the later, more specific phrase "at the right hand of God the Father Almighty." Rufinus's creed has "holy church" where the later creed refers to the "holy catholic church." And Rufinus's creed is missing the concluding phrase of the later Apostles' Creed, "and the life everlasting." Of course, none of these differences create any actual dissonance between the creed Rufinus comments on and the later Apostles' Creed, but the differences would have been unthinkable if the apostles had actually composed a fixed creed in the first century. Had that really happened, the church would surely have worked to maintain the wording of the creed without variation. Instead, what took place was the gradual evolution of a creed that was by no means in its final form in 404, as Rufinus was writing.

Furthermore, in Rufinus's commentary, he refers repeatedly to differences between his creed and other creeds around at the time. Usually he contrasts his creed with the Greek creeds, while still insisting that there is no difference in substance between them. Occasionally, though, he contrasts his creed with other Western creeds, as, for example, when he comments that the Roman Creed does not describe the descent into hell.[3] Clearly, then, there was not just a single creed from the first century onward. There were several, probably many, that were well known at the beginning of the fifth century. These various creeds agreed in content, but not in exact wording. Thus, we can conclude that Rufinus's creed was not so much *the* Apostles' Creed as it was a step along the way to the fixed form of that creed.[4] In fact, the first time in

3. Rufinus, *Commentary on the Apostles' Creed* 18, p. 52.
4. Frances Young summarizes: "But the Apostles' Creed as we now have it cannot go back to the apostles. For one thing, it is not identical word for word with the creed to which this legend is first attached, though clearly it is a later descendent of what we call 'the Old Roman

our extant literature that this creed was even *called* the Apostles' Creed was only some fifteen years before Rufinus wrote. Ambrose of Milan (an Italian, like Rufinus) described it with that title in a letter written in 389 or 390.[5] As we mentioned in chapter 1, the Apostles' Creed underwent a long history of development, not reaching its final form until the early eighth century. In fact, scholars disagree on how early it should be called the Apostles' Creed. Some use that phrase to describe it throughout its history of development, from about 150 to 700, on the grounds that there was enough continuity in its wording for it to bear the same name the entire time. Others, focusing on the amount of change in wording over time, call earlier versions the "Old Roman Creed" and reserve the name "Apostles' Creed" for the document as it developed from 400 to 700. We will follow the latter practice and thus not speak again of the Apostles' Creed until chapter 6. The Old Roman Creed, in contrast, is part of the focus of this chapter.

Instead of a single creed with a fixed form throughout Christian history, there were many creeds with variations in wording, and these creeds gradually assumed fixed forms. Where then did the creeds come from if not from a single meeting of the apostles? And how did they move from variable to fixed in form? These are the questions we need to consider in this chapter, and to do so, we must start much earlier than the time of the apostles.[6]

Going Way Back: The Primal Creed-like Affirmation

It is commonly and persuasively argued that the initial source of all Christian creeds was a statement from well over a millennium prior to the time of Christ and the apostles. In Deuteronomy 6:4, the Lord says through Moses, "Hear,

---

Creed.' Secondly, neither the Old Roman Creed nor the Apostles' Creed have been used in the Greek church, which produced its own formulae, similar in style and pattern but not the same in wording. All these different credal formulae, including the Old Roman Creed as well as Eastern forms, emerge around the turn of the third century, and cannot be traced in earlier Christian literature." *The Making of the Creeds* (London: SCM, 1991), 2.

5. Ambrose of Milan, *Epistle* 42.5, in *Saint Ambrose: Letters*, trans. Mary Melchior Meyenka, FC 26 (Washington, DC: Catholic University of America Press, 1954), 227. Ambrose writes of those who deny the virgin birth, "Let them believe the creed of the Apostles which the Church of Rome keeps and guards in its entirety."

6. The classic scholarly work on the process by which the creeds were formed is Kelly, *Early Christian Creeds*. More recent and even more detailed is Jaroslav Pelikan, *Credo: Historical and Theological Guide to Creeds and Confessions of Faith in the Christian Tradition* (New Haven: Yale University Press, 2003). Works that are less detailed and addressed to a more popular audience include Gerald Bray, *Creeds, Councils and Christ* (Downers Grove, IL: InterVarsity, 1984); Young, *Making of the Creeds*; Carl R. Trueman, *The Creedal Imperative* (Wheaton: Crossway, 2012); Justin S. Holcomb, *Know the Creeds and Councils* (Grand Rapids: Zondervan, 2014).

O Israel: The Lord our God, the Lord is one." Of course, this is not actually a creed, since a creed is a statement by the people about God, in whom we believe, whereas this is a statement from God to the people. Nevertheless, one can argue that this statement functioned as a creed, focusing the attention of the people of Israel on the one, undivided God in whom they believed. Jaroslav Pelikan's appraisal is typical: "Behind and beneath all the primitive creeds of the apostolic and subapostolic era there stands the primal creed and confession of the Christian church, *The Shema*. . . . *The Shema* did not, of course, arise from within the history of Christendom at all; rather, the history of Christendom may in a real sense be said to have arisen from it."[7]

If we consider the Shema (the word is Hebrew for "hear," the first word of Deut. 6:4) in the context of ancient Near Eastern thought, we can easily recognize why it was so formative for the people of Israel. As the nations around Israel envisioned the world, it was controlled by a host of gods and goddesses, none all-powerful, who competed with one another for power over the cosmos and the people in it. Human life was thus imagined to be a bewildering task of guessing which god to appease at which time, so as to gain the smoothest passage through the chaos of the world. To make matters even worse, people were never sure whether the gods wanted them to be there at all—many origins accounts saw this world as an accidental by-product of a primordial clash between gods. In vivid contrast to these accounts of the world and of humanity's place within it, the first words of the Bible proclaim, "In the beginning, God created the heavens and the earth" (Gen. 1:1). There was, in fact, no jumble of gods fighting one another, no guesswork for humankind about which gods to try to placate. There was only one God, present in the beginning, who made absolutely everything that exists outside himself. The Shema of Deuteronomy 6 is the explicit affirmation of what is implicit in Genesis 1:1: there is the one true God, and there is everything else. It is as if the Bible is drawing a hard line between God on one hand and all else that exists on the other.

This metaphysical line is ineradicable and unbridgeable, and its presence shapes everything about the Jewish (and later Christian) faith. We are in a *dependent* position with respect to God the Lord. We do not try to bend him to our will; we exist to serve his will. We do not manipulate him; he directs us. But we are also in a *confident* position with respect to the Lord. He is the only one out there, and he has no division of will within himself, so we need have no divisions in our loyalty to him. We never need to wonder whether there is another god waiting in the wings whom we need to buy off or appease. We

7. Pelikan, *Credo*, 374.

are free to serve the one, undivided God with our own undivided loyalty. This was the lesson that Israel had to learn in the midst of the pagan, polytheistic world of the ancient Near East, and above all else, the Shema encapsulated this lesson. It rightly stood at the very center of Israel's faith.

By the first century, the Jewish world had thoroughly imbibed the absolute monotheism of the Old Testament. But as the Christian church moved out of that world into the pagan world of Africa, Europe, and Asia, the mainly gentile church had to learn the same lesson in a different kind of pagan world, filled with a different but equally complex array of imagined gods and goddesses. Into this new but basically similar world the church now had to affirm again that there is a hard line between God and everything else. The Lord is the only, undivided God of the universe, who made everything and to whom everything is subservient. As Paul eloquently puts it in 1 Corinthians 8:5–6, "For although there may be so-called gods in heaven or on earth—as indeed there are many 'gods' and many 'lords'—yet for us there is one God, the Father, from whom are all things and for whom we exist." The most basic affirmation of ancient Israel has become—in a context at once different and yet fundamentally similar—the most basic affirmation of the church as well.

Indeed, still today this is the most basic affirmation of the Christian faith, although again the context has changed. Today the imagined gods and goddesses are not outside us, but within. We fancy that we can shape reality as we see fit—whether by living in virtual reality when real reality doesn't suit us, or even by altering aspects of our reality that humankind has always previously regarded as fixed and given. No longer do we bow before images of wood and stone that we have made. Instead, we bow before ourselves, declaring ourselves to be sovereign over our own worlds and demanding that others submit to reality as we construe it, imagine it, or even refashion it. In this context of radical self-worship, Christians must yet again confess, "There is one God, the Father, from whom are all things and for whom we exist." There is a hard line between God and what he has made, and we are below that line. We are not meant to reimagine reality but to serve God within it.

A Glorious Complication: Creedal Language in the New Testament

Of course, in the first century the Christian church did not simply need to relearn the central lesson of Israel's faith in a new context. There was also another stunning truth—seemingly in conflict with the first—that had to be learned and wrestled with. In fact, you may have noticed that in the biblical quotation above, we stopped in the middle of a sentence. The rest of 1 Corinthians 8:6 reads, "and one Lord, Jesus Christ, through whom are all things and through whom we exist." Here we must notice the striking parallels between the way the one God, the Father, is described and the way the Lord Jesus Christ is depicted. The Father is the one *from whom* everything exists and *for whom* we exist; Jesus Christ is the one *through whom* we and all other things exist. How can Paul combine in a single verse such restrictive language about God the Father and such tantalizingly similar language in describing Jesus?

Paul is hardly the only New Testament writer to do this. In fact, if Genesis 1:1 is the background for the creed-like affirmation of the Shema, then perhaps one can fairly say that John 1:1 is the background for Paul's creed-like affirmation in 1 Corinthians 8:6.[8] John's Gospel begins with "in the beginning," an obvious reference to Genesis 1:1. But before describing an action—creation—taking place in the beginning, John describes a relationship that was already present: "In the beginning was the Word, and the Word was with God, and the Word was God. He was in the beginning with God. All things were made through him, and without him was not anything made that was made" (John 1:1–3). Here we see the Word distinguished from God ("was the Word"), set in relationship to God ("was with God"), and identified with God ("was God"), just as Paul distinguishes Christ from God ("one God . . . and one Lord"), sets him in relationship to God, and identifies him with God (the last two by using the title "Lord" to describe him). Furthermore, John and Paul both affirm that all things were made *through* the Word/Lord.

The question of how Jesus Christ can be both distinct from God and identified with God was indeed an urgent one, and it complicated the creedal affirmation of one God considerably. But such complexity did not lead the New Testament writers to retreat from the affirmation that Jesus Christ is the Lord. As we saw on the first page of this book, in Romans 10:9–10, Paul links the salvation of the Christian to the confession that "Jesus is Lord."

Along with confessing the identity of Jesus with God, the New Testament writers also affirm creed-like summaries of the saving events of Christ's life. Paul describes the gospel in 1 Corinthians 15:3–4 as follows: "For I delivered to you as of first importance what I also received, that Christ died for our sins in accordance with the Scriptures, that he was buried, that he was raised on the third day in accordance with the Scriptures." Similarly, in Philippians 2:5–11 Paul affirms in creed-like fashion that Christ

---

8. Of course, Paul wrote 1 Corinthians several decades before John wrote his Gospel. We mean here that the relationship between God and the Word described in John 1:1 is the background to the confession Paul makes in 1 Cor. 8:6, even though the actual writing of John 1:1 came later.

did not count equality with God a thing to be grasped, but emptied himself, by taking the form of a servant, being born in the likeness of men. And being found in human form, he humbled himself by becoming obedient to the point of death, even death on a cross. Therefore God has highly exalted him and bestowed on him the name that is above every name, so that at the name of Jesus every knee should bow, in heaven and on earth and under the earth, and every tongue confess that Jesus Christ is Lord, to the glory of God the Father.

So we see that the New Testament writers complicate the creedal affirmation of faith in one God by affirming with equally creedal force that Jesus Christ is to be identified with that one God, and by attaching particular creed-like significance to the events of Christ's life, death, and resurrection. The line between God and everything else is no less hard than it was before, but Christians affirm that Jesus belongs above that line, and yet lived an earthly life as one below it.

There is yet another complication in the nascent creedal affirmations of the New Testament. Some of them confess not only God/Father and Jesus/Lord but also a third person. Paul concludes 2 Corinthians with a famous benediction: "The grace of the Lord Jesus Christ and the love of God and the fellowship of the Holy Spirit be with you all" (13:14). And of course, we have already seen that in Matthew 28:19 Jesus commands Christians to baptize "in the name of the Father and of the Son and of the Holy Spirit." While the Holy Spirit receives far less attention in the New Testament than Jesus does, the creed-like affirmations in these and other passages indicate that he, too, belongs above the hard line that divides God from all created things.

One could adduce many more biblical passages,[9] but the ones we have considered should be sufficient to demonstrate that the divinely inspired writers of the New Testament make affirmations that have a creedal ring to them and that these affirmations tend to include at least two of the following four elements:

1. A confession of the one God, the Father
2. A confession of Jesus Christ, linked to the Father by calling him "Lord" or "Son"
3. A summary of the events of Christ's earthly life, death, and resurrection
4. An affirmation that the Holy Spirit is linked to the Father and Son

9. See the long discussion of creed-like elements in the New Testament in Kelly, *Early Christian Creeds*, 8–29.

From the New Testament's reflection on and additions to the Shema, then, we find the beginnings of the creedal impulse among Christians.

Creed Writing in the Second and Third Centuries

Our sources for second- and third-century Christianity are relatively few and fragmentary. As a result, we do not have extant texts of full creeds from these centuries, but a number of writings in our possession include references to or citations of creed-like statements embedded in longer discussions, just as the New Testament Letters that we mentioned in the previous section include such citations. Accordingly, scholars are able to conclude that the creedal impulse latent in the New Testament documents continued into the second and third centuries and to reconstruct what these primitive creeds likely said. From what we can tell, they were of two major types: (1) creeds beginning with Christ, focusing on summaries of his earthly life, and (2) creeds that were explicitly threefold in structure and dealt at least in a rudimentary way with the Spirit as well as the Father and the Son. From the second category emerged threefold symbols associated with baptism that dominated the creedal landscape prior to the fourth century. In this section we will look at examples of these types.

Creeds Focused on Christ and Summarizing His Life

In their massive work on the creeds, Jaroslav Pelikan and Valerie Hotchkiss argue that New Testament scholars have identified the core of early Christian proclamation: one God, creator of heaven and earth; his only Son, born of the virgin Mary, crucified under Pilate, raised from the dead, and returning to judge the world; the Holy Spirit, who inspired the prophets and gives life to the church.[10] This was the story that early Christians proclaimed, and these were the three actors in the story. Pelikan and Hotchkiss conclude, "It does not appear to be stretching the available evidence to suggest, therefore, that there was some such stock outline at the foundation of Christian preaching, which was passed on from one preacher to the next both by the laying on of hands at ordination and by a system of apprenticeship."[11]

In fact, we see such summaries of the events of Christ's life presented in quasi-creedal form in the earliest postbiblical Christian writings. Ignatius was a very early bishop of Antioch in Syria (today the city is in southeastern

10. CCFCT 1:10.
11. CCFCT 1:10.

Ignatius was martyred in the Colosseum.

Turkey rather than in modern Syria) who was one of the earliest prominent Christians to be arrested for his faith, transported to Rome, and killed by wild beasts in the Roman Colosseum. As he was being taken from Antioch to Rome in about AD 107, he wrote several letters to the leaders of the churches that he visited on the way, and his letter to the church in Smyrna (modern Izmir in western Turkey) contains the following affirmation:

> I glorify Jesus Christ, the God who made you so wise, for I observed that you are established in an unshakable faith, having been nailed, as it were, to the cross of the Lord Jesus Christ in both body and spirit, and firmly established in love by the blood of Christ, totally convinced with regard to our Lord that he is truly of the family of David with respect to human descent, Son of God with respect to the divine will and power, truly born of a virgin, baptized by John in order that all righteousness might be fulfilled in him, truly nailed [to the cross] in the flesh for us under Pontius Pilate and Herod the tetrarch (from its fruit we derive our existence, that is, from his divinely blessed sufferings), in order that he might raise a banner for the ages through his resurrection for his saints and faithful people, whether among Jews or among Gentiles, in one body of his church.[12]

12. Ignatius of Antioch, *To the Smyrnaeans* 1.1–2, in *The Apostolic Fathers: Greek Texts and English Translations of Their Writings*, ed. Michael W. Holmes (Grand Rapids: Baker, 1999), 185. Also in CCFCT 1:40.

Here we should notice the focus on who Christ is as a person. Ignatius directly calls him "God," and yet he insists on Christ's lineage from David "with respect to human descent" and his sonship to God "with respect to the divine will and power." Ignatius further insists on the genuineness of Christ's life story: "*truly* born of a virgin," "*truly* nailed in the flesh." This early creed-like proclamation is strikingly similar to the sermons of the book of Acts, especially in the way it begins with Christ, rather than with God the Father.

About a third of the way through the second century, Justin, a young philosopher from Samaria (in the center of modern Israel), was converted to Christianity. After finding his way to Rome, he addressed two apologies for the Christian faith to the Roman emperor, Antoninus Pius. Justin was martyred for refusing to worship the Roman gods around the year 165. In his *First Apology*, written about 155, he describes the Christian way of life and then asserts,

> Our teacher of these things is Jesus Christ, who was also born for this purpose, and was crucified under Pontius Pilate, procurator of Judea in the time of Tiberius Caesar, and we shall show that we worship him rationally, having learned that he is the Son of the true God himself, and holding him in the second place, and the prophetic Spirit in the third rank. For they charge our madness to consist in this, that we give to a crucified man second place after the unchangeable and eternal God, begetter of all things, for they do not know the mystery involved in this, to which we ask you to give heed as we expound it to you.[13]

Three things are noteworthy about this affirmation. First, Justin's summary of Christ's life events is quite short, but he goes to great lengths to situate that life in the midst of Roman history that the emperor would know. Second, he describes the Son as holding "second place" after the Father. To us, this assertion is immediately suspicious, maybe scandalous. His statement certainly was problematic, and the church later learned to express the Father-Son relationship much more accurately. But we see here an early attempt to address what we called the "glorious complication" of the Son's identification with the Father. The third thing to note in this passage is that it mentions the Spirit, albeit placing him in the "third rank." The natural way to think of the trinitarian persons is to rank them in order, and Justin has done so without sufficiently reflecting on the significance of the fact that the New Testament does not always list them in the order Father, Son,

13. Justin Martyr, *First Apology* 13, in *The First and Second Apologies*, trans. Leslie William Barnard, ACW 56 (New York: Paulist, 1997), 31. Also in *CCFCT* 1:46.

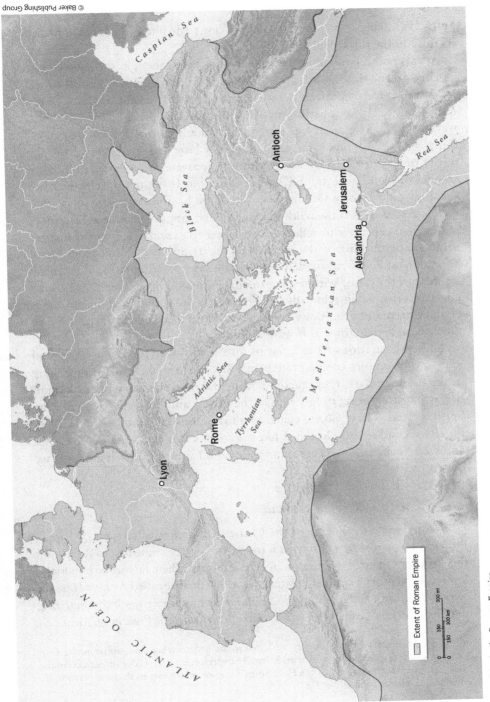

Key cities in the Roman Empire

Spirit.[14] The church had much more thinking to do about the way it affirmed its faith in the three persons.

At this point, contemporary readers may be rather aghast that someone so close to the time of the apostles could fail to recognize the full equality of the three trinitarian persons. But our surprise on this point grows out of an overly simplistic way of looking at Christian history. We tend to think that the church was purer and had a better understanding of all things Christian in its early years, and only later did it fall away from the purity of the gospel. Such an appraisal is accurate in some ways and with respect to some aspects of Christian life, but it fits the development of theology quite poorly. On that issue, it would be more accurate to say that the church *possessed* the truth through the writings of the New Testament but needed centuries to reflect on how best to *express* that truth. Justin's problematic ranking of the persons of the Trinity is a classic example of an understandable but inadequate initial effort at articulating the central mystery of the faith. With respect to our discussion in chapter 1, he is like a new convert speaking clumsily because he has not yet learned the grammar of the Christian faith. As we will see, the church got better at this kind of theological articulation as it went along.

These affirmations from Ignatius and Justin were typical of early and mid-second-century creedal statements. Taking their cue from the preaching in the book of Acts, they started with Christ and the story of his human life, while attempting to link him to the Father and, in Justin's case, to the Spirit as well. These Christ-centered affirmations began to be replaced in the late second century by creed-like statements that started with the Father and were specifically structured in a threefold way. To such statements we now turn.

Creeds with a Threefold Structure

The first great theologian of the Christian church was Irenaeus of Lyons. Probably born in Smyrna (in what is today Turkey), he came first to Rome and then to Lyons in Gaul (southeastern France today), where he was bishop in the late second century. His greatest work was a long treatise called *Against Heresies* (written ca. 180), and in about 190 he also wrote a shorter work summarizing the Christian faith, called *Demonstration of the Apostolic Preaching*. Although

---

14. See Matt. 28:19, in which they are listed in the order Father, Son, Spirit, and 2 Cor. 13:14, in which the order is Son, Father, Spirit. The variations in the order of persons in the New Testament writings may be the Holy Spirit's way of reminding us that the persons are equal and can be listed in any order.

he wrote in Greek, this summary of the faith is preserved only in an Armenian translation.[15] Early in the *Demonstration*, Irenaeus makes this affirmation:

> And this is the order of our faith and the foundation of [the] edifice and the support of [our] conduct: God, the Father, uncreated, uncontainable, invisible, one God, the Creator of all: this is the first article of our faith. And the second article: the Word of God, the Son of God, Christ Jesus our Lord, who was revealed by the prophets according to the character of their prophecy and according to the nature of the economies of the Father, by whom all things were made, and who, in the last times, to recapitulate all things, became a man amongst men, visible and palpable, in order to abolish death, to demonstrate life, and to effect communion between God and man. And the third article: the Holy Spirit, through whom the prophets prophesied and the patriarchs learned the things of God and the righteous were led in the path of righteousness, and who, in the last times, was poured out in a new fashion upon the human race renewing man, throughout the world, to God.[16]

In this passage, we should immediately recognize the shift in vantage point compared to Ignatius and Justin. Rather than starting with Jesus's earthly life and ministry as they did, Irenaeus begins with the Father and considers the Son in terms of his eternal relationship to the Father. Then and only then does he turn his attention to the Son's action of becoming man and the purposes for the incarnation. As a result, one can think of this creedal statement as having a threefold structure—one "article" for each of the persons of the Trinity—and the section on the Son moves from his eternal being to his actions, both in creation and in redemption. It is also worth noting that while Irenaeus *numbers* the persons, he does not *rank* them one above another. In the generation between Justin and Irenaeus, there has already been much progress toward a more accurate understanding of the Trinity.

Statements beginning with the earthly life of Jesus, such as those we have seen by Ignatius and Justin, followed the pattern of the Synoptic Gospels.

---

15. Readers may be surprised that we could fail to possess a writing in the language in which it was written. We need to remember that the New Testament is vastly better preserved than any other writing from the ancient world. Among patristic writings, it is wonderful if we possess one complete manuscript of a work in the language of its composition. More often, we possess only fragments in the original language, or only a translation (as in the case of the *Demonstration*), or in some cases only fragments of translations in various languages. Readers may also be surprised that the non-Greek language in which we have the *Demonstration* is Armenian. Remember that the church was present far beyond the Greek- and Latin-speaking worlds very early in Christian history. Armenia, in fact, became officially Christian earlier in the fourth century than the Roman Empire did.

16. Irenaeus of Lyons, *The Demonstration of the Apostolic Preaching* 6, in *On the Apostolic Preaching*, trans. John Behr, PPS 17 (Crestwood, NY: St. Vladimir's Seminary Press, 1997), 43–44. Also in *CCFCT* 1:50.

In contrast, affirmations such as this one by Irenaeus follow the pattern of John 1 more closely—beginning with the Trinity in eternity and then moving to the incarnation. Thus, both kinds of creedal statements have biblical precedent. Over time, though, the threefold pattern exhibited by Irenaeus came to predominate. The main reason for this is that creedal statements were used not merely for proclamation/preaching, but especially in connection with baptism. Matthew 28:19 provided the pattern for trinitarian baptism, and Jesus's specific mention of all three persons under the one "name" in that passage provided the rationale for the development of baptismal symbols in which one confessed each person sequentially and was immersed after each confession. Thus, the baptismal use of creeds—growing out of the Lord's command—came to dictate the pattern that future creeds followed. We will now consider these developments.

Creeds in Connection with Baptism

In the late nineteenth century a very early manual on Christian worship and practice was discovered, called the Didache (the Greek word means "teaching"). This manual was written in Greek and came from Syria. It was written no later than the middle of the second century, and perhaps even the late first century. Thus it may be the oldest nonbiblical Christian writing we possess and could even predate the latest New Testament books. The Didache contains the following famous description of baptism:

> Now concerning baptism, baptize as follows: after you have reviewed all these things [that is, the patterns of Christian life and morality on which the work concentrates], baptize "in the name of the Father, and of the Son and of the Holy Spirit" in running water. But if you have no running water, then baptize in some other water; and if you are not able to baptize in cold water, then do so in warm. But if you have neither, then pour water on the head three times "in the name of the Father, and Son and Holy Spirit."[17]

This passage is not really creedal in character, since it contains no affirmation beyond its quotation of Matthew 28:19. Nevertheless, in a sense it set the stage for the development of baptismal symbols by describing the way the early Christians connected the words of Jesus's command with the act of baptism. It is also interesting to note the preference for cold, running water, as well as the allowance for a different technique (pouring rather than immersion) if circumstances dictated a change.

17. Did. 7.1–3, in Holmes, *Apostolic Fathers*, 259. Also in CCFCT 1:42.

Much more specific than the Didache was a work called the Apostolic Tradition, written in Rome in about 215 and ascribed to Hippolytus. This work is believed to derive from the mid- and late second-century practices of the church at Rome. The document's description of baptism is as follows:

> When the person being baptized goes down into the water, he who baptizes him, putting his hand on him, shall say: "Do you believe in God, the Father Almighty?" And the person being baptized shall say: "I believe." Then holding his hand on his head, he shall baptize him once.
>
> And then he shall say: "Do you believe in Christ Jesus, the Son of God, who was born of the Holy Spirit and the Virgin Mary, and was crucified under Pontius Pilate, and was dead and buried, and rose again the third day, alive from the dead, and ascended into heaven, and sat down at the right hand of the Father, and will come to judge the living and the dead?" And when the person says: "I believe," he is baptized again.
>
> And again the deacon shall say: "Do you believe in the Holy Spirit, in the holy church, and in the resurrection of the body?" Then the person being baptized shall say: "I believe," and he is baptized a third time.[18]

This is a very early instance of an interrogatory creed, in which the three headings of the faith (one on each person of the Trinity) were expressed as questions to which the person being baptized gave his or her assent. Here we should notice that in spite of the interrogatory formula, the threefold structure is very similar to the affirmation we saw from Irenaeus in the previous section. Note also that we are now beginning to see additional affirmations placed after the confession of faith in the Holy Spirit: the church and the resurrection of the body. Such lists of affirmations—things *that* one believes as distinct from the three persons *in whom* one believes—continued to expand throughout the patristic period. Over time, the questions began to be expressed as declarative statements, and three-part declaratory creeds started to emerge. In the next section we will consider two such declaratory creeds.

Two Paradigmatic Early Creeds

One should remember that we do not possess in manuscript form actual creeds from the second and third centuries. Instead, we possess creed-like affirmations embedded in longer writings. Nevertheless, scholars can be very confident that at least by the third century, declarative creeds did exist and were used in connection with baptism. Furthermore, by piecing together

---

18. Hippolytus, *Apostolic Tradition* 21, in CCFCT 1:61.

evidence from many sources, scholars are able to be quite confident about the wording of those creeds. The following table gives English translations of the two most important reconstructed creeds of the era before the fourth century. On the left is the Old Roman Creed (which, as we have seen, is called the Apostles' Creed by those who seek to emphasize its continuity with the later form of the creed with that name), which was used in Rome in both Latin and Greek[19] as early as the middle of the second century. On the right is a Greek creed from the Eastern church, which may have been the prototype for various Greek baptismal symbols used in the third century.

The Old Roman Creed	A Prototypical Greek Creed
I believe in God the Father almighty;	We believe in one God, the Almighty, Maker of all things visible and invisible;
and in Christ Jesus His [only] Son, [our Lord,]	and in one Lord Jesus Christ, his only-begotten Son, begotten of the Father before all ages;
Who was born from the Holy Spirit and the Virgin Mary,	through whom also all things came to be;
Who under Pontius Pilate was crucified and buried,	who for us came down from heaven and became incarnate, was born of the Virgin Mary and was crucified under Pontius Pilate and was
on the third day rose again from the dead,	buried, and rose on the third day in accordance with the Scriptures, and ascended into heaven,
ascended into heaven,	and is seated at the right hand of the Father,
sits at the right hand of the Father, whence he will come to judge the living and the dead;	and will come in glory to judge the living and the dead;
	of his kingdom there will be no end.
and in the Holy Spirit, the holy Church, [the remission of sins,] the resurrection of the flesh [, eternal life].[a]	We believe also in one Holy Spirit, the giver of life, and in one holy catholic and apostolic church, one baptism of repentance for the forgiveness of sins, in the resurrection of the dead, in the kingdom of heaven, and in life everlasting. Amen.[b]

a. This creed is reconstructed from many sources. Chief among them are Rufinus's *Commentary* (already considered at the beginning of this chapter) and a fourth-century Greek writing by Marcellus of Ancyra that includes a quotation of the creed with interpolations. The phrase "eternal life" is in the Greek writing, but not in Rufinus's Latin writing. The Latin and Greek reconstructions, as well as the English translation, may be found in J. N. D. Kelly, *Early Christian Creeds*, 3rd ed. (London: Longmans, 1972), 102. Scholarship since Kelly's time has suggested that the other phrases we have placed in brackets may not have been present in the creed until the fourth century. See Liuwe H. Westra, *The Apostles' Creed: Origin, History, and Some Early Commentaries*, Instrumenta patristica et medievalia 43 (Turnhout: Brepols, 2002), 68.

b. This reconstruction was proposed in August Hahn, *Bibliothek der Symbole und Glaubensregeln der alten Kirche*, 3rd ed. (1897; repr., Hildesheim: Olms, 1962), document 122. The English translation comes from *CCFCT* 1:14.

We should take note of the major differences between these two symbols. First, and most obvious, the Eastern creed is considerably more specific on

19. Until the late second century, Greek was more widely spoken than Latin even in Rome itself.

almost every point. Regarding the Father, it emphasizes *one* God and asserts that he has created all things visible and invisible (an emphatic idiom in Greek for emphasizing that God made everything, akin to the Hebrew idiom "the heavens and the earth," which also means "everything"). The Western creed did not include that assertion at this point in its development, but when it later gained that phrase, it used the Hebrew idiom rather than the Greek one. It is also worth noting that the Greek word translated as "almighty," *pantokratōr*, conveys not so much the ability of God to do anything he chooses as the fact that he rules over all beings. This word comes into Latin as *omnipotens* and thus into English as "almighty," but it would be better to render it as "all sovereign" or "the ruler over all" to make the emphasis of the Greek word clear. Surprisingly, the Greek symbol does not use the word "Father" to describe God, perhaps because it uses that word in the next paragraph on the Son.

In the paragraph on Christ, the Greek creed begins with the preincarnate relation of the Son to the Father and describes the Son's role in creation, both of which are missing from the Western symbol. The phrase "begotten of the Father before all ages" strikes modern ears uneasily, as if there were a time when the Son did not exist and he was begotten in time but before the universe was created. This idea underwent considerable refinement in the fourth century, on the way to the Nicene Creed. The Greek creed not only is more specific about the incarnate life of Christ but also describes the entire economy of the incarnation as the Son's coming down from heaven for us, again following John's descriptive paradigm rather than that of the Synoptic Gospels. Both creeds include the second coming for judgment, but only the Eastern creed mentions the eternal duration of the Son's kingdom.

The Eastern symbol has little to say about the Holy Spirit (he is "the giver of life"), but even this is more than in the Western creed, which offers only "in the Holy Spirit." Among the affirmations appended to the end, the Western creed affirms only the "holy church," whereas the Eastern creed calls the church "one, holy, catholic, and apostolic." Only the Eastern creed connects forgiveness of sins to baptism (see Acts 2:38)—if the Western creed even mentions forgiveness of sins at all at this time period, since that phrase may have been added later—and only that creed mentions the kingdom of heaven.

As we have already seen, the Old Roman Creed (the Western one) had many similarities to the later Apostles' Creed and can certainly be seen as a step along the way to that symbol. Likewise, the reconstructed Eastern baptismal symbol was quite similar to the later Nicene Creed, and we may regard it (or more likely, the various different local symbols derived from it in the East) as part of the basis for the Nicene Creed. The difference is that in the West the Old Roman Creed evolved into the Apostles' Creed by a gradual process, but in the East the delegates at Nicaea and then Constantinople intentionally fashioned the Nicene Creed using the various baptismal symbols as models.

Conclusions

In this chapter we have seen that the creedal impulse, derived from the Shema and developed into the creed-like assertions of the New Testament, continued in the second and third centuries. Affirmations of a creedal sort, focusing on the life of Christ, were embedded into the proclamation of the gospel and found their way into summaries of that proclamation in longer Christian documents. Over time the structure of these creedal summaries began to be more threefold, with one paragraph dedicated to each person of the Trinity and with the Father as the starting point rather than the incarnate Christ. At the same time, three-part baptismal questions (interrogative creeds) began to be restructured into three-part declarative baptismal symbols. At the center of all such creeds—interrogatory or declarative—was the communal expression of faith in the Father, in the Son, and in the Holy Spirit.

As far as content goes, we have seen that there was variety in the details, but nevertheless, the various symbols evinced a strong consensus about the persons of the Trinity and the saving events of Christ's life. Some of the earliest statements seem to modern ears to subordinate the Son and Spirit to the Father, but the reconstructed Greek symbol at least makes a start toward excluding such subordination by emphasizing that the Son is "only-begotten" and "begotten before all ages," and by calling the Spirit "the giver of life." Gerald Bray sums up this era of creed writing appropriately: "It must be concluded that many different texts [of baptismal symbols] were in use without provoking friction or dissent. The main reason for this must be that the trinitarian pattern and the extended exposition of the life and work of Christ are standard features common to them all. Points of difference are minor and seldom have doctrinal implications of their own."[20]

At this point, we may be a little bit uncomfortable, because the major distinctive of Protestant Christianity, justification by faith, does not seem to be included in these outlines of the Christian faith at all. But before we get too suspicious, we need to consider that part of the point of justification by faith—in Paul's Letters and in Reformation teaching—is to remind us that we are not the objects of our own faith. We depend for salvation not on what we have done or can do, but on what Another has done and is doing. This is why we so insistently contrast faith (directed toward Another) with works (which

20. Bray, *Creeds, Councils and Christ*, 99.

we could regard as faith directed toward our own abilities). Here we should recognize that this is what early Christian preaching and creedal summaries were doing, but in a different way. By telling the story of Jesus and by naming the Father, Son, and Spirit as the actors in that story, Christian preachers in the New Testament and the early church were specifically *not* describing our own action or performance. The omission of what we do from the statements was just as significant as the inclusion of the story of Jesus in those statements. By that very omission and inclusion, preachers were calling their audiences to look elsewhere than themselves—to the Father, Son, and Spirit—for their salvation. One could say that the very act of telling the story of Jesus (as the Gospels did, as the New Testament preachers did in the book of Acts, and as the preachers and symbol writers of the early church did) is just as much an affirmation of justification by faith as we make when we—following Paul in Romans and Galatians—actually expound on that phrase itself. If Protestant readers can remain attuned to what the creeds don't say as much as to what they do say, we may find some of our suspicions allayed. Indeed, we may find that talking about the God in whom we are to trust is just as compelling a way to foster trust in him alone as talking about justification by faith directly!

At this point in our story, we stand in the third century, surrounded by a number of local baptismal symbols that agree in substance but differ in details. How did we go from these varied local creeds to more fixed and universally approved statements such as the Nicene Creed and (in a different way and to a lesser degree) the Apostles' Creed? The main factor providing incentive for such fixing and universalizing of the creeds was the conversion of the Roman Empire to Christianity. As we prepare to focus on the great conciliar gatherings and their products—the Nicene Creed and the Chalcedonian Definition—let us now turn to Constantine and the massive reshaping of the Roman world in the early fourth century.

3

A Christian Empire and Creedal Standardization

On October 28, 312, one of the most momentous battles in world history took place just north of Rome. It was the critical battle in the struggle for control of the Roman Empire that had begun after Emperor Diocletian abdicated the throne in 305, and it pitted the young general Constantine, ruler over the northern and western portions of the empire, against Maxentius, who controlled Italy and the central regions. Constantine had brought his troops over the Alps by the rugged Via Flaminia, down to the Milvian Bridge over the Tiber River, the final gate before entry into Rome itself.

Had Maxentius been a prudent strategist, he would have remained in Rome, utilizing the abundant stockpiles of food and munitions, the support of his allies, and above all the city walls that Constantine would need to breach if he hoped to take the city. Yet Maxentius preferred to attack openly rather than appear to cower in his palace,[1] so he sent his troops down to the Milvian Bridge. The original stone bridge had been destroyed, and Maxentius had a series of flat, wooden pontoons erected atop boats and linked across the Tiber, allowing for a quick, if shaky, crossing on October 27. The strategy proved to be Maxentius's downfall. Once the soldiers crossed, the river was now at their

---

1. There are three ancient accounts of the battle, from Christian historians Eusebius and Lactantius and from the pagan historian Zosimus. For the Christian accounts, see Eusebius, *Life of Constantine* 1.37–38, in NPNF[2] 1:492–93; and Lactantius, *The Deaths of the Persecutors* 44–45, in *Lactantius: The Minor Works*, trans. Mary Francis McDonald, FC 54 (Washington, DC: Catholic University of America Press, 1965), 190–92.

The Battle at the Milvian Bridge by Charles Le Brun

back, and so an army encircling them could pin them in place. Constantine attacked with strength the next day once Maxentius was across. First he sent his cavalry to break Maxentius's less-disciplined horsemen, and then he struck with his foot soldiers. Eventually Maxentius sought to retreat to Rome, but the pontoon bridges collapsed in the mayhem, drowning horses and men. Maxentius, too, fell into the river and attempted to swim to the opposite bank. He drowned, and thus ended the civil war in the Roman West. "The hand of God was over the battle line," wrote the Christian historian Lactantius years later.[2]

Two questions, one narrow and the other broad, arise as we consider this battle. First, why did Maxentius not stay in Rome, where he could easily have warded off a potential invasion by Constantine's forces? And second, what does this have to do with the Christian church, and especially with Christian creeds? These questions are closely intertwined, and to answer them we need to go back deeper into Constantine's story and that of the church in the Roman Empire.

Maxentius

Persecution of the Church in the Roman World

The popular Christian image of the church in the Roman Empire is one of constant and brutal persecution for the entire first three centuries. This image is not completely wrong, but it certainly is exaggerated. The reality was that at any given time and place, there might be intense local persecution,[3] but it was rarely widespread or long lasting. This pattern of local persecution was broken by two major periods of empire-wide persecution of Christians, the first under Decius and Valerian in the 250s, and the second, sometimes called the Great Persecution, under Diocletian in the early fourth century.

Before we get any further with this story, though, we need to pause for a reminder that Christianity was never confined to the Roman Empire, and the circumstances of Christians outside that empire were usually very different from within it. Indeed, the church in Persia flourished without persecution during the periods when the Romans were persecuting Christians. Why? Because the Persians hated the Romans enough that they looked with kindness

2. Lactantius, *Deaths of the Persecutors* 44, p. 191.
3. For example, the persecution in Italy in 64–68 under Nero, during which Peter and Paul were executed, or the persecution in Asia Minor (modern Turkey) in 95–96 under Domitian, which may form the backdrop for the book of Revelation. Other intense local persecutions came in Gaul (France) in 177–78, and in Achaia (Greece), Africa (Tunisia), Gaul, and Egypt in 202–3. See Lactantius, *Deaths of the Persecutors* 2–5, pp. 138–43.

on anyone—such as Christians—whom the Romans didn't like! Once the Romans stopped persecuting Christians in the fourth century—the story we are in the process of considering—the Persians started persecuting them within their own empire, and the "Great Persecution of Persia" in the 340s was far more devastating than the Roman persecutions had been.[4]

The Roman emperor Diocletian, who took the throne in 284, divided the empire into what was called the tetrarchy, in which there were two chief rulers (Augusti), each ruling over half of the empire, each assisted by a junior ruler (a Caesar). Diocletian himself was Augustus over the East, while Maximian was Augustus over the West. Galerius was Diocletian's Caesar and his closest adviser, while Maximian's Caesar in the West was Constantius Chlorus, Constantine's father. Diocletian was a devout pagan who, like many emperors before him, considered the glory of Rome to derive from its faithful worship of the Roman gods. So he was wary of Christians, Manichaeans,[5] Jews, and any others who refused to worship the old Roman gods, but he had Christians on his staff and maybe even in his family, and he usually left them alone. Diocletian was turned step-by-step to embrace persecution after receiving ominous prophecies from the oracle of Apollo, by the urging of Galerius (a much more fanatical pagan than Diocletian), and finally in 299 by the failure of a ritual sacrifice to produce the desired oracular word from the gods, a failure that the pagan priests attributed to "profane persons"—Christians—who had disrupted the sacrifice. Diocletian began weeding Christians out of the army, and then, at the urging of Galerius, he issued the first of four edicts of persecution on February 23, 303. The edict called for the razing of churches, the seizure of Scriptures, and the expelling of any Christians remaining in governmental or military positions, as well as forbidding Christians to assemble.[6]

The results, while very uneven, were horrifying in some places. Nicomedia (north-central Turkey today), the site of the imperial palace from which

4. See Samuel H. Moffett, *A History of Christianity in Asia*, vol. 1, *Beginnings to 1500*, 2nd ed., American Society of Missiology Series 36 (Maryknoll, NY: Orbis, 1998), 137–47.

5. Manichaeanism was a dualistic sect that arose in Persia and spread throughout the Near East of late antiquity. It was very popular in the Roman world and, like Christianity, pulled people away from worship of the old Roman gods. Augustine of Hippo, the great North African theologian, was a Manichaean before his conversion to Christianity in 386.

6. The story of the Great Persecution is told in many places. Eusebius's and Lactantius's accounts are especially gripping and form the basis for modern Christian retellings. See Eusebius, *Ecclesiastical History* 8, in *Eusebius Pamphili: Ecclesiastical History, Books 6–10*, trans. Roy J. Deferrari, FC 29 (Washington, DC: Catholic University of America Press, 1955), 163–205; Lactantius, *Deaths of the Persecutors* 7–16, pp. 144–56. A good entry point into the primary sources is David M. Gwynn, *Christianity in the Later Roman Empire: A Sourcebook*, Bloomsbury Sources in Ancient History (London: Bloomsbury Academic, 2015). See also Peter J. Leithart, *Defending Constantine: The Twilight of an Empire and the Dawn of Christendom* (Downers Grove, IL: IVP Academic, 2010).

Diocletian issued the first edict, felt the wrath of Rome first and hardest. Indeed, persecution was intense in Asia Minor (Turkey), Palestine, and Egypt for most of the next twenty years (with one major interval of peace), until 324. In Latin North Africa (Tunisia and Algeria today), persecution led by the Augustus Maximian was almost as intense as in the East for two years, but ended abruptly in late 304. In Gaul and Britain, where the Caesar Constantius Chlorus had little enthusiasm for the persecution, there was almost no loss of life; he simply burned down a few churches to satisfy the emperor that he had complied with the edicts.

From the Great Persecution to Milvian Bridge

In May 305 Diocletian took the unprecedented step of abdicating as emperor, and he retired to his palatial villa in current-day Croatia. Maximinus Daia, Galerius's nephew, replaced him as Augustus in the East. At the same time, Diocletian orchestrated the retirement of the Western Augustus, Maximian, thus leaving Constantius Chlorus in charge. According to Lactantius, Galerius orchestrated the double abdication and planned to replace Constantius with his friend Licinius, thus shoring up his own power.[7]

Constantius's first wife was Helena, apparently a woman of humble circumstances. The couple's son Constantine spent his youth far from his parents, serving in Diocletian's army in the East and joining Galerius's court after Diocletian's retirement. After much pleading from Constantius, Galerius allowed Constantine to join his father for the British campaign. In July 306 Constantius died at York—the extreme western fringe of the empire—and as he died he named Constantine, in his mid-30s, as his successor. Back in Rome, Maximian's son Maxentius, envious of Constantine's elevation to power in the far West, seized power over Rome and Italy, thus setting up the inevitable struggle with Constantine for control of the western half of the empire.

And so we return to the Battle of Milvian Bridge. Why did Maxentius not stay in Rome? By 312, the Christians in the West had been basically free of persecution for eight years, and the eastern reaches of the empire had been free of persecution since 311, although it soon began again. Galerius had died of cancer in 311, and Licinius and Maximinus Daia now controlled the East. October 28, 312, marked the sixth anniversary of Maxentius's seizure of power in Italy; he was popular with the people, and he was convinced that any undertaking would succeed. Peter Leithart summarizes well: "It seemed a propitious moment for him to confront his enemy, and his confidence was

---

7. See Lactantius, *Deaths of the Persecutors* 19–20, pp. 161–63.

buoyed by an oracle that reported, with the ambiguity characteristic of all oracles, that 'the enemy of Rome' would soon be defeated. He believed he was engaged in a battle of gods, a religious war, one in which he upheld the traditional worship of the empire."[8] Thus inspired, he crossed the Tiber on October 27, planning to do battle the next day.

On the other side of the river, as Constantine prepared to face Maxentius, he, too, saw himself in a religious war, and he needed a god on whom to rely to ward off the power of the pagan gods whom Maxentius trusted. What happened on October 27, the day before the battle, is described by Lactantius: "Constantine was warned in quiet to mark the celestial sign of God on his shields and thus to engage in battle. He did as he was ordered. He inscribed the name of Christ on the shields, using the initial letter X, crossed by the letter I with its top portion bent. Armed with this sign, the army took the sword."[9] Eusebius's account is much more effusive:

> He considered, therefore, on what God he might rely for protection and assistance. While engaged in this enquiry, the thought occurred to him that, of the many emperors who had preceded him, those who had rested their hopes in a multitude of gods, and served them with sacrifices and offerings, had in the first place been deceived by flattering predictions, and oracles which promised them all prosperity, and at last had met with an unhappy end, while not one of their gods had stood by to warn them of the impending wrath of heaven. . . . He judged it to be folly indeed to join in the idle worship of those who were no gods . . . and therefore felt it incumbent on him to honor his father's God alone. . . . Accordingly he called on him with earnest prayer and supplications that he would reveal to him who he was, and stretch forth his right hand to help him in his present difficulties. And while he was thus praying, a most marvelous sign appeared to him in heaven. . . . He saw with his own eyes the trophy of a cross of light in the heavens, above the sun, and bearing the inscription, CONQUER BY THIS.[10]

As we see, the details of these accounts vary, but the essential features are the same: Christ appeared to Constantine and provided an emblem under which his army gained victory over Maxentius. There has long been debate about exactly what the emblem was, but the common view for most of Christian history has been that it comprised a chi-rho or Christogram, an emblem in which the first two letters of Christ's name in Greek (χ and ρ) were combined in such a way as to make the shape of a cross.

---

8. Leithart, *Defending Constantine*, 65.
9. Lactantius, *Deaths of the Persecutors* 44, p. 191.
10. Eusebius, *Life of Constantine* 1.37–38, in NPNF² 1:489–90.

The chi-rho symbol

More important than the exact emblem, however, is Eusebius's claim that Constantine sought to combat Maxentius's reliance on pagan gods by reliance on the one true God. On the eve of the most important battle of his life, Constantine embraced the Christian faith, and a day later Rome—recently the chief persecutor of the church—was controlled by one who identified himself by the name and emblem of Christ. Maxentius's decision to leave Rome to meet Constantine at the Milvian Bridge makes perfect sense if one sees the conflict—as everyone at the time did—as a clash of competing gods. In the minds of people who saw the conflict this way, Maxentius's gods were routed by Constantine's new God, Christ.

Toleration and Consolidation

Meanwhile, back in the East the situation was changing rapidly. In 313 Licinius married Constantine's sister (a devout Christian), painted a Christian symbol on his own banner, ordered his army to pray to the Christian God, and routed his rival, Maximinus Daia, in Byzantium. That same year, Licinius and Constantine—now the only two rulers of the Roman Empire—wrote a series of letters concerning the toleration of Christians and granting freedom of religion to everyone but privileged status to the Christian faith. These letters are often triumphantly labeled the Edict of Milan, but in fact they did little more than preserve the status quo. Persecution had ceased in the West by 306, and it had more or less stopped in the East in 311. Licinius later had a change of heart and reinstituted persecution of Christians in the East as part of his last attempt to unseat Constantine. The final battle came on September 18, 324, at Chrysopolis near Nicomedia, where the persecution had begun twenty-one years earlier. Constantine prevailed, and now control of the entire Roman Empire was in the hands of one man, a Christian.

From the moment of Constantine's rise to power the Christian world knew of no other description of his conversion than "miracle." Eusebius, who had chronicled the harrowing stories of the early martyrs, turned to write a history of Constantine's life shortly after the emperor's death. From the vantage point of someone who witnessed the transition from persecution to acceptance, Eusebius was so in awe of Constantine that he wrote, "I stand as it were without power of speech or thought and unable to utter a single phrase."[11]

But Constantine was a man of apparent contradictions. He claimed to give allegiance to the Prince of Peace while being a ruthless and vindictive emperor. He murdered his wife and son while supporting the church-building efforts of his mother, Helena. His enemies feared yet respected the reach of his power, and his supporters, particularly among Christians, mixed popular praise for his rule with breathless exhilaration that the fires of persecution had ceased.[12]

It would be a lie to say that the transformation of Roman religion was immediate or even permanent. In the fourth century there was a rush to embrace the Christian faith, but not a few of these new converts approached Christ with Roman assumptions about what a god was to do on their behalf. Constantine, for all the might of the emperor that lay behind his faith, could not rupture the heritage of pagan belief with the wave of his hand. Much hard work lay ahead in discipling the new converts—indeed, in converting those who were allegedly but not truly converted already. Be that as it may, Christianity in the Roman Empire changed more dramatically through Constantine's rise to power than at any other point in history. Again, we need to remember that Christianity was also present outside the Roman Empire. In fact, Rome was not even the first kingdom to embrace the faith. Osrhoene, a small kingdom in what is today eastern Turkey, may have become the first Christian kingdom in the late second century. And in the early fourth century, Armenia, Ethiopia, and Georgia became officially Christian prior to Rome.

---

11. Eusebius, *Life of Constantine* 1.3, in NPNF[2] 1:482.
12. Wrestling with these seeming contradictions in Constantine's life is the major purpose of Leithart, *Defending Constantine*.

But Rome was by far the largest empire to adopt the Christian faith in ancient times, and its conversion had the most dramatic effect on the church as a whole.

At this point, it is important to say something about our use of geographical terminology. One of Constantine's first acts as sole Roman emperor was to commission the building of a glorious new capital on the site of the ancient city of Byzantium. This new city, Constantinople, was soon to become the center of the Christian world, as

Constantine on
an official coin

© Baker Publishing Group

well as the administrative center of the Roman Empire. As a result, Rome itself diminished in prestige a great deal, and the Christian West became more isolated from the East. Thus, while technically there continued to be a single Roman Empire, it is more accurate to refer to distinct political entities in the eastern and western parts of the Roman world. Modern historians typically refer to the eastern regions, including the capital, as Byzantium or the Byzantine Empire. In the West there was a substantial power vacuum after the removal of the capital, and this vacuum eventually was filled by tribes from north of the Alps. It is common to hear that Rome fell in 476,[13] the year German soldier Flavius Odoacer deposed the last native Roman to rule Italy. In reality, it was only the western regions of the Roman Empire that "fell," since "Rome" was actually governed from Constantinople. Eventually, Frankish rulers united the Western Christian world into what is grandiosely called the "Holy Roman Empire." In light of these realities, in roughly the first half of this book we use "Roman Empire" to refer to the entire Roman (Christian) world, "Byzantium" or "Byzantine Empire" to refer to the eastern Roman (Christian) world, and "Western Christian world" or "Frankish realms" to refer to the West. Beginning with part 3, we will have reached the point that it will become appropriate to speak of "Western Europe," "medieval Europe," and even of the "Holy Roman Empire" (with the understanding that the last of these consisted not of Western Europe as a whole but mainly of what later became Germany).

13. A position made famous in the eighteenth century by Edward Gibbon, *History of the Decline and Fall of the Roman Empire.*

Conclusions

With all of this tumultuous history in mind, we are ready to address the broad question that we posed near the beginning of this chapter: What does all of this have to do with early Christian creeds? The short answer is that the conversion of the empire meant that church life and imperial life became closely intertwined, and thus the desire for theological articulation of the faith—the creedal impulse—began to be combined with the need for imperial unity and stability. Within a year of his conversion, in 313 Constantine was called on to resolve a theological/ecclesiastical dispute (the Donatist schism) in faraway North Africa, and before he had consolidated his power in 324 he was made aware of a great theological crisis (the Arian controversy) brewing in the Eastern Christian world. While Constantine probably had little understanding of the theological issues at stake, he definitely had an interest in seeing the church adopt a unified confession of faith. In short, the conversion of the empire meant that the need for imperial unity put pressure on the church to standardize its various creedal formulations, to make a visible show of unity before the whole of Roman society.

Of course, this imperial pressure raises more questions. Elsewhere Fairbairn has expressed them like this: "Did imperial pressure force the church to adopt creedal statements even though such creedal uniformity was not really essential to the Christian faith? Did such creedal statements produce only a surface unity while masking deep divisions in the way Christians understood Christ? Or was there a genuine consensus about the person of Christ, a consensus that was brought to light under imperial prodding but not imposed by that pressure?"[14] Since standardized Christian creeds emerged only after the conversion of the Roman Empire, it is tempting to assume that imperial pressure was what produced the uniformity that the creeds provided, and thus that the uniformity was merely superficial. But in the chapters that follow we will argue that there really was a genuine consensus behind the creeds, and thus that imperial prodding did not impose unity but rather provided the occasion for demonstrating a unity that was already there. We are now ready to turn to the Christian church's greatest theological crisis, the Arian controversy, which led to Christianity's most widely accepted creed, the Nicene Creed.

14. Donald Fairbairn, *Grace and Christology in the Early Church*, Oxford Early Christian Studies (Oxford: Oxford University Press, 2003), 3.

4

The Nicene Creed

A Creed for the Entire Church

On May 20, 325, at the imperial resort city of Nicaea in what is today Iznik, Turkey (near Istanbul on the Asian side of the Bosporus), some three hundred bishops from throughout the Christian world gathered. Eusebius describes the momentous occasion this way:

> As soon, then, as the whole assembly had seated themselves with becoming orderliness, a general silence prevailed, in expectation of the emperor's arrival. . . . And now, all rising at the signal which indicated the emperor's entrance, at last he himself proceeded through the midst of the assembly, like some heavenly messenger of God, clothed in raiment which glittered as it were with rays of light, reflecting the glowing radiance of a purple robe, and adorned with the brilliant splendor of gold and precious stones. Such was the external appearance of his person; and with regard to his mind, it was evident that he was distinguished by piety and godly fear.[1]

It would be difficult to overstate how awe-inspiring this spectacle must have been to the assembled bishops. Constantine's defeat of Licinius in nearby Chrysopolis—and with it the final end of the Great Persecution in the Roman Empire—was less than a year in the past. Bishops who had spent their lives coping with an antagonistic Roman state could scarcely believe their eyes

---

1. Eusebius, *Life of Constantine* 3.10, in *NPNF*[2] 1:522.

The city of Nicaea

as a Christian emperor (who had even paid their travel expenses) opened a theological council to proclaim the Christian faith to the world. Over the next month, the bishops produced a creed affirming the church's faith that the Son is just as fully God as the Father, a creed they thought would crush the new heresy of Arius (more on him in this chapter) and bring peace to the church. For the rest of Christian history, the names "Nicaea" and "Constantine" were forever linked in celebration of this crowning moment of achievement.

The only problem was that the story didn't play out according to the script.[2] The unity of the Christian empire, symbolically portrayed with such vividness at Nicaea, proved to be rather elusive in actuality. Arius did more or less recede from prominence after the council, but an Arian-like heresy reared its head again in the 340s, dominating the church's attention and eventually forcing the convening of another great council in Constantinople in 381. The creed promulgated at Nicaea on June 19, 325, was not, in fact, what we today call the "Nicene Creed"—at least not exactly. To make matters worse, many modern scholars suggest that there never was any unity, any consensus about the Christian faith at all. In what has come to be the classic statement, R. P. C. Hanson asserted in 1988, "Should this state of affairs be called a

2. For an excellent, detailed overview of this history, see John Behr, *The Nicene Faith*, 2 vols. (with continuous pagination), Formation of Christian Theology 2 (Crestwood, NY: St. Vladimir's Seminary Press, 2004), 69–122. See also Leo Donald Davis, *The First Seven Ecumenical Councils (325–787): Their History and Theology* (Collegeville, MN: Liturgical Press, 1983), 33–133.

controversy, or a search in a fog, a situation when 'ignorant armies clash by night'? Another important point to realise about the period . . . is that it was not a history of the defence of an agreed and settled orthodoxy against the assaults of open heresy. On the subject which was primarily under discussion there was not as yet any orthodox doctrine."[3]

These are strong and troubling words. How did all this happen? How could a short, universally accepted summary of the Christian faith—the Nicene Creed—emerge from such chaos? Was there really no consensus about God until the end of the fourth century?[4] These are the questions that concern us in this chapter, and to begin answering them, we need to look more closely than we have so far at the interface between the Christian faith and the Greco-Roman thought world.

Salvation in Greco-Roman Thought and in Christianity

In Greco-Roman society, as in many pagan societies, there was great variety in how one described god (or the gods, or the divine realm, or ultimate reality), and also great variety about what a person had to do in order to attain to the realm of god or the gods (or to gain salvation, if one wants to say it that way). But what the many different gods and paths to god had in common was that whatever one thought had to be done, human beings had to do it themselves. Varying religions offered competing versions of self-salvation. In the many popular religions of the Roman world, salvation was accomplished through rituals that allegedly united practitioners to one or another of the Roman gods. In contrast, the great thinkers of the Greco-Roman philosophical scene prescribed varied approaches to ethical behavior while usually insisting that the path to union with the gods was a matter of ethics and morality, not just ritual observance. In both low and high forms, pagan religions started from the premise that we could and must rise up to the divine realm ourselves.

In sharp contrast, Christianity affirms that what is necessary for people to be united to the true God is not something that fallen human beings can do

3. R. P. C. Hanson, *The Search for the Christian Doctrine of God: The Arian Controversy, 318–381* (1988; repr., Grand Rapids: Baker Academic, 2005), xviii.

4. The classic scholarly treatment of this complicated controversy is Hanson, *Search for the Christian Doctrine of God*. Recent works that see more consensus than Hanson does include Behr, *Nicene Faith*; Lewis Ayres, *Nicaea and Its Legacy: An Approach to Fourth-Century Trinitarian Theology* (New York: Oxford University Press, 2004). More recent still, and perhaps the best place to start, is Khaled Anatolios, *Retrieving Nicaea: The Development and Meaning of Trinitarian Doctrine* (Grand Rapids: Baker Academic, 2011).

Altar of Zeus at Pergamum, a symbol of salvation for the Greco-Roman world

themselves. It follows, therefore, that if we are to be saved, God has to come to us. Scripture describes God's descent to us in many ways, such as God's calling of Abraham, God's leading of Israel out of Egypt, and the establishment of Israel as a nation. But all of these events are precursors to two main descents: the incarnation of the Son and the descent of the Holy Spirit to indwell believers. In short, our salvation is accomplished because the Son of God has come down to live *among* us, and the Holy Spirit has come down to live *within* each of us.[5]

From this biblical-theological logic that God had to come down to save us and that this coming down was accomplished primarily through the incarnation of the Son and the indwelling of the Spirit, two implications follow readily:

1. The Son and the Spirit have to be *just as fully and equally God* as the Father is. Otherwise, it wouldn't be *God* who came down to save us, and we would be left with the impossible task of saving ourselves.
2. The Son really had to *come down* through the incarnation. Otherwise, we would again be left with the impossible task of rising up to God on our own.

As you look at these assertions, you'll recognize that we have already seen them in the early creed-like affirmations and baptismal symbols of the second and third centuries. Those statements focused either on putting the Son and the Spirit "above the line" with God, or on describing Christ's human life "below the line" after he came down. Indeed, we argued in chapter 2 that this focus on God, Christ, and the Holy Spirit was the early church's way

5. We should note here that these were the two main past descents. Two others will come in the future: the second descent of Christ to earth, and finally the descent of the Father as he brings heaven with him and establishes the new heavens and new earth.

of stressing the same point that Protestants are making when they discuss Pauline justification by faith.

God

Creation

Distinction between God and creation

The theological background to Nicaea was rooted in the church's response to the highest form of pagan philosophical thought. Remember that from popular religion to Greco-Roman philosophy, pagan thought in the ancient world focused on the means by which the human being could rise up to the divine realm. The most influential of the Greek philosophies was Platonism,[6] which by the first century AD affirmed the existence of a high god to whom human souls sought to be united. By the third century, Platonism had postulated a series of unequal divinities, the high god (called the "One"), the "Logos" or "Word," and the "World Soul" or "Spirit." Here, of course, there were astonishing verbal parallels to the Christian Trinity, but the parallels were misleading. In Platonism, the three divinities were not remotely equal. The One was seen as far above the Word, which in turn was above the World Soul. Furthermore, the lower divinities were regarded as rungs on a ladder, and with the help of the World Soul and the Word, a human soul was thought to be able to climb up to the high god, the One.[7]

What this means, of course, is that Platonic philosophy explicitly affirmed that human beings were able to rise up to god and that the lower divinities were aids to help us make that ascent. In this way, Platonism, for all its philosophical sophistication, was not markedly different from any other pagan religion. It affirmed self-salvation, as did all the rest. In fact, by the third century, famous Platonists were claiming that it would be unworthy of the One to pay any attention to human beings, or to anything else outside itself. (We use the word "itself" intentionally, since Platonists viewed the high god as being impersonal.) The high god, the One, could and must focus only on

6. Modern scholars distinguish three phases in the development of the Platonic tradition after Plato's death in 348 BC: the period of Platonism until about 100 BC; the age of Middle Platonism, from around 100 BC to AD 200; and the time of Neoplatonism from the third century forward. For simplicity, we follow the ancient practice of referring merely to Platonism, without distinguishing Middle Platonism from Neoplatonism as moderns do.

7. The greatest of the third-century Platonic philosophers was the Egyptian Plotinus. For an example of his hierarchical view of god and of salvation as the ascent of the soul to the One, see Plotinus, *Enneads*. A useful anthology, with extensive selections from the Enneads, is Jason L. Saunders, ed., *Greek and Roman Philosophy after Aristotle*, Readings in the History of Philosophy (New York: Free Press, 1966).

itself, and so any thought of its descending to the human realm to help human beings was unthinkable.[8]

From this explanation, it does not seem that the church would have had any trouble distinguishing its thought from Platonic teaching. But the problem, as you may have guessed, was the similar terminology. When people steeped in Greco-Roman thought forms read the Bible, it was easy for them to identify the God of the Bible, the Father, with the high god of Platonism. Likewise, it was easy to identify the Son with the Word (indeed, John's Gospel even calls him "the Word"), and to equate the biblical Holy Spirit with the Platonic World Soul. As people unwittingly made such identifications, they could easily treat the vast amount of biblical discussion about ethical living as instruction in how to rise up to God. The fundamental distinctives of Christianity—not just a Trinity but a Trinity of *equal* persons, and the insistence that God had to come down to us—could be lost as philosophically minded thinkers read the Bible through lenses that owed more to Platonism than to a scriptural worldview.

The most famous and influential of the early Christian Platonists was Origen of Alexandria (located on the Nile delta in Egypt), who lived from about 185 to 253. He was a brilliant thinker and a rigorous ascetic who taught at a famous catechetical school (that is, a school for instructing young Christians in the faith). In the early third century, Origen wrote a work titled *On First Principles*, which could be called the first systematic theology book in Christian history. Although he wrote the work in Greek, we possess it completely only in a Latin translation that many scholars believe is inaccurate, and so it is difficult to establish what Origen actually taught. But if we go by the work *On First Principles* as we have it, the vision that it gives us of the Christian faith is a strange one indeed. The work describes human souls as having always existed in a disembodied state, and in that state all but one of the souls (that of Jesus) rebelled against God and "fell." God then chose to create the physical world as the place where these fallen souls could work their way back to him, and he united each soul with a body for that purpose. Salvation, as Origen conceived it (again, if we can trust *On First Principles* as we have it), consisted of the soul's struggles to rise up to God, and Jesus (who never fell away from God to begin with) served primarily as a guide to enable the souls to make the upward trek.

It is not hard to recognize that this vision of Christian life owes too much to Platonism and not enough to a biblical view of the world. In fact, *On First*

---

8. Plotinus famously claimed, "The Supreme as containing no otherness is ever present with us; we are present with it when we put otherness away. It is not that the Supreme reaches out to us seeking our communion; we reach towards the Supreme; it is we that become present." *Ennead* 6, ninth tractate, in Saunders, *Greek and Roman Philosophy*, 270.

Origen

Principles specifically states that the Son is lower than the Father and that the Spirit is lower than both Father and Son.[9] Here was the unequal Trinity of Platonism, coupled with a Platonic view of salvation as the task of humans to rise up to God. How could someone as brilliant as Origen make such a bad mistake? Well, we need to remember again that the text of his masterwork as we have it may not reflect very well what he actually wrote. But even if it does, we should realize that when Christianity and one's own cultural worldview *sound* very similar, it is hard for people to recognize where they differ. The verbal similarities make it easy to interpret the gospel too much in light of one's own culture. It could happen to anyone—even Origen—and in different ways maybe even to us.

Origen's thought was regarded by many as being problematic, but it was enthusiastically embraced by others, and we label the ascetic movement that he

9. Origen, *On First Principles* 1.3.5, in *Origen: On First Principles*, trans. G. W. Butterworth (Gloucester, MA: Peter Smith, 1973), 33–34.

started as Origenism. Many Christian Origenists were monks and nuns who were already inclined to see Christianity in terms of their ascetic efforts, and under Origen's influence they interpreted Christian life as an upward movement of the soul toward God. The role of the incarnation—the downward movement of God to us—was thus less valued. Consequently, it was easy for followers of Origen to forget that the Son was equal to the Father and instead to interpret him as a subordinate divinity, more akin to the Platonic understanding of the Word than to the biblical understanding.

The Outbreak of the Arian Controversy (318–25)

In the early fourth century, a man by the name of Arius arrived in Alexandria. He was from Antioch (on the coast of the Mediterranean, in what was then Syria but is today southern Turkey) and studied under one of Origen's followers, Lucian of Antioch. Arius regarded salvation as an upward movement of the soul to God, and he saw the Son as a figure between God and humanity who could thus help us in that ascent.[10] Arius was also a rigorous logical thinker, and he believed that the Bible's teaching on creation from nothing (that is, that everything outside God was created by God; nothing existed independently as an equal to him) meant that even the Son had to be created. In this way, Arius took Origen's belief that the Son was lower than the Father to its logical conclusion: if there really was a hard line between God (uncreated) and everything else (created by God), then it would seem that the Son (who in Arius's mind "must" be lower because the Platonic Trinity of unequals was influencing Arius as well as Origen) would have to be below that line, and thus a creature.

In 318 or 319, as the recently converted Constantine was still solidifying his power over the eastern regions of the Roman Empire, Arius wrote a letter to Alexander, the bishop of Alexandria. Part of the letter reads,

> We acknowledge one God, the only unbegotten, the only eternal, the only one without cause or beginning, the only true, the only one possessed of immortality, the only wise, the only good, the only Sovereign, . . . the begetter of his only Son before endless ages; through whom he made both the ages and all that is; begetting him not in appearance but in truth, giving him subsistence by his own will, [begetting him] immutable and unchanging, the perfect creation of

10. For an excellent treatment of Arius's view of salvation, see Robert C. Gregg and Dennis E. Groh, *Early Arianism: A View of Salvation* (Philadelphia: Fortress, 1981). See also Anatolios, *Retrieving Nicaea*, 122, where he contrasts Arius's "portrayal of Christ as an upwardly mobile god whose overall career is one of promotion, progress, and advance" with Athanasius's view of "Christ as the descending, self-humbling God."

God. . . . The Son, timelessly begotten by the Father, created and established before all ages, did not exist prior to his begetting, but was timelessly begotten before all things; he alone was given existence [directly] by the Father. For he is not eternal or co-eternal or equally self-sufficient with the Father.[11]

Here we should notice that the issue was not whether the Father is unbegotten and the Son begotten. Everyone in the fourth century understood the Son to be somehow begotten from the Father, or the Bible would not have called him "Son." The issue was not even whether the Son was begotten before the universe was created, since even Arius asserted that the Son was begotten "before all ages." The issue was whether there was once when there was no Son, and therefore whether the Son was eternal or not. Arius clearly believed that there *was* once when there was no Son (not quite "a time when there was no Son," since this was before time, but nevertheless the Son "was not before he was begotten"). If there was once when the Son was not, then the Son was a creature. Christ goes below the hard line separating God from all that he has made, not above the line. For Arius, "begotten" and "created" were synonymous, and the begotten/created one must somehow be after the one who begat/created him.

Father

Christ and Creation

Arianism sees the Son as created.

In one sense, Arius's thought here is perfectly logical. With human beings, begetting is an action that takes place in time, and a son has to be younger than his father. If we think in terms of this human analogy of begetting, then we would seemingly be forced to agree with Arius. Furthermore, in Greek the word for "having been begotten" (*gennētos*) was almost identical to the word for "having come into existence" (*genētos*). The two words differed by only one letter, were pronounced the same way, and functioned as synonyms in all cases where they were used of human beings. So Arius was working from the biblical idea that everything except God was created by God, but he was imbued with a philosophical mind-set that saw the Son as lower than the Father, and he was speaking a language in which the word for being a son sounded like and functioned the same way as the word for coming into existence. We can hardly be surprised that with these mental tools in hand, Arius called the Son a creature. Furthermore, since Arius (like many of Origen's followers) saw salvation

---

11. Rowan Williams, *Arius: Heresy and Tradition*, rev. ed. (Grand Rapids: Eerdmans, 2001), 207–11. Also in CCFCT 1:77.

as our task of rising up to God, he felt no urgency for the Son to be coeternal with and equal to the Father. The Son, he incorrectly thought, was the one who would lead us up to God—one creature rising up so that other creatures could follow him and rise up themselves. All Arius was doing was taking the common Platonic-influenced reading of Christianity to its logical conclusion.

Therein lies the rub. Mistakes that are bad enough to be called heresies rarely arise full-blown out of nowhere. They start out as seemingly small mistakes whose significance is not immediately noticed, and only when someone pushes the mistaken logic to its conclusion does the church as a whole recognize that there is something seriously amiss. Arius's letter, and especially the bold assertions in the portions of the letter we have quoted, led the church to recognize the problems with any "Christianity" that placed the Son lower than, and later than, the Father.

The Council of Nicaea (325)

Arius's bold proclamations in his letter to Alexander led to several years of letter-writing frenzy and the convening of a small synod[12] in Syrian Antioch, which condemned Arius's teaching. The leader of that synod, Hosius of Cordoba (Spain), was Constantine's theological adviser, and he recommended that the emperor call a larger council to confirm that synod's decision. Constantine complied by calling a council to meet in Ancyra (present-day Ankara, the capital of Turkey), but he then moved the council closer to the imperial court in Nicomedia,[13] and it met in Nicaea from May 20 to June 19, 325. Constantine invited all 1,800 Christian bishops living within the Roman Empire. Delegates came from all reaches of the Roman world and beyond, and estimates of the actual attendance ranged from 250 to 318.

The bishops assembled at Nicaea included a number of radical anti-Arians, including Constantine's adviser Hosius, Alexander of Alexandria, and Alexander's deacon, Athanasius, who was then in his late twenties and who went on to dominate the Arian controversy for the rest of his life. Arius was joined by a few vocal followers from Libya (where his influence was strongest), and he also had a major ally in Eusebius of Nicomedia (not the same person as the church historian Eusebius of Caesarea). The majority of

12. An ecclesiastical gathering was called a *synodos* in Greek or a *concilium* in Latin. In English, we normally use the Greek-derived word "synod" for a small council and the Latin-derived word "council" for a major one.

13. The new imperial capital of Constantinople was under construction at this point, so the imperial court was residing on the Asian side of the Bosporus. Constantinople was dedicated in 330.

the bishops entered the council without a clear idea of what the issue was or even what was wrong with describing the Son as being lower than the Father, but Alexander, Hosius, and company quickly convinced them of the need to reject Arius's teaching.

The question of what to affirm instead of Arius's teaching was more complicated, and since we do not have actual minutes from this council,[14] we do not know the exact proceedings. But from accounts written by those who were present, it appears that various baptismal symbols were brought forward as models for the writing of a creed and that Hosius was most instrumental in producing the Creed of Nicaea. The new creed was formally ratified on June 19, 325. Remarkably, only three people refused to sign: Arius himself (who was a presbyter, not a bishop) and two Libyan bishops, Theonas and Secundus. All three were exiled, and Arius's writings were condemned.[15]

The Creed of Nicaea

The table below contains the reconstruction of a prototypical Greek creed (discussed in chap. 2) next to the Creed of Nicaea (with the key Greek terms left untranslated for now).

If one sets aside the untranslated Greek words for a moment, it is clear that the Creed of Nicaea had many similarities to the early Eastern baptismal symbols from which it was modified. (Keep in mind that what we have on the left is a reconstruction; what the bishops at Nicaea likely had in front of them were various symbols similar to one another, of which this reconstruction is an approximation.) We see the same basic structure, with a paragraph on each person of the Trinity, and a division of the paragraph on Christ into sections on who he is and what he has done for our salvation. The content of the Creed of Nicaea is in harmony with the reconstructed earlier symbol, and there is even some word-for-word agreement.

At the same time, the differences are striking. The paragraph on the Holy Spirit is reduced to a bare affirmation, without the various other affirmations (church, baptism, resurrection, etc.) normally mentioned along with the Holy Spirit. The description of Christ's life and work is actually shorter as well, but the description of who he is in relation to the Father is much longer. Most

---

14. Detailed "acts" (akin to what we call "minutes," but more stylized and meant as public documents), as well as lists of all bishops present, first appeared with the Third Ecumenical Council in 431.

15. For ancient accounts of the council, see Socrates, *Ecclesiastical History* 1.8–9, in NPNF[2] 2:8–17; Eusebius, *Life of Constantine* 3.7–14, in NPNF[2] 1:521–23; Sozomen, *Ecclesiastical History* 1.7, in NPNF[2] 2:253.

A Prototypical Greek Creed	The Creed of Nicaea
We believe in one God, the Almighty, Maker of all things visible and invisible;	We believe in one God the Father All Governing, creator of all things visible and invisible.
and in one Lord Jesus Christ, his only-begotten Son, begotten of the Father before all ages; through whom also all things came to be; who for us came down from heaven and became incarnate, was born of the Virgin Mary and was crucified under Pontius Pilate and was buried, and rose on the third day in accordance with the Scriptures, and ascended into heaven, and is seated at the right hand of the Father, and will come in glory to judge the living and the dead; of his kingdom there will be no end.	And in one Lord Jesus Christ, the Son of God, begotten from the Father as only begotten, that is, from the *ousia* of the Father, God from God, Light from Light, true God from true God, begotten not created, *homoousios* with the Father, through whom all things came into being, both in heaven and in earth; Who for us men and for our salvation came down and was incarnate, becoming human. He suffered and the third day he rose, and ascended into the heavens. And he will come to judge both the living and the dead.
We believe also in one Holy Spirit, the giver of life, and in one holy catholic and apostolic church, one baptism of repentance for the forgiveness of sins, in the resurrection of the dead, in the kingdom of heaven, and in life everlasting. Amen.[a]	And [we believe] in the Holy Spirit.
	But, those who say, Once he was not, or he was not before his generation, or became to be out of nothing, or who assert that he, the Son of God, is of a different *hypostasis* or *ousia*, or that he is a creature, or changeable, or mutable, the Catholic and Apostolic Church anathematizes them.[b]

a. August Hahn, *Bibliothek der Symbole und Glaubensregeln der alten Kirche*, 3rd ed. (1897; repr., Hildesheim: Olms, 1962), document 122; translation in CCFCT 1:14.

b. John H. Leith, ed., *Creeds of the Churches: A Reader in Christian Doctrine, from the Bible to the Present*, 3rd ed. (Atlanta: Westminster John Knox, 1982), 30–31 (modified by restoring the key terms to Greek). Also in CCFCT 1:159.

revealing of all, however, is the addition of anathemas, a list of incorrect statements about Christ. Notice that the church did not simply condemn the statements; it condemned the people who affirmed these things of Christ. Taken together, the changes clearly indicate the contextual origin of this creed. It was almost exclusively an attempt to address the problems of Arianism. It did so by affirming in much stronger language than had been used previously the Son's equality with the Father and by vehemently rejecting those who affirmed the Son to be noneternal or a creature or mutable. Symbols designed for use in a fairly general setting (baptism) were modified to deal with a very specific heresy: the placing of the Son below the hard line that divides God from all that he has created.

Furthermore, in spite of the controversial terms that we have left untranslated, it is crystal clear what this creed is claiming. It strongly affirms the *derivation* of the Son from the Father through the repetition of the words "begotten" and "from." It just as strongly affirms the *identity* between the Son and the Father: not only is the Son *from* God, but he *is* God; not only is he *from* light, but he *is* light. Even though it does not try to explain what divine begetting involves, it does insist that in the case of God, being begotten is different from being made/created. In all of these ways, the creed places the Son on the same side of the creator-creature divide as the Father. Also clear is the creed's insistence that for our salvation, the Son "came down" through the incarnation. Indeed, the second paragraph/article of the creed unequivocally affirms both of the points that we argued were the main assertions of the later Nicene Creed: for us to be saved, God had to come down, and thus the Son has to be fully equal to the Father. Since this is indeed so clear, and since the creed was so obviously focused on rejecting the Arian heresy, one might indeed wonder why this creed and the condemnation of Arius did not bring the controversy to an end. As we asked at the beginning of this chapter, why did the dispute drag on for some fifty-six years after this?

To answer that question, we need to notice two other things about this creed. First, and most obvious, the mention of the Holy Spirit is woefully inadequate. Indeed, this is just a placeholder. It is as if the bishops were reminding themselves that they needed to say something about the Holy Spirit, but they weren't doing so now because all their attention was on the Son.

Second, there are three complex and controversial Greek philosophical terms included in this creed: *ousia*, *homoousios*, and *hypostasis*.[16] The first of these, *ousia*, is perhaps the easiest to understand, since its usage did not vary much over time. The word *ousia* is from the word for "being," and it was understood as the innermost reality of an entity; it was that which made the entity *be* what it was. One could say that *ousia* is the "stuff" an entity is made out of, that enables us to see that it is *x* and not *y*. But when the word refers to God, this description doesn't work, because God isn't made out of any stuff. So it is better, when applying this word to God, to say that *ousia* is the collective total of whatever characteristics God possesses (perfect love, justice, power, etc.) that enable us to recognize him as God and not some other being. There was general agreement in the ancient world about *ousia*, and it can be satisfactorily rendered as "substance" or "essence." So when

16. For an excellent discussion of the words *ousia* and *hypostasis*, as well as the related words *physis* and *prosōpon* (which we will encounter in the next chapter), see John A. McGuckin, *St. Cyril of Alexandria: The Christological Controversy; Its History, Theology, and Texts*, reprint ed. (Crestwood, NY: St. Vladimir's Seminary Press, 2010), 138–45.

the creed states that the Son is "from the Father's *ousia*," this means that he is begotten bearing the same characteristics (what later theologians called attributes) as the Father, in contrast to all creatures the Father has made, which have a different character.

With this understanding of *ousia*, the adjective *homoousios* was intended to mean that whatever made God be God, the Son was *the same* in that way. It is translated as "consubstantial," "coessential," "one in essence," or "one in being," and the idea is that if the possession of characteristics *a*, *b*, and *c* indicates that an entity is God rather than a created being, then the Son possesses *a*, *b*, and *c* just as the Father does. If one considers the human analogy for a minute, you as a human being can *make* anything you want, and the product need not bear any resemblance to you. But you can *beget* (if you are a man) or *conceive* (if you are a woman) only a human being substantially like you, not an entity utterly different. In the same way, to say that the Son is begotten from the Father and even from the Father's substance is to assert the fundamental identity between the two. Even though the usage of the word *ousia* was very stable in the fourth century, and thus one might think that *homoousios* would likewise be quite clear, it turned out to be perhaps the most controversial word in Christian theological history, as we will see shortly.

The third philosophical word in the creed is *hypostasis*. Unlike *ousia*, this word changed dramatically in usage over the course of the fourth century. At this point early in the century, it was used as a synonym for *ousia*, to refer to the underlying substance that made something what it was. Over the course of the fourth century, though, the word began to be used of the concrete manifestation of the underlying substance—that is, more in the sense of "person" than "substance." As this chapter progresses, we will watch that shift, along with the considerable confusion associated with it. For now, though, notice that the creed uses the word *hypostasis* as a synonym for *ousia* when it condemns those who say that the Son is "of a different *hypostasis* or *ousia*." If the Son were of a different essence/substance/character from the Father, he would be a creature rather than God.

At this point, the obvious question is why the bishops gathered at Nicaea used these philosophical words in the creed to begin with. Why didn't they simply use biblical language? In fact, this question often turns into an accusation, as some modern scholars and even laypeople bemoan the "fact" that the church fathers transformed the gospel into some sort of Greek philosophical system. Before we accept that negative judgment, however, we need to recognize two things. First, an overly philosophized version of Christianity was what led to Arius's thought, not that of the church. Such philosophizing was what the church was arguing against, not what the bishops themselves were trying to do.

Another thing we need to recognize is that the bishops at Nicaea were driven to use nonbiblical language in order to make clear the difference between Arius and themselves. We have mentioned above that Athanasius was present at Nicaea as an assistant to Bishop Alexander of Alexandria. The bishop died three years later, and Athanasius became bishop of Alexandria. He then spent the remaining forty-six years of his life defending the Council of Nicaea in the midst of the myriad attacks that council faced. In the heat of those attacks in the mid-350s, Athanasius penned his *Defense of the Nicene Definition*, and part of his argument in that crucial work concerned the very question of why the bishops at Nicaea departed from biblical words. Athanasius wrote that at the council, as various biblical expressions were suggested for inclusion in the creed, the Arians

> were caught whispering to each other and winking with their eyes, that "like" and "always," and "power," and "in Him" were, as before common to us and the Son. . . . But the bishops discerning in this too their dissimulation, were again compelled on their part to collect the sense of the Scriptures, and to re-say and re-write what they had said before, more distinctly still, namely, that the Son is "one in essence" [*homoousios*] with the Father; by way of signifying, that the Son was born from the Father, and not merely like, but the same in likeness, and of shewing that the Son's likeness and unalterableness was different from such copy of the same as is ascribed to us, which we acquire from virtue on the ground of observance of the commandments.[17]

This striking window into the inner workings of the council shows that the bishops felt compelled to use nonbiblical words in order to "collect the sense of the Scriptures" in a way that would make clear the fundamental difference between their thought and that of Arius. At the most basic level, as we have seen, Arius argued for an essential similarity between Christ and us. Arius's Christ, like us, was below the hard line separating God from all else. Arius's Christ, like us, needed to advance, to rise up to God. In sharp contrast, the framers of the Creed of Nicaea wanted to affirm that Christ started out by being fundamentally *unlike* us and *like* God. He was and is above the hard line, not below it. We are works that God makes; Christ is the Son whom God has begotten, and thus he is "not made." He is the one "through whom all things came to be," rather than one of the things that came to be. This Son, who was fundamentally like his Father and unlike us, *became like us* when he

17. Athanasius, *Defense of the Nicene Definition* 20, in NPNF[2] 4:163–64.

"came down and became incarnate." For Arius, salvation was an upward action: first the Son and then his followers had to rise up to God. For the bishops at Nicaea—indeed for the Christian faith as a whole—salvation involved the downward action of one who was truly God coming to earth to live as truly human. And at the center of the creed's affirmation of this stark difference lay the word—admittedly not a biblical word but one deemed necessary by the bishops—*homoousios*, "one in essence" or "consubstantial."[18]

Father, Son

Creation

The Nicene understanding of the Son

When we consider the Creed of Nicaea as a whole, it should be fairly obvious that its polemical character (the inclusion of anathemas) and extreme disproportion (great specificity about the Son's eternal being, but relatively little about his earthly ministry and nothing of substance about the Holy Spirit, the church, etc.) would hardly make it suitable as a liturgical creed. It simply did not have the flow and balance that liturgical usage required. Furthermore, the word *homoousios* had a problematic past and raised the suspicions of many bishops that the creed itself was heretical in a different way than Arius's thought was heretical. These problems led to a complicated and confusing aftermath to the Council of Nicaea, and to this we now turn.

The Aftermath of Nicaea (325–57)

Although Arius was exiled, his banishment did not last long. Some two and a half years after the Council of Nicaea, he submitted to Constantine a confession of faith that, though silent about the word *homoousios*, was satisfactory to the emperor (who was, of course, a theological novice). Constantine requested that the bishops reinstate Arius, but Alexander of Alexandria refused to honor the request. After Athanasius replaced Alexander in 328, he also refused to reinstate Arius. Athanasius thus began his episcopacy on rather rocky terms with the imperial throne and under a cloud of suspicion with the many Eastern bishops who were loyal to the throne.

18. Behr comments helpfully, "Prior to the council, the term [*homoousios*] did not carry a precise meaning, but had been used in various, more or less loose, ways. Neither does the term appear to be an integral part of anyone's theological vocabulary. . . . All the indications point to the term being introduced into the creed because it was known that Arius and his most ardent supporters objected to it." *Nicene Faith*, 157.

By the late 330s, it was obvious that many bishops were uneasy with the word *homoousios*. The word had been used in the past to indicate not merely that Father and Son shared the same identity/character/nature, but that they were actually numerically one—that is, (to use later terminology) the same person. This was the heresy of Sabellianism (also called Modalism or Modalistic Monarchianism), associated with Sabellius, an early third-century Roman teacher. Sabellianism affirmed a single person of God, called the Son-Father, who manifested himself in different ways (or modes) at different times. In the Old Testament period, he showed himself as Judge and Father, in the time of Christ as Son, and in the church age as Spirit and Helper. But these different manifestations did not have independent existence as distinct persons. A variant of the same idea, associated with Paul of Samosata (on the banks of the Euphrates River in ancient Syria, but today underneath the Ataturk Dam in southeastern Turkey) in the third century and Marcellus of Ancyra (Ankara, modern capital of Turkey) in the fourth century, was the teaching that the Word was not a distinct person from the Father but an aspect of God, and this aspect was manifested in the Son Jesus during his earthly life. In other words, an impersonal aspect of God was perfectly exhibited in the man Jesus, who was in a sense adopted as Son of God. The third-century council that had ruled against Paul of Samosata actually condemned the use of the word *homoousios*. Not surprisingly, then, many Eastern bishops opposed Nicaea's use of that word.

Nicaea had set a precedent for the writing of a general (as opposed to a purely local) creed whose wording was affirmed and used throughout the Christian world. But because of the concerns about the word *homoousios*, by about the year 340 many bishops thought it wise to try to write new creeds avoiding the controversial word. Among the most famous of the many creeds written in the 340s and 350s were the Dedication Creed,[19] written in Syrian Antioch in 341; the Western Creed of Sardica, written in 343 in what is today Sophia, Bulgaria;[20] and the Macrostich or Long-Lined Creed, produced in Syrian Antioch in 344.[21] These and other creeds of the time avoided the use of the word *homoousios* and described the Son in other, more traditional ways. It is not always clear whether they were meant as replacements for the Creed of Nicaea (although Athanasius took most of them that way and called them "Arian") or whether they were meant as explanations of Nicaea.[22] Thus, it is

19. See *CCFCT* 1:89.
20. See *CCFCT* 1:91–93.
21. See *NPNF*[2] 4:462–64.
22. Fairbairn has argued that the "Western Creed of Sardica" was meant as a commentary on Nicaea rather than as a replacement. See Donald Fairbairn, "The Sardican Paper, Antiochene

The eastern and western halves of the Roman Empire

also difficult to tell which of these creeds should be classified as "Arian" and which as "Nicene." The confusion created by the word *homoousios* had made it difficult to tell who was saying what, who was on which side. Indeed, the church historian Socrates, summing up the confusion over the objectionable word and admitting that he didn't understand the issues, wrote, "It seemed not unlike a contest in the dark; for neither party appeared to understand distinctly the grounds on which they calumniated one another."[23]

Adding to the confusion was the fact that, at the same time, Roman imperial politics were a blur that eclipsed even the complicated situation leading to Constantine's accession earlier in the century (described in chap. 3). Constantine died in 337, leaving the empire to his three sons. Constantius controlled the eastern portions, Constantine II ruled Britain and Gaul, and Constans ruled Italy and the Balkans. Like his father, Constantine II sought to extend his rule from the far west into Italy, but he was killed in 340 in his unsuccessful campaign to control Rome itself. Thus, Constans now controlled the entire West and Constantius the East. This arrangement lasted until 350, when Constans was assassinated, leading to a new power struggle that left Constantius as sole emperor until his own death in 361. At that point, his nephew Julian, who renounced Christianity for paganism, ruled for a brief eighteen months before dying in battle in 363, at which time the empire returned to Christian hands and became more stable, as Jovian assumed the throne.

These imperial power struggles were intertwined with the shifting and confusing theological alliances. Most notably, Constans was a strong supporter of the Creed of Nicaea, Constantius generally favored the anti-Nicene bishops, and Julian sought to create havoc in the church by pitting all groups of Christians against one another. All three of these emperors wielded the tool of banishment (and reinstatement of bishops banished by others) to try to shore up their support. Bishops of various persuasions were banished by one emperor or another and then reinstated by a different emperor, leading to an almost constant migration of bishops from region to region from 340 to 363. Athanasius himself was exiled five different times for a total of seventeen years, sometimes to the West and sometimes to the Sahara Desert in Upper Egypt. Cyril of Jerusalem and other bishops likewise spent more than a decade in one exile or another, several years at a time.

So what do we make of all this confusion? One way to handle it would be to distinguish groups of Christians by the key words they used to describe the Son's relationship to the Father. One party, led by Athanasius, insisted

---

Politics, and the Council of Alexandria (362): Developing the 'Faith of Nicaea,'" *Journal of Theological Studies*, n.s., 66, no. 2 (2015): 653–66.
   23. Socrates, *Ecclesiastical History* 1.23, in NPNF² 2:27.

on the word *homoousios*, "one in essence," as the best word. Another group, led by Basil of Ancyra and George of Laodicea (in western Turkey today), preferred instead to speak of the Son as *homoios kat' ousian*, "like according to essence," and they insisted that this was not the same thing as *homoousios*. Yet a third group, which was actually led by the emperor Constantius (whose major goal was to remove *ousia* language from the Creed of Nicaea because it had fostered so much controversy), advocated the expression *homoios kat' energeian*, "like in activity." Finally, a small group of people led by Eunomius and Aetius insisted that the Son was *heterousios*, "unlike in essence." Thus, it would appear that there were four major factions in the decades after Nicaea.

However, we suggest that among these four groups, there were actually only two fundamentally different viewpoints. One view, what Athanasius and later Christian historians have called Arianism, affirmed that the Son had to rise up to God and, in doing so, could lead us up. This was the faith of those who called the Son "unlike in essence" and of those who called him "like in activity." The other view, what has later been called Nicene Christianity or simply orthodoxy, affirmed a fully divine Son who had to come down to accomplish our salvation. This was the faith of those who called the Son *homoousios* and of those who called him "like according to essence," although in the 350s the groups using those different expressions did not realize their fundamental agreement. The following table may help to clarify the situation:

Group	What the Group Said	What the Group Meant
Homoousian Party	*homoousios* ("one in essence")	The Son shares God's nature and is the one who has come down to save us.
Homoiousian Party	*homoios kat' ousian* ("like according to essence")	The Son is exactly like God in nature and is the one who has come down to save us.
Homoian Party	*homoios kat' energeian* ("like according to activity")	The Son acts in the way God does in order to rise up to God.
Heterousian Party	*heterousios* ("unlike in essence")	The Son, although different in character from God, acts in the way God does in order to rise up to God.

From this table, perhaps it should be clear that the various words being used masked a basic dichotomy, the same dichotomy that we have seen throughout this story of creeds. Can we rise up to God, or does God have to come down to us? If the latter, then the Son who comes down has to be just as fully God as the Father. We believe that in the 350s most of the church was actually in agreement on this fundamental point (that is, most bishops belonged to one or the other of the first two groups in the table above), and only the diverse terminology prevented them from seeing that agreement.[24] How, then, did the church emerge from what Socrates called "a contest in the dark"?

Emerging from the Darkness (357–62)

The various creeds that were written in the 340s and early 350s did not overtly take a stand against the Creed of Nicaea, and we have seen that it was not always clear whether they were meant as replacements for it or as explanations of it. That deference toward Nicaea abruptly ended in the summer of 357, when a small group of bishops met in Sirmium (in modern-day Serbia) at the insistence of Emperor Constantius. These bishops issued a creed that prohibited the use of "essence" language (expressly forbidding the use of the terms *homoousios* and *homoios kat' ousian*) and explicitly stated that the Son was subordinate to the Father. Their discussion of the incarnation dropped the famous statement that the Son "came down," although it did speak of his taking flesh.[25] The next several years saw Constantius move with increasing boldness to compel bishops throughout the empire to embrace this faith in a creaturely Son who rose up to the Father, and his efforts galvanized the church into more unified action against him. Hilary of Poitiers (from France, but at this time he was in exile in the East) labeled this creed the Blasphemy of Sirmium,[26] and both Hilary and Athanasius insisted that *homoios kat' ousian* was the same thing as *homoousios*.[27]

Nevertheless, reconciling the *Homoiousian* and *Homoousian* parties was tough work, with little progress until Constantius died in 361 and the pagan Julian the Apostate became emperor. In an effort to foment chaos by pitting Christians one against another, Julian reinstated all of the exiled bishops, regardless of their theological leanings. Many of these bishops were in exile in Upper Egypt, and they sailed down the Nile to Alexandria before dispersing to their various episcopal sees. Before they left town, Athanasius called a council in the spring of 362, at which key terminological stumbling blocks were removed, allowing the church's consensus to emerge into daylight. The main issue, mentioned earlier in this chapter, was that some Eastern bishops

---

24. For a fuller explanation, see Donald Fairbairn, "The Synod of Ancyra (358) and the Question of the Son's Creaturehood," *Journal of Theological Studies*, n.s., 64, no. 1 (2013): 111–36.

25. Athanasius gives the full text in *On the Synods* 28, in NPNF[2] 4:466.

26. Hilary of Poitiers, *On the Synods* 10, in NPNF[2] 9:6.

27. See Athanasius, *On the Synods* 41, in NPNF[2] 4:472. See also the whole of Hilary's *On the Synods* in NPNF[2] 9.

were using *hypostasis* as a synonym for *ousia* (that is, using both to mean "essence," as the Creed of Nicaea itself had done in the anathemas), and thus were speaking of one *hypostasis* in God. Athanasius himself used the word this way. Others were using *hypostasis* more in the sense of "person," and thus were speaking of three *hypostaseis* in God. Athanasius insisted that the groups explain themselves so that each group could recognize that the other was trying to say the same thing it was, and then he subtly encouraged terminological standardization by advocating the expression "three *hypostaseis* and one *ousia*" ("three persons and one essence"). At the same time, Athanasius guided the assembled bishops in affirming the *homoousios* as the standard way to profess the Son's equality with the Father.[28]

This council was of crucial significance in bringing about reconciliation between the groups that had been battling in the night. While one could see it is a compromise or a manufactured unity, the way we have presented the entire controversy strongly suggests that it was actually the unveiling of a consensus that was already present, a consensus long obscured by political machinations and terminological confusion. The way was now paved for the reaffirmation of Nicaea as a creed for the entire church. The Council of Alexandria also called attention to the need for creedal language about the Holy Spirit.

Further Struggles (362–81)

The emerging consensus did not mean that the political battles related to Nicaea were over. While the West was more pro-Nicene, anti-Nicene imperial policy still continued in the East. Symptomatic was the fact that when Athanasius died in 373 and his brother Peter was chosen as bishop, the government refused to ratify the election and instead installed an Arian, Lucius. These political battles continued throughout the 370s until Theodosius I, a Nicene, gained control of the Eastern empire in 379, again restoring religious peace to the Roman world.

At the same time, the theological issues under consideration turned from the Son in eternity to his incarnate state, and from the first two persons of the Trinity to the Holy Spirit. In the 360s and 370s a friend of Athanasius, Apollinaris from Laodicea in Syria,[29] began to argue for a view of Christ in which the Word took the place of his human mind. While the church did respond to

28. See Fairbairn, "Sardican Paper," 675–78.
29. This was not the same city as the Laodicea in western Asia Minor (Turkey), one of the seven churches of the book of Revelation.

Pasabag (Valley of the Monks) in Cappadocia in modern Turkey

Apollinaris at the time, this issue pertains more to the Chalcedonian Definition than to the Nicene Creed, so we will consider it in the following chapter.

Much more directly related to the Nicene Creed was the question of the Holy Spirit. In the latter part of the fourth century, a group called Macedonians emerged who affirmed the equality of the Son to the Father but denied that of the Holy Spirit. In response, shortly before Athanasius died, he wrote two long letters in which he addressed the status of the Holy Spirit with respect to the Son and the Father. In these letters he used the word *homoousios* to describe the Holy Spirit's relation to the Father, thus strongly emphasizing the equality of the Spirit to the other persons.[30]

After Athanasius's death, the mantle of leadership fell to three brilliant theologians from the region of Cappadocia in what is today central Turkey. Two of these were Basil of Neocaesarea (normally called Basil the Great) and his brother Gregory of Nyssa, two of ten children from a devout Christian family. Educated by their older sister, Macrina, herself one of the best-educated Christians of the time, they became leaders of fourth-century monasticism and church politics, as well as great theologians. Both of them wrote treatises arguing against the thought of Eunomius (the major Arian-like theologian

30. Athanasius, *First Letter to Serapion* 1.27.4, in *Works on the Spirit*, trans. Mark Del-Cogliano, Andrew Radde-Gallwitz, and Lewis Ayres, PPS 43 (Yonkers, NY: St. Vladimir's Seminary Press, 2011), 96.

of the time). Basil also wrote a major work on the Holy Spirit against the Macedonians, in which he argues that the Spirit possesses the titles and attributes ascribed to the Father and Son, and that he is worshiped together with the Father and Son. Thus, he should be seen as God in the same way as the Father and Son.[31] The third of the "Great Cappadocians" was Basil's and Gregory's best friend, Gregory of Nazianzus (often called Gregory the Theologian). He was one of the great orators of the early church, and his *Five Theological Orations* on the Trinity provide one of the best examples of mature trinitarian theology as it developed in the late fourth century.[32]

Basil died in 379, about the time that Theodosius was consolidating his power over the empire. Theodosius enforced the Nicene faith throughout the Eastern empire and even had Gregory of Nazianzus installed as bishop of Constantinople in November 380. At about the same time, Theodosius called for a council to meet in Constantinople in May 381.

The Council of Constantinople (381)

About 150 bishops, all from the eastern part of the empire, gathered in Constantinople for the council. They included Gregory of Nazianzus (now bishop of Constantinople) and Gregory of Nyssa, Cyril of Jerusalem, Meletius of Antioch (who presided at Theodosius's request), and surprisingly, thirty-six Macedonians, whom Theodosius had invited in the confidence that they could be won over to the affirmation of the Spirit's equality. The council began with the sudden death of Meletius (Gregory of Nyssa preached the funeral oration) and then the election of Gregory of Nazianzus to preside. The Macedonians, however, walked out of the conference rather than assent to the Nicene faith. Furthermore, delegates from Egypt raised objections to the way Theodosius had named Gregory as bishop of Constantinople, and Gregory promptly resigned and departed. After all of these matters had been sorted out, the council was finally able to get to work, and it was Cappadocian theology that dominated. The Nicene faith was reaffirmed, and the full deity of the Holy Spirit was proclaimed. Apollinarianism was condemned, although we will consider that in the next chapter.[33]

31. See St. Basil the Great, *On the Holy Spirit*, trans. Stephen M. Hildebrand, PPS 42 (Yonkers, NY: St. Vladimir's Seminary Press, 2011).

32. See St. Gregory of Nazianzus, *On God and Christ*, trans. Frederick Williams and Lionel Wickham, PPS 23 (Crestwood, NY: St. Vladimir's Seminary Press, 2002).

33. See the accounts of the council in Socrates, *Ecclesiastical History* 5.8, in NPNF[2] 2:380; Sozomen, *Ecclesiastical History* 7.7, in NPNF[2] 2:121; Theodoret, *Ecclesiastical History* 5.8, in NPNF[2] 3:135–36.

Since we don't have minutes of the council, we don't know more specifically what its inner workings were, and incredibly enough, there is some question about whether it even approved what we call the Nicene Creed. That document (properly called the Nicene-Constantinopolitan Creed, as opposed to the Creed of Nicaea from 325) makes its earliest appearance in our extant literature only in 451, and many church fathers between 381 and 451 seem to have been unaware of it. Accordingly, some have argued that the Council of Constantinople did not approve a creed at all. However, J. N. D. Kelly has argued convincingly (and subsequent scholars have agreed) that what we call the Nicene Creed was approved at Constantinople in 381. His conclusion is worth quoting:

> The Council of Constantinople did in fact, at some stage in its proceedings, endorse and use C [= the Nicene-Constantinopolitan Creed], but in doing so it did not conceive of itself as promulgating a new creed. Its sincere intention was simply to confirm the Nicene faith. That it should do this by adopting what was really a different formula from that of Nicaea may appear paradoxical to us, until we recall that at this stage importance attached to the Nicene teaching rather than to the literal wording.[34]

With this complicated history behind us, and with the startling possibility that the Nicene Creed did not even come from the Council of Constantinople set aside, we are now finally ready to look at the creed itself.

The Nicene Creed

The table below contains the Creed of Nicaea from 325, printed and discussed earlier in this chapter, displayed beside the Nicene Creed of 381. A quick read-through will show the obvious similarity between the two documents. Both profess faith in each of the persons of the Trinity in turn. Both emphasize the role of Father and Son in creation. Both stress the equality of the Son to the Father prior to rehearsing the events of his earthly life. Both include the word *homoousios*, since the long struggle over that word concluded with its general acceptance as a description of the Son's relationship to the Father. Both mention the Holy Spirit. And in both cases, the statement that the Son "came down" for our salvation holds pride of place at the very center of the creed.

34. J. N. D. Kelly, *Early Christian Creeds*, 3rd ed. (London: Longmans, 1972), 325. See also Davis, *First Seven Ecumenical Councils*, 121–22.

The Creed of Nicaea	The Nicene Creed
We believe in one God the Father All Governing, creator of all things visible and invisible.	We believe in one God the Father All Governing, creator of heaven and earth, of all things visible and invisible.
And in one Lord Jesus Christ, the Son of God, begotten from the Father as only begotten, that is, from the *ousia* of the Father, God from God, Light from Light, true God from true God, begotten, not created, *homoousios* with the Father, through whom all things came into being, both in heaven and in earth;	And in one Lord Jesus Christ, the only-begotten Son of God, begotten from the Father before all time, Light from Light, true God from true God, begotten not created, *homoousios* with the Father, through Whom all things came into being;
Who for us men and for our salvation came down and was incarnate, becoming human. He suffered and the third day he rose, and ascended into the heavens. And he will come to judge both the living and the dead.	Who for us men and because of our salvation came down from heaven, and was incarnate by the Holy Spirit and the Virgin Mary and became human. He was crucified for us under Pontius Pilate, and suffered and was buried and rose on the third day, according to the Scriptures; and ascended to heaven, and sits on the right hand of the Father and will come again with glory to judge the living and dead. His kingdom shall have no end.
And in the Holy Spirit.	And in the Holy Spirit, the Lord and life-giver, Who proceeds from the Father, who is worshiped and glorified together with the Father and Son, Who spoke through the prophets;
	And in one holy, catholic, and apostolic Church. We confess one baptism for the remission of sins. We look forward to the resurrection of the dead and the life of the world to come. Amen.[a]
But, those who say, Once he was not, or he was not before his generation, or became to be out of nothing, or who assert that he, the Son of God, is of a different *hypostasis* or *ousia*, or that he is a creature, or changeable, or mutable, the Catholic and Apostolic Church anathematizes them.[b]	

a. John H. Leith, ed., *Creeds of the Churches: A Reader in Christian Doctrine, from the Bible to the Present*, 3rd ed. (Atlanta: Westminster John Knox, 1982), 33 (modified by restoring the key terms to Greek). Also in *CCFCT* 1:163.

b. Leith, *Creeds of the Churches*, 30–31 (modified by restoring the key terms to Greek). Also in *CCFCT* 1:159.

At the same time, a glance at the proportions of the creeds reveals important differences. The section on the eternal identity of the Son is actually shorter in the Nicene Creed than in the earlier creed, whereas the discussion of the events of his earthly life is longer. The anathemas are missing entirely from the Nicene Creed. And most strikingly, the bare affirmation of the Holy Spirit in the Creed of Nicaea is expanded to a whole paragraph in the Nicene Creed, followed by traditional affirmations (church, resurrection, etc.) missing from the earlier creed. We saw earlier in this chapter that the Creed of Nicaea was ill-suited to liturgical life because of the anathemas and the lack of proportion (especially the lengthy section on the eternal Son). Now we see that the Nicene Creed has restored more normal proportions (less on the eternal Son, more on his earthly life) and removed the anathemas, and thus that it is much more suitable as a liturgical summary than the earlier creed. The creed emerged from various baptismal symbols and was modified substantially at Nicaea in 325 in order to refute Arianism with precision and power. Now, at Constantinople it has been modified again to restore it to a more traditional liturgical style, with less detail on the now-settled issue of the Son's equality to the Father, but much more detail on the now-controversial equality of the Holy Spirit, and more phrases about Christ's life and the various appended affirmations recouped from baptismal symbols.

In fact, the style of the Nicene Creed is so much more liturgical than that of its predecessor that scholars generally agree it is not actually a modification of the Creed of Nicaea. Again, we do not know the details of what happened at Constantinople, but scholars today think that the bishops assembled there did not take the Creed of Nicaea as their starting point and modify it into the Nicene Creed. Rather, scholars think that some other, more liturgical creed of the time was the starting point for their work.[35] Be that as it may, it is clear that the bishops at Constantinople were developing the *faith* of Nicaea by addressing a new situation (in which the full equality of the Spirit was at issue), even if their base text was not the Creed of Nicaea itself but some other document in harmony with it. Hanson's conclusion is important: "We can, I believe, conclude with fair confidence that those who drew up C [the Nicene Creed] and those who knew of its existence and probably taught and used it for the next fifty years did not think of it as a new, separate creed from N [the Creed of Nicaea] . . . but simply as a reaffirmation of N, an endorsement of what it really meant by means of a little further explanation."[36]

If we move past these general comparisons to a more detailed analysis, other differences between the creeds emerge. The statement "of a different *hypostasis* or *ousia*" in the anathemas of the earlier creed implied an identification of those two words. As we have seen, by now they were no longer

---

35. See Kelly, *Early Christian Creeds*, 301–25; Davis, *First Seven Ecumenical Councils*, 121–23; Hanson, *Search for the Christian Doctrine of God*, 816–17; Behr, *Nicene Faith*, 377.
36. Hanson, *Search for the Christian Doctrine of God*, 820.

regarded as synonyms, and the formula "one *hypostasis* or *ousia*" has been replaced by "three *hypostaseis* and one *ousia*." Removing the anathemas in the Nicene Creed allows this terminological change to become standard without the awkwardness of having to explain the old word usage in the creed of 325. Thus, the Nicene Creed bears tacit witness to this sharpening of trinitarian terminology without actually using that terminology.

Furthermore, "from the *ousia* of the Father" and "God from God" in the Creed of Nicaea are both missing from the Nicene Creed. These omissions are, in fact, major planks in the scholarly argument that the council must have been working from a different base than the original Creed of Nicaea, since it would be unthinkable that anyone at this point would object to those phrases. However, it is still possible to explain the omissions on the assumption that the base was the Creed of Nicaea and the bishops at Constantinople dropped these phrases intentionally. Perhaps they were simply trying to shorten this section of the creed. (After all, "true God from true God" occurs later, so including "God from God" as well is unnecessary.) Or perhaps their desire was to focus on the persons in relationship to one another, rather than on the abstract idea of *ousia* or essence. It is noteworthy that *homoousios* (which, of course, was retained) is an adjective, the use of which serves to stress the relationship of the Son to the Father, not to call attention to essence per se. *Ousia*, in contrast, is a noun that forces one to focus on essence. Perhaps the final wording of the Nicene Creed—with no mention of *ousia* in the noun form, or for that matter, of *hypostasis*—is attempting to focus not so much on the *concept* of three persons with one essence, as on the three persons *themselves*, who are, in fact, equal and share the same set of characteristics.

By far the most significant difference between the two creeds is the addition of a lengthy discussion of the Holy Spirit in the Nicene Creed. This new discussion establishes the Spirit's equality with the Father and Son by calling him "the Lord and life-giver." Notice here that just as the Son is called "Lord," so the Spirit is called "Lord." Just as the Son is the agent of creation, so the Spirit is the one who gives life. The equality of the persons is not handled in abstract terms but by describing them in relation one to another. Then comes the famous affirmation, "Who proceeds from the Father." This assertion parallels the description of the Son as "begotten from the Father." The Son's deity has to do with his relation to the Father, who is God, and the Spirit's deity has to do with a different kind of relation to the Father, who is God. Again, the persons are described in relation one to another, not in the abstract. At this point, some Western readers will recognize that their version of the creed reads "from the Father *and the Son*." We will consider this later addition to the Latin version of the creed in chapters 7 and 10. For now, it is enough to point out that the phrase "Who proceeds from the Father" comes directly from Jesus's words in John 15:26. Although Jesus *sends* the Spirit to descend on the disciples, the Spirit's *eternal* relation is described as "Who proceeds from the Father." Here the creed is reproducing exactly the wording of the biblical text.

The next great affirmations have to do with the Spirit's work in time (he "spoke through the prophets") and our response to him ("worshiped and glorified together with the Father and Son"). This phrase is reminiscent of Basil the Great's major argument in his work *On the Holy Spirit*, that we worship the Holy Spirit just as we worship the Father and Son. Thus, the Holy Spirit must be and is equal to the other persons, in contrast to what the Macedonians argued. Like the Son, the Holy Spirit goes above the hard line separating God from everything he has made.

Among the beliefs appended to the paragraph on the Holy Spirit in the Nicene Creed, the first and most striking is the belief "in one holy, catholic, and apostolic Church." The four adjectives used to modify the word "church" in this phrase are often called the "marks of the church," and different groups within Christendom have long understood the oneness, holiness, catholicity, and apostolicity of the church in different ways.[37] Moreover, there is great disagreement on how one should understand the relation of this assertion to the ones about the Holy Spirit. Protestants are inclined to see the church, forgiveness of sins, resurrection, and the life of the age to come as works that the Holy Spirit brings about.[38] Thus, one could say that Protestants take "believe in the church" in the sense of "believe that there is one, holy, catholic, and apostolic church."[39] Roman Catholics tend to take "believe in" more strongly here and

37. For an introduction to the various interpretations of these marks of the church, see Alister E. McGrath, *Christian Theology: An Introduction*, 5th ed. (Oxford: Wiley-Blackwell, 2011), 390–99.

38. See, for example, J. I. Packer, *The Apostles' Creed* (Wheaton: Tyndale, 1977), 74–77; Alister E. McGrath, *"I Believe": Understanding and Applying the Apostles' Creed* (Grand Rapids: Zondervan, 1991), 118–24. Although both are commenting on the Apostles' Creed, their words about the church apply equally to the Nicene Creed, and McGrath's discussion actually deals with the phrase from the Nicene Creed, not found in the Apostles' Creed! Both show a Protestant understanding of the church as the work of the Holy Spirit and what could be called a minimalistic reading of the force of "believe in" with reference to the church.

39. Long before Protestantism began, Rufinus, in his *Commentary on the Apostles' Creed*, elucidated this distinction between belief in God and belief that there is a holy church. He writes, "Had the preposition IN been inserted, the force of these articles would have been identical with that of their predecessors. As it is, in the clauses in which our faith in the Godhead is laid down, we use the form, IN GOD THE FATHER, IN JESUS CHRIST HIS SON, and IN THE HOLY SPIRIT. In the other clauses, where the theme is not the Godhead but created beings and saving mysteries, the preposition IN is not interpolated. Hence we are not told to believe IN THE HOLY CHURCH, but that the Holy Church exists, speaking of it not as God, but

to focus on the role of the church as an extension of the incarnation, drawing its life from Christ and mediating his grace to the world.[40] Eastern Orthodox Christians are more likely to insist that "belief in" has the same force with respect to the church as it does with respect to the Father, Son, and Spirit. We do not just believe that there is a holy, catholic, and apostolic church. Instead, they argue, we believe *in* that church just as we believe *in* Father, Son, and Spirit.[41] We will consider these differences in the understanding of the church—as well as related matters that may trouble Protestants, such as the connection between baptism and forgiveness—in chapters 8 and 9.

Conclusions

In this chapter we have surveyed the convoluted history behind the drafting of the Creed of Nicaea at the First Ecumenical Council in 325 and the eventual adoption of what we call the Nicene Creed at the Second Ecumenical Council at Constantinople in 381. From this survey, though, it may not appear that the chapter subtitle—"A Creed for the Entire Church"—is warranted. Indeed, it may seem that the Nicene Creed is merely the statement of faith that won out, and that it did so only because of the political success of Constantine in the early part of the fourth century and Theodosius toward the end. How can we claim that this is truly a universal creed?

To recognize the universality of the creed, we need to grasp three things. First, on the fundamental question—"Can we rise up to God, or does God have to come down to us?"—the vast majority of people who called themselves Christians in the fourth century were in agreement. We cannot rise up to God on our own; God must come down. So a Son who was a creature like us, who could merely lead us up to God, would do us no good. Likewise, a Spirit who was a creature could not be the "Lord and life-giver" who unites us to God. The complicated terminological issues often obscured the depth and breadth of the agreement, but that consensus was there, and when it was brought to the surface, the church rallied in agreement.

---

as a Church gathered together for God." Rufinus, *A Commentary on the Apostles' Creed* 36, trans. J. N. D. Kelly, ACW 20 (New York: Newman, 1955), 71.

40. See, for example, Luke Timothy Johnson, *The Creed: What Christians Believe and Why It Matters* (New York: Doubleday, 2003), 254–57.

41. See, for example, Anna Marie Aagaard and Peter Bouteneff, *Beyond the East-West Divide: The World Council of Churches and "the Orthodox Problem"* (Geneva: WCC Publications, 2001). Bouteneff writes, "The Church emerges not only as a community of believers, not only as something that we believe *exists*, but as something we believe *in* in the same way we believe in God—Father, Son and Holy Spirit" (p. 20).

Second, in order to grasp the creed's universality we need to recognize that imperial pressure was not what produced this consensus, even though imperial prodding led the church to articulate it. The clearest evidence of this is that when Constantius tried to unify the church around a statement of faith that subordinated the Son to the Father, that tried to silence discussion of theological terminology, and that omitted the crucial phrase "he came down," the church rose up in opposition, bringing its internal disputes to resolution and speaking with a united voice. Emperors could and did demand creeds, could and did lean hard on the church to say this rather than that in a creed, but could not successfully overturn the will of the church, try as they might.

A third thing we need to do in order to grasp the universality of the creed is to remember that the faith it enshrines was accepted not just under pressure, but willingly, and not just in the Roman Empire, but also outside the reach of Constantine's or Theodosius's coercive power. Indeed, all groups still in existence today that call themselves Christian have accepted the faith of Nicaea.[42] It is true that organized Arian Christianity took hold among the Gothic and Vandal tribes north of the Alps in the fourth century, largely through the work of the missionary Ulfilas. But this Arian Christianity was absorbed into Nicene Christianity by the early sixth century, and no officially Arian group remained after that time. Kelly's eloquent conclusion, quoted in chapter 1 of this book, is worth repeating: "Of all existing creeds it is the only one for which ecumenicity, or universal acceptance, can be plausibly claimed. . . . It is thus one of the few threads by which the tattered fragments of the divided robe of Christendom are held together."[43] This creed truly is, more than any other document penned by human beings, a creed for the entire church.

As we bring this chapter to a close, it is worth making one more point. Christians are fond of saying that the Nicene Creed is too complicated, too philosophical, too hard to understand. If this chapter has succeeded in doing anything, it has shown that the situation producing the creed *was* complicated—maybe more so than any other theological debate in Christian history. Nevertheless, the Nicene Creed that emerged was not an abstruse theological treatise, the property of bishops and theologians alone. While a parade of philosophical and theological terms marched across the stage during the fourth-century controversies, the only one that remained in the final form of the creed was *homoousios*, "consubstantial." For the most part, the

---

42. In the Eastern churches, for more than fifteen hundred years the Nicene Creed has been the baptismal symbol and has also been recited during the celebration of the Eucharist. It is recited during the eucharistic celebration in Roman Catholic and Anglican churches as well. Many Lutheran and some Reformed Protestant churches recite it during Advent and Lent.

43. Kelly, *Early Christian Creeds*, 296.

creed relied on language accessible to ordinary people. Sometimes we make the mistake of equating the Nicene Creed with the complexities of either the period that produced it or our later theological discourse based on it. In particular, the word "essence" dominates Protestant discussions of the Trinity, and few of us realize that the word does not occur as a noun in the final form of the Nicene Creed. Although the way the final wording came about was complicated, it is striking that the creed focuses not on "essence" and "person" as concepts, but on the Father, the Son, and the Spirit.

Turn back a few pages and read it again, on its own, without the assumption that it is too complicated for you to understand. It is really quite simple: we believe in one God who made everything; we believe in his eternal Son, equal to him, who came down for our salvation, to do for us what we could not do ourselves; we believe in his eternal Spirit, worshiped just as much as he and the Son are, who makes us alive. This is the Nicene faith. Indeed, this is the Christian faith, to which believers throughout history and throughout the world have been dedicated. The Nicene Creed is for everyone.

5

The Chalcedonian Definition

Explaining the Nicene Creed

Early in the previous chapter we discussed what we called the biblical-theological logic that God had to come down to save us through the incarnation of the Son and the indwelling of the Spirit. We argued then that two things follow from this logic:

1. The Son and the Spirit have to be *just as fully and equally God* as the Father is. Otherwise, it wouldn't be God who came down to save us, and we would be left with the impossible task of saving ourselves.
2. The Son really had to *come down* through the incarnation. Otherwise, we would again be left with the impossible task of rising up to God on our own.

As we saw, the first of these points was the issue of the fourth century, as the church penned the Nicene Creed to articulate the full equality of the Son and Spirit to the Father. We also saw that the church stated the second point through the creed's affirmation that for us and our salvation, the Son "came down from heaven, and was incarnate." However, at least in the early part of the Arian controversy, the church did not reflect in much depth on what it meant for the Son to come down. This issue began to gain prominence in the 360s, and as we saw, it was addressed briefly at the Second Ecumenical Council. But it was the fifth century before this issue truly rose to the surface,

Painting of the Council of Chalcedon by Vasily Surikov

leading to two more ecumenical councils (the third, at Ephesus in 431, and the fourth, at Chalcedon in 451). At Chalcedon, in response to great imperial pressure to produce a new creed, the assembled bishops responded instead by repeating both the Creed of Nicaea and the Nicene Creed, and issuing a definition explaining and developing the faith of Nicaea with more specificity about the incarnate Son.

We also mentioned earlier that unlike the Nicene Creed, universally accepted in the Christian church, the Chalcedonian Definition has proven to be strikingly divisive. Along the way to that definition, four councils were held (including two competing councils meeting at the same time in Ephesus in 431, one of which is now considered ecumenical), reaching seemingly disparate conclusions. The church in what was then eastern Syria (eastern Turkey, Iraq, and Iran today) rejected the Third Ecumenical Council at Ephesus. After Chalcedon, other churches in the non-Greek-speaking Eastern Christian world (Egypt, Ethiopia, Armenia, and western Syria) rejected its definition of the faith. If the process leading to the Nicene Creed seems chaotic up to the drafting of the creed itself, the process surrounding Chalcedon looks chaotic and fractured both before and afterward. There are many scholars who argue that there was no consensus at all about Christ in the early church.[1]

Therefore, the question of what claim the Chalcedonian Definition can make to universality is an urgent one. In this chapter we address this question by surveying the events and theological debates that led to Chalcedon and analyzing the Chalcedonian Definition itself, and by considering the reasons for the rejection of Chalcedon in many parts of the Christian East. In the process, we make the perhaps surprising argument that in spite of its divisiveness, the Definition expressed a profound consensus about Christ on the part of virtually the whole Christian church.[2]

The Beginnings of Controversy: Apollinarianism

We mentioned Apollinaris in the previous chapter, and now it is time to return to his thought in more detail. He was a friend of Athanasius and a staunch defender of the Nicene faith, and he was also one of the key early thinkers dealing with the question of what it meant for the Son or Word (the *Logos* in Greek) to become fully human. Apollinaris thought that to be fully human was to be an enfleshed spirit or a spirit in a body. In other words, he thought that if one was both immaterial (spirit) and material (body), then one was human. On the surface, this makes perfect sense. God and angels are completely spiritual, with no material component. Animals are fully physical, with no spiritual component. Only human beings are both spiritual and material. Thus, it is correct to say that being both spiritual and material is a *necessary* condition of being human. But is this a *sufficient* condition, or are there other

1. A particularly forceful, but by no means uncommon, expression of the view that there was no consensus about Christ is Philip Jenkins, *Jesus Wars: How Four Patriarchs, Three Queens, and Two Emperors Decided What Christians Would Believe for the Next 1,500 Years* (New York: HarperOne, 2010). Note, for example, his claim that "Chalcedon was not the only possible solution, nor was it an obvious or, perhaps, a logical one. Only the political victory of Chalcedon's supporters allowed that council's ideas to become the inevitable lens through which later generations interpret the Christian message" (p. xi).

2. The classic scholarly treatment of patristic Christology, including the Councils of Ephesus and Chalcedon, is Aloys Grillmeier, *Christ in Christian Tradition*, vol. 1, *From the Apostolic Age to the Council of Chalcedon (451)*, 2nd rev. ed. (Louisville: Westminster John Knox, 1988). See also Leo Donald Davis, *The First Seven Ecumenical Councils (325–787): Their History and Theology* (Collegeville, MN: Liturgical Press, 1983), 134–206. An excellent recent treatment of the politics of the controversy, albeit with a rather superficial view of the theological issues, is George A. Bevan, *The New Judas: The Case of Nestorius in Ecclesiastical Politics, 428–451 CE*, Late Antique History and Religion 13 (Leuven: Peeters, 2016).

conditions that must also be met before one can be considered fully human? Apollinaris believed that this was a sufficient condition for being human, whereas the church quite quickly responded to the contrary.

From this starting point, Apollinaris articulated a picture of the incarnate Christ in which the Logos took the place of the human mind in Christ. His idea was that if a spirit enfleshed is a human being, then for the Logos, who was already a spirit, to become human, he needed to take to himself only a human body. He did not need a human mind (usually called a "rational soul" in Greek) in order to be human. With respect to the Creed of Nicaea (of which he was a strong proponent), Apollinaris argued in effect that when the Logos "came down" through the incarnation, for him to come all the way down to the point of being human required only the assumption of flesh, not a human mind. Postulating a human mind in Christ would complicate any attempts to understand his psychology (if you will), and Apollinaris sought to avoid what he thought was an unnecessary complication.[3]

Let us step back for a minute and consider Apollinaris's thought. First, we need to recognize that this is not as severe a mistake as that of Arius and his followers. Apollinaris was emphatically not saying that we could rise up to God and needed only a leader. He insisted, as did Athanasius and the church as a whole, that God the Son had to come down to us. His problem was that his conception of what it meant to be human—and thus what it meant for the Son to come all the way down to a human level—was inadequate. To say this differently, he understood the *movement* of salvation correctly as a downward move on God's part, but he did not correctly grasp the full *extent* of this movement.

We saw in the previous chapter that as early as the Council of Alexandria in 362 it was recognized that the Logos needed to assume a human mind as well as a body for our salvation, and at the Council of Constantinople in 381 Apollinarianism was condemned, albeit without explanation. But the church father primarily responsible for responding to the problem with Apollinaris's thought was Gregory of Nazianzus (also called Gregory the Theologian), one of the three Great Cappadocians, whom we met in the previous chapter. Probing the implications of the incarnation to a depth that few previously had reached, Gregory recognized that the salvation Christ accomplished through the incarnation could reach only as far as his incarnation extended. In other words, if the Logos took on himself only a body, then the healing and salvation

---

3. Apollinaris's writings survive only in fragments. A convenient place to find translations of these collected fragments is Richard A. Norris Jr., ed., *The Christological Controversy*, Sources of Early Christian Thought (Philadelphia: Fortress, 1980), 107–11. See especially fragments 22, 25, 72, 129.

that he brought would extend only to the body. But the roots of sin do not lie in the body, because the body simply does what the mind or rational soul commands it to. When we sin, the problem is not fundamentally that our bodies act recalcitrantly against what we want to do, although that may be true in limited instances. More often, and more fundamentally, the problem is that we *want* to sin, and so we do. The problem, at heart, lies in the mind (and even more deeply in the will, which will be part of our discussion in chap. 8).

Shortly after his withdrawal from the Council of Constantinople, Gregory wrote two letters to his deputy priest Cledonius in 382. In the second of these letters, he insisted,

> Whoever has set his hope on a human being without mind is actually mindless himself and unworthy of being saved in his entirety. The unassumed is the unhealed, but what is united with God is also saved. Had half of Adam fallen, what was assumed and is being saved would have been half too; but if the whole fell he is united to the whole of what was born and is being saved wholly. They are not, then, to begrudge us our entire salvation or to fit out a Savior with only bones and sinews and the picture of a human being.[4]

Gregory's phrase "the unassumed is unhealed" went on to become one of the most famous catchphrases in Christian theological history. It perfectly encapsulated the need for the Son to take a full humanity—not just a body, but also a human mind (rational soul), human emotions, the ability to be tempted (although he did not actually sin; see Heb. 4:15)—in order to save us. While Apollinaris's mistaken concept of what it meant to be human was understandable, a Christ who took on himself merely flesh and not also a human mind could not have extended salvation to the sphere that needs it the most: the complicated and fallen realm of the human mind and will. If Christ had been the way Apollinaris said he was, that kind of Christ could not have saved us. Thus, the Logos must have assumed, and did assume, a human mind as well as a human body when he came down and was incarnated to accomplish our salvation.

An Unusual Response to Apollinarianism

As was the case with the initial condemnation of Arianism, so also here in the initial condemnation of Apollinarianism, this might have been the end

4. St. Gregory of Nazianzus, *Second Letter to Cledonius* 5, in *On God and Christ*, trans. Frederick Williams and Lionel Wickham, PPS 23 (Crestwood, NY: St. Vladimir's Seminary Press, 2002), 158.

Antioch in Syria

of the controversy. But it wasn't, because the specter of Apollinaris loomed large over the thought of three influential Christian thinkers (all from Syrian Antioch), whom the church later dubbed collectively as Nestorians and labeled their thought Nestorianism. These were Diodore, who was bishop of Tarsus (the apostle Paul's hometown in what is now southern Turkey) in the late fourth century; Theodore, who was bishop of Mopsuestia (near Tarsus) in the late fourth and early fifth centuries; and Nestorius, who became the bishop of Constantinople in 428.[5]

Diodore, Theodore, and later Nestorius saw Apollinarianism not as a mistake that should force a more thorough consideration of what it means to be human, but as an error so catastrophic that it demanded a complete rethinking of the incarnation. They undertook this rethinking by concentrating on the question of to whom one should ascribe the various events of Christ's life. Previously, theologians such as Athanasius and the Cappadocians had adopted a rubric of "as God / as man" and had described different actions and events by saying that God the Son incarnate did some of these things in a way befitting God, and others in a way befitting man. They emphasized, however, that it was the same person, God the Son or the Logos, who did both sets of actions. For example, in the year 380, in his famous *Oration* 29 on the Son, Gregory of Nazianzus asserted, "As man he was baptized, but he absolved sins as God. . . . As man he was put to the test, but as God he came through victorious. . . . He hungered, yet he fed thousands."[6] In contrast to this "as God / as man" approach, Diodore and Theodore became convinced that the human events (in the example just above, being baptized, being put to the test, and hungering) needed to be ascribed to a human being considered

5. In the nineteenth century, scholars linked these three thinkers together with others from the area around Antioch—Eustathius, Severian, John Chrysostom, John, and Theodoret—into an "Antiochene School" and began to depict the christological controversy as a clash between that school and the "Alexandrian School." We believe that this way of telling the story, while still very common and present in most textbooks, gives the mistaken impression that the two "schools" were equally represented and that the Chalcedonian Definition was simply a compromise between them. Therefore, we don't tell the story in this way in this chapter. For a brief explanation of why we disagree with this common approach to the controversy, see Donald Fairbairn, "The One Person Who Is Jesus Christ: The Patristic Perspective," in *Jesus in Trinitarian Perspective: An Intermediate Christology*, ed. Fred Sanders and Klaus Issler (Nashville: B&H Academic, 2007), 80–92. For more of the details, see the works by Fairbairn and others cited in that chapter.

6. St. Gregory of Nazianzus, *Oration* 29.20, in *On God and Christ*, trans. Frederick Williams and Lionel Wickham, PPS 23 (Crestwood, NY: St. Vladimir's Seminary Press, 2002), 87.

independently of the Son. In particular, they insisted that the crucifixion and death of Christ must be ascribed to an independent man, not to God the Son. Thus, with Apollinarianism in the background, these thinkers articulated an understanding in which Jesus was a man whom the Logos indwelt, granting him grace, aid, and cooperation in a way somewhat similar to the way the Holy Spirit does as he indwells believers.[7]

At this point, you might think that this means the Logos and the man were two separate persons. This has been the common charge leveled against the thought of Diodore and Theodore both in ancient and modern times, and they were very well aware of it. To see how they responded to it, we need to go into a little more detail about terminology. You may remember that in the previous chapter we saw that *ousia* and *hypostasis* started out as synonyms, both meaning approximately "essence." During the fourth century, though, *hypostasis* began to be used more in the sense of "person." There are two more terms we need to consider now. The first is *physis*, which is normally translated as "nature," but which many in the fifth century used in the sense of a "personal nature," an entity acting according to its characteristics or attributes. The second word is *prosōpon*, which originally meant "mask," in reference to the mask an actor in a Greek drama wore in order to indicate the character he was playing. By the fifth century, *prosōpon* was normally used in the sense of "person," and thus as a synonym for the newer use of *hypostasis*. But Diodore, Theodore, and Nestorius used it sometimes in the sense of "person" and sometimes in the sense of an external presentation (more literally like the mask to which the word originally referred).[8]

If this sounds confusing, perhaps it would be helpful to think of the four Greek words as representing a spectrum from the innermost "essence" of something to the outermost "presentation." The order would normally be like this: *ousia, physis, hypostasis, prosōpon.*

There are at least four ways to group the words in this spectrum so as to refer to what we now call the two natures and the one person of Christ. Three of these ways are presented in the table below, and the fourth will come up later in this chapter.

In this table the lines indicate where one can logically make hard distinctions so as to group certain words and use them as synonyms. In the first case, *ousia* is used to mean "essence," and *physis, hypostasis,* and *prosōpon*

---

7. The understanding of Christ described in the next few paragraphs is explained in detail in Donald Fairbairn, *Grace and Christology in the Early Church*, Oxford Early Christian Studies (Oxford: Oxford University Press, 2003), 21–62.

8. For more detail on these words, we refer readers again to John A. McGuckin, *St. Cyril of Alexandria: The Christological Controversy; Its History, Theology, and Texts*, reprint ed. (Crestwood, NY: St. Vladimir's Seminary Press, 2010), 138–45.

First Way (Most of the early fifth-century church)	Second Way (Most of the church after Chalcedon)	Third Way (Diodore, Theodore, and Nestorius)
ousia = essence	*ousia* = essence	*ousia* = essence
	physis = nature	
physis = personal nature		*physis* = personal nature
hypostasis = person	*hypostasis* = person	*hypostasis* = person
prosōpon = person	*prosōpon* = person	
		prosōpon = presentation

are all words for "person." This was the way most of the church was using the words in the early fifth century. In the second case, *ousia* and *physis* become words for "essence/nature," and the words *hypostasis* and *prosōpon* become words for "person." This constituted a change in the use of *physis*—moving it from one side of the line to the other—and it was the way most of the church wound up using these words after about 450, as we will see later in this chapter. But for Diodore, Theodore, and Nestorius, the word usage was more like the third column, in which *ousia* meant "essence," *physis* and *hypostasis* were words for "person," and *prosōpon* was more external even than "person," referring to how Christ appeared on earth.[9]

Why does this bewildering terminology matter? Because just as in the fourth century, even more so in the fifth and following, different uses of these words made it hard for the people involved in the discussions to understand what others were saying.[10] Diodore, Theodore, and Nestorius spoke of two *physeis* in Christ, and one *prosōpon*. If we translate these phrases as "two natures" and "one person," this sounds very acceptable to us. But when we recognize how they were using the words, we see that what they meant was two persons, the Logos and the assumed man, who *appear* as one external presentation because one doesn't actually see the Logos; one sees only the man. Furthermore, they argued that the word "Christ" was something of a corporate term that could encompass both the Logos and the assumed man, and this understanding of the word "Christ" enabled them to say that Christ is both divine and human. The Logos is divine, and the man is human, and since "Christ" is the man indwelt

9. This is an oversimplification. Actually, Theodore and Nestorius sometimes used *prosōpon* as a synonym for *hypostasis/physis* (thus, to mean roughly "person") and sometimes (as in Nestorius's famous phrase "*prosōpon* of union") to mean "external presentation." This latter use of *prosōpon* is the one described in the paragraph above.

10. This was neither the first nor the last time that terminology proved to be confusing in a theological controversy. Differing word usage has almost always been one of the factors leading to theological disagreements. We will see similar cases of terminological confusion at later intervals throughout this book.

Portrait of Nestorius by Romeyn de Hooghe

by the Logos, "Christ" is both divine and human. Most of the time, though, they used the word "Christ" to refer to the assumed man, Jesus. Thus, the picture that emerged from their thought was that of Christ as a uniquely graced man, a man who received grace from the indwelling Logos in a greater way than we do from the indwelling Holy Spirit. Christ, the man, had the task of rising up to God with the help of the indwelling Logos, and in a similar but not identical way, we have the task of rising up to God with the help of the indwelling Holy Spirit. Thus, Christ is much more similar to us than he is different. He is not God the Son who has come down to save us, but rather he is a divinely indwelt man who can lead us up to God.

If you can follow this line of reasoning through the tangled terminology to the conclusion at the end of the last paragraph, then you may be thinking that Diodore's, Theodore's, and Nestorius's understanding of Christ militates against the phrase in the Nicene Creed that we have argued was central, the statement that for us and for our salvation, the Son *came down.* How could they square their understanding with the creed? In short, they interpreted the creed differently from the way most of the church did. They argued that the creed began by introducing the term "Christ," which referred to both the Logos and the man, and then proceeded to describe first the Logos (in the statements "light from light, true God from true God," etc.) and then the man (in the descriptions of the life and ministry of Christ).[11] Thus, in their understanding, the two halves of the creed's second paragraph referred not to who the Son was and then to what he did, but to two distinct persons described consecutively, first the Logos and then the man. The phrase "came down" was of little significance in their minds.

11. See Nestorius's explanation of the Nicene Creed in his *Second Letter to Cyril*, in Norris, *Christological Controversy*, 136.

The Church's Response to Nestorianism

Now we are ready to consider the way the church responded to the thought of Diodore, Theodore, and Nestorius. The preeminent theologian leading the response was Cyril of Alexandria, a great student of Athanasius's writings (although he was not born until a few years after Athanasius died and thus did not study under him personally) who was bishop of Alexandria in Egypt from 412 until his death in 444. Cyril's thought was based above all else on the downward action of God to restore human beings to the status they had lost through the fall. Early in his career, he wrote against Arianism by insisting on the full equality of the Son to the Father and by distinguishing (as Athanasius had done) between the Logos, who is "Son by nature," and human beings, who become "sons by grace or adoption." His mantra was that only the Son by nature could make us sons by grace. As Nestorianism came to the church's attention, Cyril began to apply the same arguments that he had used against Arianism to the new error. Just as Athanasius and others had argued that the Logos was always Son, rather than becoming Son by advancing toward God, so Cyril argued that Christ was always Son, rather than becoming Son by advancing. Closely connected to this was his insistence that as a person, Christ *is* God the Son who has become incarnate. The issue, in his mind, was not *whether* Christ was one person (whatever one meant by *prosōpon*); it was *who* that one person was and is. Christ is the *same person* before and after the incarnation; he is the Logos incarnate, eternal and equal to the Father. The incarnation was an act by which the Logos, who was already a *person*, became a *human* person. It was not an act by which a *separate* human person was united to the Logos. Cyril emphasized this in many ways, but he is most famous for a single, easily misunderstood slogan, "one incarnate *physis* of God the Logos." In this phrase, Cyril meant *physis* in the sense of "personal nature," and he was emphasizing that the Logos is a single person after the incarnation, rather than saying that the Logos and the man are separate persons. As we will see, this phrase became the source of enormous controversy after Cyril's death.[12]

It may come as a surprise that Cyril and others used many of the same arguments that they had used previously in opposition to Arianism. Why? After all, Diodore, Theodore, and Nestorius were staunch Nicenes, who themselves insisted on the full eternality and equality of the Son and the Spirit to God the Father. Why rehash old arguments? The answer, we suggest, is that Cyril realized that although this new teaching was by no means the same as Arianism,

---

12. See Fairbairn, *Grace and Christology*, 61–132. For the significance of "one incarnate *physis* of God the Logos," see 126–29.

it amounted to the same thing as Arianism. The bottom line was that both Arianism and Nestorianism *put our salvation in the hands of one who was not fully God*. Arianism did this by arguing that the Son was a creature. Nestorianism did this by arguing that even though the Son was above the hard line and equal to the Father, Christ was a creature, a graced man, rather than being God the Son himself. In both cases, a creature could do nothing but lead us up to God; he could not come down to save us because he was not really God the Son. But if—as Scripture and the church insisted—we could not rise up to God ourselves, then for us to be saved, God had to come down. Nestorius's Christ, like Arius's Son, was not God who had come down. Nestorius's Christ, like Arius's Son, could not save us. Thus, the specter of Apollinaris's mistake pushed Diodore, Theodore, and Nestorius into one that was arguably even bigger, and ironically more like the mistake of Arianism—seeing salvation as an upward movement of humanity in imitation of a "redeemer" who should more properly be called a "leader" or "trailblazer."

Therefore, in contrast to what we may think and to the way many textbooks describe the controversy, the crucial issue in dispute was not whether Christ was both divine and human (that was agreed, although there was still a need to explore further what it meant to be human). Nor was the dispute primarily about how to balance divinity and humanity, without overemphasizing one or the other. Nor still was it mainly about the terminology of "two natures" and "one person," although obviously that was an important factor. Instead, the central issue was the personal continuity of the preincarnate Logos with the earthly man Jesus. Are the Logos and the man distinct persons who can be counted together as a single presentation because the Logos indwells the man? Or is the man Jesus the same person who has always been the Father's Son? To say it yet another way, is Christ a graced man, a divinely inspired man? Or is he the one, true, eternal Son of God himself?

When one states the question this way, it should be clear that the vast majority of Christians, both in the fifth century and subsequently, believed and believe that Christ is the eternal Son of God himself, who has come down and become incarnate to save us. If Theodore, Diodore, and Nestorius were not saying this—if they really were saying that Christ was divine only in the sense of being indwelt and empowered by God, and that he was redeemer only in the sense of being able to lead us up to God—then why was their thought not instantly recognized as being problematic and rejected? Why was there a controversy? Why did the controversy split the church into groups that remain separate to this day? The short answer is that—as in the fourth century, so also in the fifth—politics and terminological misunderstandings obscured the consensus that was present, but in this case the obscuring (if we are right to call it that) persisted not for decades but for centuries, indeed for a millennium and a half so far. We need now to turn to the history of the controversy.

The Controversy Comes to a Head (428–31)

In the year 428, a hotly contested election was held to choose the new bishop of Constantinople.[13] None of the competing factions was able to garner majority support for its candidate, and eventually a complete outsider, Nestorius, was chosen. He was philosophically brilliant but politically rather naive in his confidence that he could resolve the long-running feuds of the capital city. One of the most important of those feuds concerned the use of the title *Theotokos* ("bearer of God") to describe Mary. To Protestant ears, this title smacks of Mariolatry, and indeed, by the fifth century attention to Mary was already excessive by later Protestant standards. At the same time, however, the word *Theotokos*, as used by theologians, was not so much about Mary as it was making a statement about her Son. The point was that the baby she bore, Jesus, was God. Only if we set aside any negative opinions we have— however justified—about popular Christian attitudes toward Mary can we understand what was going on in 428.

Shortly after he assumed the episcopal see of Constantinople, Nestorius began to argue that Mary was not, strictly speaking, the bearer of God, and he advocated the use of the title *Christotokos* to describe Mary, rather than *Theotokos*.[14] The famous rejoinder from the monastic community was, "If Mary is not, strictly speaking, the bearer of God, then her Son is not, strictly speaking, God." Soon thereafter, Cyril jumped into the fray, writing to the Egyptian monastic community as well as to Emperor Theodosius II and others in the imperial court, and initiating a tense correspondence with Nestorius himself.[15]

The tension reached a boiling point in the summer of 430, when Pope Celestine held a synod in Rome that condemned Nestorius and demanded that he recant his errors and affirm the faith of Rome and Alexandria. Celestine asked Cyril to enforce the Roman synod's demand, and Cyril wrote a harsh letter to Nestorius, to which he appended twelve statements (known as the

13. For an excellent discussion of the events up to and including the Council of Ephesus, see McGuckin, *St. Cyril of Alexandria*, 10–120. See also Bevan, *New Judas*, 77–236; Grillmeier, *Christ in Christian Tradition*, 1:414–519; Davis, *First Seven Ecumenical Councils*, 134–67.

14. See Nestorius, *First Sermon against the* Theotokos, in Norris, *Christological Controversy*, 123–31.

15. See L. R. Wickham, ed., *Cyril of Alexandria: Select Letters*, Oxford Early Christian Texts (Oxford: Oxford University Press, 1983).

Twelve Anathemas or Twelve Chapters) that Nestorius was supposed to sign.[16] For example, the fourth anathema condemned those who denied that Christ was God, and therefore that Mary was *Theotokos*, and the fifth anathema condemned those who claimed that Christ was a God-bearing man, rather than the Son by nature. Nestorius, of course, could not accept these anathemas, but they were so strongly worded that they aroused the suspicions of other bishops in Syria as well: John of Antioch, Theodoret of Cyrrhus, and Andrew of Samosata. At about the same time (autumn 430), Theodosius II called for an ecumenical council to meet the next summer in Constantinople, but the site was later changed to Ephesus. The furor over Cyril's anathemas ensured that the council, when it did meet, was deeply divided.

The Council of Ephesus and Its Aftermath (431–33)

In fact, the word "divided" is hardly sufficient to describe what happened. The various groups of bishops began trickling into Ephesus in early June 431. Nestorius came with sixteen from around Constantinople, Memnon of Ephesus assembled fifty-two from what is today Turkey, and Cyril brought fifty from Egypt. John of Antioch and the contingent of Syrian bishops were late in arriving, as was the small group of legates from the pope. While those already present in Ephesus waited for the others to arrive, Nestorius, on one hand, and Cyril and Memnon, on the other, conducted massive public-relations campaigns seeking to gain adherents to their sides. Around June 20, word arrived from John that he would be there in a week and that if he was delayed, Cyril should start without him. John doubtless meant that Cyril should start without him if he was delayed beyond the week stipulated, but Cyril took the message at face value (John was, after all, already delayed) and opened the proceedings immediately, on June 21, 430.

Cyril and the council of about two hundred bishops summoned Nestorius three times, and when he refused to come to defend himself, they read out a selection of his writings and condemned him on the basis of those works. When John and the Syrian party arrived, Nestorius immediately ushered them into his camp and explained what had happened. John was livid at Cyril for starting without him, and he met with Nestorius and about fifty bishops in another council (called the *conciliabulum*, or "little council"), which condemned Cyril and Memnon. Finally, the papal legates arrived and sided with Cyril's council. When Theodosius heard of these events, he

---

16. This is the *Third Letter to Nestorius*, with the anathemas appended. See Wickham, *Cyril of Alexandria*, 29–33.

inexplicably affirmed *both* councils and had Cyril, Memnon, and Nestorius deposed and imprisoned. Finally, in October 431, Theodosius was persuaded to side with Cyril's council, and he restored Memnon and Cyril to their sees while sending Nestorius back to his monastery in Antioch. The letter writing continued for two more years until finally, in 433, Cyril and John agreed to a joint statement (called the "Formula of Reunion"), bringing temporary peace to the church. At that time, Nestorius was banished to a Saharan oasis in Upper Egypt, where he spent the remaining two decades of his life.

Without a doubt, then, the proceedings at Ephesus were a mess. In fact, it is hard to argue with those who claim that there was no consensus at all about Christ—after all, a would-be ecumenical council had just devolved into a regional shouting match, with Syria and Constantinople on one side, and Egypt and most of what is today Turkey on the other. How could this *not* be a clash between two rival groups? Furthermore, the later agreement between Cyril and John looks for all the world like a political compromise. How can one *not* consider it to be a mere rapprochement, bereft of any actual consensus?

There are two crucial pieces of evidence that help us to see that there was more consensus at Ephesus than people realized and that fit the story of this council into the themes we have been developing in this chapter so far. First, in the autumn of 430, before he saw Cyril's anathemas, John of Antioch wrote Nestorius a letter in which he urged him to accept the title *Theotokos* for Mary. In the letter he specifically argued that the title *Theotokos* served to safeguard the fact that it was really God the Logos who took on himself the economy of the incarnation for our sakes. By writing in this way, John showed that he agreed with Cyril on this crucial point.[17] Second, sometime during the correspondence between John and Cyril after Ephesus, one of them made a change in the Formula of Reunion (which we will quote and discuss shortly) that they were considering, and both of them agreed to the change. It had to do with clarifying the fact that Jesus after the incarnation was the same one who had always been the Father's Son.[18] Taken together, these two pieces of evidence indicate that in spite of John's dislike of Cyril's anathemas and his anger at the way Cyril conducted the council, he and Cyril basically agreed on the fundamental point that God the Son came down to save us, that Christ was God the Son incarnate himself. Furthermore, it appears that John simply did

---

17. See Donald Fairbairn, "Allies or Merely Friends? John of Antioch and Nestorius in the Christological Controversy," *Journal of Ecclesiastical History* 58, no. 3 (2007): 383–99. Fairbairn's translation and commentary on this part of the letter are on pp. 391–92.

18. For a discussion of this change, see Fairbairn, *Grace and Christology*, 212–15.

not realize that Nestorius was *not* saying the same thing. While he remained ignorant of his friend's view of Christ, his actions were guided by his anger at Cyril. But later, once he realized what Nestorius was actually teaching, he reconciled with Cyril and agreed to Nestorius's deposition. If this is correct, then at Ephesus in the fifth century, just as in the fourth century previously, there was a consensus that was obscured by other factors, a consensus that eventually came to light.

With this history behind us, let us now examine the Formula of Reunion, to which John and Cyril agreed in 433. The text is as follows:

> Therefore we confess that our Lord Jesus Christ, the only-begotten Son of God, is complete God and complete human being with a rational soul and a body. He was begotten from the Father before the ages, as to his deity, but at the end of the days the same one was born, for our sake and the sake of our salvation, from Mary the Virgin, as to his humanity. This same one is *homoousios* with the Father, as to his deity, and *homoousios* with, as to his humanity, for a union of two *physeis* has occurred, as a consequence of which we confess one Christ, one Son, one Lord. In accordance with this concept of the unconfused union, we confess that the holy Virgin is the bearer of God, because the divine Logos was made flesh and became a human being and from the moment of conception itself united to himself the temple which he took from her. And as to the things said about the Lord in the Gospels and apostolic writings, we know that theologians make some common as applying to one *prosōpon*, and divide others as applying to the two *physeis*, and teach that some are appropriate to God in accordance with Christ's deity, while others are lowly in accordance with his humanity.[19]

Several things about this confession are noteworthy. First, it emphasizes very strongly the oneness of Christ. There is "one Christ, one Son, one Lord." Second, and crucially important, it emphasizes that the one "born . . . from Mary the Virgin, as to his humanity" is the "same one" as the one "begotten from the Father before the ages, as to his deity." This confession is not interpreting the creed the way Nestorius did. Instead, it emphasizes through the phrase "the same one" the personal continuity between the eternal Son and the man born of Mary. Jesus is *not* a man indwelt by the Logos; he *is* the Logos incarnate. Third, and also very important, the confession uses the phrases "one *prosōpon*" and "two *physeis*," thus indicating that it is using the word *physis* not in the old way, to mean "person," but in a new way, to mean "nature." Cyril accepted this way of speaking even though his normal

---

19. Norris, *Christological Controversy*, 141–42 (translation modified and with the key terms restored to Greek). Also in CCFCT 1:169–71.

use of *physis* had been more like "person," because the confession makes sufficiently clear that there is one person, the Logos incarnate. Like Athanasius in 362, Cyril in 433 was willing to adopt word usage different from his own as long as the central theological point was clear.

The Formula of Reunion brought a temporary truce to the christological battles, and in very significant ways it paved the way for the Chalcedonian Definition. As we will see, the phrase "the same one" and the language of "two *physeis*" figured prominently in that definition. On the road to Chalcedon, however, there was much more drama.

The Opponents of Ephesus: The Assyrian Church of the East

After the peace brought about by the Formula of Reunion, Nestorius was banished in 436, and Theodosius demanded that all bishops throughout the Byzantine Empire assent to the formula. A relatively small number of bishops on the eastern fringes of the empire refused to comply. Their churches were already linked by geography to others farther east, outside Byzantium's orbit (and thus not subject to Theodosius's decrees), forming a group known collectively as the East Syrian or Persian church. As word spread of what had happened, these churches joined together in opposition to the Council of Ephesus and became an identifiably separate group, today called the Assyrian Church of the East (usually called the Nestorian Church in Western textbooks).[20] The Church of the East did and does affirm the first two ecumenical councils and the Nicene Creed, but rejected and rejects the Council of Ephesus and subsequent councils. This church also formally rejected and rejects the Chalcedonian Definition.

Beginning in the fifth century, the Church of the East lived in virtually complete isolation from the rest of Christendom. It possessed an extraordinary missionary zeal, having already taken Christianity deep into India before the fifth century and launching a major mission to China in the seventh century.[21] Indeed, one testimony to the church's success is that when Marco Polo wrote his *Travels* in the late thirteenth century, he mentioned the presence of "Nestorian" churches throughout the Middle East, India, central Asia, and

20. For the history of this separation, see Samuel H. Moffett, *A History of Christianity in Asia*, vol. 1, *Beginnings to 1500*, 2nd ed., American Society of Missiology Series 36 (Maryknoll, NY: Orbis, 1998), 186–207.

21. For the history of the Persian, Indian, and Chinese churches, see Moffett, *History of Christianity in Asia*, vol. 1. See also the Chinese Christian sutras dating from the seventh and eighth centuries, described and translated in Martin Palmer, *The Jesus Sutras: Rediscovering the Lost Scrolls of Taoist Christianity* (New York: Ballantine, 2001).

especially Mongol China.[22] The Church of the East also engaged in deep and substantive dialogue with Islam throughout what we call the Middle Ages,[23] and its long history of coping with life in the Muslim world could provide great insight to the Western Christian world today, as we increasingly must come to terms with Islam.

But is the Church of the East actually Nestorian? This is a difficult and complicated question, the answer to which depends as much on scholars' assessments of what Nestorianism is and whether one considers it a problem as on what scholars actually think that the Church of the East teaches.[24] Nevertheless, if one considers Nestorianism to be a genuine heresy in which Christ as a divinely indwelt man leads us up to God (as we have argued in this chapter), there are at least three possible lines of reasoning for arguing that the Church of the East is not heretical. First, although the Church of the East did not agree to Nestorius's deposition and banishment, it has never regarded him as its premier teacher. It does not call itself Nestorian as the West does. The refusal to accept Nestorius's deposition certainly derived at least partly from anti-Byzantine political sentiment rather than theological rationale, and that may even have been the major reason for it.

Second, it appears that the Church of the East has understood the word *hypostasis* in a different way from the Byzantine churches, and thus that terminological confusion contributed to its rejection of the Council of Ephesus. You may remember that by the late fourth century, the church as a whole had begun using *hypostasis* in the sense of "person," and thus it affirmed three *hypostaseis* of the Trinity and one *hypostasis* of Christ. However, the Church of the East, writing in Syriac, used a word to translate *hypostasis* that clearly aligned with the older use of *hypostasis* in the sense of "essence."[25] In order to

22. Marco Polo mentions Nestorian churches in three places in the Middle East (Mosul, Baghdad, and Tabriz), three places in central Asia (Kashgad, Yarkand, and Uyghuristan), six places in Cathay (Erguiul, Egrigaia, Tenduk, Khanbaliq, Chang'anfu, and Guangyuan), and six places in southern China (Qarajang, Baoying, Ziangyangfu, Zhenjiangfu, Changshou, and Xingzai).

23. See, for example, the famous dialogue between Timothy, patriarch of Baghdad, and Mahdi, Islamic caliph of Baghdad, in 781. The text is translated in *Woodbrooke Studies: Christian Documents in Syriac, Arabic, and Garshūni*, vol. 2, ed. and trans. Alphonse Mingana (Cambridge: W. Heffer and Sons, 1928).

24. Another way of making a case for the orthodoxy of the Church of the East is to argue that Nestorianism is not a real heresy. This is the pathway taken by much twentieth-century scholarship, followed by Moffett, *History of Christianity in Asia*, 1:175–80, 305–7. In our opinion, this line of reasoning is inadequate because we believe Nestorianism really was a heresy.

25. See *The Book of Marganitha*, an apologetic work written around 1300 to explain the Church of the East's Christology to Western Christians. The work was published in English in 1988 by the Literary Committee of the Assyrian Church of the East and is available online at http://www.nestorian.org/book_of_marganitha_part_i.html.

grasp this difference, let us look again at the table that we considered earlier in this chapter. As we print the table again, we will leave out the first way and add a fourth, that of the Church of the East:

Second Way (Most of the church after Chalcedon)	Third Way (Diodore, Theodore, and Nestorius)	Fourth Way (Church of the East)
ousia = essence	*ousia* = essence	*ousia* = essence
physis = nature	———————————	*hypostasis* = substance
———————————	*physis* = personal nature	*physis* = nature
hypostasis = person	*hypostasis* = person	———————————
prosōpon = person	———————————	*prosōpon* = person
	prosōpon = presentation	

If this table is accurate, it seems that the Church of the East had three words for "essence/nature/substance" and one word for "person." As a result, this church argued for two *hypostaseis* in Christ, considered in the sense of two substances, essences, or natures (divine and human). But to Byzantine or Western ears after the fifth century, this sounded like an affirmation of two *persons* in Christ, and thus sounded heretical. When these differences in the ways the key words were used are taken into consideration, it is possible that in spite of the long-standing split between the Church of the East and Byzantine Christianity, the groups were making the same basic affirmation about Christ.[26]

A third line of reasoning is that modern ecumenical discussions have led many to the conclusion that the Church of the East holds to a Christology consistent with that of Ephesus and later Chalcedon, albeit expressed in different terminology.[27] Especially noteworthy is the joint declaration issued by the Roman Catholic Church and the Church of the East in 1994, a declaration that expresses the Christian faith while avoiding disputed terminology altogether. This declaration insists on the incarnation as the downward movement of the Son for our salvation and states that Christ is not a man in whom God resides but is the same God the Word, begotten of the Father before the universe.[28]

Be that as it may, the Church of the East separated from the rest of Christendom in protest of the Council of Ephesus and has remained separate for

26. For a similar perspective on the complicated terminological issues, see Jaroslav Pelikan, *The Christian Tradition: A History of the Development of Doctrine*, vol. 2, *The Spirit of Eastern Christendom (600–1700)* (Chicago: University of Chicago Press, 1974), 39–49.

27. See Ronald G. Roberson, *The Eastern Christian Churches: A Brief Survey*, 7th rev. ed. (Rome: Edizioni Orientalia Christiana, Pontifical Oriental Institute, 2008), 16.

28. Roberson, *Eastern Christian Churches*, 186–88.

the rest of its history (so far). But back in the Byzantine Empire, the situation was no less cloudy, and we need to turn our attention back to that realm.

Christological Confusion (441–49)

The peace that John of Antioch and Cyril of Alexandria forged in 433 on the basis of the Formula of Reunion did not survive their deaths in 441 and 444.[29] It often happens that the students of a great teacher are more rigid and less nuanced than their master, and this certainly was the case with Cyril's students, especially his successor as bishop of Alexandria, Dioscorus. We have seen that Cyril's mantra was the catchphrase "one incarnate *physis* of God the Logos," and that in using this phrase he intended *physis* in the sense of "person," or better, "Son." There is a single Son of God, the eternal Logos or the Only-begotten One, and he is the one who has come down and become man for our salvation. However, during the course of his negotiations with John of Antioch, Cyril recognized that others were using the word *physis* differently, and he was willing to accept the use of *physis* to mean "nature" (and thus, to accept the language of two *physeis* in Christ), as long as it was crystal clear that the one born of Mary was the same one who had always been the Father's Son. Thus, Cyril willingly signed the Formula of Reunion, which started with the affirmation of the personal continuity between the Logos and the incarnate Christ, and then used the language of two united natures to describe the incarnation itself.

In contrast to Cyril himself, Dioscorus and others used *physis* rigidly in the sense of "person," and to them, any two-*physeis* language must be Nestorian. (Such language indeed would have been Nestorian if *physis* were meant in the sense of "personal nature" or "person.") A similarly rigid follower of Cyril was Eutyches, an aging monastic leader in Constantinople and the spiritual adviser to the imperial court. Eutyches, likewise using the word *physis* to mean "personal nature" or "concrete nature," refused to speak of two natures after the incarnation, although he was willing to grant that divinity and humanity were two natures before they were united, and thus he could sanction the phrase "out of two natures." Eutyches was vigorously opposed by Theodoret of Cyrrhus (near Tarsus in what is today southern Turkey), who, without

---

29. For the events up to and including the Council of Chalcedon, see Grillmeier, *Christ in Christian Tradition*, 1:520–54; Davis, *First Seven Ecumenical Councils*, 170–204. For an introduction to Chalcedon, as well as the acts (akin to minutes), see Richard Price and Michael Gaddis, trans., *The Acts of the Council of Chalcedon*, 3 vols., Translated Texts for Historians 45 (Liverpool: Liverpool University Press, 2005). See especially 1:17–56. See also Bevan, *New Judas*, 237–339.

naming Eutyches directly, criticized anyone who spoke of Christ's humanity as if it had been absorbed into his deity.[30] It is worth noting that we do not know whether Eutyches himself ever taught this, but Theodoret's characterization of his thought has been attached to Eutyches's name ever since. If this was, in fact, what Eutyches taught, such an absorption would have effectively meant the nullification of Christ's genuine humanity.

This renewed debate set the stage for two small councils in diametric opposition each to the other. The first was a "home synod" in Constantinople (that is, a council called rather quickly and including only those bishops who were already present in and around the capital) in November 448, chaired by Flavian, who had become bishop of Constantinople in 446. At this council a formal trial of Eutyches was conducted, his thought was condemned, and the formula "two *physeis*" was officially approved. Shortly after this council, in 449, Pope Leo I (Leo the Great) wrote his famous *Tome to Flavian*,[31] in which he condemns Eutyches, insists on the formula "in two natures after the union,"[32] and correctly points out that the phrase "out of two natures" made no sense because the human nature did not exist prior to the incarnation. In spite of these helpful affirmations, Leo's *Tome* led to great debate later because it included three statements that appeared to treat the natures independently, as if each could operate on its own. Nevertheless, Leo unequivocally affirmed the continuity between the Logos and the incarnate Christ.[33]

Dioscorus was furious at the condemnation of Eutyches and, perhaps even more important, at the departure from Cyril's language, and he called a competing council in Ephesus in August 449. At this council Dioscorus refused to read Leo's *Tome* publicly, reinstated Eutyches, and had Flavian declared heretical. When Leo heard of this, he dubbed the Ephesine council of 449 a "robber synod" and worked to undo its decrees, but Theodosius was solidly in favor of it. Thus, within five years of Cyril's death and eight years of John of Antioch's, their hard-won peace had completely fallen apart, and it seemed that no consensus could be reached at all. Again, we find that the situation was a complete mess.

In July 450, Theodosius II died in a horseback-riding accident, ending his forty-two-year reign as Byzantine emperor. The power struggle that followed

30. See Donald Fairbairn, "The Puzzle of Theodoret's Christology: A Modest Suggestion," *Journal of Theological Studies*, n.s., 58, no. 1 (2007): 100–133.

31. Translated in Norris, *Christological Controversy*, 145–55.

32. Leo was writing in Latin, in which language the distinction between *natura* ("nature") and *persona* ("person") was far more clear-cut than it was in Greek. Obviously, our English theological terms, with the equally clear-cut distinction between them, come directly from the Latin words.

33. See Fairbairn, *Grace and Christology*, 218–20.

saw Theodosius's sister Pulcheria marry Marcian, a Roman senator, and name him as emperor. In one of his first acts as emperor, Marcian called for an ecumenical council to meet in 451.[34] Originally meant for Nicaea, the council was moved to nearby Chalcedon as the bishops were assembling in September 451.

The Council of Chalcedon (October 451)

On October 8, 451, about 370 delegates gathered in the martyrium of St. Euphemia in Chalcedon to hold the first of sixteen sessions before concluding on November 1. The mood was contentious from the outset, since Leo's legates demanded that Dioscorus be removed without even a trial, and other delegates called for the removal of Theodoret. It took much patient work to sort through the various writings and accusations and come to judgment about each case. Along the way, there were tense moments, such as the session at which it seemed that Pope Leo's *Tome* might be deemed heretical, which would have led to an immediate walkout by the papal legates. There were also surprising moments such as the formal reading of the Nicene Creed of 381, when it was discovered that many bishops were not familiar with it, since they had continued using the Creed of Nicaea from 325. At all times, the bishops felt the weight of the imperial command to draft a new creed, a command that they deliberately resisted as they instead produced a "definition." Throughout the proceedings, the standard of christological orthodoxy (next to Scripture, of course) was Cyril of Alexandria.[35] His *Second Letter to Nestorius* and his letter to John of Antioch accepting the Formula of Reunion were the touchstones to which other writings and bishops were compared. Indeed, Cyril received all the credit for the Formula of Reunion, although John of Antioch surely played a role in its final form, and Theodoret may have been the original author. When Leo's *Tome* was under attack, Theodoret defended the pope by pointing out that Cyril had written much the same thing. While modern scholars have tended to regard Chalcedon as a compromise, as a merely negative document, or even as a victory for Cyril's opponents, this

---

34. Bevan, *New Judas*, 1–2, 232–30, brings forward several little-known sources indicating that Marcian actually recalled Nestorius from exile in order to present him at the council, receive from him a recantation of his past errors, and restore him to communion with the church. According to these sources, Nestorius died either before he began the journey or on the journey itself. While these sources may be trustworthy and may reflect Marcian's intentions accurately, in our opinion the assembled bishops would not have agreed to Nestorius's restoration.

35. See the perceptive analysis of the theology of Chalcedon in Price and Gaddis, *Acts of the Council of Chalcedon*, 1:56–75.

is not the way the bishops assembled at Chalcedon understood their task. Instead, both Roman contributions (from Leo) and Syrian ones (the Formula of Reunion and Theodoret's arguments) were held up to the light of Cyril's focus on the single sonship of Christ. By treating Cyril with such deference, the assembled bishops were also affirming one way of interpreting the Nicene Creed—the way that Cyril and

Chalcedon

most others took it, as a proclamation of Christ as the only-begotten Son who had come down for our salvation. Thus they tacitly rejected Nestorius's way of taking the creed as a discussion of the "Christ" composed of Logos and assumed man.

The work of drafting a definition of the faith fell to a committee consisting of the three papal legates, six bishops from Syria, and six from Greece, Macedonia, and Asia Minor (western Turkey today). The definition was presented and debated on October 20, and a modified form was agreed upon on October 22 and promulgated ceremonially on October 25. It is several pages in length and affirms and quotes both the Creed of Nicaea and the Nicene Creed.[36] What is new in these several pages is one paragraph about the incarnate Son, which normally is considered by itself to be the Chalcedonian Definition. The placement of this paragraph after the solemn recitation of both creeds shows that the delegates considered their work to follow directly in the footsteps of the Nicene fathers of the fourth century. We turn now to this paragraph.

The Chalcedonian Definition

The following is the new paragraph of the Chalcedonian Definition, with the key terms restored to Greek. We have also used boldface type for the central portion of the paragraph in which the key terms occur.

> We, then, following the holy Fathers, all with one consent, teach men to confess one and the same Son, our Lord Jesus Christ, the same perfect in Godhead and the same perfect in manhood, the same truly God and truly man, of a reasonable soul and body; consubstantial with the Father according to the Godhead, and the same consubstantial with us according to the Manhood; in all things

36. See the convenient translation of the most important pages of the acts in Norris, *Christological Controversy*, 155–59.

like unto us, without sin; begotten before all ages from the Father according to the Godhead, and in these latter days the same, for us and for our salvation, born of the Virgin Mary, the God-bearer, according to the Manhood; one and the same Christ, Son, Lord, Only-begotten, **to be acknowledged in two *physeis* inconfusedly, unchangeably, indivisibly, inseparably; the distinction of *physeis* being by no means taken away by the union, but rather the property of each *physis* being preserved, and concurring in one *prosōpon* and one *hypostasis*, not parted or divided into two *prosōpa*,** but one and the same Son and only begotten, God the Word, the Lord Jesus Christ, as the prophets from the beginning have declared concerning him, and the Lord Jesus Christ himself has taught us, and the Creed of the holy Fathers has handed down to us.[37]

The portion of this paragraph in bold is the part that Western readers usually consider to be the most important, because this is the part that attempts to clarify the terminology for "person" and "nature." The bishops at Chalcedon follow the Formula of Reunion and Leo's *Tome* in speaking of two *physeis* in Christ. By doing so, the Chalcedonian Definition associates the word *physis* with *ousia*, the essence/nature/substance, the set of properties that defines what it means to be God or man. In fact, notice that the Definition even uses the word "property" to describe the union of natures—the properties of both divinity and humanity come together in the one person of Christ. On the other hand, the Definition clearly associates *prosōpon* with *hypostasis*; both are words for "person," and Christ is one *prosōpon/hypostasis*. This terminology was a departure from the way Cyril had normally used the words, and it brought much-needed clarity to discussions of Christ.

Nevertheless, it would be a mistake to think that the purpose of the Definition was merely to bring terminological clarity. The following is the same paragraph, with the Greek terms now translated into English, with the paragraph divided up, and with both bold and italic highlighting used in order to illustrate what we believe is the main affirmation of Chalcedon.

We, then, following the holy Fathers, all with one consent, teach men to confess **one and the same Son, our Lord Jesus Christ,** *the same* perfect in Godhead and *the same* perfect in manhood, *the same* truly God and truly man, of a reasonable soul and body; consubstantial with the Father according to the Godhead, and *the same* consubstantial with us according to the Manhood; in all things like unto us, without sin; begotten before all ages from the Father according to the

---

37. Philip Schaff, ed., *The Creeds of Christendom, with a History and Critical Notes*, 3 vols., 6th ed. revised by David Schaff (1877; repr., Grand Rapids: Baker, 1998), 2:62–63 (translation slightly modified and with the key terms restored to Greek). Also in *CCFCT* 1:181.

Godhead, and in these latter days *the same*, for us and for our salvation, born
of the Virgin Mary, the God-bearer, according to the Manhood;

one and the same Christ, Son, Lord, Only-begotten, to be acknowledged in
two natures inconfusedly, unchangeably, indivisibly, inseparably; the distinction
of natures being by no means taken away by the union, but rather the property
of each nature being preserved, and concurring in one Person and one Subsistence, not parted or divided into two persons, but **one and the same Son and
only begotten, God the Word, the Lord Jesus Christ,**

as the prophets from the beginning have declared concerning him, and the
Lord Jesus Christ himself has taught us, and the Creed of the holy Fathers has
handed down to us.[38]

First, notice the three phrases in boldface type. These could be called framing statements, since they serve to divide the significant portions of the
paragraph into two parts. The first part deals with the full deity and the
full humanity of the Lord Jesus Christ, and the second deals with the terminology of two natures and one person used to describe him. Furthermore,
notice that the framing statements get more specific as they go along, and
the increasing specificity serves to emphasize the personal continuity between the Logos and the man Jesus. "Christ" is not a word for describing
two persons, the Logos and the man. Rather, the Lord Jesus Christ is one
and the same Son (the first framing statement). He is the same one who
has always been God's Only-begotten (the second framing statement). He
is the same one who has always been the Word/Logos (the third framing
statement).

Second, notice the italicized phrase "the same," which occurs five times in
the paragraph about the divinity and humanity of Christ. The word "same"
in these cases is masculine in Greek, and it emphasizes that the person described as consubstantial with the Father is the same one who is consubstantial with us. Note especially the unequivocal insistence (reminiscent of
the Formula of Reunion as well as the Nicene Creed) that the one who was
begotten from the Father eternally is the same one who is born of the Virgin
Mary for our salvation. These five instances of "the same [one]," coupled
with the three occurrences of "one and the same," mean that in a single
paragraph the bishops are repeating *eight times* that Jesus and the Logos are
the same person. This is the central affirmation of the Chalcedonian Definition. Jesus is not a man indwelt by the Logos so that the man can lead us
up to God. He is the Logos who has come down to become human so that
he could save us.

38. Schaff, *Creeds of Christendom*, 2:62–63.

In the process of making this central affirmation, the bishops clarified what it meant to be human by emphasizing against Apollinarianism that Christ's humanity includes a rational soul as well as a body, and by stressing against Eutychianism that the properties of divine and human natures remain discernibly different after the union. But the main confession is that God's only-begotten Son has himself personally come down to save us. Seen in this way, the Chalcedonian Definition is indeed a clarification of the central affirmation of the Nicene Creed. And just as Arianism was the primary target of the Nicene Creed, so here Nestorianism (certainly not the same heresy, but amounting to the same thing in that it, too, places our salvation in the hands of a nondivine being—a leader rather than a savior) is the major target in view. We are back where we started: Can we rise up to God, as both Arianism and Nestorianism implied? If not (as the church insisted), then God had to come down to us, which means that the fully divine Son had to come all the way down to the level of true human life.

The Opponents of Chalcedon: The Oriental Orthodox Churches

Chalcedon was the best-attended of the ecumenical councils, so most of the bishops in the Byzantine Empire either signed it or had it signed on their behalf. But among the lower clergy and especially the monastic communities in the Christian East, there was deep suspicion that the Chalcedonian Definition was either implicitly or explicitly Nestorian because of its adoption of the formula "in two *physeis*." Chalcedon's deposition of Dioscorus was a source of outrage in Egypt, where a rabid allegiance not merely to Cyril's thought, but especially to his one-*physis* terminology, was the norm. In Syria as well there were many who saw Chalcedon as Nestorian, and Antioch—ironically, the same city that had produced Theodore and Nestorius—was the home of Cyril's most ardent supporter and Chalcedon's most vocal critic, Severus of Antioch.[39] The opposition to Chalcedon was so strong that in many episcopal sees anti-Chalcedonian bishops were elected and served at the same time as Chalcedonian bishops in a tense rivalry. The reputation of Chalcedon in the East became so bad that in 482, the Byzantine emperor Zeno and Acacius, patriarch of Constantinople, sought to reestablish unity by bypassing Chalcedon altogether and advocating instead a confession, the *Henotikon*, based only on the first three ecumenical councils. This ploy largely backfired, since Rome broke

---

39. A very helpful anthology of Severus's writings is Pauline Allen and C. T. R. Hayward, trans., *Severus of Antioch*, Early Church Fathers (London: Routledge, 2005).

fellowship with Constantinople because the *Henotikon* did not explicitly affirm Chalcedon, whereas others in the East rejected the document because it did not explicitly condemn Chalcedon.[40]

In fact, virtually the entire non-Greek-speaking Christian world was uneasy about Chalcedon, and over the course of the late fifth and early sixth centuries, the anti-Chalcedonians developed separate church hierarchies and other structures, thus sealing the schism. These churches—Coptic (in Egypt), Ethiopian, Eritrean, Syrian, Armenian, and much later Malankaran (in India)—have continued in fellowship with one another but in separation from the Byzantine and Roman churches up to the present day. They are collectively called Oriental Orthodox, although many Western books refer to them as Monophysite, from the Greek words for "single *physis*." The Western opinion has long been that because they affirm only a single nature in Christ, they are heretical in the opposite way that Nestorianism is heretical. But if you have been able to follow the terminological discussions in the last two chapters, you can probably guess that this appellation is inaccurate. In fact, the Oriental Orthodox churches have continued to use the word *physis* in its earlier sense, akin to "person," and thus their affirmation of one *physis* should be understood as "one person," not "one nature."[41]

Over the course of this chapter, we have described, and depicted in tabular form, four major ways of understanding the relation between the Greek words *ousia*, *physis*, *hypostasis*, and *prosōpon*. The first way, in which *ousia* was the only word for "essence/nature," and *physis*, *hypostasis*, and *prosōpon* were all words for "person," was the way most of the church used the words in the early fifth century, and the Oriental Orthodox continued to use the words this way. The second way, in which *ousia* and *physis* were words for "essence/nature," and *hypostasis* and *prosōpon* were words for "person," was the word usage sanctioned by Chalcedon. The third way was that of Theodore and Nestorius, who saw *ousia* as the word for "essence/nature," *physis* and *hypostasis* as the words for "person," and *prosōpon* more like "external presentation. The fourth way, we argued, was the usage of the Church of the East, which saw *ousia*, *hypostasis*, and *physis* as words for "substance/essence/nature," and only *prosōpon* as a word for "person." Setting aside

---

40. For an English translation of the *Henotikon*, see W. H. C. Frend, *The Rise of the Monophysite Movement: Chapters in the History of the Church in the Fifth and Sixth Centuries* (Cambridge: Cambridge University Press, 1972), 360–62.

41. For Severus's use of *physis* and *hypostasis* as synonyms, see, for example, *To Nephalius*, in Allen and Hayward, *Severus of Antioch*, 59–66. See also the discussion in Pelikan, *Christian Tradition*, 2:49–61.

Theodore's and Nestorius's usage (the third way), we repeat the others in the table below:

First Way (Oriental Orthodox churches)	Second Way (Chalcedonian churches)	Fourth Way (Church of the East)
ousia = essence	*ousia* = essence	*ousia* = essence
	physis = nature	*hypostasis* = substance
physis = personal nature		*physis* = nature
hypostasis = person	*hypostasis* = person	
prosōpon = person	*prosōpon* = person	*prosōpon* = person

If this table is accurate, the Oriental Orthodox apparently were using the word *physis* differently from the Chalcedonians, whereas the Church of the East was using the word *hypostasis* differently from the Chalcedonians.

The Oriental Orthodox churches have never been as remote from Byzantine and Western Christianity as the Church of the East has been. As we will see in chapter 8, there were two major attempts by Byzantium to reconcile with the Oriental Orthodox, one in the sixth century and the other in the seventh. Nevertheless, for a millennium and a half the Oriental Orthodox churches have had a substantially separate history from the Chalcedonian (Eastern Orthodox, Roman Catholic, and later Protestant) churches. In the twentieth century, increasing contact led to significant theological discussions, and a groundbreaking meeting in August 1964 between Oriental and Eastern Orthodox theologians produced recognition of their substantial agreement.[42] Subsequent ecumenical discussions have continued to explore and proclaim that agreement.[43]

Conclusions

Just as was the case with the Nicene Creed in the fourth century, so also with the Chalcedonian Definition in the fifth, one could easily argue that there was no consensus at all. In both cases, one could insist, the production of a creed/definition was the result of favorable political fortunes for one party among several. Indeed, just as Constantine's and Theodosius I's political consolidation in the fourth century paved the way for the Creed of Nicaea

42. See the record of these proceedings in *Greek Orthodox Theological Review* 10, no. 2 (1964–65).

43. For the declarations resulting from some of these ecumenical discussions, see Roberson, *Eastern Christian Churches*, 193–220.

and then the Nicene Creed, so also the unexpected death of Theodosius II led directly to the political environment in which the Chalcedonian Definition could be written.

We have also seen in this chapter that unlike the situation with the Nicene Creed (which at least produced unity at the end of a messy controversy), there never was any complete unity related to Chalcedon. The Third Ecumenical Council at Ephesus in 431 actually consisted of two competing councils at the same time, and the 440s saw two more competing councils take place less than a year apart. Ephesus and Chalcedon tore the Christian East into three major factions that remain separate to this day, more than fifteen hundred years later. It is no wonder that many people believe that there never was a consensus about the identity of Jesus Christ.

Throughout this chapter, however, we have tried to suggest that beneath the messy surface of the various councils and the bitter splits occasioned by the Chalcedonian Definition, there *was* a consensus, one that grew directly out of the Nicene Creed's insistence that the Son "came down" for our salvation. Differences in the use of the words for "natures" and "person" in Christ meant that this consensus was obscured. Political allegiances—particularly anti-Byzantine sentiment in the non-Greek-speaking Christian East—hardened the differences from merely obscuring consensus to rejecting outright any possibility that there could be any. Then long centuries of isolation deprived the various Christian bodies of opportunities to lift the veil and consider whether there might be any commonality beneath the divisions. But through all of that, we have argued, a consensus was present, and it has been rediscovered in the twentieth and twenty-first centuries.

What, then, are we to make of the Chalcedonian Definition? Perhaps it is best to accept it as *a way* to express the consensus truth that God the Son personally came down and became a man so that he, the Son, could live, die, and be raised as a man for our salvation. Chalcedon's way of expressing this—with its helpful but divisive terminological innovation and its rather philosophical language—is hardly the only way to express this truth. Christians can express and have expressed the same faith using other words, or using the same words differently. Here we should remember that the Chalcedonian Definition was never meant to stand on the level of the Nicene Creed, let alone on the level of Scripture. It was meant as an explanation of the Son's "coming down" enshrined at the center of the creed. Understood correctly, it serves that purpose very well. Misunderstood, it divides tragically. But what is universal about the Chalcedonian Definition is not its word usage, its terminology, or its philosophical tenor. Instead, what is universal is the faith that it proclaims—the faith that the baby born from the Virgin Mary is the same person who has always been the Father's only Son. Unlike the Nicene Creed, the Chalcedonian Definition has not been accepted by all Christians. But the vast majority of Christians throughout history have affirmed the same Son, and the same downward movement of that Son to earth for our salvation, that Chalcedon sought to proclaim.

6

■■■■■■ ■ ■■■■■■ ■ ■ ■ ■■■■■■■■■■■ ■ ■ ■

The Apostles' Creed

A Regional Creed with Traditional Authority

In chapter 2 we saw that in spite of the legend that Rufinus detailed for us, there were multiple Christian creeds in the first few centuries, with significant differences in wording, but not in content. In the second and third centuries, these creeds were most commonly associated with baptismal liturgies, and foremost among them was the baptismal symbol of the Roman Church, which some call the Apostles' Creed and others refer to as the Old Roman Creed. In the fourth and fifth centuries, the crises over the Trinity and Christology led to the ecumenical councils that produced two great conciliar statements, the Nicene Creed and the Chalcedonian Definition, which were the subjects of chapters 4 and 5. In the Eastern churches, the Nicene Creed eventually replaced the local symbols completely, but this was not the case in the West, where local and regional baptismal symbols continued to flourish alongside the conciliar statements. By the early eighth century, these regional creeds coalesced into the final form of the Apostles' Creed, which in the ninth century and following assumed a place comparable in traditional authority to the Nicene Creed, although it never garnered the universal sanction of an ecumenical council.

Thus, in this chapter we consider the way the Old Roman Creed was standardized into the Apostles' Creed, and we examine the distinctive teaching of that Western creed.[1] To begin doing this, we need to return to Rufinus and the time period around 400, when the Roman Creed was first called the "Apostles' Creed."

The Apostles' Creed (circa 400)

At the end of chapter 2 we printed scholars' reconstructions of the Old Roman Creed and a prototypical Greek creed. In the case of the former, brackets indicated words and phrases that recent scholars think were added in the fourth century and thus were not part of the earliest forms of the Old Roman Creed. In order to highlight the changes in the creed between the second and late fourth centuries, we reprint this text below on the left, with the bracketed phrases removed altogether. On the right is the creed as suggested by Rufinus in the year 404, with the changes in boldface type.

The Old Roman Creed (second and third centuries)	The Apostles' Creed (ca. 400)
I believe in God the Father almighty;	I believe in God the Father almighty;
and in Christ Jesus His Son,	and in Christ Jesus His **only** Son, **our Lord,**
Who was born from the Holy Spirit and the Virgin Mary,	Who was born from the Holy Spirit and the Virgin Mary,
Who under Pontius Pilate was crucified and buried,	Who under Pontius Pilate was crucified and buried,
on the third day rose again from the dead, ascended into heaven,	on the third day rose again from the dead, ascended into heaven,
sits at the right hand of the Father, whence he will come to judge the living and the dead;	sits at the right hand of the Father, whence he will come to judge the living and the dead;
and in the Holy Spirit, the holy Church, the resurrection of the flesh.[a]	and in the Holy Spirit, the holy Church, **the remission of sins,** the resurrection of the flesh.[b]

a. See J. N. D. Kelly, *Early Christian Creeds*, 3rd ed. (London: Longmans, 1972), 102; Liuwe H. Westra, *The Apostles' Creed: Origin, History, and Some Early Commentaries*, Instrumenta patristica et medievalia 43 (Turnhout: Brepols, 2002), 68.
b. Kelly, *Early Christian Creeds*, 102.

A glance at the two versions of the creed presented here shows only two changes. First is a strengthening of the brief statement on the identity of Christ: he is God's *only* Son and can be described with the same phrase "our

1. This chapter and the next one require us to overrun the stated time period for part 1 of this book (100–500) and to consider some events of the sixth through eighth centuries. Nevertheless, the reason for considering the era of the creeds to have ended ca. 500 is that the Apostles' Creed was in nearly its final form by that time and the Athanasian Creed was written about that time.

Lord" used to describe the Father. Second is the addition of "the remission of sins."

But why were these additions made? On this point, Rufinus has a revealing comment. Discussing the initial statement of belief in God the Father, he writes,

> I think it appropriate to mention that certain additions are to be found in this article in some churches. No such development, however, can be detected in the case of the church of the city of Rome. The reason, I suppose, is that no heresy has ever originated there. . . . Elsewhere, to the best of my understanding, the presence of heretics seems to have occasioned the insertion of clauses, the idea being that they would help to exclude novelties of doctrine. For my part, I propose to base myself on the text to which I pledged myself when I was baptized in the church of Aquileia.[2]

Several points are noteworthy in this passage. First, Rufinus acknowledges that there are differences between the local creeds in different cities. This is no surprise because, in fact, he discusses those local differences as he works his way through the assertions of the creed.

Second, and most striking, Rufinus suggests, somewhat tentatively, that the reason why the Roman creed is shorter than the creeds of other cities is that there have been no heresies in Rome that necessitated the addition of extra phrases. Leaving aside the question of whether it is true that no heresy had originated in Rome, the important thing for us to notice is that creeds grew as new mistakes forced them to. For example, it may have initially seemed sufficient to affirm that Jesus is God's Son. But as various inadequate understandings of his divine sonship were articulated, the church recognized that it was necessary to be more specific: Jesus is God's *only* Son, who is called "our Lord." Indeed, the vastly greater specificity of the Nicene Creed on this point grows directly out of the fact that the Eastern church was rocked by the Arian controversy. The Western church, feeling the effects of that controversy from more of a distance, felt compelled to add to its affirmation of Jesus as God's Son, but did not feel the compulsion to add nearly the detail that the Eastern church did. According to Rufinus, the Roman church did not suffer from heresies (at least not from *its own* heresies—heresies originating there), and so its creed could remain shorter than the creeds of other cities.

The third point to note is that Rufinus's exposition is based not on the Old Roman Creed per se but on the baptismal symbol of Aquileia in Italy, the symbol

---

2. Rufinus, *A Commentary on the Apostles' Creed* 3, trans. J. N. D. Kelly, ACW 20 (New York: Newman, 1955), 31–32.

that he recited at his own baptism. This is why we have to reconstruct the Old Roman Creed from Rufinus's commentary and other sources. He does not actually quote that creed but simply mentions the places where it differs from his own baptismal symbol. This admission is striking: in a work whose very title is *A Commentary on the Apostles' Creed*, Rufinus's base text, so to speak, is the baptismal symbol of Aquileia rather than the Old Roman Creed. It seems that in spite of his legend about the composition of the creed, Rufinus is using the phrase "Apostles' Creed" not to indicate a single, set creed, but more generally to refer to the constellation of Latin creeds that he considers in his commentary.

Thus, by the turn of the fifth century, the Western creedal world had already seen the gradual expansion of its creeds to combat new mistakes, and this expansion was going on at a faster rate in other regions under the Latin umbrella than it was in Rome itself. As the phrase "Apostles' Creed" first began to be used, and as the additions and refinements that later characterized the final form of the Apostles' Creed came into existence, the emerging form of the creed was, ironically, less associated with Rome itself than it was with other Latin-speaking regions. The road from the Old Roman Creed to the final Apostles' Creed does not seem to have gone through Rome!

Toward the Apostles' Creed

The earliest appearance of the Apostles' Creed in its final form comes in a compendium of Christian doctrine written for Benedictine monks engaged in missionary work in the region of Lake Constance (on the borders of Germany, Austria, and Switzerland today). The author of the document was St. Priminius, and it can be dated between 710 and 724, the time period when Charles Martel (about whom more later) was rising to power. The creed in almost identical form also shows up in liturgical documents from the same time period in Gaul (modern France) and Ireland.[3] How then did we go from a Roman creed to which an Italian writer bore witness in about 400 to a somewhat enlarged and much more standardized creed in the early eighth century, whose witnesses all hailed from north of the Alps?

Not surprisingly, the story is exceedingly complex. In a recent scholarly work, Liuwe Westra has dedicated 180 pages to regional variations in the Latin creed in Africa, the Balkans, Italy, Gaul, and Spain, and his "brief" tabular summary of these variants comprises twenty-three pages![4] The short version

---

3. See J. N. D. Kelly, *Early Christian Creeds*, 3rd ed. (London: Longmans, 1972), 398–404.
4. Liuwe H. Westra, *The Apostles' Creed: Origin, History, and Some Early Commentaries*, Instrumenta patristica et medievalia 43 (Turnhout: Brepols, 2002), 99–276, 540–62.

of this story[5] is that as early as the sixth century, when Rome itself was still using a creed more like the Old Roman Creed than like the later Apostles' Creed, a creed much more like the latter was already in use in southern Gaul (southeastern France today). Southern Gaul was ripe with theological ferment (or, to put it negatively, rife with potential heresies), making it a place in need of greater creedal specificity to keep the heretics at bay. Thus, it seems that the creedal evolution—always proceeding faster away from Rome than in Rome itself—was fastest there.

In order for a creed to reach final form, however, it needs not just an accelerator but also eventually a set of brakes to bring additions and changes to a close. If the Western creedal ferment in the sixth and seventh centuries was most aggressive outside Rome and especially in Gaul, where, when, and how did the brakes get applied? To answer this question, we need to look to the great reshaping of the Western Christian world in the eighth and ninth centuries. We have seen that St. Priminius, who gave us the first written evidence of the final form of the creed, worked in the realm of Charles Martel in what is today southern Germany. In 732 Charles was the victorious general in the fateful Battle of Tours (in France), which halted the Muslims' advance into central Europe and forced them back into Spain. As vast swaths of Asia were conquered by the Crescent,[6] and as the Byzantine world faced repeated attacks from Arab and later Turkish Muslims, northern Europe was spared and was able to develop without fear of the Muslim invaders. The next several generations saw the rise of the Carolingian Dynasty in France and Germany, as Charles Martel was succeeded by his son Pepin ("the Short")[7] and then his grandson Charlemagne, who reigned in the late eighth and early ninth centuries.

Part of the impetus for the rise of the Carolingians was an increasingly close trans-Alpine alliance between the crown and the papacy, and one of the major conditions for such an alliance was that the crown would advocate for liturgical uniformity throughout northern Europe. In 754 Pepin signed an agreement with Pope Stephen II to bring about liturgical conformity throughout the Frankish realm, based on Roman practice. Closely related to this liturgical movement was a strong push for increased education and morality among the laity. The Frankish kings demanded that all subjects of the realm learn the Lord's Prayer and the creed. As a practical matter,

5. For a modest summary of the details, see Kelly, *Early Christian Creeds*, 411–34. For an exhaustive treatment, see Westra's work, *Apostles' Creed*.

6. The culminating battle came in 751 at Talas in what is today Kyrgyzstan. There the Arabs defeated the Chinese and became the world's supreme military power.

7. The Fairbairn family would like you to know that our dog is named after Pepin the Short.

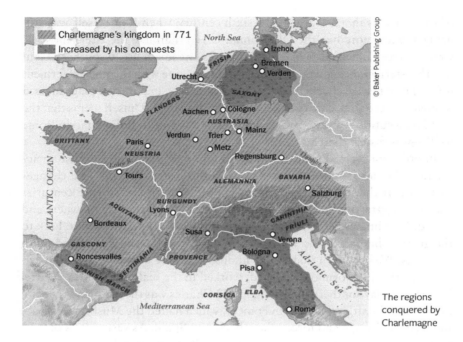

The regions conquered by Charlemagne

it was only the clergy who were interrogated about their knowledge of the basics of the faith, but nevertheless the push for better education created a need for a standardized creed that all could learn and recite. Thus, we see that the impetus for creedal uniformity in the East came with the Arian controversy, but in the West it came four centuries later with a pressing need for basic education.

In 811–13 Charlemagne wrote to the metropolitan bishops in his realm, asking for details about their baptismal liturgies and the creeds recited in those ceremonies. The results of this inquiry show that by this time the final form of the Apostles' Creed was the dominant symbol of the Frankish kingdom. Charlemagne's purpose was to standardize *Frankish* practice according to what was done in Rome, as per his father's agreement with the pope. But one of the eventual results was that Rome—after centuries of using the Old Roman Creed and even the Nicene Creed in its baptismal liturgy—finally accepted the Gallo-Frankish document that we know as the Apostles' Creed as its baptismal symbol. We do not know how or even exactly when this shift took place, except that it was sometime after the ninth century. J. N. D. Kelly's conclusion is worth quoting verbatim: "In persuading Rome to accept a new baptismal confession, the church beyond the Alps was merely handing back to her, enriched and improved, that same venerable rule of faith which she

The Coronation of Charlemagne by Raphael (1483–1520)

herself had compiled in the second century as an epitome of the everlasting gospel."[8]

With this history in mind, we are ready to examine the distinctive teaching of the Apostles' Creed itself,[9] and we will do this by comparing the final form with the form Rufinus knew in about 400 and with the Nicene Creed.

The Distinctiveness of the Apostles' Creed

In chapter 2 we compared the Old Roman Creed with a reconstructed prototypical Greek creed, and we noted that the Greek creed was more specific on almost everything. As the Arian controversy pushed the Greek church into even greater precision, the disparity grew ever greater. While the Nicene Creed is not nearly as philosophical as the controversies out of which it grew, it does contain some philosophical language and a great deal of detail about the Son and the Spirit with respect to the Father. None of that specificity is present in any early Western creed, or even in the expanded and final Apostles'

8. Kelly, *Early Christian Creeds*, 434.

9. There are many books analyzing the Apostles' Creed. See, for example, Michael Horton, *We Believe: Recovering the Essentials of the Apostles' Creed* (Nashville: Thomas Nelson, 1998); Alister E. McGrath, *"I Believe": Exploring the Apostles' Creed* (Grand Rapids: Zondervan, 1991); Justo González, *The Apostles' Creed for Today* (Louisville: Westminster John Knox, 2007); J. I. Packer, *Affirming the Apostles' Creed* (Wheaton: Tyndale, 1977).

Creed. As a result, for the most part the Apostles' Creed stands as a general summary of common Christian beliefs, without elaboration. At the same time, however, there are several affirmations in the Apostles' Creed that are not present elsewhere, as we will now see.

In the table below, the left column displays the Apostles' Creed as it was known to Rufinus in about 400; in the center is the final form of the Apostles' Creed, and the right column gives the Nicene Creed. Boldface type indicates additions to the Apostles' Creed between 400 and 700, and underlining indicates teaching found in the Apostles' Creed that is not present in the Nicene Creed.

A glance at the boldface type shows that there are seven noteworthy changes or additions in the Apostles' Creed between 400 and 700.[10] Of these, three are clearly reminiscent of the Nicene Creed (or perhaps earlier Eastern creeds): the addition of "creator of heaven and earth," of "catholic" to "the holy Church," and of "the life everlasting."[11] The other four changes/additions constitute the "new" teaching of the Apostles' Creed, not present either in Western antecedents or in the Eastern creed. These four are as follows:

1. Increased specificity about the conception and birth of Christ. Other creeds describe his birth "from the Holy Spirit and the Virgin Mary"; the Apostles' Creed specifies, "*conceived* by the Holy Spirit, *born* of the Virgin Mary."
2. Increased specificity about the death of Christ. Other creeds speak of crucifixion, suffering, and/or burial; this one alone adds death.
3. The addition of "he descended into hell."
4. The addition of "the communion of saints."

We will now consider each of these unique features in turn.

Christ's Conception and Birth

Why does the Apostles' Creed provide greater specificity about Christ's conception and birth than other creeds do? There seem to be two possible reasons. First, the phrase reflects a more attentive reading of the annunciation account in Luke 1 than we see in other creeds. Second, and probably more important, the detail in the Apostles' Creed reflects a need to shore

10. Or eight, if one considers changing the session at the right hand "of the Father" to "of God the Father Almighty" to be noteworthy.
11. Remember that this phrase was present in a Greek version of the Old Roman Creed from the fourth century.

The Apostles' Creed (ca. 400)	The Apostles' Creed (ca. 700)	The Nicene Creed (381)
I believe in God the Father almighty;	I believe in God, the Father Almighty, **creator of heaven and earth;**	We believe in one God, the Father All Governing, creator of heaven and earth, of all things visible and invisible;
and in Christ Jesus His only Son, our Lord, Who was born from the Holy Spirit and the Virgin Mary, Who under Pontius Pilate was crucified and buried, on the third day rose again from the dead, ascended into heaven, sits at the right hand of the Father, whence He will come to judge the living and the dead;	And in Jesus Christ, His only Son, our Lord, Who was **conceived** by the Holy Spirit, born of the Virgin Mary, **suffered** under Pontius Pilate, was crucified, **dead** and buried. **He descended to hell,** on the third day rose again from the dead, ascended to heaven, sits at the right hand of **God** the Father **Almighty,** thence He will come to judge the living and the dead;	And in one Lord Jesus Christ, the only-begotten Son of God, begotten from the Father before all time, Light from Light, true God from true God, begotten not created, *homoousion* as the Father, through Whom all things came into being, Who for us men and because of our salvation came down from heaven, and was incarnate by the Holy Spirit and the Virgin Mary and became human. He was crucified for us under Pontius Pilate, and suffered and was buried, and rose on the third day, according to the Scriptures, and ascended to heaven, and sits on the right hand of the Father, and will come again with glory to judge the living and dead. His kingdom shall have no end.
and in the Holy Spirit, the holy Church, the remission of sins, the resurrection of the flesh.[a]	I believe in the Holy Spirit, the holy **catholic** Church, **the communion of saints,** the forgiveness of sins, the resurrection of the body, **and the life everlasting.** Amen.[b]	And in the Holy Spirit, the Lord and life-giver, Who proceeds from the Father, Who is worshiped and glorified together with the Father and Son, Who spoke through the prophets; and in one holy, catholic, and apostolic Church. We confess one baptism for the remission of sins. We look forward to the resurrection of the dead and the life of the world to come. Amen.[c]

a. J. N. D. Kelly, *Early Christian Creeds*, 3rd ed. (London: Longmans, 1972), 102.

b. John H. Leith, ed., *Creeds of the Churches: A Reader in Christian Doctrine, from the Bible to the Present*, 3rd ed. (Atlanta: Westminster John Knox, 1982), 24–25. Also in *CCFCT* 1:669.

c. Leith, *Creeds of the Churches*, 33 (modified by restoring a key term to Greek). Also in *CCFCT* 1:163.

up the understanding of the Holy Spirit by distinguishing his role in the incarnation from that of Mary. We have seen that the Nicene Creed contains a whole paragraph about the Holy Spirit, in addition to the brief statement about his role in Jesus's birth. The Apostles' Creed, lacking such a stand-alone discussion of the Holy Spirit, helps to identify him with the Father and the Son by distinguishing him from Mary: the Holy Spirit is the actor who brought about the conception, but Mary was the one through whom the birth took place.

Public Domain / Wikimedia Commons

The Annunciation by Leonardo da Vinci (1452–1519)

In fact, as he wrote his commentary in 404, Rufinus evidently already felt the need to distinguish the Holy Spirit's role in the conception from Mary's. In his long discussion of the virgin birth, he writes, "He is born by the Holy Spirit from the Virgin. . . . What you are expected to understand here is that He who, as you have already learned, was born ineffably from the Father had a shrine constructed for Him by the Holy Spirit in the recesses of the Virgin's womb."[12] Mary's womb was the location of the incarnation, but Rufinus makes clear that the Holy Spirit was the agent accomplishing it. Incidentally, after his discussion of "and in the Holy Spirit," Rufinus gives a long account of the inspiration of the biblical books and the canon of Scripture. This account serves to fill out the brief mention of the Holy Spirit in the creed itself and corresponds to the Nicene Creed's affirmation "who spoke through the prophets."[13]

Thus, what appears to be a mere detail in the Apostles' Creed likely grew out of a recognition in the Western church that the bare affirmation "in the Holy Spirit" needed creedal supplementation. The Apostles' Creed provides this supplementation in a way different from, but complementary to, the Nicene.

Christ's Suffering and Death

The second distinctive feature of the Apostles' Creed is its more comprehensive treatment of Christ's suffering and death. The Latin creed in Rufinus's time mentioned suffering and burial, and the Nicene Creed mentioned

12. Rufinus, *Commentary on the Apostles' Creed* 9, p. 42.
13. Rufinus, *Commentary on the Apostles' Creed* 37–38, pp. 72–74.

The Crucifixion by Hermann tom Ring (1521–96)

crucifixion, suffering, and burial. The final Apostles' Creed affirms that Jesus "suffered under Pontius Pilate, was crucified, *died*, and was buried." Of course, there is no inconsistency between the creeds here, for the affirmation of burial certainly implies the recognition of the preceding death. But is there any significance to the addition of the word "died"? It would certainly be reasonable to answer this question negatively. On the other hand, we suggest that the addition of this word sometime between 400 and 700 may indicate that the Western church was already beginning to place more emphasis on the death of Christ itself than it had previously done, and the beginnings of this shift in emphasis eventually led to a rethinking of the atonement in the eleventh century.

As we have seen throughout this book thus far, the church always affirmed the *account* of Christ's incarnation, life, death, and resurrection. The facts of this history, recounted in varying degrees of detail, were part and parcel of all early creeds. But early creedal statements did not explain exactly how to interpret the death of Christ, and even more notably, the early symbols did not explain the relation between Christ's death and forgiveness of sins, even though the creeds grew out of baptismal ceremonies dramatizing (or conveying) forgiveness of sins, and many creeds specifically mentioned such forgiveness. To Protestant eyes, this failure to connect the death of Christ to the forgiveness of sins may well rank as one of the greatest problems with early Christian thinking.

In defense of the church fathers, we could point out that the question they were concerned with—whether Christ was really God the Son living and dying as a man, or merely a man inspired by the Logos—is even more central than the question of how to interpret Christ's death. Perhaps one is not in a position to interpret the death until one has successfully dealt with the question of who it was who died. The Chalcedonian Definition made clear who it was who was *born* for our salvation, but the explicit extension of that affirmation to the question of who it was who *died* came later, at the Fifth Ecumenical Council in 553 (which we will consider in chap. 8). So it should not surprise us that attention to the *interpretation* of Christ's death, rather than just the *fact* of it, did not come until later in Christian theological history. In the meantime, the addition of "died" to the final Apostles' Creed may be a tantalizing foreshadowing of the great atonement discussions that were coming.

Christ's Descent into Hell

By far the most famous of the additions in the final Apostles' Creed is the assertion that Christ descended into hell. The question of whether this assertion belongs in the creed, and of whether it is biblical even if it does so belong, has been a lively one since the time of the Reformation and has been reargued with new vigor in American theological journals (especially *Westminster Theological Journal* and *Journal of the Evangelical Theological Society*) since 1990.[14] Before we can begin assessing the significance or truthfulness of this addition, let us return to Rufinus to get the basic facts. He writes, "In the creed of the Roman church, we should notice, the words DESCENDED INTO HELL are not added, nor for that matter does the clause feature in the eastern churches. Its meaning, however, appears to be precisely the same as that contained in the affirmation BURIED."[15] One could take this to mean that "he descended into hell" means nothing more than "he was buried," but that

---

14. For an excellent summary of both the Reformation and contemporary debates, see Jeffery L. Hamm, "*Descendit*: Delete or Declare? A Defense against the Neo-Deletionists," *Westminster Theological Journal* 78 (2016): 93–116. Among its many strengths, Hamm's article covers in more detail the points that we are about to make concerning Rufinus.

15. Rufinus, *Commentary on the Apostles' Creed* 18, p. 52.

is not actually what Rufinus intends. Later in his discussion, he asserts that Psalms 22:15; 30:9; and 69:2[16] prophesy Jesus's descent into hell,[17] and that this is what Peter was referring to in 1 Peter 3:18–20. Finally, on the basis of John 12:32 and Matthew 27:52–53, Rufinus claims that the purpose of the descent was so that Jesus could bring back from hell as spoils of his victory those who had been held as prisoners there.[18]

It is clear, then, that Rufinus affirmed Jesus's literal descent into hell and that the descent was present in his own baptismal symbol, that of Aquileia. In fact, even though the descent was not present explicitly in the Nicene Creed, it did feature in some earlier Eastern symbols, and Kelly argues persuasively that the Western church added it as a result of Eastern influence.[19] Therefore, it is not the case that Rufinus believed that "descended into hell" meant nothing more than "was buried." Rather, he believed that when a creed mentioned only burial, the (literal) descent into hell was implicit in the creedal use of the word "buried." Accordingly, although the clause made its way into the Apostles' Creed relatively late, it did have a long pedigree and widespread affirmation earlier. We cannot justly argue that the church's early faith did not include Christ's descent into hell.

Since that is the case, what does the strange clause mean? First, we need to recognize that in the Old Testament, Sheol (translated as "Hades" in Greek and "hell" in English) signified simply the grave or the undifferentiated underworld, the place of the dead. Thus, in the earliest patristic affirmations of Jesus's descent into hell, the claim likely meant no more than that he died.[20] But by Rufinus's time, the descent into hell held considerably more significance. What did Rufinus mean in saying that Christ descended into hell to bring from there the spoils of his victory?

To understand this, we need to return to a point we have made just above, that the early church focused more on the person of Christ (who was it who was born and died on the cross?) than on how to interpret that death by crucifixion. In the first Christian millennium, when theologians did specifically interpret the death of Christ, they tended to do so in one of two ways. Both interpretations started from the premise that the major problem of sin was that it made us captives to death and the devil, and so the solution was to overcome the powers that enslaved us and set us free. (Notice the

---

16. These are the Psalm numbers as printed in the English Bible. The Vulgate, following the Septuagint, numbers these as 21:16; 29:10; and 68:3.

17. Rufinus, *Commentary on the Apostles' Creed* 28, p. 61.

18. Rufinus, *Commentary on the Apostles' Creed* 29, pp. 62–63.

19. Kelly, *Early Christian Creeds*, 379.

20. See Kelly, *Early Christian Creeds*, 378–83.

difference between this starting point and the common Protestant assumption that the major problem of sin has to do with guilt.) From this starting point, the church fathers described the death either as the overcoming of death and the devil by the act of dying itself, or as a divine ransom paid to Satan in order to trick him into overstepping his authority (that is, to trick Satan into releasing his captives in order to gain Christ, whom he regarded as more valuable than all the captives but whom he could not hold captive in death because Christ was sinless).[21] Sacrificial or "substitutionary" images for the death were also present in the early church but did not come to dominate the understanding of the atonement until much later, and only in the Western church.

In both of these early views, the key aspect of the atonement was God's gaining victory over the powers of death and the devil so as to liberate the people who were held captive to those powers. With this approach to the death of Christ in the background, the descent into hell was understood as either the announcement of victory (Christ went into hell to announce to Satan's minions that he, rather than Satan, had won) or as the actual liberation of Old Testament believers who were unjustly held by the devil but who could not be freed until Christ had won the victory. The second of these is what Rufinus affirms in his *Commentary on the Apostles' Creed*.

Therefore, the insertion of the clause "he descended into hell" into the Apostles' Creed reflected a widespread understanding of the nature of Christ's work, in which victory over hostile powers was central and in which a literal descent was seen as crucial either to the liberation of the human beings held captive by demons or to the proclamation of the victory over those demons that Christ had won.

In the later Western church, and especially in Protestantism, as the atonement began to be seen exclusively in terms of guilt, satisfaction, and forgiveness, it seemed to many that the descent into hell needed either to be reinterpreted (as Christ's taking on himself the full penalty of our sins) or dropped from the confession of faith. The result has been the longstanding debate in Protestant circles about this clause of the creed that we mentioned at the beginning of this section. What Protestants should probably ask themselves, however, is whether the primacy of satisfaction in their understanding of the atonement actually means that Christ's work

21. For the first of these views (which could be called simply the "victory" view), see, for example, Gregory of Nazianzus, *Oration* 45.22, in NPNF[2] 7:431. For the second (the "ransom to the devil" view), see, for example, Gregory of Nyssa, *Great Catechetical Oration* 23, in NPNF[2] 5:493–94. Rufinus himself shared Gregory of Nyssa's view. See Rufinus, *Commentary on the Apostles' Creed* 16, p. 50–51.

had nothing to do with victory. Admittedly, we are unlikely today to affirm that Old Testament believers had to remain in hell until Christ liberated them, since we are more likely to claim that God could have and did dispose himself toward the saints of old on the basis of the atonement that he later made through Christ (see Rom. 3:25), and thus could accept them into his presence as soon as they died. But at the same time, do we not want to affirm that victory was a significant part of what Christ was accomplishing through his death and resurrection? If we do want to acknowledge the importance of victory in the atonement, then the puzzling affirmations in 1 Peter 3:18–20 may make us open to the possibility that Jesus descended into hell to proclaim victory over the demonic powers. This affirmation in the creed, interpreted in one of the ways the early church understood it, is worth taking seriously today.

The Communion of Saints

The last of the distinctive affirmations in the Apostles' Creed is the inclusion of the phrase "communion of saints." In this phrase, the Latin word translated as "saints" can be either masculine or neuter, and thus it can refer either to communion/fellowship with holy people or to participation in holy things. The first of these is the way the phrase has been taken for most of Christian history (hence the English translation, which resolves the ambiguity of the Latin phrase), but in the Middle Ages it was common to take the word as referring to holy things—that is, the sacraments. Remember that the Nicene Creed mentions baptism in connection with the forgiveness of sins, whereas the Apostles' Creed affirms "remission of sins" with no mention of baptism. Thus, it appears that the interpretation "participation in holy things" as a reference to the sacraments arose in an attempt to redress an omission in the creed. If one takes the word for "saints" as masculine, and thus as referring to holy people, the phrase is still ambiguous, since it is not clear whether it has in view official saints (that is, people whom the Roman Catholic Church has formally canonized) or saints in the New Testament sense of "believers." Finally, there is ambiguity about whether the phrase is referring to fellowship with living believers or departed believers.[22]

Thus, the phrase "communion of saints," though it appears on the surface to be one of the most clear-cut and innocuous statements in the creed, is actually among the slipperiest. It can be, and has been, interpreted in various ways in keeping with the different ecclesiologies of various Christian groups.

22. See Kelly, Early Christian Creeds, 388–95.

Conclusions

In this chapter we have seen that there was a long and winding road from the brief second-century symbol produced in Rome, to its gradual expansion (mainly away from Rome, and especially in Gaul) from 400 to 700, to its adoption as the standard creed of the Frankish world in northern Europe by about 800, to its eventual acceptance as the standard creed in Rome itself. At this point, it should be no wonder that many scholars distinguish between the Old Roman Creed and the Apostles' Creed. At the same time, we should not forget the continuity that provides justification for laypeople and some scholars to call the Western symbol "the Apostles' Creed" from the very beginning of its history.

Precisely because the Apostles' Creed began as a baptismal symbol and never lost its moorings in liturgical usage, it remained shorter and more general than the elaborate creeds put forward at Nicaea in 325 and Constantinople in 381. This brevity and the creed's liturgical cadence have made it far easier to memorize and recite than the Nicene Creed (let alone the Creed of Nicaea!), and for a thousand years it has been the main—but not the only—creed for use in public worship among Western Christians who value creeds.[23] During that long history, the Apostles' Creed has garnered a great deal of respect and a profound level of authority. In the Western Christian world, that authority is so strong that many writers refer to it as universal or as uniting all of Christendom.[24]

We need to recognize two things, however. First, Western Christendom does not constitute all of Christendom. The Eastern churches have never given the Apostles' Creed the level of respect that they accord to the Nicene Creed, although they have informally accepted it. Second, and closely related, *traditional* authority is not the same as *conciliar* authority. The Apostles' Creed has a widespread and long-standing traditional authority, but as we have emphasized previously, only the Nicene Creed has universal conciliar sanction.

Nevertheless, the Apostles' Creed is of great value, focusing clearly on the threefold affirmation of faith in God, in his Son, and in his Spirit, while also

23. The Apostles' Creed has been used in daily offices in Roman Catholicism since the Middle Ages, and it is also used on most days in the Anglican daily offices. It is recited weekly in many Lutheran and Reformed Protestant churches. Of course, it is also the baptismal symbol of all Western churches that recite a creed during the baptismal ceremony.

24. Note, for example, Philip Schaff's famous overstatement from more than a century ago: the Apostles' Creed is "the best popular summary of the Christian faith ever made within so brief a space. . . . It is the bond of union between all ages and sections of Christendom." *The Creeds of Christendom, with a History and Critical Notes*, 3 vols., 6th ed. revised by David Schaff (1877; repr., Grand Rapids: Baker, 1998), 1:15.

providing brief references to many of the major points of Christian doctrine. It moves easily from God the Father Almighty, to the human life of his only Son our Lord, to the Holy Spirit and his work among us. In the process, it provides hooks on which to hang more lengthy discussions of the great doctrines of the faith to which it merely alludes. Even when we base those longer discussions only on the Apostles' Creed, we rely on the Nicene Creed and the Chalcedonian Definition, as well as innumerable other theological discussions, to fill in the gaps. As a result, perhaps it is best to regard the Apostles' Creed as a skeleton on which the whole of Christian faith and doctrine can be hung. Although it did not come directly from the apostles, it does bring cohesion and structure to their proclamation of the gospel.

7

The Athanasian Creed

A Creedal Anomaly with Staying Power

In a collection of sermons by early sixth-century bishop Caesarius of Arles (in Gaul), there is a preface that reads in part, "And because it is necessary, and incumbent on them, that all clergymen, and laymen too, should be familiar with the Catholic faith, we have first of all written out in this collection the Catholic faith itself as the holy fathers defined it, for we ought both ourselves frequently to read it and to instruct others in it." Following the preface is the full text of what we now call the Athanasian Creed, with the title "The Catholic Faith of Saint Athanasius the Bishop."[1]

We should note straightaway that in this reference (recorded history's first direct mention of the document), the Athanasian Creed is not called a creed. It is a document allegedly representing Athanasius's "faith," one that was meant for study by clergy and laity, not for liturgical recitation per se. It was not called a symbol until the thirteenth century; before that time it was dubbed "The Faith of Athanasius" or "The Catholic Faith." Furthermore, the Athanasian Creed differs from others we have encountered in that it emerged neither through baptismal usage nor through conciliar deliberations. In both respects,

---

1. See J. N. D. Kelly, *The Athanasian Creed* (New York: Harper & Row, 1964). Kelly's work has so thoroughly settled the historical questions related to the Athanasian Creed that there has been little scholarly work on that document subsequently. Much of this chapter is indebted to Kelly's work (as indeed much of the discussion in the previous chapters has been indebted to his work on other creeds).

the document scarcely seems to warrant its later categorization as a creed. And as we have already seen in chapter 1, it was not written by Athanasius. In fact, a well-known saying among creedal scholars is that there are only two things about the Athanasian Creed that are certain: it is not Athanasian, and it is not a creed. Thus, in this chapter we call the document "The Catholic Faith"[2] as well as the "Athanasian Creed." It is ironic that a document never meant as a creed, and not regarded as such until some seven hundred years after its composition, is revered as a creed today not only by Roman Catholics but also by those Protestants who affirm creeds. As we will see later in this book, most Protestant confessions that mentioned creeds included this as one of the creeds they affirmed.

What, then, is the story behind this odd document? How did it originate, and how did it take its place alongside the Apostles' and Nicene Creeds? These are the questions that we take up in this chapter.

Dispensing with the Attribution to Athanasius

As we consider the origins of "The Catholic Faith," we should begin by justifying the now-universal belief that it was not written by Athanasius. First of all, it was written in Latin rather than Greek, and, in fact, it was not translated into Greek until at least the late twelfth century. Furthermore, there is no evidence that either Athanasius or any of his many Greek followers knew of it. The Byzantine world seems to have been largely unaware of it until the twelfth century. Third, the document's theological terminology clearly presupposes a Western, Latin milieu and dates from a time later than Athanasius. As we have seen, the language for person and substance was still in flux in Athanasius's time but was set by the time of this document, and as we will see later in this chapter, the document represents a later Western development in the way theology was conceptualized. Finally, the document affirms what theologians call the "double procession of the Holy Spirit"; that is, it claims that the Spirit proceeds from the Father and the Son, whereas the Nicene Creed had stated simply that he proceeds from the Father. This, too, is a Western development (if not actually subsequent to the time of Athanasius). From all of these considerations, it is clear that the document was written in a Latin theological milieu later than the end of the fourth century, and thus that its author could not have been Athanasius.[3]

2. Scholars today normally call it the *Quicunque* (Latin for "whoever"), which is the first word of the document as written in Latin.
3. See Kelly, *Athanasian Creed*, 2–3.

Nevertheless, in the West, where it originated, "The Catholic Faith" was associated with Athanasius's name and benefited enormously from his prestige. As part of the Carolingian effort to improve education, Charlemagne sought to impress on the clergy not only the Apostles' Creed and the Lord's Prayer but also "The Catholic Faith of St. Athanasius." After the split between East and West (which we will discuss in chap. 10), the Western church began to insist that the East give attention to the Athanasian Creed. By the late fourteenth century, the West had been so successful in this endeavor that the Easterners concluded that the document was by Athanasius, although they insisted that the double procession of the Holy Spirit was a Western interpolation. But when modern Western scholarship began to question Athanasian authorship in the sixteenth and seventeenth centuries, the Eastern Orthodox Church decisively rejected the document.[4] Thus, we see that the Athanasian attribution emerged in the West (as did the document itself) and was foisted on the East with only temporary success. In spite of the name, the Athanasian Creed is a Western document through and through. Athanasius himself had nothing to do with it.

The Composition and Early Use of "The Catholic Faith"

Where and when, then, did the document originate? It seems certain that Gaul was the place of writing, just as it was the place where Caesarius first quoted the document. There have been many scholarly attempts to pinpoint the location more precisely by comparing the document's Latin style to that of Gallic writers, and to pinpoint the date by locating the theological language of the document within the flow of the trinitarian and christological controversies. These inquiries, over more than two hundred years of scholarly work, have led to a general conclusion that "The Catholic Faith" came from the orbit of the monastery at Lérins and the episcopal see of Arles. It had to have been written after the year 416, the publication date of the masterpiece On the Trinity by the North African bishop Augustine of Hippo (since it obviously depends on that great work)[5] but before the end of Caesarius's episcopate in 542 (since he quotes it in the sermon collection mentioned above). Suggested authors are Hilary of Arles and Vincent of Lérins in the early fifth century, and Caesarius of Arles himself in the sixth. J. N. D. Kelly convincingly argues for late fifth- or early sixth-century authorship by someone under Caesarius's tutelage (but not Caesarius himself), and he concludes,

4. See Kelly, *Athanasian Creed*, 42–48.
5. We will turn our attention to Augustine of Hippo in depth in chap. 9.

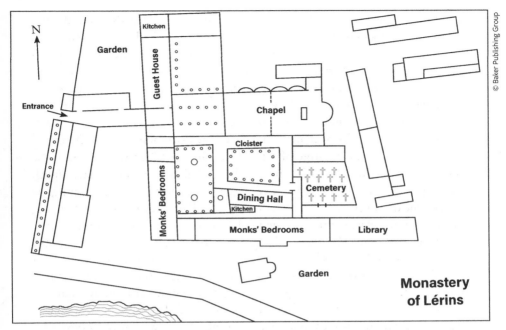

Lérins Abbey

The connexion of the creed with the monastery at Lérins, its dependence on the theology of Augustine and, in the Trinitarian section, on his character-istic method of arguing, its much more direct and large-scale indebtedness to Vincent, its acquaintance with and critical attitude towards Nestorianism, and its emergence at some time between 440 and the high noon of Caesarius's activity—all these points, as well as the creed's original function as an instru-ment of instruction, have been confirmed or established by our studies. . . . Only the name of the actual author eludes us.[6]

In addition to the question of the time and place of writing, another im-portant issue is what the function of "The Catholic Faith" was. If it was not originally a creed, what was it? To answer this question, we need to go back to the collection of Caesarius's sermons in which we first find the document. In the preface, from which we quoted at the beginning of this chapter, Caesarius indicates that "all clergymen, and laymen too" should be familiar with the faith. The focus on clergy in this assertion suggests that the initial purpose of the document was to provide a template that clergy could use to master the central theological dogmas of the Christian faith. While laypeople are

6. Kelly, *Athanasian Creed*, 123.

mentioned, they may well have been secondary in Caesarius's mind. Be that as it may, the document was originally meant to be studied and mastered, not to be recited liturgically. The Athanasian Creed was also cited by a council held around 670 in Autun in Burgundy (central France today). The council decrees, "If any priest or deacon or cleric cannot recite without mistake the creed which, inspired by the Holy Spirit, the apostles handed down, and the Faith of the holy primate Athanasius, he should be episcopally censured."[7] Again, we see that the primary audience of the document was the clergy.

Over time, as the prestige of "The Catholic Faith" grew, it began to be inserted into prayer books for liturgical use. This started in the late eighth century, and in the ninth century it began to be recited, and even sung, as part of the daily services. The document was still used as a tool for educating and examining clergy, but its growing place in the liturgy meant that, for the first time, it began to be regarded as a creed. By the middle of the thirteenth century, medieval writers began to speak of three creeds, and the Athanasian Creed's place next to the Apostles' and Nicene Creeds was assured. A document written (as far as we know) by a single person rather than by a council or by the hand of liturgical development, and intended for educational purposes rather than liturgical ones, had become a creed with staying power.[8]

The Structure of "The Catholic Faith"

The Athanasian Creed is a masterpiece of balanced affirmations presented in almost poetic form. It consists of forty-two verses, each containing a single assertion or proposition that is directly linked to those before and after it. The verses are usually numbered, and in this chapter we cite them by verse numbers. Unlike any of the creeds we have encountered thus far, "The Catholic Faith" is not structured either around the three persons of the Trinity or around the events of Christ's life, death, and resurrection. Instead, it is organized into two major sections, one on the Trinity as a whole (vv. 3–28), rather than separate articles on each of the persons, and the other on the incarnation and life of Christ (vv. 29–41).

At the beginning and end of the document are affirmations that the faith described in these two major sections is the catholic faith (vv. 1–2, 42). Let us first look at these framing statements.

7. See Kelly, *Athanasian Creed*, 41.
8. Today the Athanasian Creed is recited on Trinity Sunday (in May or June) in Roman Catholic and in many Lutheran churches. Its use in Anglicanism is declining, although some churches still use it on select days in the daily services.

[1]Whoever desires to be saved must above all things hold the catholic faith.

[2]Unless one keeps it in its entirety inviolate, one will assuredly perish eternally.

[42]This is the catholic faith. Unless one believes it faithfully and steadfastly, one will not be able to be saved.[9]

One should notice immediately that the focus of this document is much different from any of the creeds we have seen previously. The early creeds covered in chapter 2, as well as the Nicene Creed and Apostles' Creed later, begin with the affirmation "I believe" or "we believe," and the focus is on the *persons* in whom we believe. This document begins not with someone in whom we believe, but with a body of beliefs—the catholic faith—that we must hold. Furthermore, this body of beliefs is regarded as a whole that one must "hold" and "keep" in its entirety in order to be saved. We have moved from creeds that profess our allegiance to God, to his Son, and to his Spirit (remember our mantra from the first chapter: the one to whom we belong is the one in whom we believe), to a document that commands us *what* to believe in order to be saved. To say it differently, we have moved from faith in some*one* to beliefs about some*thing*, from faith in the *God* who has sent his Son and Spirit for our salvation to belief in *doctrines* about the Trinity and the incarnation.

This shift may or may not be striking to you. As a guess, we suspect that the more familiar you are with Western theology, the less surprising (or even noticeable) this shift will be to you. Why? Because the Athanasian Creed reflects the direction that Western theology was already heading at the time of its composition. Subsequent Western theology in the Middle Ages and later continued this focus on doctrines, on things that we must (or should, or may, or do, or do not, or cannot) affirm. That shift has distinct advantages, most notably that it enables great theological precision (as is apparent from most substantial volumes of Western theology by both Catholics and Protestants). But at the same time, we should recognize what is lost in the process. Affirming truths *about* God is not the same thing as dedicating one's life *to* God. Assent to doctrines does not necessarily imply allegiance or faith. By shifting the focus to doctrines, the Western church opened up the possibility that systematic theology might become divorced from the actual living of a life dedicated to God, his Son, and his Spirit. This divorce does not always take place, and it is surely unintentional when it does, but notice that what makes

9. Here and in the subsequent sections of this chapter we use the translation from Kelly, *Athanasian Creed*, 17–20. Also in CCFCT 1:676–77.

the divorce possible is the shift from persons to doctrines, from the ones in whom we believe to the things that we believe.

As we recognize that the Athanasian Creed represents a shift in the way the Christian faith is articulated, let us turn to its teaching on the Trinity and the incarnation to see how this shift plays out.

The Trinitarian Teaching of "The Catholic Faith"

The section on the Trinity (vv. 3–28) begins as follows:

> [3]Now this is the catholic faith, that we worship one God in Trinity and Trinity in Unity,
> [4]without either confusing the persons or dividing the substance.
> [5]For the Father's person is one, the Son's another, the Holy Spirit's another;
> [6]but the Godhead of the Father, the Son, and the Holy Spirit is one, their glory is equal, their Majesty coeternal.

Here we should acknowledge the importance of the word "worship," which mitigates to some degree the claim we made in the previous section. This document is not merely about concepts, about doctrines. It stresses the one God whom we worship. Remember that the Nicene Creed affirms that the Holy Spirit is "worshiped and glorified together with the Father and Son," and the statement in verse 3 of this document that "we worship one God in Trinity" seems to be getting at the same truth. However, the very next phrase, "Trinity in unity," shifts the focus from the persons themselves to the concepts. Verse 4 introduces the terms "person" and "substance," and the phrasing of verse 5 clearly focuses on concepts rather than on the persons themselves. The writer could have asserted, "The Father is one person, the Son is another, and the Spirit is another." That would have kept the focus on the persons themselves, while stressing that they are distinct as persons. But by claiming "the Father's person is one, the Son's another, the Holy Spirit's another," the writer accentuates the concept of person over the persons themselves. Interestingly, verse 7 is more successful at focusing on the persons, because it stresses what they share: Godhead, glory, and eternal majesty.

The document continues its discussion of unity and Trinity by focusing on attributes that the persons share:

> [7]Such as the Father is, such is the Son, such also the Holy Spirit.
> [8]The Father is increate, the Son increate, the Holy Spirit increate.

⁹The Father is infinite, the Son infinite, the Holy Spirit infinite.

¹⁰The Father is eternal, the Son eternal, the Holy Spirit eternal.

¹¹Yet there are not three eternals, but one eternal;

¹²just as there are not three increates or three infinites, but one increate and one infinite.

¹³In the same way the Father is almighty, the Son almighty, the Holy Spirit almighty;

¹⁴yet there are not three almighties, but one almighty.

¹⁵Thus the Father is God, the Son is God, the Holy Spirit God;

¹⁶and yet there are not three gods, but there is one God.

¹⁷Thus the Father is Lord, the Son Lord, the Holy Spirit Lord;

¹⁸and yet there are not three lords, but there is one Lord.

¹⁹Because just as we are obliged by Christian truth to acknowledge each person separately both God and Lord,

²⁰so we are forbidden by the catholic religion to speak of three gods or lords.

Notice that to some degree this paragraph follows the pattern of earlier theology discussed in chapter 4. Treating the substance or essence of God as a set of attributes, earlier theologians taught that Father, Son, and Spirit all share each of those characteristics. So also here: Father, Son, and Spirit are each uncreated. Each is infinite. Each is eternal. Each is almighty. Thus, each is God, and each is Lord.

At the same time, however, there is a difference here. Following Augustine, the author of "The Catholic Faith" does not treat the attributes as characteristics that God *has*; he treats them as what God *is*.[10] So, for example, he asserts that even though Father, Son, and Spirit are each almighty, there is one almighty, not three. An earlier theologian, or an Eastern theologian from this time period, would have been more likely to say that there *are* three who are almighty, but since they share all power, they constitute one God and Lord, not three. In the hands of this writer, the person-centric focus of that earlier way of speaking is transformed into an attempt to balance the *concepts* of unity and Trinity by asserting in a quasi-mathematical way that three persons are each almighty, but there is one almighty, not three. A new focus on concepts rather than persons, and a new emphasis on what one could call "mathematical symmetry" as a tool to deal with the Trinity, are reflective of shifts in the Western theological world after Augustine.

Having discussed the unity of the persons in this new, Western way, the author of "The Catholic Faith" turns to the relations between the persons:

10. For a discussion of the way Augustine's trinitarian theology influenced this document, see Kelly, *Athanasian Creed*, 80–84.

[21]The Father is from none, not made nor created nor begotten.

[22]The Son is from the Father alone, not made nor created but begotten.

[23]The Holy Spirit is from the Father and the Son, not made nor created but proceeding.

[24]So there is one Father, not three Fathers; one Son, not three Sons; one Holy Spirit, not three Holy Spirits.

[25]And in this Trinity there is nothing before or after, nothing greater or less,

[26]but all three persons are coeternal with each other and coequal.

[27]Thus in all things, as has been stated above, both Trinity in unity and unity in Trinity must be worshipped.

[28]So one who desires to be saved should think thus of the Trinity.

This paragraph shows the same desire for mathematical symmetry that we have seen throughout the trinitarian section, but its main affirmations are identical to what earlier theologians had said, with one exception. Like earlier theologians and creeds, this document emphasizes the equality and eternity of the three persons. Like earlier theologians and creeds, it stresses that the Father is from nothing and the Son is from the Father, not made but begotten (see the Nicene Creed's "begotten not made").

The exception, though, is that "The Catholic Faith" asserts, "The Holy Spirit is from the Father and the Son, not made nor created but proceeding." This is an early affirmation of the "double procession of the Holy Spirit" or the *Filioque*. The Latin word *Filioque* means "and from the Son," and both the word and the phrase "double procession" refer to the affirmation that the Holy Spirit eternally proceeds from both of the other persons, not just from the Father.[11] Remember that the Nicene Creed has affirmed the procession of the Holy Spirit "from the Father," without commenting one way or another on whether he also proceeds from the Son. In the West it was common for theologians to affirm the double procession of the Spirit, whereas Greek theologians tended either to disavow any such double procession or to use the phrase "from the Father *through* the Son" rather than "from the Father *and* the Son."

The question of what difference it makes whether one affirms or denies the *Filioque* is a complicated one that later played a role in the eventual

11. In John 14:16 Jesus describes the Father as sending the Holy Spirit, and in John 15:26 he says that he will send the Spirit from the Father. Clearly, then, both Father and Son send the Spirit into the world to accomplish his mission. But in John 15:26 Jesus also affirms that the Holy Spirit proceeds from the Father, and this is the source of the language to that effect in the Nicene Creed. The question—which cannot be resolved merely exegetically—is whether the Son's sending the Spirit into the world implies that the eternal procession of the Holy Spirit is also from the Son as well as from the Father.

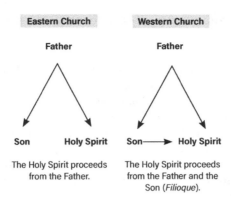

schism between the East and the West. For now, it is sufficient for us to recognize that if one denies the *Filioque*, the implication is that the Father, *as a person*, is the focus of trinitarian doctrine. The Father is uncaused, from no one and nothing. He is God pure and simple. The Son is God because of his eternal relation to the Father—he is eternally begotten from him. The Spirit is God because he, too, has an eternal relation to the Father—he eternally goes forth or proceeds from him. This way of speaking maintains the focus on the persons that we have argued was characteristic of early trinitarian theology. In partial (but by no means complete) contrast, the affirmation of the *Filioque* is usually related to a view of the Trinity that focuses on mathematical symmetry, the balancing of oneness and threeness. In such a model, drawing a line (metaphorically speaking) connecting the Son and the Spirit, to go along with the lines already drawn connecting the Father and Son and connecting the Father and Spirit, provides balance and helps to illustrate the equality of the persons. The debate over the *Filioque* thus has to do more with which model of the Trinity one uses than with the actual question of whether one can demonstrate biblically that the Spirit proceeds from both of the other persons. We will return to the question of the *Filioque* in chapter 10. Let us now turn to the christological teaching of the Athanasian Creed.

"The Catholic Faith" on the Incarnation

In this section of the document, the author adheres much more closely to the creedal language of those who have gone before him. The focus throughout is on the person of God the Son. While the Nicene phrase "came down" does not occur, the incarnation as an action by which the eternal Son came to earth to suffer for us is clear. The following is the first paragraph of this section:

> [29]It is necessary, however, to eternal salvation that one should also faithfully believe in the incarnation of our Lord Jesus Christ.
> [30]Now the right faith is that we should believe and confess that our Lord Jesus Christ, the Son of God, is equally both God and man.
> [31]He is God from the Father's Substance, begotten before time; and he is man from his mother's substance, born in time.
> [32]Perfect God, perfect man composed of a rational soul and human flesh,
> [33]equal to the Father in respect of his divinity, less than the Father in respect of his humanity.

Notice in verse 30 that the first assertion regarding "our Lord Jesus Christ" is that he is the Son of God. This affirmation precedes the insistence that he is "equally both God and man" and sets the stage for the descriptions of verses 31–33. This Son of God is "God from the Father's Substance,"[12] and as such, was begotten before time. He (clearly "the same one," although this document does not spell that out) is also "man from his mother's substance, born in time."[13] The structuring of the paragraph around a single person, the eternal Son, who has always been God and who is now man as well, is reminiscent of the Chalcedonian Definition. Notice also the affirmation that Christ's humanity includes "a rational soul and human flesh." This assertion was almost ubiquitous after the late fourth century as a way of disavowing Apollinarianism.

The next paragraph is as follows:

> [34]Who, although he is God and man, is nevertheless not two but one Christ.
> [35]He is one, however, not by transformation of his divinity into flesh, but by the taking up of his humanity into God;
> [36]one certainly not by confusion of substance, but by oneness of person.
> [37]For just as rational soul and flesh are a single man, so God and man are a single Christ.

In verses 35–36 we see language almost identical to that which Vincent of Lérins earlier used to combat Nestorianism,[14] as our author insists that the

---

12. Notice that this is a phrase from the Creed of Nicaea that was dropped in the final form of the Nicene Creed.

13. Even after Chalcedon it was common in the West to use the word "substance" rather than "nature" to describe the divine and human within Christ.

14. In his *Excerpta*, which have not been translated into English.

eternal Son did not merely indwell the man Jesus; rather, he took humanity into his own person. The body-soul analogy, while certainly incomplete, was almost universal as a description of the christological union.

Finally, "The Catholic Faith" discusses the actions of the incarnate Christ.

[38]Who suffered for our salvation, descended into hell, rose from the dead,
[39]ascended to heaven, sat down at the Father's right hand, whence he will come to judge living and dead:
[40]at whose coming all men will rise again with their bodies, and will render an account of their deeds;
[41]and those who have behaved well will go to eternal life, those who have behaved badly to eternal fire.

Here, along with a standard recitation of the events of Christ's earthly life, two things are noteworthy. First, the Athanasian Creed affirms the descent into hell, which by this time had been added to the Apostles' Creed as well. Second, in contrast to the Apostles' Creed (which merely affirms that Christ will judge the living and the dead), this document affirms the basis for Christ's judgment: the deeds/behavior of those being raised from the dead. To Protestant ears, the focus on behavior in verse 41 may be unnerving. If we are on the lookout for anything that smacks of "works righteousness" and a denial of justification by faith, we seem to have found the smoking gun here.

Well, maybe, or maybe not. Whenever our works-righteousness antennae are engaged, we need to remember that there is a lot of "works" language in the New Testament, including references to judgment on the basis of works.[15] Of course, in the big picture, what we do is the fruit of the transformation that God has already made in us through Christ and the Holy Spirit, but if biblical authors can refer to judgment on the basis of works without always painting the big picture, so can the Athanasian Creed. We should not jump immediately to condemn a writing on the basis of a statement such as this.

At the same time, Protestant fears that this document is sliding into medieval works righteousness are probably somewhat justified. The document began by insisting that in order to be saved, one has to keep "the catholic faith" (a body of doctrines). Now, at the end, it is claiming that judgment will be based not merely on assenting to the doctrines, but also on works. Here we see, at the beginning of the Middle Ages, a movement toward insisting on works in addition to faith, which later incited the reaction that we call the Reformation. But notice the logic of this movement. If one reduces faith

15. See, for example, the parable of the sheep and the goats in Matt. 25, as well as 2 Cor. 5:10 and Rev. 22:12, not to mention James 2.

from allegiance to a person down to assent to doctrines, then one needs to add something in order to do justice to the biblical picture of Christian life. But if one were to maintain the focus on faith as allegiance to a person (again, remember "the one to whom we belong is the one in whom we believe"), then it would be fairly obvious that such allegiance would lead to a transformed life, a life characterized by good works. In other words, the felt need to bring works into a document like this may stem from a shift away from allegiance to God, his Son, and his Spirit. The divorce of theological language from Christian life, already underway at the time "The Catholic Faith" was composed, may have contributed to what eventually was a skewed perception of the relation between faith and works by the late Middle Ages.

Conclusions

The Athanasian Creed certainly is a creedal anomaly. It was not composed by the person whose name it bears or even in the language he spoke or the part of the Christian world where he lived. It was not originally intended as a creed and only very gradually began to be used liturgically. It has rarely been accepted outside the Western Christian world and has recently fallen into disfavor even there. It is hardly used in public worship today. Yet it did have a lot of staying power and rose to the rank of the Western church's third creed in the High Middle Ages, a position it still holds in Roman Catholicism and Lutheranism today, if nowhere else.

What are we to make of this odd document? We have seen that in spite of its unusual origin and historical pathway, it does have much to teach us. Its balanced phrases provide a simple way of emphasizing truths as complex as, for example, that Father, Son, and Spirit share the same attributes, or that the same Son is both eternal in his begetting from the Father and temporal in his birth from Mary. While it is hard to recite, it is worth reading and meditating on. That, in fact, was what it was originally meant for!

Nevertheless, there are problems with the document as well. We have seen that the trinitarian discussion in "The Catholic Faith," while not actually at odds with the earlier creeds (Eastern and Western), does represent a significant shift in the way the doctrine of the Trinity is articulated. At the time of its writing, Western theology was beginning to strike out on its own course, and this document both reflected and, as it became more widely used, cemented that new direction. Readers of this book may disagree on whether that new direction was a good one, but it should at least be clear that the shift from focusing on the trinitarian persons as the ones in whom we believe, to focusing on doctrines, is potentially dangerous.

With the writing of the Athanasian Creed around the year 500, we bring the era of the creeds to a close, even though the Apostles' Creed underwent some minor revisions later. In part 2 we will examine the very different ways in which the Eastern and Western churches explored the theology of the creeds from 500 to 900. As we will see, the different directions that they took eventually led to the split between East and West into what we today call Eastern Orthodoxy and Roman Catholicism. To that story we now turn.

Exploring Creedal Theology

(500–900)

8

Clarifying Chalcedon in the East

By the year 500, the Nicene Creed had become firmly established throughout the Christian world, the Chalcedonian Definition was on the books, and the Apostles' Creed was nearing its final form (although it did not reach complete fixity until some two hundred years later). Furthermore, by 500, the anomaly that was later called the Athanasian Creed had already been written or was soon to see the light of day. The great era of the creeds was essentially over. Thus, one might have expected that as the sixth century dawned, we would find a Christendom united around its great creedal statements, especially if, as we have argued, those statements expressed a profound consensus about the heart of the Christian faith.

Alas, at least on the surface, such unity was very far from being present in the year 500. As we saw in chapter 5, outside the Byzantine Empire the Church of the East had broken ties with the rest of Christendom several decades earlier and spent the next fifteen hundred years in substantial isolation, in spite of its affirmation of the Nicene Creed. In that chapter we also saw that the new terminology of the Chalcedonian Definition (in which *ousia* and *physis* were both words for "nature/essence," and *hypostasis* and *prosōpon* were words for "person") was deeply divisive in the Byzantine Empire as well, and many Eastern Christians in Egypt, Syria, and even Greece were convinced that Chalcedon was Nestorian. We have also seen that Emperor Zeno's *Henotikon*, a political attempt at shoring up unity by avoiding Chalcedon altogether, backfired spectacularly, since Rome interpreted that document as an insult to the authority of Chalcedon and accordingly broke fellowship with Constantinople. Thus, the year 500 saw a Christian world in unprecedented—and to many people, unimaginable—discord.

To Byzantine Christians at the time, not all splits were created equal. The rift with the Church of the East was of relatively little concern, since that church was far removed from life in Byzantium. Of more significance was the split with Rome, but by now the Western Christian world represented the fringes of the "Roman" world and was becoming more and more Frankish, so this split as well was of less than titanic interest. By far the most important to the Byzantines was the rift with the Syrian and Coptic (Egyptian) churches that were later called Oriental Orthodox. Indeed, the fact that Zeno wrote the *Henotikon* had already showed that shoring up unity with Syria and Egypt was important enough that he thought it was worth sacrificing the Council of Chalcedon to try to achieve it. And over the next two hundred years, Byzantium made two more major efforts at reconciliation with the anti-Chalcedonian churches, leading to the Fifth and Sixth Ecumenical Councils in 553 and 681. Both efforts were politically unsuccessful, but both produced important clarifications of the Chalcedonian Definition. Then another great crisis rocked the Byzantine world, calling for yet another ecumenical council in 787. With these three councils, the Eastern church probed the incarnation to a depth that the Western church never matched. In this chapter we consider each of these three ecumenical councils as explorations and clarifications of the Chalcedonian Definition.

Theopaschitism and the Fifth Ecumenical Council (553)

As we have argued throughout this book, a central affirmation of the Christian faith is that we cannot rise up to God on our own, so God must come down to save us. This truth takes pride of place in the Nicene Creed, and we argued that amid the various affirmations of the Chalcedonian Definition, the most insisted-on claim was that the baby born from Mary was "the same one" who had eternally been the Father's only Son. What Chalcedon did not do, though, was extend this claim from the birth of Christ to his death. The most poignant way to phrase the christological question is to ask who it was who died on the cross. Who was it who cried out, "My God, my God, why have you forsaken me?" (Matt. 27:46)? Was it a man indwelt by the Son who suffered and died, or was it God the Son himself who suffered "as man," in his humanity? Although Cyril of Alexandria had repeatedly insisted that it was really God the Son who died on our behalf (always qualifying the claim by saying that he died in his humanity, not in his divine nature per se), Chal-

Man of Sorrows by Geertgen tot Sint Jans

cedon did not address this question directly.

People who were suspicious of the terminology used in the Chalcedonian Definition were inclined to think that the council was dividing Christ into two distinct persons, the Logos and the man Jesus. To such people, the omission of the death of Christ from the Definition suggested that if Chalcedon *had* pronounced on that issue, the council would have denied that the Son himself suffered on the cross and would have assigned the death only to the man Jesus. The theological term for this issue is "theopaschitism," derived from the Greek words for "God" and "suffering." While virtually everyone in the early church would have denied that God was capable of suffering in his own nature, most also insisted that God (the Son) genuinely suffered as a person through the humanity that he assumed into his person at the incarnation. Western Christians today often handle this issue by saying something like "the divine nature didn't suffer; only the human nature did."[1] While perhaps not technically false, this statement is basically meaningless, since natures do not do anything at all; persons do. We argued in chapter 5 that natures are sets of characteristics that enable persons who possess those natures to do certain things. God, by virtue of possessing the divine nature, cannot suffer. Humans, by virtue of possessing a human nature, can suffer. But if Christ, as a person, is God the Son, then that person, God the Son, could truly suffer by virtue of the human nature that he possessed after the incarnation. To connect this idea to what we have seen previously: since it was really God the Son who was born as a man for our salvation, then it was really God the Son who died as a man, in his humanity, for that salvation. One can, and we

---

1. As we will see in chap. 14, this issue was a major point of tension between Martin Luther and Huldrych Zwingli in the sixteenth century.

believe one should, see this affirmation as an extension of what Chalcedon stated when it claimed that the one born from Mary was the same one who had eternally been the Father's Son.

The affirmation that God the Son suffered on the cross in his humanity was thus a way of demonstrating to the anti-Chalcedonian churches that Chalcedonians did not divide Christ into distinct persons, and thus that Chalcedon was not actually Nestorian. In the 510s, a group of ardently pro-Chalcedonian monks from Scythia (modern Romania) sought to link the language of the Chalcedonian Definition directly to the theology of Cyril, and a hallmark of their effort was the insistence that one person of the Trinity suffered in the flesh.[2] While the monks' efforts to bring their case to both Constantinople and Rome proved ineffectual (for various reasons that had little to do with the merits of their case), they caught the attention of a young man in the imperial court, Justinian, who was the nephew of the Byzantine emperor Justin. Justinian himself became emperor in 527.[3]

Justinian was the first emperor to be a significant theologian. Building on the connections made by the Scythian monks, he proposed a two-plank plan to clarify the teaching of Chalcedon, to convince the anti-Chalcedonian churches of the East that they and the Chalcedonians shared the same faith, and to convince the West that the East was not abandoning Chalcedon's authority. The first plank was the promulgation of the theopaschite affirmation that one of the Trinity suffered in the flesh. The second plank was the condemnation of three entities collectively known as the "Three Chapters." These were the person and writings of Theodore of Mopsuestia, certain writings by Theodoret of Cyrrhus, and a letter to Mari the Persian attributed to Ibas of Edessa. As we saw in chapter 5, Theodore was Nestorius's teacher and, in many ways, the father of Nestorianism. Justinian proposed condemning his entire corpus of writings. Theodoret took part in the small countercouncil at Ephesus in 431 led by John of Antioch and wrote several treatises against Cyril of Alexandria.

---

2. See "The Chapters of John Maxentius" (the leader of the Scythian monks), in *Fulgentius of Ruspe and the Scythian Monks: Correspondence on Christology and Grace*, trans. Rob Roy McGregor and Donald Fairbairn, FC 126 (Washington, DC: Catholic University Press of America, 2013), 235–36.

3. For the fuller story of the Scythian monks, see McGregor and Fairbairn, *Fulgentius and the Scythian Monks*, 3–21. For the broader picture of events leading to the Fifth Ecumenical Council, see Richard Price, trans., *The Acts of the Council of Constantinople of 553, with Related Texts on the Three Chapters Controversy*, 2 vols. in 1, Translated Texts for Historians 51 (Liverpool: Liverpool University Press, 2009), 1:1–41. See also Leo Donald Davis, *The First Seven Ecumenical Councils (325–787): Their History and Theology* (Collegeville, MN: Liturgical Press, 1983), 207–53; Aloys Grillmeier and Theresa Hainthaler, *Christ in Christian Tradition*, vol. 2, *From the Council of Chalcedon to Gregory the Great, Part 2: The Church of Constantinople in the Sixth Century* (Louisville: Westminster John Knox, 1995), 317–473.

Justinian I

Justinian proposed condemning these writings against Cyril, but not everything else that Theodoret wrote. The letter to Mari was written in the aftermath of Ephesus and was very critical of the council and of Cyril. Justinian proposed condemning this letter and suggested (rather speciously) that Ibas was not actually the author. By insisting on the theopaschite formula and condemning the Three Chapters, Justinian hoped to demonstrate that Chalcedonians were not closet Nestorians.

In May and June of 553, the Fifth Ecumenical Council was held in Constantinople. Justinian was not present, but he carefully scripted the council to achieve the goals that he had laid out.[4] The council issued no new creed or definition, but in its official summary of the proceedings it strongly emphasized its adherence to the four previous ecumenical councils and the inconsistency of the Three Chapters with the decrees of those councils, especially with the Nicene Creed and the Chalcedonian Definition.[5] The council promulgated fourteen canons, all phrased in the form of anathemas.[6] Three of these are especially important for our purposes. The third canon condemned anyone who said that "the [Word] of God who works miracles is not identical with the Christ who suffered, or alleges that God the Word was with the Christ who was born of woman, or was in him in the way that one might be in another, but that our lord Jesus Christ was not one and the same, the Word of God incarnate and made man."[7] The fifth canon anathematized anyone who tried "to introduce into the mystery

---

4. For the full acts, see Price, *Acts of the Council of Constantinople.*

5. For this summary, see Norman P. Tanner, ed., *Decrees of the Ecumenical Councils*, vol. 1, *Nicaea I to Lateran V* (Washington, DC: Georgetown University Press, 1990), 107–13. Also in CCFCT 1:185–201.

6. For these canons, see Tanner, *Decrees of the Ecumenical Councils*, 1:114–22. Also in CCFCT 1:201–15.

7. Tanner, *Decrees of the Ecumenical Councils*, 1:114. Also in CCFCT 1:201.

of Christ two subsistences [*hypostaseis*] or two persons, and having brought
in two persons then talks of one person only in respect of dignity, honor or
adoration, as both Theodore and Nestorius have written in their madness
. . . [or who] falsely represents the holy Synod of Chalcedon, making out that
it accepted this heretical view by its terminology of 'one subsistence.'"[8] The
tenth canon stated, "If anyone does not confess his belief that our lord Jesus
Christ, who was crucified in his human flesh, is truly God and the Lord of
glory and one of the members of the Holy Trinity: let him be anathema."[9]

It is worth noting that the acts of the council do not include direct reference to the teachings of Origenism, but there is a strong tradition indicating
that the council also addressed Origenism and condemned it, and canons
condemning Origenism have long been associated with the council.[10] If, as
is almost certain, the council actually condemned Origenism as well as the
Three Chapters, then this means that it dealt with the roots of both great
heresies of the early church. Arianism grew out of Origenistic teaching, as
we saw in chapter 4, and Nestorianism was the child of Theodore's teaching,
as we saw in chapter 5.

Despite the elaborate scripting of the council, it was not successful in
achieving its political aims. Most of the Syrian and Egyptian churches continued to regard Chalcedon as a Nestorian document, and at about this time
they began developing church structures that were permanently separate from
those of the Chalcedonians. Pope Vigilius was extremely ambivalent about
the council. He had actually been summoned to Constantinople in the 540s
to broker an agreement on the matter, and he accepted the canons only very
reluctantly and under intense imperial pressure. Many in the West believed
that condemning the Three Chapters constituted a denial of the authority
of the Council of Chalcedon, since the delegates at that council had agreed
to seat both Theodoret and Ibas. Because of this chilly Western reception,
many modern scholars regard the Fifth Ecumenical Council as a mistaken
aberration that, like Ephesus in 431, overemphasized Christ's unity at the
expense of his full humanity.

In contrast to that interpretation, we believe that this council—for all its
messiness—should be seen as a legitimate development from Chalcedon, indeed, as a clarification of Chalcedon by extending its thought from the birth
to the death of Christ.[11] Since it was really God the Son who was born for

---

8. Tanner, *Decrees of the Ecumenical Councils*, 1:116. Also in CCFCT 1:203–5.
9. Tanner, *Decrees of the Ecumenical Councils*, 1:118. Also in CCFCT 1:209.
10. See Price's discussion of this issue in *Acts of the Council of Constantinople*, 2:270–80.
11. See Price's outstanding explanation of the council in *Acts of the Council of Constantinople*, 1:59–75. Note in particular his explanation on p. 73 of the common scholarly inter-

us, it was really God the Son who died for us. He died in his humanity, not in terms of his deity per se, but the person who hung on the cross bearing the sin of the world was God's eternal Son himself, who humbled himself not only to the point of incarnation but even to the point of death on the cross. While the council did not achieve its political goals, it did the Christian world a far greater service by stating this crucial implication of Chalcedon. The Fifth Ecumenical Council was a theological success, even though it was a political failure. But because it failed politically, the Eastern Christian world was still left with the task of trying to reconcile the Syrian and Egyptian churches to Byzantium.

Monotheletism and the Sixth Ecumenical Council (680–81)

At the beginning of the seventh century, the Sassanid Persians conquered much territory on the eastern flanks of Byzantium, and there were constant threats from Slavic peoples to the north as well. But in the 620s, the Byzantine emperor Heraclius was successful in retaking Syria, Egypt, and Armenia for Byzantium. This event highlighted the desirability of reunion between the Chalcedonians and anti-Chalcedonians, since they were now once again in the same political orbit. Then, after Muhammad's death in 632, Arab armies swept through the Middle East and North Africa, taking control of vast swaths of the Roman Empire. These threats made the need for internal unity in the remaining Christian lands especially urgent, and Heraclius, together with Sergius, patriarch of Constantinople, engaged in intense negotiations with the anti-Chalcedonians of Syria, Egypt, and Armenia as well.

From these negotiations emerged a new strategy: the affirmation of a single activity in Christ, even though he possesses two natures. This idea is called monenergism, from the Greek words for "single activity." In the early 630s, Sophronius of Jerusalem opposed this teaching by insisting that activity is a function of nature, not of person. When Sergius wrote to Pope Honorius to inform him of the debate in the East, Honorius responded by rejecting the language of "single activity" and instead offering the complementary expression "single will" (referred to as monotheletism, from the Greek words for "single will"). Sergius accepted the new terminology and prepared an imperial

---

pretation. In contrast to that interpretation, Price concludes (and we agree), "The miaphysite rejection of Chalcedon as Nestorian showed that the Definition was open to misinterpretation, and it was evasive on one major issue, the propriety of theopaschite expressions. I would therefore argue that the canons of 553, so far from narrowing or distorting the vision of Chalcedon, imported a welcome clarification, and one that the great majority of the fathers of Chalcedon, Cyrillian in their loyalties, would have applauded."

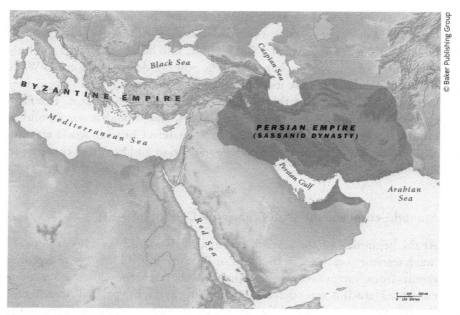

The Sassanid Persian Empire

decree (the *Ecthesis*), which Heraclius promulgated in 641, making monothe-letism official imperial doctrine for the moment. After Heraclius died in 641, his successor, Constans II, attempted to put a lid on the brewing controversy over the new policy by issuing another edict (the *Typos*) forbidding anyone to speak of either one will or two wills in Christ![12]

The major opponent of monotheletism was Maximus the Confessor, who had been an official under Heraclius in the 610s but had left to pursue the monastic life. He left Byzantium in 626, settling eventually in North Africa. From Carthage, Maximus argued that since in the Trinity there are three persons and one nature, and also one will, the will must be a func-tion of the nature, not the person. Since Christ has two natures, and will is a function of nature, he must have two wills, divine and human, rather than one. In addition to this point of trinitarian logic, Maximus based his argument on the even more significant soteriological conviction that the unassumed is unhealed. If the Logos did not assume a human will at the incarnation, then the will was not saved. In making this point, Maximus extended the soteriological logic that Gregory of Nazianzus had used three

12. For an overview of the controversy, see Andrew Louth, *Maximus the Confessor*, Early Church Fathers (London: Routledge, 1996), 7–16; Davis, *First Seven Ecumenical Councils*, 258–87.

hundred years earlier to combat Apollinaris's contention that the Logos took the place of the human mind in Christ. Just as the salvation of humanity must have involved the Son's taking a human mind on himself, so also our salvation must have involved his taking a human will on himself. To say it differently, if the mind is that aspect of humanity that most needs salvation and healing, then within the mind, it is not simply the cognitive ability that needs healing, but even more so the will. What most makes us unable to rise up to God on our own is the recalcitrance of our sinful wills, and the healing of the human will must have taken place through the Son's assumption of a human will at the incarnation. As a result of Maximus's arguments, we can see that unlike theopaschitism (which, because it affirmed a central truth related to salvation, was an appropriate way of seeking to reconcile Chalcedonians and non-Chalcedonians), monotheletism was an inappropriate, and indeed heretical, way of attempting such reconciliation. A Christ without a human will distinct from his divine will could not bring salvation to our human will.

Maximus also insisted that if one were to renege on saving doctrine for the sake of political compromise, as the imperial edict commanded, then the silence itself was heretical. To be silent on an issue of such import was simply not an option. This argument is important evidence that the church was, when necessary, willing to stand up to the emperor. While the church welcomed any help the emperor could give in the service of the truth (as in the case of the church's acceptance of Justinian's lead in the sixth century), it did not tolerate imperial orders that arose out of a misunderstanding of saving doctrine. In such cases, prominent churchmen were willing to stare down the empire. Maximus himself suffered terribly for his bravery. He was tried in imperial court in 654 and exiled to Thrace (northeastern Greece) upon his refusal to recant. He was again tried in 661, and when he would still not recant, his right hand and his tongue were cut off, and he was sent to exile in the Caucasus, where he died the next year.[13] Finally, the imperial attitude changed as Constans was assassinated in 668, and his son Constantine IV replaced him.

Following Maximus's lead, in 678 Pope Agatho condemned monotheletism. Then under Constantine's auspices, the Sixth Ecumenical Council met in Constantinople over a nine-month period in 680–81. The council

13. See the following anthologies of Maximus's works: George C. Berthold, ed., *Maximus Confessor: Selected Writings*, Classics of Western Spirituality (New York: Paulist Press, 1985); Louth, *Maximus the Confessor*; Paul M. Blowers and Robert Louis Wilken, trans., *On the Cosmic Mystery of Christ: Selected Writings from St. Maximus the Confessor*, PPS 25 (Crestwood, NY: St. Vladimir's Seminary Press, 2003).

published an exposition of the faith[14] that linked its work to the five previous ecumenical councils and named the major heretics whom those councils condemned: Arius at the First Ecumenical Council, Macedonius (who opposed the full deity of the Spirit) and Apollinaris at the Second, Nestorius at the Third, Eutyches and Dioscorus at the Fourth. In the case of the Fifth Ecumenical Council, the exposition stated the following: "with the fifth holy synod, the latest of them, which was gathered here [in Constantinople] against Theodore of Mopsuestia, Origen, Didymus and Evagrius, and the writings of Theodoret against the twelve chapters of the renowned Cyril, and the letter said to have been written by Ibas to Mari the Persian."[15] Didymus and Evagrius were noteworthy Egyptian followers of Origen in the fourth century, so this comment indicated that the Fifth Ecumenical Council had in fact condemned Origenism as well as the Three Chapters. The council thus showed that it understood itself to be following the lead of all five previous councils, not merely correcting an overemphasis on the part of the Fifth.

The exposition named the promulgators of the monothelete heresy (including the former pope Honorius and the former patriarch of Constantinople Sergius) and described the heresy as "a single will and a single principle of action in the two natures of the one member of the holy Trinity, Christ our true God," and specifically links this mistake to that of Apollinaris.[16] The council praised the current emperor (without naming him) for his part in reversing the previous heretical imperial policy and sanctioned the report of Pope Agatho in which he condemned monotheletism. It likewise affirmed Leo's *Tome* and the letters of Cyril of Alexandria.[17]

The council paraphrased the Chalcedonian Definition, with significant additions taken from the canons of the Fifth Ecumenical Council, and then it addressed the issue at hand as follows:

And we proclaim equally two natural volitions or wills in him and two natural principles of action which undergo no division, no change, no partition, no confusion, in accordance with the teaching of the holy fathers. And the two natural wills not in opposition, as the impious heretics said, far from it, but his human will following, and not resisting or struggling, rather in fact subject to his divine and all powerful will.[18]

14. See Tanner, *Decrees of the Ecumenical Councils*, 1:124–30. Also in CCFCT 1:219–29.
15. Tanner, *Decrees of the Ecumenical Councils*, 1:124–25. Also in CCFCT 1:219.
16. Tanner, *Decrees of the Ecumenical Councils*, 1:126. Also in CCFCT 1:221.
17. Tanner, *Decrees of the Ecumenical Councils*, 1:126–27. Also in CCFCT 1:223.
18. Tanner, *Decrees of the Ecumenical Councils*, 1:128. Also in CCFCT 1:225.

In this assertion we see clearly both the similarity between Christ and us, and the distinction. Like us, he has a fully human will. We as sinful human beings reject and refuse to follow God's will; we use our human wills in opposition to God. But unlike us, Christ submits his human will fully to the divine will, which in his case is his own divine will, not that of another. We need to remember again that after the incarnation, Christ lived in two ways at once, "as God" and "as man." His *human* submission to the divine will was a crucial part of his obedience by which he accomplished our salvation. Without the possession of a fully human will, he could not have submitted *humanly* to the divine will. The unassumed is unhealed. The church here built on a crucial truth that it had previously recognized and brought greater clarity, precision, and depth to its understanding of Christ.

In rejecting the concept of a single energy or will in Christ, the Chalcedonian church effectively shut the door on the possibility of reconciliation with the Oriental Orthodox churches. After about the year 700, they, like the Church of the East previously, went their own way and had less and less contact with the churches of the Byzantine and Frankish worlds.

Iconoclasm and the Seventh Ecumenical Council (787)

In the spring of 717, the Byzantine Empire was in chaos, as the previous two decades had seen a series of coups with no sustained imperial rule. The Arab armies that had swept through much of the Middle East in the previous century were taking advantage of the unrest to make preparations for a massive siege of Constantinople, which began in the summer of that year. But before the siege could begin, a Byzantine general, Leo III, seized power and led his armies in a narrow but successful defeat of the Arabs, who finally withdrew after a full year of laying siege. Leo III brought stability to the empire, reigning until 741. But Leo also brought something else. In 726 he issued a decree forbidding the use of icons in worship and demanding their destruction.

Visual imagery had long been important in Christian worship. From crude cave art in the second century to the elaborately decorated cathedrals of Constantine's and later Justinian's time, the visual had always held a place alongside the spoken and written word. Today, the word "icon" refers to an image painted on wood according to a specific artistic style and meant for use in liturgical worship, but in the eighth century the word (Greek *eikōn*, "image") referred not only to paintings but also to other forms of religious art such as mosaics, frescoes, and statues. Images, understood thus, were common in the church from at least the fourth century. In the sixth century,

Modern Orthodox
icon of Christ Pan-
tocrator (Church
of St. Alexander
Nevsky, Belgrade)

the role of icons in the Byzantine world began to change, as their veneration
in worship increased and they began to hold significant public functions.
Indeed, an icon of Mary *Theotokos* was believed to have been responsible
for Leo's victory in 718, so when he issued his decree eight years later, he was
bucking long-established trends.[19]

This increasing role for the visual was not without its detractors, however.
Some Christians believed that icons fell under the condemnation of the second
of the Ten Commandments. Others found them embarrassing, especially since
Islam—the new menace on the borders of the empire—rejected all religious
pictures as idolatrous. Leo's decree probably grew out of the influence of these
simmering pockets of disapproval, but his action put him in direct conflict with
the church's major leaders. He was immediately opposed by both Germanus,
patriarch of Constantinople, and Pope Gregory II, who wrote with uncommon directness that ecclesiastical matters were not the prerogative of the
emperor. (Here again we see that as intertwined as the empire and the church
were, churchmen were not afraid to criticize the emperor when necessary.) In

19. For the background to the controversy, see St. John of Damascus, *Three Treatises on the
Divine Images*, trans. Andrew Louth, PPS 24 (Crestwood, NY: St. Vladimir's Seminary Press,
2003), 7–9. For the history of the dispute, see Davis, *First Seven Ecumenical Councils*, 290–319.

addition to patriarch and pope, the most important defender of icons was John of Damascus, a Syrian government official who worked for the Muslim caliph in his early life and then became a monk near Jerusalem. Although he never set foot in Byzantine territory, he was the greatest Byzantine theologian and apologist of his time.

After Leo's decree, John of Damascus wrote three treatises in favor of icons between 726 and 740.[20] In these treatises John makes three major arguments. First, he insists that "image" is a central motif in Scripture—for example, Christ is the image of the invisible God, and the Old Testament contains images that foreshadow the New Testament. Second, he distinguishes worship (*latreia* in Greek) from veneration (*proskynēsis* in Greek), arguing that the first is due to the persons of the Trinity alone, but the second can also be given to others—saints and their icons—as a way of honoring them without actually worshiping them. Thus, the veneration of icons did not constitute idolatry, which would be the worshiping of someone or something besides God. Third, John argues that while it is certainly impossible to represent God as he is in himself, it is not only possible but *necessary* to depict in visual form the incarnate—and therefore visible—Son. Icons were, above all else, emblems of the incarnation, and the painting of icons was the major way the church proclaimed the truth that God the Son has become visible through that incarnation.[21]

The controversy continued off and on for nearly 120 years, and throughout that period, the opponents of icons, called "iconoclasts" (smashers of icons), always came from the ranks of emperors and their officials. Every major church theologian, patriarch of Constantinople, and pope was an "iconodule" (servant of icons), also called an "iconophile" (friend of icons). Nevertheless, the iconoclasts produced some substantial theological arguments, which they put forward at a council controlled by Emperor Constantine V (a more violent enemy of icons than his father, Leo III, had been) in 754 in Hiera (near Chalcedon). In addition to arguing that there was no clear mandate for icons in the pre-Constantinian church, the iconoclasts insisted that the veneration of icons forced one into either idolatry or Nestorianism. Their argument was that an iconodule, in depicting Christ in a painting, was representing the divine, which cannot be represented. This was idolatry. If iconodules protested by saying that they were representing only the humanity of Christ, not the divinity, the iconoclasts would then claim that they were therefore dividing

20. These are translated in *Three Treatises on the Divine Images* (Louth).

21. In addition to the treatises themselves, see Andrew Louth, *St. John Damascene: Tradition and Originality in Byzantine Theology*, Oxford Early Christian Studies (Oxford: Oxford University Press, 2002), 193–208.

the deity and humanity of Christ. This was Nestorianism. In a clear retort to the iconodules' argument that the incarnation demanded the making of icons, the iconoclasts claimed that the only permissible visible representation of the incarnation was the Eucharist.[22]

After Constantine V's death in 775, his son Leo IV became emperor. He was married to Irene, a woman devoutly attached to icons. Leo died in 780, leaving his ten-year-old son as nominal emperor, but the actual power fell to Irene, who reigned until 803. Spurred on by Tarasius, patriarch of Constantinople, Irene called a council to reverse the decisions of the iconoclastic council of 754. Originally begun in Constantinople in 786, it was interrupted by the army (still loyal to Constantine V and to iconoclasm) and reconvened more than a year later, in September 787, in Nicaea. The doctrinal statement of this Seventh Ecumenical Council[23] followed the now-familiar pattern of reciting the Nicene Creed and affirming the previous councils, as well as naming the heretics condemned at those councils.[24] Again, we see that the councils saw themselves as moving in a straight line of development and as building on the previous councils. Viewed from this line of development, the council of 754 was an aberration, like some other nonecumenical councils before it.[25]

After this rehearsal of past heresies, the council continued:

> To summarize, we declare that we defend free from any innovations all the written and unwritten traditions that have been entrusted to us. One of these is the production of representational art; this is quite in harmony with the history of the spread of the gospel, as it provides confirmation that the becoming man of the Word of God was real and not just imaginary, and as it brings us a similar benefit.[26]

Here we see a direct link between the incarnation and the making of visual images. By celebrating the visual/material rather than denigrating it, the church affirmed that God truly became material and visible. The council went on to affirm that churches were to be adorned with visual images of various kinds, depicting not only Christ but also Mary, angels, saints, and the cross. As justification for this adornment of churches, the council asserted,

22. For the decrees of the iconoclastic Council of Hiera, see *NPNF²* 14:543–46.
23. See Tanner, *Decrees of the Ecumenical Councils*, 1:133–38. Also in *CCFCT* 1:233–41.
24. Tanner, *Decrees of the Ecumenical Councils*, 1:134. Also in *CCFCT* 1:235.
25. For example, the smaller council at Ephesus in 431, and the councils at Constantinople in 448 and Ephesus in 449.
26. Tanner, *Decrees of the Ecumenical Councils*, 1:135. Also in *CCFCT* 1:237.

The more frequently they [the images] are seen in representational art, the more are those who see them drawn to remember and long for those who serve as models, and to pay these images the tribute of salutation and respectful veneration [*proskynēsis*]. Certainly this is not the full adoration [*latreia*] in accordance with our faith, which is properly paid only to the divine nature, but it resembles that given to the figure of the honored and life-giving cross, and also to the holy books of the gospels and to other sacred cult objects.[27]

Notice the clear distinction between veneration and worship; the latter is given only to God, but the former may justly be paid to other persons and objects as well.

This council was meant to bring iconoclasm to an end once and for all, but it did not do so. Subsequent emperors also espoused iconoclastic policies, until the controversy finally came to a close with the death of the last iconoclastic emperor, Theophilus, in 842. The following year a small synod was held in Constantinople, declaring the council of 787 (rather than the council of 754) to be the Seventh Ecumenical Council and affirming its decrees. The link between icons and the incarnation was so central to Eastern Christian consciousness that the close of the iconoclastic controversy in 843 has been celebrated ever since as the "Triumph of Orthodoxy."

Many Protestant readers may be profoundly uneasy about the decisions of the Seventh Ecumenical Council, perceiving the veneration of icons and other material objects as idolatry, in spite of the church's insistence to the contrary in the eighth century. We may be prone to say that, in this case, the church made the wrong decision. For those of us who do feel this way, there are two things we should recognize.

First, it is important to distinguish between what the theologians gathered at the council intended and what actually happens in much of popular Christian worship. It may very well be the case that some, or many, worshipers in Eastern Orthodox churches are paying more attention to the saints and icons than to Christ. It may even be that they are worshiping the icons instead of Christ, and thus that they are falling into idolatry. It may be that the teachers of the church are not doing as much as they should to prevent that from happening. But be all that as it may, what the Eastern church intended and intends is not that people worship saints and icons. Instead, the intention is that the icons point either to Christ or to the saints whom they represent, and the saints point to Christ, who has made them saints. Saints are saints not "on their own" (remember, the whole import of patristic theology is that we cannot rise up to God on our own), but are so because of their relationship to

---

27. Tanner, *Decrees of the Ecumenical Councils*, 1:136. Also in CCFCT 1:237.

Christ. Icons and other forms of visual art are meant to convey relationship, and understood in this way, they deserve to be taken seriously.

Second, it is worth recognizing that much of Protestantism has a rather anemic theology of the visual and the material. Protestants are adamantly opposed to Gnosticism and utterly committed to the truth that God has become human, but at the same time, our reaction to medieval Roman Catholicism has given us a somewhat antimaterial view of spiritual reality.[28] We tend to divide easily between the spiritual and the material, and even in the material realm, between the visual and the auditory. We as a tradition are formed by the reading and preaching of the Word, by the text and its oral exposition, as well we should be. But can the image (the visual and material) not come to the aid of the textual and the oral in proclaiming the message of salvation? If we as Protestants disagree with either the theology of the Seventh Ecumenical Council or (more likely) the actual practice of Eastern Orthodox Christians, we need to ask ourselves: Do we have a positive theology of the visual, one that is more than merely a reaction against the Middle Ages? If not, do we need one?

Conclusions

In this chapter we have seen the way the Eastern church (with some involvement from the popes and other Western leaders) explored and deepened the theology of the Nicene Creed and the Chalcedonian Definition through three more ecumenical councils. There certainly are elements of this story that are troubling. The intertwining of Byzantine politics, and especially the major roles played by some of the emperors, could sow doubt in our minds about the veracity of the councils' doctrinal decisions. But we should remember that context is always a part of theological formulation, and context has to do with social and political factors as well as "religious" ones. This was no more or less true in the case of the ecumenical councils than it was in the case of the Reformation confessions that we will examine later in this book. We should also remember that the church was never blind in its allegiance to the emperor. During the monothelete and iconoclastic controversies, the church did not hesitate to oppose emperors whose policies they saw as threats to saving doctrine, just as had been the case in the Arian controversy centuries earlier. In light of that willingness to go toe-to-toe with emperors (and pay the political price for doing so), we should regard the church's compliance with Justinian during the theopaschite controversy as an indication that the

---

28. For the origins of this Protestant attitude, see our discussion of Zwingli in chap. 14.

bishops agreed with him, not as an indication that he was simply dictating to a submissive church. The process by which the councils reached their conclusions was indeed messy and full of politics, but the conclusions they reached nevertheless represented the mind of the church as a whole at that time.

If we step back from the gritty details of these councils, we can see that all of them followed a common trajectory. It was a trajectory set up by the question that we asked early in this book and have repeated at many points: "Can we rise up to God, or does God have to come down to us?" The first two ecumenical councils, at Nicaea in 325 and Constantinople in 381, stressed that the Son and the Spirit are just as fully God as the Father. If it were not so, it would not be *God* coming down to save us through the incarnation and the indwelling of the Spirit. The next five councils proclaimed and explored what it meant for the Son to come *all the way down* for our salvation. The Third and Fourth Ecumenical Councils, at Ephesus in 431 and Chalcedon in 451, taken together, emphasized that it was really God's eternal Son who was born for our salvation, and because he was really born as a man, he possesses divine and human natures. The Fifth and Sixth Ecumenical Councils, at Constantinople in 553 and in 680–81, clarified what it meant for God the Son to come down: the one who suffered on the cross was indeed God's eternal Son, and he possessed a human will through which he could bring healing to our fallen wills. Finally, the Seventh Ecumenical Council, in 787, constituted a ringing endorsement of the reality of the incarnation: God the Son really did come down to the material realm; he became visible—a fact that Protestants can all affirm even if they do not agree with the connection that the council insisted on between that fact and the making of visible images.

With the last of the seven councils, the greatest period of theological ferment in the Eastern Christian world came to a close. But what about the West? We have seen that various popes played bit parts in the later ecumenical councils, but essentially those great meetings were the work of the Christian East, not the West. During the period from 500 to 900, the West was consolidating its own theological heritage and moving in directions that were, while not actually contradictory, at least very different. We now turn to that story.

9

The West Charts Its Own
Theological Course

As we have told the story of the great creeds, a parade of important Christian thinkers, as well as major political figures, has marched across these pages. But amid the flurry of names—some famous and others less so—it has perhaps been surprising to you that the most famous name from the entire patristic period has rarely been mentioned. That was Augustine of Hippo, the brilliant theologian, bishop, polemicist, and spiritual writer who lived from 354 to 430 in Latin North Africa. We have thus far mentioned him only in connection with the date of the Athanasian Creed and its trinitarian theology. How could someone become by far the best-known person in the early church while still figuring rather minimally in our story?

The answer to this question provides an appropriate on-ramp to the story of Western theology in the Middle Ages, and thus to the story of the Reformation and its confessions. Augustine has played only a minor role in our story so far because, by accidents of geography and timing, he took no part in the great councils leading to the Nicene Creed and the Chalcedonian Definition. He had not yet become a Christian at the time of the Second Ecumenical Council in 381 and had already died by the time of the Third Ecumenical Council in 431. (He did receive an invitation to it, since the emperor did not know he was dead.) He also lived far from the regions of what is today western Turkey, where the great discussions of those issues took place. And yet Augustine became the most famous person in the early church because he engendered the thought of the *Western* church from the early Middle Ages up to the present day. In introducing the theology of the Middle Ages, Jaroslav Pelikan writes, "There is, at least since the apostles, no figure in Christian history who has so dominated a millennium with his teachings as Augustine did."[1] He had such dominance because of his utterly central role in the controversies and discussions that were formative in shaping the development of *Western* theology.

To say this a different way, as time went on, Eastern and Western theology focused on significantly different issues, and while the Eastern emphases directly related to the central affirmations of the *creeds*, the Western emphases set the stage for the great debates that produced medieval and Reformation *confessions*. From 500 to 900, as the East was consolidating the heritage of Nicaea and Chalcedon by going deeper into Christology, the West was consolidating the heritage of Augustine's thought, especially on three issues. The first of these was the *justification* of the Trinity, in partial contrast to the focus on the *persons* of the Trinity that had characterized earlier trinitarian theology and continued to be the Eastern focus for several more centuries. The second issue was the understanding of the church, its authority, and especially its sacraments. The third issue, closely related to the second, was the theology of grace, especially as it pertained to questions of human free will or lack thereof.

In this chapter, therefore, we consider these three defining issues of Western theology up to the early Middle Ages. In each case, we will go back to Augustine's own thought (although of course he lived prior to the year 500) and then mention the way the church developed Augustine's thought in the first few centuries after his death. By doing this, we will set the stage not only for the schism between East and West (to be covered in chap. 10) but especially for the great Western developments leading to the Reformation that will dominate our story in parts 3 and 4 of this book.

The Justification of the Trinity

In our discussion of the Athanasian Creed in chapter 7, we noted that the document focused less than other creeds on the trinitarian persons themselves and more on the *concepts* of person and essence/substance, and we also noted

---

1. Jaroslav Pelikan, *The Christian Tradition: A History of the Development of Doctrine*, vol. 3, *The Growth of Medieval Theology (600–1300)* (Chicago: University of Chicago Press, 1978), viii.

Public Domain / Wikimedia Commons

Ulfilas among the Gothic tribes

that in this respect, the author of the Athanasian Creed was following Augustine. Earlier, in chapter 4 on the Nicene Creed, we mentioned in passing that the Arian missionary Ulfilas had great success among the Gothic and Vandal tribes north of the Alps in the fourth century. Those groups, we commented, initially converted to Arian Christianity but were absorbed into Nicene Christianity by the early sixth century. It is now time to take up these points that we mentioned in passing earlier and fill in the rest of the story.

The Goths and Vandals were the famous "barbarians" who overran and took control of the western part of the Roman Empire in the fifth century. The sack of Rome in 410 by the Visigoths was the first time in nearly eight hundred years that the Eternal City had fallen to a foreign invader. The Vandals took Spain in 409 and Latin North Africa in 429–30, and they were at the gates of Hippo in August of 430, as Augustine lay dying. At the time of their conquests, both tribes were (Arian) Christian, and they were profoundly in awe of the great Roman civilization that they conquered. As a result, they did far less damage to the cities, and killed far fewer people, than one might have expected. Goths and/or Vandals and Romans began the complicated task of learning to live together in Italy and North Africa. For our purposes, the most significant aspect of this new social arrangement was that Arianism remained a live option in the Western Christian world long after it had more or less vanished from the East. This lingering Arian presence provided the backdrop against which Augustine wrote one of his three great masterpieces, *On the Trinity*.[2]

2. The other two were his *Confessions*, the first great spiritual autobiography in Christian literature, and his *City of God*, a majestic summary of human history as a conflict between the forces opposed to God (the "city of man") and God's kingdom (the "city of God"). The *City of God* is regarded as Christianity's first great work of political theology and philosophy of history, and it is sometimes referred to as the last great work of classical Latin prose.

Augustine's *On the Trinity* was one of the most tightly organized works of the patristic period. It consists of fifteen books, the first and last of which state and restate the doctrine of the Trinity. Books 2–4 consider the biblical development of the doctrine, books 5–7 examine the doctrine logically, and books 8–14 consider the human being as an image of the Trinity before returning to the Trinity itself in book 15.[3] In the biblical portion of the work (books 2–4), Augustine focuses firmly on the persons of the Trinity, and his argument for demonstrating that the Son and the Spirit are equal to the Father in some ways parallels the earlier Eastern discussions of the Arian controversy. He starts with the one God, the Father, and he marshals biblical evidence to show that the Son and the Spirit are so united to the Father that they constitute one God with him. They go above the hard line separating God from all that he has created.

In the logical section (books 5–7), however, Augustine focuses much more on the *concept* of unity in diversity or oneness in threeness. He asserts, "There is at least no doubt that God is substance, or perhaps a better word would be being; at any rate what the Greeks call *ousia*."[4] Remember that earlier the church had written of God's essence as something that he *possesses*, but here Augustine identifies the essence as what God *is*. This shift set the stage for subsequent Western discussions of the Trinity to focus on the essence as a quasi-entity in itself, which became a hallmark of Western trinitarian doctrine. Augustine also misunderstands the new use of *hypostasis* in Greek theology to mean "person." Thinking that the Greeks still meant "substance" when they wrote *hypostasis*, he claims in a famous passage,

> For the sake of talking about inexpressible matters, that we may somehow express what we are completely unable to express, our Greek colleagues talk about one being, three substances, while we Latins talk of one being or substance, three persons, because as I have mentioned before, in our language, that is Latin, "being" and "substance" do not usually mean anything different. And provided one can understand what is said at least in a puzzle, it has been agreed to say it like that, simply in order to be able to say something when asked "Three what?"[5]

Augustine thought that the Greeks were speaking in a puzzle that was ultimately insoluble: they were saying that God is one something and three somethings at the same time. Augustine's solution to this seemingly insoluble

---

3. For an excellent discussion and schematic rendering of the work's structure, see Edmund Hill's introduction to Augustine, *The Trinity*, trans. Edmund Hill, Works of Saint Augustine 1/5 (Hyde Park, NY: New City Press, 1991), 21–27.

4. Augustine, *On the Trinity* 5.3, in Hill, *Trinity*, 190.

5. Augustine, *On the Trinity* 7.7, in Hill, *Trinity*, 224.

puzzle was to justify the juxtaposition of oneness and threeness (what we called "mathematical symmetry" in chap. 7 on the Athanasian Creed) by appealing to other instances of such oneness and threeness—created images of the Trinity. These images—especially memory, intellect, and will within the human mind, and lover, beloved, and love among humans—dominate books 8–14 of *On the Trinity*.

These middle and latter books of *On the Trinity* set the course of Western trinitarian doctrine in the centuries after Augustine. As we have already seen, as early as the Athanasian Creed—written no more than a century after *On the Trinity*—the concept of unity in diversity already figured prominently, and this focus continued in subsequent Western theological history. The task of trinitarian theology began to be seen less as studying the persons in their relationship one to another and more as justifying the mathematical symmetry of oneness and threeness, with the concept of essence at the center of that enterprise. An unintended consequence of this new approach was that trinitarian language in the West became somewhat different from the language of both Scripture and the church's earlier way of speaking.

This new approach to the Trinity in the West did not derive simply from the misunderstanding of Greek trinitarian terminology. The lingering Arianism that prompted Augustine to write *On the Trinity* was another factor forcing the Western church not merely to assert that the three persons constituted one God, but to justify how that could be possible. The need for such justification also pushed Augustine and other Western theologians to the affirmation that the Spirit proceeds from the Father and the Son, as a way of explaining the unity and equality between the Father and the Son.[6] As Henry Chadwick memorably puts it, "Augustine thought the Arians could drive a coach and horses through a doctrine of the Trinity which excluded the Son from the coming forth of the Spirit from the Father. We should therefore say that the Spirit proceeds from the Father and the Son."[7] Augustine's affirmation of the Spirit's procession from the Son as well as the Father became virtually universal in the Western Christian world. We have already seen the same affirmation in the Athanasian Creed, and Augustine's most brilliant North African disciple, Fulgentius of Ruspe, was an eager proponent of the *Filioque* in the early sixth century as well.[8]

6. For Augustine's affirmation of the *Filioque*, see *On the Trinity* 4.29; 15.29, in Hill, *Trinity*, 174, 419.

7. Henry Chadwick, *East and West: The Making of a Rift in the Church, from Apostolic Times until the Council of Florence*, Oxford History of the Christian Church (Oxford: Oxford University Press, 2003), 27.

8. See Fulgentius, *To Peter on the Faith* 4; 54, in *Fulgentius: Selected Works*, trans. Robert B. Eno, FC 95 (Washington, DC: Catholic University of America Press, 1997), 61–63, 93–94.

Augustine of Hippo by Antonio Rodríguez

At a small council in Toledo, Spain, in 589 the Nicene Creed was read aloud, as was customary, and if the acts of the council are to be trusted, it was read with the addition of the *Filioque* (for the first time of which we are aware). The delegates at that council had no intention of modifying the creed, and thus we must conclude either that they inherited a creed to which the word had already been added or that the acts as we have them have been modified from the way the creed was originally read. At any rate, it was in Spain that the *Filioque* first made its way into the creed, before the year 600.[9] The issue of the *Filioque*, as well as the less obvious but more fundamental issue of approaching the Trinity through the rubric of oneness and threeness, rather than persons in relationship, played a role in the split between East and West, and we will return to these issues in chapter 10.

The Church, Its Sacraments, and Its Authority

Long before the time of Augustine, the Western church had begun placing much more emphasis on the nature of the church itself than had been the case in Eastern theology. Two schisms, both closely related to persecutions of Christians by the Roman Empire, pushed the church to the front and center in the attention of Western theologians, including Augustine himself.

The first schism came in the midst of the persecutions under the emperors Decius (249–51) and Valerian (257–58). During these persecutions, a large number of Christians renounced their faith either by offering sacrifices to the Roman gods or by bribing Roman officials to write them certificates saying

9. See A. Edward Siecienski, *The Filioque: History of a Doctrinal Controversy*, Oxford Studies in Historical Theology (Oxford: Oxford University Press, 2010), 68–69.

that they had done so, though they had not. During the interval between the Decian and Valerian persecutions, many Christians who had lapsed sought readmission into the church, and in Rome a dispute arose over what conditions should be imposed on those who sought to repent and return. Pope Cornelius allowed anyone who sought readmission to come back to the church, thus advocating a broad view of the church as a hospital for the spiritually sick, a hospital willing to take anyone into its fold. He was opposed by Novatian, who insisted that by lapsing during persecution, a person had irrevocably abandoned the Christian faith and should not be reinstated but should remain in lifelong repentance. Novatian thus stood for an extremely rigorous understanding of the church as a society of saints. The disagreement grew so sharp that Novatian's followers broke with the Roman church and consecrated him as a rival bishop of Rome. After Cornelius's death, his successor, Stephen, continued the same policy of easy readmission to those who lapsed during the Valerian persecution, and the Novatian church remained separate.[10]

As this was happening in Rome, Cyprian, bishop of Carthage in North Africa, who himself had escaped persecution by fleeing the city, argued for a mediating position. In his work *On the Unity of the Catholic Church*, he argues that splitting the church was a far worse sin than lapsing during persecution, since a church splitter such as Novatian endangered not only his own soul but those of his followers as well.[11] We should notice here the assumption that the Novatian church was not the true church, and therefore that its members could not be saved. In Cyprian's mind, the church as a visible, united body was essential for salvation.[12] He also argued that any who lapsed during persecution should be readmitted if they brought forth suitable evidence of repentance.

After the Diocletian persecution (which, in the West, lasted from 303 to 306), the same problem arose, as many who had lapsed during persecution sought readmission to the church. But this time around, the major issue was not whether such people could be readmitted (everyone except the few Novatians believed they could), but whether sacraments performed by people who had lapsed during persecution were rendered invalid by their sin. In 311, Caecilian was chosen as bishop of Carthage, but the bishop who consecrated him, Felix, allegedly had lapsed during the persecution by giving up his copies

---

10. See Allen Brent, introduction to St. Cyprian of Carthage, *On the Church: Select Treatises*, trans. Allen Brent, PPS 32 (Crestwood, NY: St. Vladimir's Seminary Press, 2006), 13–29.
11. St. Cyprian of Carthage, *On the Unity of the Catholic Church* 19, in *On the Church: Select Treatises*, trans. Allen Brent, PPS 32 (Crestwood, NY: St. Vladimir's Seminary Press, 2006), 173.
12. For an especially clear statement of this view, see St. Cyprian of Carthage, *On the Unity of the Catholic Church* 23, p. 178.

of the Scriptures to Roman officials who sought to destroy them. Many North African bishops, believing Caecilian's consecration to be invalid because of Felix's prior sin, rejected him and chose Majorinus as bishop, leading to a rupture in the North African church. After Majorinus's death, the bishops who followed him then chose Donatus, who gave his name to the schismatic movement, Donatism. Like the Novatians before them, the Donatists saw the church as a pure body of saints, and they believed that sacraments could be valid only if the faith and life of both the celebrant and the recipient were pure. As justification for their belief, they pointed to the fact that Cyprian (by now a hero of North African Christianity) had argued similarly during the Novatian schism.[13]

Unlike the Novatians in the third century, the Donatists in the fourth century captured the hearts and minds of many of the common people in North Africa, and by the end of that century they actually outnumbered the Catholic Church in that region. With Catholic Christianity thus reeling, its leaders needed a champion who could best the Donatists with both argument and oratory. They chose Augustine—at the time a brilliant young rhetorician turned monk—and elected him bishop of Hippo in 396, largely so that he could officially fight the battle with the Donatists.

Augustine lost little time in commencing this battle, and he spent the first decade of the fifth century immersed in the struggle with Donatism. Most significant for our purposes is his work *On Baptism, against the Donatists*, published around 400. In this work he tackles the question of the validity of a sacrament by dividing "validity" into three parts: genuineness, correctness, and profitability for one's salvation. Baptism, Augustine argues, is *genuine* whenever it is performed in the name of the Father, Son, and Holy Spirit, whether done in a Catholic church or a Donatist church. He argues that baptism is done *correctly* only when it is performed in a Catholic church. So Donatist baptism was genuine but not done rightly. Finally, Augustine insists that baptism is *profitable* for one's salvation only if that person is *now* in the Catholic Church, regardless of where he or she had been baptized.[14] Again, notice the assumption that only in the true church, the Catholic Church, could one be saved, even though one could genuinely receive baptism or another sacrament elsewhere.[15]

---

13. The classic treatment of this schism is William Frend, *The Donatist Church: A Movement of Protest in Roman North Africa* (Oxford: Clarendon, 1952). See also J. Patout Burns and Robin M. Jensen, eds., *Christianity in Roman Africa: The Development of Its Practices and Beliefs* (Grand Rapids: Eerdmans, 2014), 47–51, 195–98.

14. Augustine develops this argument throughout *On Baptism* 1. See especially the summary in 1.2, in *NPNF[1]* 4:412.

15. See also Burns and Jensen, *Christianity in Roman Africa*, 214–18.

In spite of Augustine's efforts, the Catholic Church could hardly be said to have won the battle against Donatism. In 411, the issue came to a head as both Catholics (including Augustine) and Donatists argued their cases before an imperial legate, Marcellinus. Augustine easily convinced Marcellinus, who then ordered strict measures to be taken against the Donatists. But in spite of these measures (including the closing and even burning of churches), Donatists by and large remained unreconciled to the Catholic Church, and they continued as a separate organization until the Arab invasion brought North African Christianity to an end in the seventh century.

What Augustine's battle with Donatism did accomplish, though, was the forging of a direction for Western Christianity. The emphasis on the church as a broad, inclusive body, incorporating everyone in a given society, became firmly entrenched and remained so up to the time of the Reformation and beyond. The belief that the validity of sacraments did not depend on the sanctity of either priest or recipient led to an ever-increasing focus on the power of the rites themselves, which eventually led to beliefs about the Eucharist that sparked the Reformation. Augustine's focus on the mediation of grace through the sacraments eventually meant that the church itself, and especially its ceremonies, lay at or near the center of people's faith, so much so that nascent Protestantism accused Catholics of putting the church in God's place. Since Donatism was the central battle of Augustine's life, it is not surprising that the legacy of the way he and others fought that battle shaped medieval Roman Catholicism in profound ways.

At the same time that Augustine's sacramentalism was dominating Western views of the church, another closely related aspect of ecclesiology was also being dramatically developed: the understanding of authority. We have already seen that in the aftermath of Chalcedon, Rome's antagonistic reactions to various Eastern developments were not the result of fundamental disagreement with, for example, theopaschitism. Instead, what most concerned Rome was the question of authority. Chalcedon had seated Theodoret and Ibas, and so a later rejection of certain writings by Theodoret and (allegedly) by Ibas looked to Rome like a denigration of the authority of the Fourth Ecumenical Council. Authority itself, rather than just the truth or falsity of particular theological assertions, was a major concern of Rome and the West.

Furthermore, it was not merely the authority of councils that was crucial to the West. The authority of bishops, and especially the preeminent authority of the bishop of Rome (the pope), was even more fundamental in the minds of Western theologians. In early Christendom there were five major episcopal sees that rose to the level of patriarchal status. Four of these (Jerusalem, Antioch, Alexandria, and later Constantinople) were in the Byzantine orbit and were

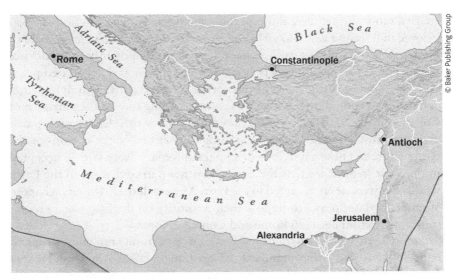

The five patriarchal cities: Antioch, Alexandria, Constantinople, Jerusalem, and Rome

largely Greek-speaking. Only one patriarchal see (Rome) was in the West and was Latin-speaking. As a result, the Christian East naturally developed an ecclesiology that involved sharing authority among various bishops, but in the West the primacy of honor that had always been afforded to Rome began to be construed as an actual authority of the Roman bishop (the pope) over the rest of Western Christendom. Indeed, as early as the 380s, Pope Damasus had argued that although the apostles came from the Greek world, the fact that Rome now possessed the bones of Peter and Paul gave it an authority superior to that of any other patriarchal see. Damasus further argued that Rome's universal authority demanded a uniformity of practice, and he set in motion a pattern of standardizing Western Christian worship practices according to what was done in Rome.[16]

After the time of Damasus and Augustine, this trend toward the increasing authority of the Roman see and the standardization of Christian practice continued, and the key period in both movements was the papacy of Gregory I (the Great) at the end of the sixth century. So pivotal was Pope Gregory in the rising stature of the papacy that his death in 604 is often considered the starting date for the Middle Ages in the West. Gregory was a man of immense piety and genuine concern for his flock. He possessed a significant family fortune, which he gave away after becoming pope in order to promote

16. See Chadwick, *East and West*, 17.

charity, monastic centers, and especially missions. For these actions he was beloved in Italy and was known by the phrase *servus servorum Dei* (servant of the servants of God), an epithet that popes use to sign their correspondence to this day. He stepped into a political power vacuum and negotiated peace with the Lombards (the latest of the northern tribes to invade Italy), further enhancing his popularity. But he was condescending toward the patriarch of Constantinople, refusing to grant him the honorary title "ecumenical patri-arch" and insisting that Rome had the right to dictate to the bishops of the entire church. These assertions of papal supremacy were widely accepted in the West (remember that there was no other patriarchal see in the Latin world) but were never accepted in the East. As we will see in the next chapter, attempts by later popes to impose their authority on the East were a major source of friction between Rome and Constantinople.[17]

Pope Gregory's vast missions work was an opportunity not only to expand papal influence but also to standardize Christian practice in the West. He sent missionaries to what is today Germany, France, Spain, and, most famously, England. The eighth-century English monk Bede gave a moving account of Gregory's sending Augustine (not the bishop of Hippo) to Kent in southeast-ern England. The account showed Gregory's pastoral concern for Augustine and his warm encouragement in the midst of the missionary's loneliness and fear at going to a barbarous people. But it also showed clearly that Gregory wanted worship in England conducted according to Roman patterns, even though there was an ancient Christian presence in Britain (Celtic Christianity) with its own patterns of worship and Christian life.[18] Bede also gave a very pro-Roman account of a later meeting at Whitby in northeastern England in the middle of the seventh century, in which the king sided with a Roman missionary, Wilfrid, in opposition to a Celtic Christian, Colman, concerning the date when Easter should be observed.[19] This account, very likely embel-lished, was indicative of the long process by which Rome sought to standard-ize Christian practice throughout the West to line up with Roman practice. In fact, we have already seen that the finalization of the Apostles' Creed was accompanied by Charlemagne's imposition of it throughout the Frankish realm in the eighth century, another example of Roman standardization.

The result of these Western ecclesiastical movements—concerning the sac-raments in particular, worship practices more generally, and the authority

17. See F. Donald Logan, *A History of the Church in the Middle Ages* (London: Routledge, 2002), 47–58.
18. See Bede, *The Ecclesiastical History of the English People*, Oxford World's Classics (Oxford: Oxford University Press, 1994), 69–74.
19. Bede, *Ecclesiastical History*, 154–59.

of the pope—was a Western church intensely focused on the church itself. Indeed, this focus on the church could be considered the defining shift that marked the movement out of the patristic period into the Middle Ages. To say it a different way, the Western church *became* the medieval Roman Catholic Church as it consolidated the Augustinian teaching about the church and sacraments, and especially as Gregory the Great consolidated Roman authority over the Western Christian world. As we will see repeatedly in part 3 of this book, questions related to papal authority and the sacraments dominated the movement toward confessionalism in the Middle Ages.

Grace and Human Action

In the latter part of the fourth century, Pelagius, a British monk, came to Rome and assembled around himself a group of ascetically minded aristocrats who looked up to him as a spiritual guide. Sometime in the first decade of the fifth century, as the Donatist controversy was at its height in North Africa, Pelagius put many of his spiritual ideas into writing through a private tract that he intended only for his spiritual disciples. He never gave that tract a name, but historians refer to it as *On Nature*. After the fall of Rome in 410, Pelagius—along with his followers and many other members of the Roman aristocracy who had the means to travel—fled Italy for the Carthage area in North Africa. There, his ideas came into conflict with those of Augustine, and a controversy (named after Pelagius) was born that set the course of Western theology to almost the same degree as the Donatist schism had done previously.[20]

Pelagius's major concern was that people have no excuses for moral laxity. He insisted that what prevented us from doing what God required was not nature but habit. From this starting point, he elaborated an understanding in which the influence of Adam on a person was that of a bad example, and the influence of Christ was that of a good example. There was no transmission of sin from generation to generation, and each person was born with the capacity to follow either Christ's example or Adam's.[21] Pelagius thus understood grace in primarily an external way, as God's teaching us what we needed to do through the law and the life of Christ. In sharp contrast, Augustine's major concern was the utter freedom of God in saving a person. When God chose to bring about transformation, there were no preceding merits on the part of

20. For a summary of Pelagius's thought and of the controversy itself, see William J. Collinge, introduction to *Saint Augustine: Four Anti-Pelagian Writings*, FC 86 (Washington, DC: Catholic University of America Press, 1992), 3–20, 93–108.

21. See Pelagius, "Letter to Demetrias," in *Theological Anthropology*, ed. J. Patout Burns, Sources of Early Christian Thought (Philadelphia: Fortress, 1981), 39–55.

the person that would compel God to save him or her. Grace worked within each person to bring about change; we did nothing to deserve it. In arguing this point, Augustine put forth a very robust view of original sin, by which the guilt accruing to Adam's sin (not just a propensity to sin) was somehow transmitted from generation to generation. Each person, Augustine taught, was born as part of a common "condemned lump" of humanity (see Rom. 9:21), and from this lump God chose through predestination which ones he would transform by his grace.[22]

The controversy was at its height from 412 through 418, although it occupied Augustine's attention until about 425. Pelagius himself fled from North Africa to Palestine in 412, and at the instigation of Jerome and Augustine, he was tried twice there in 415 and acquitted on technicalities both times. Jerome appealed to Pope Zosimus, who also acquitted Pelagius in 417. Finally, after Zosimus's death, Pope Innocent and three Western synods all condemned Pelagius in 417–18. Several of Pelagius's followers eventually made their way to Constantinople, where Nestorius harbored them and even wrote to Pope Celestine in 430 that he wanted to reopen the case of Pelagianism. In 431, the Council of Ephesus condemned Pelagianism in one of its minor actions, almost certainly as a simple courtesy to the pope.

The church's seeming reluctance to condemn Pelagianism probably did not indicate that there was much sympathy for his thought. Instead, there seems to have been a lot of confusion about what he actually taught, since he argued that what he had written in *On Nature* was never meant for public consumption and thus, to use modern idiom, inadmissible in court. Furthermore, many in the Western church believed that Augustine had overstated his case, especially in regard to original sin. There seems to have been a consensus that while Pelagius was wrong, Augustine may not have been right either. His stark view of original sin and his strongly predestinarian concept of grace were suspicious to most Christian thinkers, and this suspicion, rather than any fundamental sympathy with Pelagius's theology, made the church slow to condemn the British monk.

In fact, the suspicion about Augustine's thought and the unanswered questions related to original sin meant that the discussion continued far beyond Augustine's lifetime. An on-again, off-again conversation on these issues, commonly referred to as the Semi-Pelagian controversy, took place between monks in North Africa and southern Gaul (France) for more than a century, from 427

---

22. See, for example, Augustine, *On Nature and Grace* 11.23, in *St. Augustine: Four Anti-Pelagian Writings*, trans. John A. Mourant and William J. Collinge, FC 86 (Washington, DC: Catholic University of America Press, 1992), 30, 40–41. See also Augustine, *On the Grace of Christ, and on Original Sin* 24; 55, in Burns, *Theological Anthropology*, 77–78, 96.

to 529. This controversy began with Augustine answering some polite questions from a few monks in North Africa and then having to defend his earlier answers to some not-as-polite monks from Gaul who believed that his view of grace threatened the ascetic striving that was so central to the monastic enterprise. In the final treatises of his life, Augustine emphasized that grace brought about the transformation of those whom God had previously predestined for salvation. He described two phases of predestination or election: first predestination to faith, and then predestination to perseverance. Only those who were chosen both to believe and to persevere would ultimately be saved.[23]

After Augustine's death in 430, the continuing discussion involved a number of people whom we have already met in this book: Vincent of Lérins, John Cassian, the Scythian monks, Fulgentius of Ruspe, and Caesarius of Arles, as well as others whom we have not had occasion to mention yet: Prosper of Aquitaine and Faustus of Riez (both from southern Gaul).[24] The long discussion came to a close (of sorts) with a synod that met in Orange (southern Gaul) in 529, convened and led by Caesarius of Arles. The Second Synod of Orange (a local synod, not an ecumenical council per se) affirmed an Augustinian view of the fall and of humanity's utter incapacity to save itself. As a result, the synod argued that when anyone came to faith and baptism, this was purely the result of God's grace.[25] At the same time, the synod departed from Augustine in its understanding of perseverance by arguing that there was no predestination either to persevere or not to persevere. Instead, any baptized Christian (one who had been predestined to believe and had been given the grace to do so) could, by cooperating with the grace offered through the church and its sacraments, continue in faith to the end and be saved.[26]

From a Protestant point of view, one could argue that this synod was splitting the baby in two by holding a view of initial faith much like that of later Calvinism, but a view of Christian life and of perseverance more like that

23. See, for example, Augustine, *On the Gift of Perseverance* 1; 9, in *St. Augustine: Four Anti-Pelagian Writings*, trans. John A. Mourant and William J. Collinge, FC 86 (Washington, DC: Catholic University of America Press, 1992), 272, 286–87.

24. For a general introduction to the Semi-Pelagian controversy, see Rob Roy McGregor and Donald Fairbairn, trans., *Fulgentius of Ruspe and the Scythian Monks: Correspondence on Christology and Grace*, FC 126 (Washington, DC: Catholic University of America Press, 2013), 11–21. For a more extended treatment, see Rebecca Harden Weaver, *Divine Grace and Human Agency: A Study of the Semi-Pelagian Controversy*, Patristic Monograph Series 15 (Macon, GA: Mercer University Press, 1996). See also Alexander Y. Hwang, Brian J. Matz, and Augustine Casiday, eds., *Grace for Grace: The Debates After Augustine and Pelagius* (Washington, DC: Catholic University of America Press, 2014).

25. Among the canons of the Synod of Orange, see canons 1, 2, 5, 8, in Burns, *Theological Anthropology*, 113–15.

26. See the synod's Definition of Faith, in Burns, *Theological Anthropology*, 119.

of later Wesleyanism. Or perhaps there was more consistency in the synod's pronouncements than later Protestants are typically willing to acknowledge. Be that as it may, the discussions of grace and human action during Augustine's lifetime and in the century afterward profoundly shaped the subsequent direction of Western theology. There was a major predestinarian controversy north of the Alps in the ninth century, and there were periodic flare-ups in the High Middle Ages. On this point as well, Augustine set the table for what came after him, and we will have occasion to return to these ideas in parts 3 and 4 of this book.

Conclusions

In this chapter we have seen that unlike the Eastern church, which in the centuries after Chalcedon delved deeper into the theology of Christ's person, the Western church in the same time period was concerned with different issues. To some degree, the different theological movements were related to different social and political situations. Byzantium was in its heyday in the sixth century, and its wealth and power gave it the leisure to explore its proud intellectual tradition. In contrast, the West faced increasing social chaos as the Goths, then the Vandals, then the Lombards invaded, and as a result, questions of authority and practice were more urgent than questions of "pure" theology. Indeed, even something as closely related to "pure" theology as the doctrine of the Trinity took a different form in the West, as intellectual pressure from Arian Goths and Vandals forced trinitarian theologians to do less probing of the relationships between the persons and more justifying of how three could be one. In addition, the West's new directions reflected and developed the concerns of its greatest thinker, Augustine, who was preeminently concerned with the sacramental mediation of grace and its outworking in the lives of believers.

However, we should be careful not to overstate the differences between these divergent directions. East and West were certainly moving apart, but their theologies may not have been inconsistent with each other. Remember the question we have asked throughout this book: "Can we rise up to God, or does God have to come down to us?" One could argue that both East and West were addressing this fundamental question. The way the Eastern church consistently handled it was by describing and probing God's coming down through the incarnation. Christology, therefore, was the "sphere" in which the question was asked. The West, while of course agreeing with the East on the need for God to come down, tended to handle the same question by discussing conversion and Christian life, and thus by trying to address the way divine grace, human action, and the rites of the church fit together as each person moved from unbelief to faith and from new birth to final glorification. As a result, questions related to the sacraments, grace, and free will, often phrased in such a way as to honor Augustine while not necessarily following him on all points, continued to arise in the Western church.

It is possible, then, that East and West were addressing the same question in different spheres of theology, and there may have been greater consistency between the diverging theologies than we often realize. Difference does not necessarily imply contradiction, and, of course, East and West did still rally around the Nicene Creed as their common profession of faith. Nevertheless, as the eighth century passed into the ninth, the increasing differences between East and West began to boil over into actual conflict, and one clause in the Nicene Creed lay near the center of the debate. That is the story of the next chapter.

10

Creedal Dissension
and the East-West Schism

In the year 858, Constantinople was abuzz. Patriarch Ignatius had been on the episcopal throne for eleven years, but the Byzantine empress Theodora and her son Michael, both of whom supported Ignatius, were losing power. There were rumors that Bardas (Theodora's brother) was involved in an incestuous relationship with his daughter-in-law, and when Ignatius publicly condemned Bardas, the ax fell on both the patriarch and the empress who had appointed him. Theodora was ousted in a coup, and Bardas took power as Caesar while leaving Michael nominally in power as emperor. Whether Ignatius was forced out by appropriate procedures or in some more underhanded way is not clear, but a legitimate patriarchal election followed, and a young layperson with a brilliant mind, a stellar education, and very good political connections was chosen as the next patriarch of Constantinople. His name was Photius.[1]

Ignatius was not without supporters, and they were livid about the replacement of their champion, a holy man with a genuine spiritual heart, with the aristocratic and perhaps a bit-too-well-connected Photius. One of Ignatius's fans, the monk Theognostos, sneaked out of Constantinople (wearing secular garb rather than his monastic habit, to avoid detection) and made his way to Rome. There he became the source of (very likely distorted) intel about Caesar

1. For the extended story of the Photian schism, see Henry Chadwick, *East and West: The Making of a Rift in the Church, from Apostolic Times until the Council of Florence*, Oxford History of the Christian Church (Oxford: Oxford University Press, 2003), 95–184.

Both Moravia and Illyricum were in dispute between the Franks and the Byzantines.

Bardas and Patriarch Photius, intel that he dutifully fed to Pope Nicholas I. Unlike the East, the West had a long-standing tradition barring the elevation of a layperson to the episcopacy without his first assuming a lower clerical rank, and Pope Nicholas therefore was inclined to side with Ignatius in the contested election. At the same time, Nicholas was primarily concerned about the question of whether the newly converted tribes in Illyricum would come under the jurisdiction of Constantinople or of Rome. The West had recently won one such jurisdictional battle, as the Moravians (in modern Slovakia) had allied with Rome and the Franks, even though they were Slavic and had gained a written alphabet for their language through the work of Byzantine missionaries, Constantine (Cyril) and Methodius. Nicholas was hoping for a similar outcome with the Bulgarian tribes, and he tried to use the disputed election as leverage to gain jurisdiction over Bulgaria. He wrote a courteous letter to Photius, to which the new Constantinopolitan patriarch responded by declaring that the East did not acknowledge the validity of any such prohibition against elevating laypeople to the episcopate.

At this point, the lid blew off the pressure cooker, and long-simmering tensions boiled over. Eventually, the tensions led to a schism between East and West that persists to the present day, and history later granted Photius the dubious distinction of playing the pivotal role in that schism. In the East he is known as Photius the Great. In the West he has long been regarded as the originator of the "Photian heresy." How did Photius bring about such an enormous rift in the church? And what does this have to do with the creeds and confessions? To answer these questions, we need to back up, gather together various threads of the story that we have already considered, and then return to the conflict between Photius and Nicholas.

The Emerging Political Rivalry between Constantinople and Rome

We saw in the previous chapter that since Rome was the only patriarchal see in the Latin-speaking world, it was easy for Latin Christians to regard Rome as possessing authority over other episcopal sees. In the East, as we have also seen, the presence of four patriarchal sees (Jerusalem, Antioch, Alexandria, and Constantinople) meant that a pattern of shared authority naturally developed, and it was more difficult for any single episcopal see to claim unique authority over others. As a result, although in theory Rome believed itself to hold authority over all of Christendom, the popes rarely tried to assert that authority over the Eastern church. (Gregory the Great's refusal to grant the patriarch of Constantinople the title "ecumenical patriarch" was a noteworthy exception.) But by the early ninth century, the political tension between Rome and Constantinople had become increasingly severe, for several reasons.

First, the rise of Islam redrew the map of the Christian world. Christianity in Latin North Africa was destroyed, leaving the Western Christian world without its erstwhile intellectual center and forcing the Latin church to move northward and westward, deeper into the Frankish realms and Britain, and eventually into the Low Countries (Belgium and the Netherlands today) and Scandinavia. In the East, Egyptian and Syrian Christians had to adapt to second-class status within newly Muslim kingdoms, and even the patriarchal sees of Jerusalem, Antioch, and Alexandria had to function in Muslim-ruled environments. This left Constantinople as the only Eastern patriarchal see that functioned in tandem with a Christian imperial government. Thus, the situations of Rome and Constantinople—cities whose episcopal sees also wielded political power that was almost unchallenged—became more similar, and rivalry between them began to emerge.

Second, the rise of the Franks, to which we have alluded at several points in the previous chapters, was accompanied by an increasingly close alliance between the Frankish government and the papacy. After Charles Martel's victory over Muslim forces at the Battle of Tours in 732, his descendants Pepin the Short and especially Charlemagne worked so closely with the papacy that the Frankish capital of Aachen (in northwestern German today) became a virtual "new Rome," paralleling Constantinople as new Rome in the East.

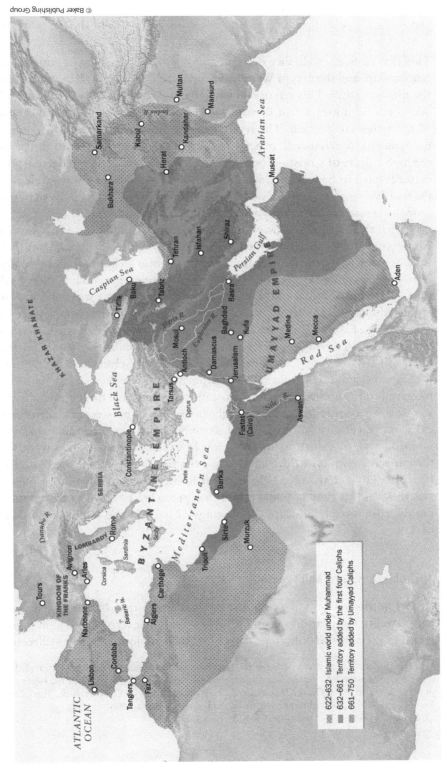

The early expansion of Islam

This Franco-Roman alliance brought about a new flourishing of education, scholarship, and the arts in Western Europe, the Carolingian Renaissance of the ninth century. This renaissance heightened tensions between East and West because it meant that Byzantium was no longer the undisputed center of Christian civilization. The regions of Europe north of the Alps—once the home of "uncivilized" tribes so backward that they posed no threat to the high culture of Constantinople—were now becoming an intellectual and cultural force to be reckoned with, and Byzantium did not always welcome the flourishing of its younger sibling with enthusiasm. This, too, added to the growing tension and rivalry between Rome and Constantinople.

Third, the increasing power and prestige of the papacy in the Western Christian world was accompanied and justified by appeals to documents that were believed to date from the early Christian centuries but that had actually been composed more recently.[2] In about 500, forged documents appeared that insisted no council (not even an ecumenical council) was valid unless approved by the pope. In the ninth century, even more spectacular forgeries emerged, the *Pseudo-Isidorian Decretals* (which professed to be papal letters from the fourth through eighth centuries) and the *Donation of Constantine* (allegedly a letter from Constantine himself to Pope Sylvester, granting him the imperial buildings in Rome and authority over the Western world as he prepared to move the capital to Constantinople). These forged documents stressed papal supremacy very strongly and served to bolster that conviction in the ninth-century Frankish world. Pope Nicholas accepted them without question and used them to justify a view in which the pope held power over the entire Christian world.[3] Thus, while the rise of Islam and the Frankish (Carolingian) renaissance helped to pit Rome against Constantinople, it was the Western view of papal power that proved to be the flashpoint igniting the combustible mixture. This brings us back to the disputed election of 858.

Nicholas, Ignatius, and Photius

After Photius's dismissive response to the papal letter, Nicholas sent two emissaries to Constantinople in 861. Their main concern was to gain papal jurisdiction over the Bulgarian tribes, but their major argument—directed

---

2. During the Italian Renaissance of the fifteenth century, Lorenzo Valla demonstrated that these documents were forgeries, and this demonstration helped set the stage for the Reformation. See Lorenzo Valla, *On the Donation of Constantine*, trans. G. W. Bowersock, The I Tatti Renaissance Library (Cambridge, MA: Harvard University Press, 2008).

3. See Chadwick, *East and West*, 95–102.

not at Photius himself but at Emperor Michael, whose Caesar had secured Ignatius's removal—was that an emperor could not depose a patriarch without appeal to the Roman see. Michael replied that while the resolution of dogmatic issues required Roman participation (in other words, doctrinal matters could not be established by merely regional synods; they required participation from the whole church), there was no dogmatic issue at stake here[4] and therefore no need to consult the pope. Nevertheless, Michael agreed to a retrial of Ignatius before the Roman legates, as a courtesy to Nicholas. At this trial, Ignatius was less than polite to the Roman emissaries, and not surprisingly, they and the council gathered around them ruled against him and in favor of Photius. But they could not prevail on the East to relinquish its claim to Bulgaria, and, in fact, soon after this Michael actually invaded Bulgaria, forcing its prince, Boris, to convert to Byzantine Christianity rather than Roman. Nicholas was furious and used his emissaries' diplomatic failure as an excuse to sack them and to hold a synod of his own in Rome in 863, at which Photius was deposed and Ignatius "reinstated."

At this point, things quickly went from bad to worse. Michael wrote what may have been the most outlandish letter in Byzantine diplomatic history,[5] in which he evidently ascribed Pope Nicholas's reinstatement of Ignatius to the ignorance of a backwater politician, while again arguing that the pope had no right to intervene in the internal affairs of Constantinople. Nicholas countered with a long justification of papal supremacy over all affairs—procedural and liturgical as well as doctrinal—of the whole church. He also held out an unexpected carrot: if both Ignatius and Photius would come to Rome with their supporters, Nicholas himself would hear the dispute. Naturally, this invitation was ignored.

At this point, it should be clear that the controversy was about questions of ecclesiastical jurisdiction, especially about whether the primacy of the pope extended to the point of his being able to intervene in internal matters of procedure in other sees. The tension was astronomical, but it was about ecclesiastical politics, not really about doctrine. In fact, we should remember that part of Michael's justification for *not* consulting Rome on the matter was that no doctrinal issue was at stake. Again, we wonder, what does this have to do with the creeds? At this point, in about the year 865, the answer to that question had to be "Nothing." But then Photius introduced into the

---

4. This was not quite true, since one of the issues was the fact that the West had been slow to recognize the authority of the Seventh Ecumenical Council, which led the East to wonder whether the Westerners actually favored iconoclasm. They didn't.

5. We write "may have been" because the letter is not extant. We know it only through Nicholas's reply.

controversy the most devastating of all charges: the Roman see's support of Ignatius in the struggle was worthless, because Rome was heretical. It had accepted the heretical notion that the Spirit proceeds from the Father *and from the Son.* Thus, with a single blow he raised the stakes of the controversy and made it into a theological debate, indeed even a creedal debate. In the process, he also bequeathed to the controversy the name by which it is normally known: the *Filioque* controversy. We have deliberately withheld that name up to this point in order to show how thoroughly this dispute began as a political, jurisdictional clash, not a doctrinal one. But now it became a doctrinal dispute, or at least it was being dressed up as one. So we need to turn back to the *Filioque* and to the way Photius used the issue against the West.

The *Filioque* as a Wedge Issue

In 866, Photius wrote an encyclical letter to the Eastern Christian bishops,[6] laying out his case against the Western church. His initial criticism of the West had to do with the Bulgarian tribes and showed the degree of ill will that now overshadowed the situation:

> For that nation had not yet been honoring the true religion of Christians for two years when impious and ill-omened men (for what else could one of the pious call them?) arising from the darkness (for they sprang from the Western regions), alas—how shall I narrate the rest? These men fell upon the nation newly established in piety and newly formed, like lightning or earthquake or a hailstorm, or rather, to speak more appropriately, like a solitary wild beast, and with feet and teeth, that is with the pressure of a shameful way of life and corrupt doctrine, ravaged and violated (as far as depended on their own audacity) the vineyard of the Lord, beloved and newly planted.[7]

The key phrase here is "shameful way of life and corrupt doctrine," and the way of life he criticized had to do with matters of Christian practice on which the West differed from the East. The Westerners fasted on Saturday but proscribed fewer foods during the Lenten fast, did not allow presbyters to marry, and repeated the rite of chrismation in certain circumstances.

The "corrupt doctrine," of course, was the *Filioque.* After listing the differences in practice, Photius wrote, "Besides the aforementioned nonsense, they even attempted to adulterate with bastard ideas and interpolated

---

6. Translated in CCFCT 1:298–308.

7. Photius, *Encyclical Letter to the Bishops of the East* 4, in CCFCT 1:299.

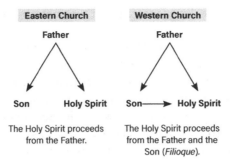

The *Filioque* controversy

words (O scheme of the devil!) the holy and sacred creed, which holds its undisputed force from the decrees of all the ecumenical councils; they make the novel assertion that the Holy Spirit proceeds not from the Father alone but also from the Son."[8] Here we see the charge that the Westerners had interpolated the Nicene Creed, which certainly was true. As we have seen, the word *Filioque* made its way into the creed in Spain prior to the end of the sixth century. By stating that the creed held its force from the decrees of all the ecumenical councils, Photius alluded to one of the key reasons for opposing the *Filioque*. Whatever one may think of the theology of the Spirit's procession, the Nicene Creed was approved by an ecumenical council—the Second in 381—and reaffirmed by all subsequent ecumenical councils without the *Filioque*. Therefore, it was reasonable to argue, as the Eastern church did, that it could be amended only through another ecumenical council.

This point serves to highlight the difference between the Nicene Creed and other creeds, as well as the different attitudes toward creeds in East and West. As we emphasized earlier in this book, the Nicene Creed was the only creed formally approved by the entire church, a fact that placed it in a different category from even the Apostles' Creed. Such a universally approved statement should not be tampered with, according to the Eastern church. So to the East, the issue was not just the theological question of whether the Spirit proceeds from both other persons of the Trinity; it was at least as much the question of whether and how one could legitimately modify the creed. The West, in contrast, saw the issue as being merely the theological question, and perhaps part of the reason for this was that the major creed to arise in the West, the Apostles', was well known to have undergone a long period of development. As a result, the idea that a change might be made in order to

8. Photius, *Encyclical Letter to the Bishops of the East* 8, in CCFCT 1:300.

articulate a theologically accurate point was not objectionable on creedal grounds in the West.

Photius then launched into a long tirade against the theology of the *Filioque*. His arguments were many and at times descended to the level of caricaturing the Western understanding, whether intentionally or not. Nevertheless, his basic idea was that affirming the double procession of the Spirit implied that there were two principles or sources of deity, and this amounted to placing the Father and the Son in opposition to each other as separate deities.[9] This is surely not what any Western theologian has ever meant, because one could, and many did, insist that the Father is indeed the sole source of deity while still arguing that the Son is involved in the Spirit's eternal procession. The Spirit proceeds from the Father with the involvement of the Son or through the Son. This was, in fact, what Maximus the Confessor had proposed in the seventh century, as a way of reconciling the Eastern and Western views on the matter.[10]

As a purely theological matter, the question of the Spirit's procession might well have been one on which East and West could have come to terms without splitting the church. But, as our discussion has shown, and as Photius's severe caricature of the Western position also demonstrated, he was not interested in coming to terms. The *Filioque* was not actually the source of the controversy that bears its name, or even the main issue of that controversy. Rather, the dispute was about jurisdiction over the Bulgarian tribes and about Rome's right to intervene in internal, nondoctrinal matters in Constantinople. The *Filioque* was simply a wedge issue, which Photius inserted into the controversy late in the day in order to rally the East to oppose the West, and in the process to affirm him (rather than Ignatius) as the proper patriarch of Constantinople.[11]

The "Fate" of the *Filioque*

In 867, Photius held a small synod that deposed Pope Nicholas for the "crimes" that he had laid out in his encyclical letter the previous year. But

9. Photius, *Encyclical Letter to the Bishops of the East* 9–23, in CCFCT 1:300–303. See also the helpful summary of Photius's argument in A. Edward Siecienski, *The Filioque: History of a Doctrinal Controversy*, Oxford Studies in Historical Theology (Oxford: Oxford University Press, 2010), 101.

10. See Siecienski, *Filioque*, 74–86.

11. Some historians manage to tell the story of this controversy without even mentioning the *Filioque*. See, for example, F. Donald Logan, *A History of the Church in the Middle Ages* (London: Routledge, 2002), 92–97.

in the same year, both Caesar Bardas and Emperor Michael were murdered, and Michael's adopted son Basil assumed the throne even though he had been Bardas's murderer and was suspected of being involved in the plot against Michael. Later that year, Pope Nicholas died (amazingly, with no foul play involved!) and was replaced by Hadrian II. This sweeping changing of the guard in both East and West left Photius in a greatly weakened political position, and synods in both Rome and Constantinople in 869–70 ruled him deposed and Ignatius reinstated as patriarch. The Constantinopolitan council (belatedly) affirmed the Seventh Ecumenical Council and the primacy of the pope in all matters, doctrinal as well as ecclesiastical. This council is today regarded by Roman Catholics as the Eighth Ecumenical Council, and the Catholic Church has continued to name its own councils as "ecumenical" up to the present time. The *Filioque* is absent from the acts of this council.

Again, however, the death of crucial players led to a change in the situation. Pope Hadrian died in 873 and was replaced by John VIII. Ignatius died in 877, after recommending that Photius (with whom he had been reconciled) replace him. Emperor Basil agreed, but this created a delicate need to gloss the acts of previous councils so as to bring about Photius's reinstatement without seeming to undermine the authority of church councils. So yet another council was held in Constantinople in 879, which secured (with some difficulty) Photius's legitimacy and left the question of jurisdiction over the Bulgarians in the hands of the emperor. At the council, the Nicene Creed was read out without the *Filioque*, and a condemnation was pronounced on those who would venture to add to the creed.[12] Thus, the act of interpolating the creed was explicitly condemned, although the theology of the double procession per se was still not addressed.

Again, we need to recognize that the issue of the Spirit's procession was never central to the so-called *Filioque* controversy, and, indeed, it was not central to the later breach in fellowship between Rome and Constantinople either. It has remained an issue of theological contention up to the present, and Photius's arguments about the negative implications of affirming the double procession have provided many Eastern theologians with justification for remaining separate from the West.[13] But in none of the flare-ups of controversy between East and West was it ever the main source of tension.

12. See Siecienski, *Filioque*, 104.
13. For example, the great twentieth-century Russian Orthodox theologian Vladimir Lossky calls the *Filioque* "the primordial cause, the only dogmatic cause, of the breach between East and West." *The Mystical Theology of the Eastern Church* (Crestwood, NY: St. Vladimir's Seminary Press, 1976), 56.

Low Points of a Growing Schism

During these complicated political maneuverings from 858 to 879, there was a brief period in the 860s during which Rome and Constantinople were technically out of fellowship with each other while the former affirmed Ignatius and the latter Photius as the rightful patriarch of Constantinople. This brief schism was a harbinger of things to come, as tensions between East and West continued to escalate from the ninth through thirteenth centuries. There were several other tense points along the way to the Great Schism that are worth describing briefly, even though they took place after the year 900, when this part of our book technically ends.

In the middle of the eleventh century, friction between Rome and Constantinople again reached a critical point, largely because of the Viking invasions of Europe in the ninth through eleventh centuries.[14] The Norsemen from Scandinavia—accomplished sailors and fierce warriors—violently captured and subdued vast territories in the British Isles, northern France, the Low Countries, and Germany.[15] By the middle of the eleventh century, they were threatening regions in southern Italy and even took Pope Leo IX captive in 1053. Since some churches in southern Italy were Greek-speaking and under the jurisdiction of Constantinople, both East and West had a stake in warding off the Viking threat. At the same time, a new slate of issues on which Eastern and Western practice differed rose to the surface, dominated by the question of whether the Eucharist should be celebrated with unleavened bread (as in the West) or leavened bread (as in the East).

In the spring of 1054, Pope Leo IX dispatched a delegation of three legates, led by Cardinal Humbert, to Constantinople. Humbert knew both Greek and Latin, but he was a headstrong man with little interest in diplomacy and thus a rather poor choice for the assignment. To make matters worse, Leo died while the delegation was en route, thus leaving Humbert technically without papal authority for his demands. Humbert was convinced that papal supremacy and Roman worship practice were both universal, and during the political negotiations he insisted on both of these. He also raised the issue of the *Filioque* through the outlandish claim that the East's *removal* of the word from the creed made it guilty of heresy. In spite of Humbert's intransigence, the Byzantine emperor Constantine IX had advised Patriarch Michael Cerularius to be tactful, and he

---

14. For these events, see Chadwick, *East and West*, 206–18; Logan, *History of the Church*, 80–88, 116–18; Siecienksi, *Filioque*, 113–15.

15. After they conquered Normandy in France, the Norsemen were sometimes called Normans, and their move from Normandy into England is referred to as the Norman Conquest.

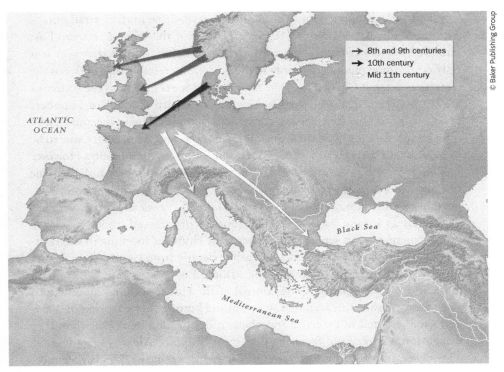

© Baker Publishing Group

Viking invasions

tried to do so as long as he could. But not surprisingly, the negotiations quickly broke down.

On July 16, 1054, Humbert and his two fellow legates went to the great cathedral Hagia Sophia, but instead of worshiping with the Greeks, Humbert placed a bull of excommunication on the altar, directed at Michael Cerularius and his supporters (not at the whole Eastern church). The document praised the emperor but accused the patriarch of many liturgical sins and, of course, of deleting the *Filioque* from the creed. A deacon tactfully removed it from the altar and handed it back to Humbert outside the church, and Humbert threw it on the ground as he and his associates hastily left the city. Eventually the bull found its way to Cerularius, who had it translated into Greek and reported to the emperor. Constantine IX had the Latin legates recalled to the city, and when they refused to explain their actions, he authorized Cerularius to pronounce an anathema. Cerularius called a hasty synod on July 24, 1054, which anathematized the authors of the bull, and subsequent hearsay insisted that the synod had actually condemned the entire Western church.

Historians disagree about the significance of these mutual anathemati-zations. While many point to 1054 as *the* date of the schism between East and West, others correctly recognize that the fateful event of that year was only one among many low points in the worsening relationship between the churches and that Christians at the time did not see the event as the source of the rift between them. Perhaps the best way to regard the saga of Humbert and Cerularius is to see 1054 as a convenient symbolic date in the middle of a four-hundred-year history of worsening separation between what came to be known as the Eastern Orthodox and Roman Catholic communions. However much significance we ascribe to 1054, though, it is clear that (again!) the issue of the Spirit's double procession played only a very minor role. Far more im-portant, yet again, was the issue of papal supremacy over the entire church.

Be that as it may, as the eleventh century progressed, there was a far greater menace than separation between the churches looming in the East-ern Christian world. The Turks, a warlike people from central Asia, began to move into what we today call the Middle East, defeating the Arabs in Syria and Palestine, thus taking control of the Holy Land and moving into Asia Minor,[16] thus threatening the Byzantine Empire. In the spring of 1095, at a small council in Piacenza (northern Italy) headed by Pope Urban II, a delegation was received from the Byzantine Emperor Alexius I Comnenos. This delegation asked for Western help in fighting off the Turkish menace, and its arrival set off the chain of events leading to the First Crusade. In November of that year, Pope Urban preached his famous sermon rallying people to the Crusade, and the first ships left in the spring of 1096. We will return to Pope Urban and the Crusades in chapter 12, but for now, only two aspects of the Crusades are directly relevant. The first is that among the many motivating factors, a prominent one was the desire to bring aid to the Greek Christians and thereby to help heal the relationship between Rome and Constantinople. Granted, it was the emperor, not the patriarch, who had asked for aid, but even so, Urban and many others in the West thought that the East might respond to magnanimous aid from the West by submit-ting to the pope and shoring up the precarious relationship. The Crusades *began* as—among other things—an attempt to bring military aid to besieged Christians in Constantinople.[17]

16. It is ironic that the land we call Turkey today had no Turkish peoples in it until the eleventh century. In fact, the Turkish migration and conquest meant that Asia Minor went from being almost 100 percent Christian (and ethnically, mostly Greek) in the year 1000 to being 90 percent Muslim (and ethnically mostly Turkish) by 1500.

17. For the rest of the story, see Jonathan Riley-Smith, *The Crusades: A History*, 2nd ed., Yale Nota Bene (New Haven: Yale University Press, 2005).

The conquest of Constantinople by the Crusaders in 1204

The other aspect that is relevant to the story of the East-West schism was a tragic series of events that unfolded in the year 1204, as the Latins readied for the Fourth Crusade. In 1201–2, Venetian merchants (who stood to gain much from Latin control of the Middle East, because it would mean much easier trade with Asia) had engaged in a massive shipbuilding program to accommodate the huge contingent of Crusaders promised. When only about a third of the expected thirty-five thousand men turned up in Venice in April 1202, and thus far less money was available to pay back the shipbuilders, the endeavor was instantly in enormous debt. To repay that debt, the Crusaders were forced to attack and plunder Christian cities on the way to the Holy Land, until word came from Alexius IV (the former Byzantine emperor who had been sacked in a coup) that if they would capture Constantinople and restore him to the throne, he would make the patriarch of Constantinople subservient to the pope. With extreme reluctance, but seemingly little choice in view of the overwhelming debt they faced, the Crusaders turned the sword on the Byzantine capital. It fell on November 24, 1204, and the spoil was used to pay off the merchants. A Latin kingdom was established with a puppet patriarch, and although Pope Innocent III condemned the attack, he did not try to hide his delight that now all of Christendom was officially under his jurisdiction.[18] The Byzantines recaptured Constantinople in 1261, but the

18. See Riley-Smith, *Crusades*, 149–60.

Byzantine Empire never again regained its former glory. Eventually Constantinople fell to the Ottoman Turks in 1453, and a half-millennium of Turkish rule over southeastern Europe began.

The sack of Constantinople in 1204 was essentially the final straw in relations between East and West. There were two major councils in the high and late Middle Ages that sought to repair the rift, one in Lyons (southeastern France) in 1274 and the other in Ferrara and then Florence (north-central Italy) in 1438–39. At both of these councils, and especially at the latter, significant progress was made on the *Filioque*, but the Western contingents also insisted on Eastern submission to the pope and compliance with Western liturgical practices. The memory of 1204 was fresh enough, even in 1439, that no assertion of papal supremacy ever gained a hearing in the East again. In the case of both councils, the agreements signed by the Eastern delegates were solidly rejected back in Constantinople.[19]

Conclusions

The schism between East and West was hardly the first split in church history, nor was it the longest-lasting one, since the christological schisms predated it by half a millennium and are also still ongoing today. But the split between Eastern Orthodox and Roman Catholic churches was the *largest* split in Christian history, sundering the vast majority of the church universal into two disunited halves. Furthermore, if one accepts the judgment that we have offered here—that the *Filioque* played only a minor role in the schism and would not, on its own, have split the church—then it becomes apparent that this was a rift occasioned by differences in practice and questions of papal authority, rather than doctrine per se. In fact, even when the *Filioque* was the issue, it was not so much the theology of the double procession per se that divided but the question of whether it was permissible to alter a creed approved by an ecumenical council. Thus, even the *Filioque* controversy itself was as much a matter of ecclesiastical authority as it was a doctrinal dividing line. That the rift was not about doctrine means that in some ways, this was the *saddest* split in Christian history.

Whatever date one gives to this schism, it is clear that the Greek and Latin churches had more or less separate histories from the thirteenth century forward. The West continued to address and develop the issues that had been important in Augustine's thought, especially the sacramental mediation of grace and the relation between grace and human action. It also continued to

19. See Siecienski, *Filioque*, 134–38, 152–72.

press the issue of papal supremacy, now with little to check the growing role of the pope in all areas of society, since the churches that pushed back against the supremacy of the papal office were no longer in the picture. Eventually, all of these issues found their detractors, and the result of growing internal Western disagreement on these issues was the Protestant Reformation.

At the same time, the East followed its own path, only rarely responding to major Western developments.[20] But as the Reformation broke, it became apparent that the Eastern Orthodox and the Protestants had at least one thing in common, an opposition to claims of absolute supremacy for Rome. This common starting point led to some tentative explorations of potential unity between Protestant Christianity and Eastern Orthodoxy and to the writing of Orthodox confessions of faith that in some ways parallel the great Protestant confessions. Thus we will have occasion to return to the Eastern Christian world in part 4 of this book. For now, though, we turn to the West and concentrate on medieval Roman Catholicism in part 3.

20. The most significant such instance was the fourteenth-century controversy between Barlaam, a Greek monk trained in Roman circles, and Gregory Palamas, who represented and defended more traditional Greek monastic practices against Barlaam's Western-influenced innovations. This controversy led to Gregory's articulation of the essence-energies distinction in describing God, one of the hallmarks of modern Eastern Orthodox theology. See John Meyendorff, introduction to *Gregory Palamas: The Triads*, Classics of Western Spirituality (Mahwah, NJ: Paulist Press, 1983), 1–22; Lossky, *Mystical Theology*, 67–90.

PART 3

From Creeds to Confessions in the West

(900–1500)

11

Setting the Stage
for Medieval Developments

In chapter 9 we saw that after the era of the creeds, Western theology began more and more to focus on issues of authority (especially papal authority) and on the church and its sacraments. Furthermore, we saw in chapter 10 that the East-West schism was not a sudden rupture but one that dragged out over several centuries. In this chapter we need to consider the years from 900 to 1100, the same period during which East and West were rapidly moving apart. In the West at this time, the pope increasingly took the lead in calling his own councils and ruling on matters of the faith. Although the medieval West produced no new creeds, pronouncements by the pope—whatever their subject—were and are considered binding on all Roman Catholic adherents. Thus, we will treat these papal decisions as *confessional*. They were not creedal because they did not focus on the three persons of the Trinity, in whom we believe and to whom we belong, but they were confessional in the sense that they spoke with binding authority about various matters of the Roman Catholic faith. Medieval Western proclamations (whether they came directly from the pope or emerged during councils called by the pope) dealt with a wide variety of issues, but two were prominent: the need for reforms in the church—both in cases where clergy had relaxed the requirement for holy living and against political rulers who threatened the church—and specific doctrines that were controversial among theologians. We will focus most of our attention on issues of theology.

In this chapter we examine three major background factors that set the stage for medieval confessional proclamations: the rise of Scholasticism (a theological movement that dramatically influenced the development of medieval thought on the sacraments), a new style of papal authority, and a new military ethos in Western Christendom. Understanding the way the Western church changed in the early Middle Ages will help prepare us to look at the major confessional proclamations of the High Middle Ages in the next chapter.

The Rise of Scholasticism

The word "Scholasticism" comes from the Latin *schola* (school) and originally simply referred to the teachings of the schools or universities.[1] Scholasticism was considered the height of learning in the Middle Ages, but for modern Christians, especially Protestants, the luster has faded from the reputation of scholastic theology. It has been viewed as a series of increasingly irrelevant debates on increasingly abstract topics, and this negative view was reinforced by fabricated stories of theologians debating the number of angels that could dance on the head of a pin. No theologian ever debated such a question,[2] but the fact that such a myth is repeated even today hints at our uneasiness with scholastic theology.

One popular misconception about scholastic theology is that it was based on a shared worldview, or set of principles, or even that it reached many common doctrinal conclusions.[3] But Scholasticism was only a method of inquiry. The point of Scholasticism was to find an appropriate way to interrogate a problem, cross-examining the evidence in the hopes of coming to a stronger conclusion. Like any method, Scholasticism could be used well in the right hands.[4] However, not all scholastic theologians were of equal caliber, and some used logic and dialectic to challenge church doctrine—some only on minor issues, though some, like Peter Abelard, did so more aggressively. One

1. For a synopsis of the scholastic method, see Alister E. McGrath, *Reformation Thought: An Introduction*, 4th ed. (Oxford: Wiley-Blackwell, 2012), 59–74. See also Steven P. Marrone, "Medieval Philosophy in Context," in *The Cambridge Companion to Medieval Philosophy*, ed. A. S. McGrade (Cambridge: Cambridge University Press, 2003), 10–50.

2. Presumably, the question would have been whether angels have substance and therefore take up space. If they do not, then an infinite number can be in the same location at once. But if they have no substance, then what are angels? Again, however, the question was never actually debated by Scholastics.

3. See David Knowles, *The Evolution of Medieval Thought* (New York: Vintage, 1962). The diversity of medieval thinking can be seen in Arthur Hyman and James J. Walsh, eds., *Philosophy in the Middle Ages: The Christian, Islamic, and Jewish Traditions* (Indianapolis: Hackett, 1983).

4. The modern approach to systematic theology, in both Protestant and Catholic contexts, is based largely on the same desire to think critically and logically about doctrine.

A medieval lecture as depicted by Laurentius de Voltolina

of the main complaints about scholastic theology, in fact, was that it was often known for denying certain beliefs rather than affirming beliefs.

When it emerged in the 900s, Scholasticism was a movement that supported the use of *dialectic* when addressing doctrinal issues. The method was not unlike a modern debate between opposing views, except that in dialectic it often was the same author wrestling through both sides of an issue. This dialectical method—as common today as it was in the Middle Ages—approached theological disputes mainly by focusing on the apparent contradictions between varying theological positions. If, for example, theologians teach both that God is beyond human reason and that we know true things about God, how are these two truths held together? A scholastic theologian would address the possible conclusions and then use a series of logical and philosophical opinions to form the best conclusion—either in favor of one position or the other, or maybe with a harmonization of both.

Perhaps the most famous work that employed this method was Thomas Aquinas's *Summa Theologiae* (thirteenth century), which follows an almost monotonous pattern: Aquinas first asks an important question—for example,

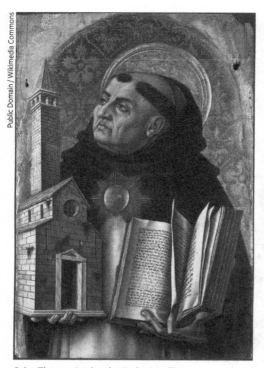

Saint Thomas Aquinas by Carlo Crivelli

"Does love exist in God?" He then weighs the rival answers, usually given in the patristic sources: (1) God has no passions, so love cannot exist, although (2) God is said to be love in the Bible. Then, ultimately, he concludes with his own judgment:[5] we must say that there is love in God.[6] When done well, the result was a pleasing balance of reason and traditional doctrine.

The scholastic method, however, was always subject to criticism on two grounds. On the one hand, the method implied that earlier theologians were guilty of error or confusion. For example, Abelard's *Sic et Non* (Yes and No) noted various inconsistent teachings on doctrine from the church fathers. Placing them side by side, Abelard hoped to provide an intellectual exercise for his readers, as they attempted to find a resolution of the inconsistency. But this gave the impression that the church fathers were less than authoritative, or worse, that they should not be trusted on every subject. Moreover, the dialectical method did not always manage to come up with a better conclusion. The Scholastics certainly assumed it to be the best philosophical method, but opponents of scholastic theology quickly found problems with dialectic, often because it relied too much on human reason. As a result, even though history remembers the medieval period as an age of Scholasticism, the use of dialectic was controversial even when it first appeared between 900 and 1000.

5. In the *Summa*, one can often find Aquinas's own theology simply by finding the paragraph that begins "I answer that." For a short, reader-friendly version of Aquinas's answers, without the laborious arguments, see Peter Kreeft, *A Summa of the* Summa: *The Essential Philosophical Passages of St. Thomas Aquinas'* Summa Theologica (San Francisco: Ignatius, 1990).

6. For a more detailed look at the *Summa*, see James F. Ross, "Thomas Aquinas, *Summa theologiae* (ca. 1273): Christian Wisdom Explained Philosophically," in *The Classics of Western Philosophy: A Reader's Guide*, ed. Jorge J. E. Gracia, Gregory M. Reichberg, and Bernard N. Schumacher (Malden, MA: Blackwell, 2003), 143–66.

The scholastic method produced storms of controversy on many issues, but for our purposes, its effects on sacramental doctrine are most important. Berengar of Tours (ca. 999–1088)[7] was a teacher of grammar and logic, and thus a proponent of the scholastic method. Early in the eleventh century, Berengar came under scrutiny over his teachings on the presence of Christ in the Eucharist. The context of this debate was the Carolingian resurgence of theological writing, which we mentioned in our previous chapter. As the Western church emerged from the collapse of the Roman Empire, theological writing was relatively sporadic and immature. But the financial support of Charlemagne and his successors in the ninth century bolstered the work of theologians and even provided them with new copies of texts previously unavailable. Berengar stood at the end of this resurgence, and he benefited from the relative comfort provided by endowments for churches and monasteries.

The books that inspired Berengar's reflections on the Eucharist were written by two leaders of the Carolingian Renaissance: Paschasius Radbertus (785–865) and Ratramnus of Corbie in northern France (d. 870). Radbertus had launched a debate in the ninth century when he published *On the Body and Blood of the Lord*,[8] arguing that the very body of Christ—the body born of Mary and crucified on the cross—was present in the bread and wine. The Catholic Church would never teach anything this stark, since it distinguished between the *natural* body of Christ and the *sacramental* body received at the Lord's Supper. But Radbertus was blistering in his criticism of those who wished to describe the Eucharist as only a mystery, without any insistence on the physical presence of Christ in the bread and wine.[9] Both his conclusion and the method he used to arrive at this answer drew other scholastic theologians to Radbertus's book. One of these was Ratramnus, who insisted that Christ's body was present *spiritually*. Ratramnus argued that asserting the physical presence of Christ was not only illogical but also unnecessary since Christ was present by the Holy Spirit.[10]

7. He is sometimes referred to as Berengarius. See Charles M. Radding and Francis Newton, *Theology, Rhetoric, and Politics in the Eucharistic Controversy, 1078–1079: Alberic of Monte Cassino against Berengar of Tours* (New York: Columbia University Press, 2003).

8. *De Corpore et Sanguine Domine.* His works can be found in PL 120.

9. Catholic thought since Radbertus, while affirming physical presence through transubstantiation, has not argued that the natural body of Christ is present. For a detailed study and a reexamination of this controversy and scholastic theology, see Toivo J. Holopainen, *Dialectic and Theology in the Eleventh Century*, Studien und Texte zur Geistesgeschichte des Mittelalters 54 (Leiden: Brill, 1996).

10. This is a common debate among Protestants, as we will see in chaps. 14 and 15. None of the Protestants, however, seemed to be aware of these debates from the earlier Middle Ages.

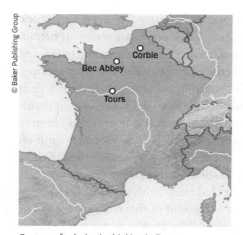

Centers of scholastic thinking in France

It should be noted that both sides affirmed a *real* presence of Christ, but they differed in the way they viewed that presence in the elements.[11] Yet, in this debate we can see at work the principles of scholastic theology. Both sides found their opponent's position illogical, in that it did not meet the standard of dialectical reason. Both sides also knew the debate had no clear precedent from the ancient church: the church fathers at times spoke in *realist* language about Christ's presence in the bread and wine, at times in *symbolic* or *spiritualist* language, but there was no unequivocal position expressed in their writings. And last, the church had not officially given a ruling on the doctrine, leaving the subject open to debate.

In the ninth-century debate, both positions had their supporters, although eventually many theologians were convinced by Radbertus's arguments for the physical presence of Christ. A century and a half later, Berengar took up the issue, but he did not agree with this majority opinion, siding instead with Ratramnus on spiritual presence. In the city of Tours, Berengar began to teach his views on spiritual presence, which eventually ignited a firestorm. Several of his students even charged Berengar with heresy. Attempting to settle the debate, two bishops examined him, but they could not agree about whether Berengar's teachings were contrary to official doctrine, especially given the precedent for spiritual presence in the works of Ratramnus. As late as 1050, there was no formal requirement for Catholics to affirm the physical presence of Christ in the sacrament.

The matter came to a head through the influence of Lanfranc of Bec (ca. 1005–89), himself an advocate of the scholastic method, albeit without a strict commitment to following dialectic or logic at all times.[12] The role of Lanfranc was important because he was already the most influential early scholastic theologian, mostly for his role in using the scholastic method

11. A good survey of eucharistic teaching in the early Middle Ages is Gary Macy, *The Theologies of the Eucharist in the Early Scholastic Period: A Study of the Salvific Function of the Sacrament according to the Theologians, c. 1080–c. 1220* (Oxford: Clarendon, 1984).

12. See H. E. J. Cowdrey, *Lanfranc: Scholar, Monk, and Archbishop* (Oxford: Oxford University Press, 2003); Margaret Gibson, *Lanfranc of Bec* (Oxford: Clarendon, 1978).

within a limited framework. His moderation allowed him to explore new ideas without inflaming the critics of Scholasticism. Lanfranc was later appointed archbishop of Canterbury, but his most influential role was as the teacher of Anselm,[13] who became the most celebrated scholastic theologian of the eleventh century and one of the greatest theologians of the entire Middle Ages. The debate over the Lord's Supper was a good staging ground for Lanfranc, since it allowed him to support the work of scholastic theologians while also criticizing those who went too far. Eventually, he brought the matter to Pope Leo IX during a regional council in Rome. The pope and the council strongly condemned Berengar and referred the case to another local council that met in France in the city of Vercelli—although Henry I of France (1031–80) barred Berengar from the council and arrested him instead.[14]

The situation grew bleak for Berengar, whose teachings went on to be condemned at no fewer than four regional councils. On at least two occasions he was forced to sign a personal confession, stating his affirmation of the physical presence of Christ in the Eucharist.[15] At the Roman assembly of 1059 he also had to add a confession on papal authority, pledging himself to be fully submissive to the decision of the pope. He admitted that he "dared to claim that the bread and the wine are . . . merely a sacrament and not the true body and the true blood of our Lord Jesus Christ." Now that his views had been rejected, however, he confessed his loyalty to the church: "But I now agree with the holy Roman Church and the apostolic throne," sharing the same view "as my lord Pope Nicholas and his holy synod." In 1079, after some doubt over his previous confession,[16] Berengar again recanted, now admitting that the very body of Christ, which "was suspended on the cross, and which sits at the right hand of the Father," is in the bread and wine.[17]

Berengar's confession was an important pivot point not only in the development of medieval doctrine but also in the evolution of the church's methods for dealing with theological controversy. As we have argued, the

13. On Anselm, see Brian Davies and Brian Leftow, eds., *The Cambridge Companion to Anselm*, Cambridge Companions to Philosophy (Cambridge: Cambridge University Press, 2005); Jasper Hopkins, *A Companion to the Study of St. Anselm* (Minneapolis: University of Minnesota Press, 1972).

14. This was likely due to political issues, especially Henry's desire to be a defender of orthodoxy. Ironically, by excluding Berengar he was overruling the pope's decree.

15. The complexity of his repeated recantations is dealt with in G. Morin, "Bérenger contre Bérenger," *Récherches de théologie ancienne et médiévale* 4, no. 2 (1932): 109–33.

16. After his first recantation, Berengar continued the fight, though on different terms. He published his *De Sacra Coena* (The Holy Supper) in part to make his case one more time, a fact that explains why a later recantation was needed.

17. Heinrich Denzinger, *The Sources of Catholic Dogma*, trans. Roy J. Deferrari (St. Louis: Herder, 1957), 144. Also in CCFCT 1:729.

language of the real presence of Christ was common in the ancient church, although no steps had been taken to define the *mode* of Christ's presence, either physically or spiritually. The controversies surrounding Berengar, however, led to new growth in the way the Western church viewed what occurred during the words of invocation as the priest declared of the bread, "This is my Body." Now that Rome had weighed in on the issue, choosing one side in the debate, the church moved permanently in the direction of affirming the physical presence of Christ in the supper. Indeed, many theologians raced to find language to accommodate the pope's view. Hildebert of Lavardin (ca. 1055–1133), a contemporary of Berengar, was the first to use the term "transubstantiation" to articulate this expanded Catholic teaching. By the twelfth century, this language was standardized, and it was officially embraced by the church at the Fourth Lateran Council (1215), which we will examine in our next chapter.

For now, it is important to realize that the medieval church usually dealt with theological issues in this same pattern. Controversies arose and were dealt with using the new scholastic method. At times, an issue would sputter out and not receive attention by the pope—as in the case of nominalism in late medieval theology or the question of whether monks should live in poverty in the thirteenth century. Such scholastic debates were hotly contested in their own day but never led the Catholic Church to alter its doctrinal language. However, when an issue was taken up by the pope or a Western council, often a debate would be settled formally by new proclamations, edicts, or papal bulls. Once formalized in this way, the new teaching became a permanent part of Catholic teaching. In cases such as that of Berengar and the presence of Christ in the sacrament, the final decision by the pope became the normative view of the Catholic faith.[18] Thus, such a papal decree could be called a "confession" as we are using the word in this book.

A New Style of Papal Authority

The controversy over Berengar, as we have seen, dealt not just with scholastic theology but also with papal authority. This controversy therefore provides an appropriate bridge to the next part of our story, the Gregorian reforms of the eleventh century leading to a new way of exercising papal authority. Pope Gregory VII (1020–85) was born Hildebrand of Sovana, and so he is often

18. The political and theological issues of the pope's power are dealt with in Brian Tierney, *The Crisis of Church and State, 1050–1300*, Medieval Academy Reprints for Teaching 21 (Toronto: University of Toronto Press, 1988).

referred to as Hildebrand and his reforms as Hildebrandine.[19] For years before his election in 1073, Hildebrand was a key figure behind the scenes in Rome and was personally responsible for the election of at least two popes. Indeed, there were few matters in which Hildebrand did not play a pivotal role—he was the one sent to France in 1054 to examine the teachings of Berengar. In that debate, he zealously supported the pope's decision to affirm Christ's physical presence in the Mass, and more generally he was often involved in the shaping of official papal decisions.

By the time Hildebrand took the papal throne, the papacy had known periods of profound moral decay. While this low level of morality was dreadful for the spiritual health of the church, the most troubling issue for Rome at the time was the papacy's entanglement with political rulers in Europe, especially the Holy Roman Emperor. According to all Catholic leaders of the day, there was no question of whether the pope should engage in political problems; rather, the issue was how to negotiate alliances with European monarchs.[20] The coronation of Charlemagne in 800 had been a watershed for the development of a unique, Western style of political government. By crowning the emperor, the pope had assumed the authority to crown future emperors, and that authority symbolized Rome's jurisdiction over the empire. Still, the papacy was not always free from political pressure. From the seventh century on, the papacy was forced to deal with a string of Roman aristocratic families that sought to subject the papal office to themselves for their own ends.[21] There was thus a tense relationship: the pope was a vital source of authority for political rulers, and yet the rulers themselves wanted to influence the church—at least to get the church's blessing on political matters, and sometimes even to the point of determining who was elected pope. At the very least, kings did not want the pope to appoint bishops without their cooperation, since they feared what bishops who were not already faithful to the king would do. In the era of feudalism, any voice that could challenge political rulers was a problem.[22]

---

19. Some sources refer to him as Hellebrand. On Gregory, see H. E. J. Cowdrey, *Pope Gregory VII, 1073–1085* (Oxford: Oxford University Press, 1998). The context of the fight between Gregory and Henry is covered in Norman F. Cantor, *The Civilization of the Middle Ages* (New York: HarperCollins, 1993).

20. A key survey of this is Tierney, *Crisis of Church and State*, 1–95.

21. Perhaps the best survey of the popes during these years is Eamon Duffy, *Saints and Sinners: A History of the Popes*, 4th ed. (New Haven: Yale University Press, 2015), chaps. 2–3. For an abridged version of the story of Gregory, see Eamon Duffy, *Ten Popes Who Shook the World* (New Haven: Yale University Press, 2011), 59–70.

22. On feudalism, the best entry into the mountain of material is F. L. Ganshof, *Feudalism*, trans. Philip Grierson (New York: Harper, 1964).

Ideally, the relationship between pope and emperor would be mutually beneficial. In moments of crisis, however, one could make life miserable for the other. Popes had been deposed by emperors, or at times the emperor nominated his own man during a papal election. In rare circumstances—such as the famous case of Thomas Becket of England—the spiritual leaders openly contested the legitimacy of a king.[23] Most of the time, bishops in powerful countries were more loyal to the king than to the church. But in not a few cases, church offices were filled by the king without first seeking approval by the pope. By the time of Hildebrand, this practice was known as *lay investiture*—the control of the ordination of a bishop (investiture) by secular rulers.[24] At times, the pope was content to allow this, or at least could do little to stop it, but problems nearly always surfaced if pope and king came to loggerheads.

As Gregory tackled this issue, it seems likely that he was driven by a mixture of vision for a renewal of papal allegiance and growing frustration over the encroachment of rulers into church matters. Gregory was not given to compassion when rulers sought to obstruct his decisions. Even those around him in the curia found his style of leadership irksome (though much of the evidence of this was inflated by his political enemies). But Gregory was not merely annoyed by lay investiture; he had already worked for years to disentangle the papacy from political influences. For example, he had played the crucial role in altering the procedure for choosing future popes to private voting by the college of cardinals—substantially the same as the procedure used today. These new rules were controversial even at the time, since the new process seemed to shut the world out of the papal election.[25] Once he was pope, Gregory continued to pursue the goal of decreasing political entanglement, especially with his condemnation of lay investiture in his *Dictatus Papae* in 1075.

The *Dictatus Papae* was one of the most important decrees for the formation of Catholic thinking on the authority of the papacy. Historians often describe the shifting attitude on papal authority in the Middle Ages not as a trickle of ideas or as a sudden lurch toward papal supremacy but as a chain of documents issued by popes during moments of crisis. The *Dictatus Papae* was at the center of this chain and paved the way for the release of the more

23. A readable biography is John Guy, *Thomas Becket: Warrior, Priest, Rebel* (New York: Random House, 2012)

24. See Uta-Renate Blumenthal, *The Investiture Controversy: Church and Monarchy from the Ninth to the Twelfth Century*, Middle Ages Series (Philadelphia: University of Pennsylvania Press, 1991).

25. It did not, in fact, remove outside influence. There were several times in the late medieval period when political or local influence played a crucial part.

sweeping bull *Unam Sanctam* by Boniface VIII, which we will discuss in our next chapter. The decree also sparked one of the most notorious fights with the Holy Roman Empire. Of course, the Catholic Church for centuries had argued for the authority of the Petrine office. But in the 1000s papal authority was based more on the practice of the pope than on detailed instructions about how Catholics were to view papal authority. At last, however, the Gregorian reforms addressed this need.

The *Dictatus Papae* was a series of basic statements, each of which demanded that Catholics recognize the authority of the pope in all matters, especially in matters of secular politics. The decree began by stressing that the pope alone was universal in the church; thus his delegate (*legatus*) sat above any regional or ecumenical council.[26] The pope was not merely to be a consultant in church matters, but, in fact, only the pope might establish new laws. Councils or synods could make suggestions, but their authority derived only from papal support. Gregory here was undermining the common practice whereby synods made decisions favored by the king, essentially making church assemblies an extension of the government.

To balance these principles, articles 18 and 21 also stated that none could overturn a decree issued by the pope. All matters had to be referred to Rome if they were to be settled officially. *Dictatus Papae* then concluded this line of thinking in article 22, which stated that "the church of Rome has never erred and, by the testimony of Scripture, will never err."[27] Consequently, article 26 continued by affirming that Catholics must hold that no one was genuinely a faithful Christian if he or she was not in communion with the pope.

Dictatus Papae had even stronger language about the authority of political rulers. Article 9 stated that "all princes are to kiss the feet only of the pope," which was not a new practice in feudal Europe but had never been enforced when it came to the relationship between princes and popes.[28] Based on the earlier practice, it would have been custom to greet each other with mutual respect, neither side implying that he was the liege. Now the new decree clearly subjugated all kings to the authority of the pope, and the language would have been read as a possible threat to the authority of Europe's rulers, including the emperor. Moreover, article 12 argued that the pope had the right to depose emperors, a right that had not been asserted by any pope before. The

26. Carl Mirbt, *Quellen zur Geschichte des Papsttums und des römischen Katholizismus* (Tübingen: J. C. B. Mohr, 1924), 146; translation in CCFCT 1:731.

27. Mirbt, *Quellen*, 146. Such language is often associated with the declaration of papal infallibility at Vatican I (1869–70), but it was expressed here eight centuries earlier by Gregory. On Vatican I, see chap. 18 in this book.

28. Mirbt, *Quellen*, 146. Also in CCFCT 1:732.

article did not give any stipulations for deposing political rulers but instead left the decision about when to do so entirely up to the pope. And finally, the document concluded by carrying the argument one step further: it stated that the pope might release subjects from their "bond of fidelity" whenever necessary.[29] These were ominous words in a feudal age.

Henry VI of Germany launched an attack on the papacy almost immediately, although we cannot be sure that he did so *because* of Gregory's decree.[30] These events are often referred to as the Investiture Crisis, one of the more sensational tales in the annals of medieval popes, told in countless textbooks and dressed up with the story of Henry standing barefoot in the snow, begging for the pope to reverse his excommunication.

The fight began when Henry, unwilling to bow to Gregory's demands, called his own council on January 23, 1076, in the city of Worms. The history of royal meddling in church affairs and Gregory's new decree made a fight inevitable, especially given that Henry was himself eager to expand the influence of the empire. The council at Worms not only defied the policies of the *Dictatus Papae* but also deposed Gregory. Two synods held by the bishops of Lombardy supported the decision of Worms, leaving Gregory no option but to respond. He excommunicated Henry, along with all his supporters at the council, and all of Henry's subjects were released from their feudal oaths to Henry if he did not relent.

Henry attempted to dig in, but he was ultimately left with a looming civil war. To heal the breach, Henry made his way to Rome, and when he discovered that the pope was headed north to Augsburg for other matters, Henry diverted his course to catch him. The showdown occurred at a castle in Canossa in northern Italy, where the pope was lodging. Henry waited outside for several days, even dressing as a penitent sinner in sackcloth.[31] We are not sure of the sincerity of Henry's penance, but even if he was playing up his remorse to the crowd, Gregory could not be seen refusing a Christian seeking restoration. The pope relented, and Henry was reinstated to the Catholic faith, although the crisis endured for several more years.

The showdown between Henry and Gregory was a test of the new Gregorian style of exercising papal authority. The *Dictatus Papae* played an essential role in shaping the medieval papacy, and future popes had ample opportunity to use these decrees to curb secular influence on the church. Gregory's efforts to establish nearly unlimited papal authority, not just in ecclesiastical matters

29. Mirbt, *Quellen*, 146. Also in *CCFCT* 1:732.
30. See Blumenthal, *Investiture Controversy*, 106–34.
31. It is unclear whether Henry stood barefoot in the snow, as most accounts state. It was enough that he had removed his royal robes and regalia, offering himself as a repentant sinner.

but on political issues as well, played a role in shaping all subsequent papal action. One generation later, the Gregorian style of papal authority also opened the door for a pope to call for a crusade to the Holy Land. This brings us to the third major background factor lying behind medieval confessional developments.

A New Military Ethos

Around the 900s, medieval Europe began to reorganize itself in new ways, and this was seen especially with the rise of the military classes.[32] These changes occurred first in the upper classes—an important community under Rome, but one that rarely participated in combat directly. However, the vanquishing of the western Roman world by the trans-Alpine tribes, as well as later pressures from Vikings and other raiding peoples, increased the need for skilled warriors. Eventually, only those with lands and revenue of their own could sustain the expenses both to train and to support this warrior class.[33]

These warriors were the basis for our myths surrounding King Arthur and our stories about medieval knights. But such myths sugarcoat the real story of the warrior classes. For most of their history, the military classes were unruly and aggressive. If a noble had too many sons and then trained those sons in war, he often risked the calamity of seeing his family divided over the sons' share of the inherited lands. To offset this problem, Europeans created the practice of *primogeniture*, a custom whereby only the firstborn son received the inheritance. Younger sons had to blaze their own trails, but once their father passed, they were often forced to take a supportive role to their elder brother—as, for example, in the Robin Hood story of Richard the Lion-hearted and his brother Prince John.[34] Not a few medieval wars were sparked by intrafamily conflict. By the 1000s, Europe's larger dynasties, especially the Frankish kingdoms, began to be carved up into what eventually became the nations of modern Europe.

We have previously noted the importance of oaths of allegiance in the feudal world. These oaths were necessary to unite those outside one's family:

32. There has been much scholarly debate in the last two generations about these warrior classes. See, for example, Constance Brittain Bouchard, *Strong of Body, Brave and Noble: Chivalry and Society in Medieval France* (Ithaca, NY: Cornell University Press, 1998).

33. On these changes, see Jean-Pierre Poly and Eric Bournazel, *The Feudal Transformation, 900–1200*, trans. Caroline Higgitt (New York: Holmes & Meier, 1991).

34. Both were historical rulers in England, although John was cast in the Robin Hood stories as an evil usurper to his brother. In actuality, Richard was off fighting in the Third Crusade, so John was serving as a regent in his absence.

the vassal swore allegiance to the lord, promising to fight in any campaigns when called on in exchange for lands of his own and security for his family in future generations. The warrior classes emerged from these vassals. Over the centuries, Europe was divided according to these oaths of vassalage, and these warrior classes, once settled, created a patchwork of estates that they governed as lesser nobles. By at least 1200, these lesser noble classes became fixed, leaving a wide gap between the upper classes and the peasantry.[35]

By the 900s the church had Christianized most of Europe, the older pagan practices had all but vanished, and the church's hierarchy now effectively extended to most of the continent. The warrior classes, however, presented a challenge in times of peace. Those trained in war found it too easy to continue fighting even without an obvious enemy. At times, the desire of some lords to gobble up the territories of their Christian neighbors proved too great.

To offset such violence, the papacy responded by issuing two decrees that led to movements bearing corresponding names: the "Peace of God" and the "Truce of God." The Synod of Charroux in 989 stated in the "Peace of God" that noncombatants were to be unharmed during any feudal campaign. These regulations expanded over the centuries to offer specific lists of those who were to be untouched—including women, children, and clergy. The "Truce of God" had a murkier origin, but its rules stipulated that all wars must take breaks during certain seasons of the year, especially on Sundays and during Lent, although by the end of the Middle Ages the list included most church holidays.

The church also aided in the creation of chivalric codes, and not a few priests or monks were responsible for writing heroic sagas about Christian knights. The purpose of these stories was to blunt the anger of the warriors, to encourage them to temper their desire for glory in battle with appropriately Christian virtue. According to the stories, a Christian knight struggled for the faith and defended those in distress. Several of these sagas, including the Arthurian legends, began to stress that the role of the warrior classes was to seek glory in the *spiritual* arena, including quests for the Holy Grail or by defending the West from the onslaught of infidels.

Both factors—the rise of warrior classes and the church's increased desire to regulate these unruly armies—were important parts of the context for medieval history after 1000. When Pope Urban II called for a crusade in 1095, he felt that it was within the scope of his power to leverage these

---

35. A recent critical study of the subject is Susan Reynolds, *Fiefs and Vassals: The Medieval Evidence Reinterpreted* (Oxford: Oxford University Press, 1994). Compare this to the older work of Ganshof, *Feudalism*.

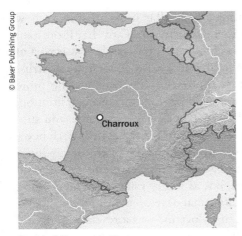

Synod of Charroux in France

warrior classes for the sake of the church. Some popes directed armies against heretics, and most wars (even between Christian nations) were instigated with the explicit blessing of the pope. By the 1500s, there were even a few cases of the pope sitting at the front of an army himself. Thus, there was within the Catholic Church an increased desire to use political force to achieve spiritual goals. For example, the rise of the Inquisition in the 1200s was driven by the church's increased reliance on military tactics against heresy. Put simply, although church and state were never united in Europe, the overlapping of church and secular politics shaped the Catholic Church for centuries.

Conclusions

In this chapter we have looked at the early medieval movement toward a confessional identity centered on the authority of the papacy. Some of the developments that we have considered—such as the issue of political power and investiture—are not typically thought to be *confessional*, at least not in the way the Reformation-era confessions are understood. But to limit the concept of "confession" to its Protestant sense is to misunderstand the comprehensive authority that came to rest with the Roman church. In Roman Catholicism (and in other Christian traditions, for that matter) it made sense to consider political power, the right to call or approve war, or other secular matters under the rubric of "confession." Moreover, these issues were frequently dealt with in the life of the medieval church, so much so that it was impossible to separate them from doctrinal issues. The Catholic Church felt that it was within its purview to rule on these matters—just as the modern Catholic Church has ruled on other "nondoctrinal" issues such as contraception, social justice, and poverty.

An equally important issue for our understanding of the medieval church is the nature of doctrinal development. Again, recognizing the contrast with later Protestantism is helpful. In the confessions of the Reformation the positions espoused derived from treating almost all matters as issues of how one properly understands the Bible. Such an attitude meant that Protestant confessions, by nature, treated doctrine as eternally true, since it was part of God's revelation. The Catholic Church, of course, also understood doctrine to be given by God's revelation, but its approach to doctrine was far more nimble. As we saw with the developments leading toward transubstantiation, the Catholic Church saw no scandal in the fact that the grammar and substance of a doctrine might evolve over time. Although the early church never ruled on the mode of Christ's presence in the Lord's Supper, the medieval church felt it appropriate to define the way Catholics were to understand the bread and wine—not as symbols, but as the physical body and blood of Christ. The Catholic approach to doctrinal development in the medieval period was based on both the notion that doctrine was a revelation of God and that such a revelation by nature could be shaped by later centuries. As we will see in chapter 16, the Council of Trent (1545–63) ratified this approach to tradition in its first session.

The best way to understand Catholic confessional identity in the medieval period is to see it as an unfolding process. Thus, what seems to Protestants a de facto change was according to Catholic teaching simply the unfolding revelation of the Holy Spirit, through the office of the papacy. In the next chapter we will consider the most important of these medieval unfoldings.

12

Catholic Confessions
in the High Middle Ages

On November 27, 1095, Pope Urban II ascended to the pulpit during the Council of Clermont (France). Popes often addressed councils—not always with a sermon, though this was not unusual during lengthy sessions. But this speech—a short, angry tirade about the expansion of Islam in the East— forever changed the church in the West.

At this time, the emperor in the East was Alexius I Comnenos (whom we met briefly in chap. 10), an anxious and restless king who spent much of his reign worried about heresy at home and Turkish armies abroad. But he was under a lot of pressure, largely because he was the nephew of the previous emperor, and he worried about ruining the dynasty. He was also under his mother's thumb, and he spent too much time worrying about upsetting her. Finally, Alexius decided to crown her instead of his wife, Irene, an act that set tongues wagging in the court. One can only imagine the strain on the marriage. Almost certainly for this reason, Alexius found it better to be off at war with the Seljuk Turks than to seek any comfort at home.

Yet the threat was not a figment of Alexius's imagination or merely an excuse to get away from a bad home situation. The Byzantine Empire was losing ground rapidly to the Seljuk Empire, an impressive Turkish dynasty that eventually spread from the Hindu Kush Mountains to the Persian Gulf. As we have seen, by the 1090s, the Turks were even advancing into Asia Minor (modern Turkey), taking them up to the gates of Constantinople. Under

Public Domain / Wikimedia Commons

Urban II and the First
Crusade

normal circumstances, the East might have called on the West to come to
its aid, but now the growing rift (discussed in chap. 10) made such a request
embarrassing for Alexius. He could not stop the Seljuk armies, however, and
so finally he sent an ambassador to the Council of Clermont to request help
from Urban II.

Urban displayed grace and generosity to the Eastern delegates. He chose
to see the problem not as a divine judgment on the East but as a call for all
Christians to restore the faith in these lands now occupied by Islam. Historians
debate Urban's goal. Did he seek to retake Jerusalem or only to alleviate the
threat to the eastern border of Asia Minor, giving Constantinople breathing
room? Perhaps most likely is that Urban was unsure of his own goals. What
we know is that he encouraged the crusade aggressively, sending preachers
throughout Europe to stoke up the will to go on crusade. Urban also had no

idea of the sheer numbers of people who would march off to the East: between twenty thousand and thirty-five thousand men—the cross on their banners, the Holy Land soon to be bathed in blood.

The First Crusade (1095–99) is an excellent point to mark the beginning of the High Middle Ages—a time of flourishing in the West, as well as rapid change in church doctrine and practice.[1] In this chapter we look at the confessional changes, especially regarding papal authority and the sacraments.

Scholasticism and Confessional Orthodoxy

In our previous chapter we discussed the rise of Scholasticism, defining it as a theological method that sought a better approach to complex issues. We argued there that Scholasticism was not always the darling of the medieval church, since not a few medieval theologians were attacked for their conclusions. At times, the method itself came under fire. Figures such as Berengar of Tours were celebrated for their intellect, as long as they did not argue against popular opinion on doctrine. We come now to one of the most famous medieval Scholastics, Peter Abelard. Remembered today for his salacious love affair with Heloise, Abelard was infamous in his own day for speculating on doctrine, especially the Trinity and salvation.[2] For this reason, he is a good example of how Scholasticism tested the boundaries of confessional orthodoxy, not always with positive results. His speculations landed him in front of councils that judged his views to be heretical on two separate occasions.

Abelard grew up in a castle, with a father who was a knight, surrounded by arms, horses, and men in training. He gave up the sword for study, however, and traveled to various parts of Europe seeking the best teachers of philosophy. He eventually settled in Paris, already known for its scholars and at the time witnessing the rise of what became Sorbonne University, the second-oldest university in Europe. There in Paris, the principal subject for Abelard was dialectic—a method of comparing two ideas in tension, followed by an examination of their weaknesses, and then settling on a solution. Abelard

---

1. The two definitive studies on the Crusades are Kenneth Setton, ed., *A History of the Crusades*, 6 vols. (Madison: University of Wisconsin Press, 1969–89); Jonathan Riley-Smith, *The Crusades: A History*, 2nd ed., Yale Nota Bene (New Haven: Yale University Press, 2005). For a quick and readable work, see Jonathan Riley-Smith, ed., *The Oxford Illustrated History of the Crusades* (Oxford: Oxford University Press, 1995).

2. For a survey of his life, see M. T. Clanchy, *Abelard: A Medieval Life* (Oxford: Blackwell, 1999). For both his life and philosophy, see Jeffery E. Bower and Kevin Guilfoy, eds., *The Cambridge Companion to Abelard*, Cambridge Companions to Philosophy (Cambridge: Cambridge University Press, 2004).

Peter Abelard

found dialectic to be the essential method for studying any doctrine. Put another way, Abelard was supremely optimistic about the ability of the mind to discover truth in all subjects, including subjects such as the Trinity and the atonement. He was also unhappy with appeals to mystery, since he felt such appeals ignored that God created us as rational beings. Christianity, of course, had never been opposed to the life of the mind, and we have seen examples of rich thinking in the early church. But Abelard wanted to approach doctrine more critically.

Abelard's dialectical approach to doctrine stood in contrast to that of Anselm (1033–1109), one of the other great dialectical thinkers of the Middle Ages and part of Abelard's generation of teachers. Anselm is always remembered for two slogans that relate to his method for theological reflection: "I believe that I may understand" (*credo ut intelligam*) and "faith seeking understanding" (*fides quaerens intellectum*).[3] Both of these slogans show that Anselm understood the role of thinking as a supplement to faith. Faith in the revelation of God was first and foremost, and without it, no truth could be grasped in theology. However, once the will took hold of God, the mind was sanctified so that it could cooperate with revealed truth, making reflection and dialectic possible. Anselm managed to hold faith and reason in balance and did not see reason as something opposed to mystery.

In contrast, Abelard took reason further than Anselm was prepared to go. While he never openly claimed that reason was superior, the pattern of

---

3. For Anselm's thought, the best place to begin is Brian Davies and Brian Leftow, eds., *The Cambridge Companion to Anselm*, Cambridge Companions to Philosophy (Cambridge: Cambridge University Press, 2005). Slightly more advanced, but still useful for students, is Jasper Hopkins, *A Companion to the Study of St. Anselm* (Minneapolis: University of Minnesota Press, 1972).

Abelard's writings showed that he saw faith or revelation as an inferior basis for truth. Reason and dialectic, therefore, wound up encroaching step-by-step into areas on which the church had refused to speculate. The anxiety for Abelard was created mostly by the fact that Greek philosophy was considered in the High Middle Ages to be the supreme example of philosophical reason. Abelard was concerned that Christian philosophy ought to occupy the same intellectual high ground, rather than allowing mystery to serve as an excuse for muddled teaching on doctrine. Abelard was also known for an arrogant style of lecturing—and, of course, his personal life was in shambles with his secret marriage to Heloise.

For our story, we will look at Abelard's teachings on the Trinity, since not a few of his contemporaries accused him of heresy and since this doctrine was a staging ground for his use of faith and reason. Abelard went beyond the Nicene Creed, primarily by claiming that the Trinity was a logical inference from the study of philosophy. God's triunity did not need to be revealed, he argued, since it could be discerned in the writings of Plato. Abelard claimed there were adumbrations of the Trinity in pagan philosophy, thus proving it was a logically defensible position.

The goal for Abelard was to reopen the Nicene Creed and see whether there was a better method for describing the Trinity. The most common tactic he took, in fact, was to explore what he called *similitudes*—analogies to explain the Trinity. The main issue in Abelard's mind was the way we understand how two things can be *different* and *similar*. Two things can be numerically the same, or substantially the same, and so on. With this as a foundation, Abelard sought an analogy in this world that might reveal a proper balance of Father, Son, and Spirit. Notice that this tactic was in keeping with the shift in Western trinitarian thought (begun as early as the Athanasian Creed and discussed in chaps. 7 and 9) from declaring faith in three persons to justifying the juxtaposition of oneness and threeness. Abelard offered several examples, the most famous of which was the analogy of wax: three pieces of wax were the same substance, but the impression on each made them different in nature.

Few in Abelard's day found his trinitarian argument compelling, and several even found it heretical—including Bernard of Clairvaux (1090–1153), who led the attack on Abelard's heresy at the Council of Sens. The council agreed and issued a number of condemnations of Abelard's teaching on the Trinity, as well as his teaching on the will, grace, and salvation. The importance of these decisions for our purposes is not only that they reaffirmed the Nicene Creed but also that they expanded Catholic teaching into other doctrines, several of which had seen no previous conciliar decisions. The statement opened by finding Abelard guilty of making too harsh a distinction between the persons of the

The archdiocese of Sens in France

Trinity—to the point of saying that "the Father is complete power, the Son some power, and the Holy Spirit no power." (Notice in his analogy of wax that the three pieces of wax were different in "nature," a claim that contradicted church teaching.) The council also condemned Abelard's use of Platonic thinking when he proclaimed that the Holy Spirit was "the soul of the world."[4]

Historians today are not convinced these decrees were fair to Abelard's theology.[5] Nevertheless, the Council of Sens followed the same pattern that we saw in chapter 11: the increasing restriction of the permissible language for articulating certain doctrines. The decrees condemned Abelard on a number of points that were beyond the scope of Scripture or patristic theology. For example, they rejected Abelard for teaching that "even chaste fear" will not be present "in the life to come."[6] The emotional capacity of the soul in heaven, of course, had not previously been part of confessional identity, but now it became such a part. These condemnations of Abelard were but one example of a process repeated often in the High Middle Ages: by responding to a small controversy with a definitive, confessional statement, the church instigated a steady amount of confessional creep—decrees added to decrees that built on one another. In the broad spectrum of issues on which such confessional creep took place, two stand out in particular: the Eucharist and papal authority. We introduced both of these themes in the previous chapter, and it is now time to return to them in earnest.

First Major Theme: The Eucharist

Simply put, there was no single doctrinal issue more important to medieval piety than the Eucharist. The Catholic affirmation of the physical presence of Christ in the Lord's Supper—later defined as transubstantiation—was also the provocation for reform movements such as those of John Wycliffe and Jan Hus, movements that arose to challenge the authority of the church.

4. Translation from *CCFCT* 1:734.
5. See Jeffrey Brower, "Trinity," in Bower and Guilfoy, *Cambridge Companion to Abelard*, 223–57.
6. *CCFCT* 1:734.

We noted in our previous chapter the evolving language about the *physical* presence of Christ in the bread and wine—a confessional demand not seen during the early church.[7] The debates surrounding the teaching of Berengar of Tours, however, played a role in launching the church into a debate over *how* Christ was confessed as present in the Eucharist. As early as the twelfth century, the language of transubstantiation had been used by theologians who wished to stress the physical nature of Christ's presence. The culmination of this line of thinking came at the Fourth Lateran Council of 1215—the twelfth ecumenical council by Roman Catholic reckoning.[8]

The pope who called the Fourth Lateran Council was Innocent III, one of the most influential popes of the medieval church. Committed to advancing the authority of the papacy, Innocent did so by action as much as by proclamation. Not only did he call the Fourth Crusade (1202–4)—a crusade that managed only to sack Constantinople and impose Western rule on the Eastern capital (as we saw in chap. 10)—but he also changed the very concept of a crusade to justify launching attacks on heretical movements in Europe (Cathars and Waldensians, to be discussed later in this chapter). But the Fourth Lateran Council is considered the most indelible mark left by Innocent III, not only because it altered the church's stance on several issues but also because its proclamation of transubstantiation was the culmination of medieval teaching on Christ's presence in the Eucharist.

The council formally gathered in the Lateran Palace in November 1215. We are told that at the opening of the council Innocent circulated a document of seventy affirmations, which the council adopted with very few changes.[9] Most of these covered important issues or reforms within the church. However, the opening statements created what the church deemed to be a new creed. This document should be styled a "confession" according to the way we are using the words "creed" and "confession" in this book, but today it is called the Lateran Creed. This was an important shift by the West, which had until now refrained from using the word "creed" for its decisions. This new creed, therefore, must be our focus.

The Lateran Creed opened with a standard affirmation of the Trinity, although it stated in passing that the Holy Spirit proceeds "from both [Father

7. The best survey on the Eucharist in the high to later Middle Ages is Miri Rubin, *Corpus Christi: The Eucharist in Late Medieval Culture* (Cambridge: Cambridge University Press, 2001).

8. The Lateran councils were those associated with the Archbasilica of St. John Lateran, located in the heart of Rome not far from the Colosseum. This is actually the cathedral of Rome, thus the cathedral of the pope. The Vatican and St. Peter's get the most attention but are in reality simply symbols of the Catholic Church, not the actual seat (*cathedra*) of the Roman bishop.

9. For more on the background of the Fourth Lateran Council, see CCFCT 1:739.

Basilica of St. John Lateran, the site of the Lateran Councils

and Son] equally."[10] The remaining portion of this creed focused on God's creation of humanity in his image and affirmed that both body and soul are by nature good—over against the teachings of Catharism, which was a quasi-Gnostic sect in southern France that held that our bodies are evil.

The Lateran Creed made three affirmations that are problematic from a later Protestant perspective. First, it affirmed that the Trinity is "undivided according to its common essence but divided according to the properties of its persons."[11] Such language reflects the shift that, as we argued in chapters 7 and 9, marked Western theological language in the Middle Ages, approaching the Trinity primarily in terms of the concepts of essence and person. Here the need to defend the Trinity against the Modalism taught by the Cathars (see below) led to the emphasis on concepts rather than on the persons themselves.

A second problem was the Lateran Creed's statement on salvation. The language is unclear, but the focus of the proclamation was entirely on works. Indeed, there was no indication that faith in Christ was even the foundation for good works. Salvation was instead tied to our imitation of Christ's incarnation, since it was said that God's taking on our human nature "showed more clearly the way of life." The final judgment will come "to render to every person according to his works, both to the reprobate and to the elect." After the resurrection, everyone will "receive according to their deserts, whether these be good or bad; for the latter perpetual punishment with the devil, for the former eternal glory with Christ."[12] Again, this seems similar

10. For our discussion of the *Filioque*, see chaps. 7 and 10.
11. Norman P. Tanner, ed., *Decrees of the Ecumenical Councils*, vol. 1, *Nicaea I to Lateran V* (Washington, DC: Georgetown University Press, 1990), 230. Also in *CCFCT* 1:741.
12. Tanner, *Decrees of the Ecumenical Councils*, 1:230. Also in *CCFCT* 1:741.

to the Athanasian Creed, and there seems to be little doubt that this is espousing a view of salvation based on works as well as faith. Moreover, since neither the Nicene Creed nor the Apostles' Creed explicitly discussed faith and works, the inclusion of works-based salvation language here is significant.

The Lateran Creed issued a third problematic declaration (to Protestants), which historians consider the most influential development in medieval Catholicism: the affirmation of transubstantiation. The decree stated that Christ's body and blood "are truly contained in the sacrament of the altar under the forms of bread and wine, the bread and wine having been transubstantiated."[13] The Lateran Creed also stressed that only a priest could bring about this miracle. The statement went on to include baptism in this type of spiritual process, since it was said that the water was consecrated by the priest. The framers of the creed did not suggest the water had been transubstantiated into anything else, but they held that the water was made holy and efficacious, just as the bread and wine became more than merely a symbol in the Eucharist.

The word "transubstantiation" is not used today beyond discussions of Catholic theology, but we use a similar word today when we refer to something being *transformed*. If we remove the prefix "trans-" from these words, we are left with two words: "form" and "substance." Both of these words are commonly used in philosophy. The form of something is its *outward* manifestation—the size, shape, and other biological features of a human person. That outward form can change, as in, say, an accident where a person loses a limb, or in the process of time where we change from youth to old age. The form can change, but we affirm that the *substance*—the essence of the person—is no different in this new form. An older person is the same substance as his or her younger self, and we certainly would never say that a person has become a different essence after losing a limb. The *form* may change—or transform—but the essence or *substance* remains the same.

The Fourth Lateran Council insisted that in the Eucharist the opposite took place: the outward form of the elements—bread and wine—was still present as the Christian took the sacrament. What changed was the *substance* of the bread and wine into the body and blood of Christ—not tasted or noticed by the senses, but affirmed by faith. Over the centuries, accounts of miracles involving the bread and wine allegedly proved that the Christian was taking the true body and blood of Christ. But these were miracles

13. Tanner, *Decrees of the Ecumenical Councils*, 1:230. Also in CCFCT 1:741.

Disputation of the Holy Sacrament by Raphael

and not the normative experience for Catholics. Indeed, the Fourth Lateran Council affirmed that the bread and wine would *look and taste the same*, while all the same they were to be *approached* as the very body and blood of Christ. To this day, the Catholic Church affirms this understanding of the Eucharist.

The influence of the Fourth Lateran Council on the view of the Eucharist, then, cannot be overstated. In some respects, the ruling of the council bore the same weight as the earlier creeds for the West until the Reformation, when all Protestant groups rejected this council. After the Reformation, however, the Catholic Church maintained the language of the Fourth Lateran Council, explicitly reaffirming the language of transubstantiation at the Council of Trent in the sixteenth century.[14] It would not be too much to say that the Catholic faith after the Fourth Lateran Council was always a faith that insisted on full adherence to its teaching on transubstantiation. From our point of view, transubstantiation was a *confessional* issue intrinsic to later Catholic identity. But from the Catholic point of view, it was a *creedal* issue, essential to the Christian faith itself. Hence the name "Lateran *Creed*."

14. See our discussion in chap. 16.

Second Major Theme: Papal Authority

Turning now to the second of our themes—the authority of the pope—we should stress again that the concept of papal authority always rested on the ironic fact that the pope was often weak against foreign kings. Until roughly 1000, the pope was controlled by several political influences, most often by the aristocracy in Rome or abroad by the Holy Roman Empire. At times, the pope was removed, or a successor chosen, simply by the will of the emperor. But as we saw in the previous chapter, the new millennium brought a new style of papal leadership. After the work of popes such as Gregory and others, the papacy began to secure its power over the earth—at least in theory. In actuality, Rome had no army and nothing to force conformity beyond threats of excommunication. In the end, threats based on spiritual authority carried the day, but not without constant reinforcing by a series of strong popes.[15]

The pope who personified this triumph of spiritual authority over secular power was Boniface VIII (1294–1303). Born Benedetto Caetani, he was an Italian who distinguished himself in both law and diplomacy. He was also, at the time of his election, a new style of pope. His predecessor was Celestine V, a man who attempted to embody the otherworldly ideal of a saint—an angelic pope to sanctify the office for a new millennium—and for his troubles was often despised for refusing to engage in the political issues required of the office.[16] In contrast, Boniface was known for his fierce opposition to his enemies, as well as a rather strong sense of ambition. He wished to return once again to the policies begun under Gregory VII and Innocent III—policies designed to curb political involvement in the church and expand the sense of the papacy's authority.

To achieve these ends, Boniface issued a bull called *Unam Sanctam* (1302), often considered to be the strongest statement of papal authority in history. In this bull Boniface took the final step of fusing salvation to papal authority, such that one could not be a true Christian without complete submission to the Roman curia. Of course, the language of papal authority had been trending this way for some time, but this was the final and most explicit articulation of such a doctrine. *Unam Sanctam* itself is quite short—only two pages in a modern printing—but the weight of its language is imposing. The decree opened with language borrowed from the Nicene Creed,

15. Two older but still indispensable studies are Walter Ullmann, *The Growth of Papal Government in the Middle Ages: A Study in the Ideological Relation of Clerical to Lay Power* (London: Methuen, 1970); Ullmann, *A Short History of the Papacy in the Middle Ages*, 2nd ed. (New York: Routledge, 2003).

16. On this background, see Eamon Duffy, *Saints and Sinners: A History of the Popes*, 4th ed. (New Haven: Yale University Press, 2015), 158–60.

"there is one holy, catholic, and apostolic church," but then it immediately added "outside this church there is neither salvation nor remission of sins." A strained trinitarian analogy followed, building on the idea of headship. The decree stated that Christ is the head of the church, but "the head of Christ, however, is God."[17] This analogy, despite its awkwardness, situated the entire point of the decree around access to salvation, since the church stood as the intermediary between God and Christ on one side, and the Christian on the other.

Since access to salvation was only through the church, the next question addressed was *how* one came to this church. Boniface continued by stressing that there were "not two heads, like a monster" over the church, but nevertheless two persons did control the church—"namely, Christ, and Christ's vicar is Peter."[18] The decree then took a swipe at the Orthodox (the "Greeks") for claiming to be part of the true church but not bending the knee to the vicar of Christ in Rome.

The central theme of *Unam Sanctam* was its sharp distinction between political and ecclesial authority. Boniface took a unique tactic, juxtaposing the human soul and the body. The opening paragraph of this discussion described the two swords—a trope often used to describe political and spiritual authority. However, these two were no longer seen as working in harmony. Rather, just as "the spiritual" was above "the material," so, too, was the spiritual authority of the pope above all authority on earth. The authority did not derive from human authority, although it was indeed wielded by a human. But to flout this authority—to challenge the pope at all—was to go against God himself.

Such was the bold ideal of *Unam Sanctam*, but the reality for Boniface was that this decree immediately led to his death. Philip IV of France (like many French kings at the time) was a rival to Boniface, and the king was not pleased with *Unam Sanctam*.[19] During Holy Week in 1303, Boniface threatened to excommunicate any who restricted the travel of French clergy—Philip was the primary person who had been doing so. By September, blood was boiling on both sides. Two of Philip's associates cornered Boniface outside the cathedral of Anagni (about fifty miles southeast of Rome) and threatened the pope directly. Boniface attempted to stand his ground, only to be slapped violently—what history books often call the

17. CCFCT 1:746.
18. CCFCT 1:746.
19. Much of this story can be found in Brian Tierney, *The Crisis of Church and State: 1050–1300*, Medieval Academy Reprints for Teaching 21 (Toronto: University of Toronto Press, 1988), 172–92.

Anagni Slap—before being imprisoned and probably beaten. He died after only a few weeks from what was reportedly a fever, though the mistreatment certainly was the true cause. To make matters more insulting, Boniface's successor lived only eight months and was followed by Clement V, a native of France. Clement not only refused to enforce *Unam Sanctam*; he also yielded to the power of the French king and moved the papacy itself to Avignon, France, where it remained from 1309 to 1377 as practically an extension of the French court.

But we should see in *Unam Sanctam* something more than the story of Boniface dying in his wretched cell. Despite the troubles related to its early implementation, the decree was and still is part of the Roman Catholic basis for papal authority, and it raises numerous challenges for both Orthodox and Protestant churches. *Unam Sanctam* tightened the noose permanently around the necks not only of those who would *challenge* papal authority but also even of those who would seek to *limit* papal authority.[20] The only path available to Christians, medieval or modern, was—and according to Roman Catholicism, still is—to submit to the office of the papacy. Essentially, unlimited papal authority had become a confessional article of faith.

Heretical and Reform Movements

Not surprisingly, several movements in the High Middle Ages arose to challenge papal authority and the role of Rome in shaping Western Christianity. These movements shared little in common beyond the desire to limit (or remove) the authority of the pope and councils in defining the confessional identity of the Christian faith. At least one of the movements—the Cathar movement in the twelfth and thirteenth centuries—taught Gnostic views of creation and salvation, views considered heretical by virtually all Christians throughout history.[21] Other movements—such as the Wycliffe movement in England—looked almost Protestant in some of their views on the authority of the Bible. But in the medieval world, all of these movements were considered heretical, largely because they rejected the authority of the papacy. We must say a few things about these movements overall, since they revealed a growing uneasiness in the West over the direction of Catholic teaching, and some of these issues returned at the time of the Reformation.

20. See, for example, our discussion in chap. 18 about ongoing ecumenical discussions with the Catholic Church.

21. The best accessible study of these medieval heresies is Malcolm Lambert, *Medieval Heresy: Popular Movements from the Gregorian Reform to the Reformation* (Oxford: Blackwell, 2002).

The first and best-known movement that opposed the Catholic Church was that of the Cathars. Many theories exist about the origin of their teachings, but it is generally believed that they adhered to a variety of older heresies. The two most cited issues in their teachings were their tendency toward Modalism in their definition of the Trinity and their quasi-Gnostic belief in a sharp division between body (evil) and soul (good).[22] In keeping with this Gnostic-style dualism, there were also some hints of a Marcionite view of God, which saw the Old Testament God as evil and the New Testament God as an expression of love. The Cathars were located mostly in southern France, in parts of the Swiss regions, and perhaps as far afield as northern Italy.

A group that is often confused with the Cathars was the Waldensians—from the same region and associated with the teachings of Peter Waldo (ca. 1140–ca. 1205).[23] The teachings of the Waldensians may not have originated with Waldo, but they are attributed to him nevertheless. The movement was known especially for reacting against the Catholic teaching on the physical presence of Christ in the Eucharist, and also for a general rejection of the opulence in the church during the High Middle Ages. Waldo himself produced a confession of faith—in many ways a forerunner to the personal confessions of faith that characterized the Reformation—in which he stresses his adherence to trinitarian orthodoxy. This confession did not spare him or his followers from persecution, however, and they were forced to withdraw to remote locations in the Alps.

These two movements were very different in theology, yet both were driven by a desire to return to a simple form of Christianity—one they claimed to see in the Scriptures—over against the lordly status of clergy in their cities. Both movements came under fire from the medieval church. The teachings of the Waldensians were condemned at the Third Lateran Council (1179), while the Cathars were condemned, as we saw, at the Fourth Lateran Council.

A third movement, the one that most embodied the challenge to Roman obedience in these centuries, was the Wycliffe movement—sometimes known as Lollardy. Today, John Wycliffe (ca. 1321–85) is often remembered as a man of the people, though in actuality he was part of the establishment. What marked Wycliffe out from his elite peers, however, was his aggressive stance against institutionalism. There was a thread of apocalyptic fervor in Wycliffe's views, glimpsed in his first published work, *The Last Age of the Church* (1356). We must remember that the fourteenth century was a time of severe anxiety

22. We discussed Modalism or Sabellianism briefly in chap 4.
23. His name is also rendered as Valdes, Valdo, Waldensius, Vaux, or Vaudes.

Georgios Kollidas/www.shutterstock.com

John Wycliffe

throughout Europe, encouraged in no small way by the outbreak of the Black Death, which left tens of millions of Europeans dead in its wake. But whatever the motivation, Wycliffe took a zealous stance against all institutions, including the church.

In his theology, then, Wycliffe was staunchly opposed to the new ideas of papal authority. He took the Fourth Lateran Council and its definition of transubstantiation as signs that the church had lost touch with the Bible. His fear of papal abuse was only made worse by the Avignon papacy and the subsequent schisms that occurred in the fourteenth century. These problems, for Wycliffe, signaled a deeper problem with the very act of relying on church institutions.

The solution for Wycliffe was to return to the Bible. Contrary to the modern popular conception, there were some editions of the Bible in English in the fourteenth century. What was not part of medieval England, however, was a Bible translated entirely into the language of the people, which in Wycliffe's day was Middle English, or an earlier form of the English spoken today and best known as the language of Chaucer's *Canterbury Tales*. The Bible was also never used in England as a tool to *challenge* the papacy, and on this point Wycliffe was at his most anti-institutional. As opposed to the Latin Vulgate of Jerome—used across Europe in Catholic churches—Wycliffe wanted to see the Bible in his mother tongue.[24]

The Wycliffe Bible—as the final product of the Wycliffe translation team became known—was not a perfect translation. In fact, it was a wooden translation of the Latin Vulgate.[25] But the Wycliffe Bible was not based on a theory

24. For a good study of the impact of the Lollard texts, see Anne Hudson, *Lollards and Their Books* (New York: Bloomsbury Academic, 2004). For students, the best book on this is David Daniell, *The Bible in English* (New Haven: Yale University Press, 2003).

25. Christopher De Hamel, *The Book: A History of the Bible* (London: Phaidon, 2001). See also Ryan M. Reeves and Charles Hill, *Know How We Got Our Bible* (Grand Rapids: Zondervan, 2018).

of linguistic excellence. It was a renegade Bible that Wycliffe hoped would inspire more Christians to leave the institutional church and embrace a simple, biblical faith. By and large, the Lollard movement was unsuccessful on its own, although it was remembered during the English Reformation and inspired English Protestants to retell the story in their own way.[26]

The Lollards were emblematic of the rise of substantive movements that criticized the established church. These challenges do not force us to assume that the Reformation was inevitable or even likely to occur, but they help us to understand why later reform movements sensed a wind in their sails when they called for reform.

Conclusions

The High Middle Ages were a curious mixture of both increased stability—at least in terms of *theories* of church authority—and rapid change within the church. Our focus in this chapter has been on the doctrinal issues that inspired confessional (or even quasi-creedal) documents, but we have also looked at the rise of anti-institutional movements that sought to overturn the medieval church in various ways. We must conclude, however, by pointing out how small these movements were and how inconsequential they were in their own time. Some—such as the teachings of Wycliffe and his followers—appeared to be a serious threat to the church, yet even so, these movements were largely gone by the time of the Reformation. By and large, the church continued to stress its authority, and, by and large, the focus on papal authority carried the day. By the Reformation in the sixteenth century, most of Europe had come to see the authority of Christ's vicar as unassailable.

In fact, because many students see the Middle Ages from the vantage point of a Reformation or modern perspective, we need to recall that the changes in medieval doctrine—even changes in the view of papal authority—did not take place quickly. Rather, they developed slowly over a period of centuries, and often in the face of controversy. It should also be noted that the Reformation did not attribute Catholic problems to the notion that the church suffered a downfall in the High Middle Ages. The Reformers argued instead that the problems were inherent in the West whenever the church began to rely heavily on church authority—especially papal authority. Early changes in the medieval period may not have been excessive, but the Reformation saw in these issues the seeds of the later Middle Ages, when doctrines were changed more

---

26. On the relatively slight influence of the Lollards, see Richard Rex, *The Lollards*, Social History in Perspective (New York: Palgrave, 2002).

dramatically. For Protestants, the primary issue was not what had changed in medieval doctrine but *on what basis* these changes were justified: papal authority or the Bible. We now turn in part 4 to the Reformation, the rise of Protestant confessionalism, and the Roman Catholic and Orthodox confessional responses to Protestantism.

The Reformation and Confessionalism

(1500–1650)

13

The Crisis of the Reformation

Around October 31, 1517, Martin Luther probably nailed a series of sentences, written in Latin, on the door of the Schlosskirche in Wittenberg.[1] These sentences, or theses, were secretly translated into German and sent around the Holy Roman Empire. Although Luther did not anticipate a full-scale reformation, his Ninety-Five Theses (as they came to be known) were regarded as a call for reform—and not simply a reform of Christian practice, since Luther even criticized the pope. It is for this reason that October 31 is remembered as the start of the Reformation—the spark that ignited Europe into schism.[2]

The Reformation turned out to be a landmark event for the church in the West. Sparked by Luther's protest in 1517, the crisis quickly spread from Wittenberg in Germany to the Swiss city of Zürich under Huldrych Zwingli. The Reformation went on to shape, positively or negatively, every country in Europe, and with the discovery of the New World and expansion around the globe, many of the tensions engulfing Europe were exported to other

1. We do not actually have hard evidence of when Luther posted the theses or whether he even posted them publicly. The story of the posting of the Ninety-Five Theses was told years later by a third party. Luther wrote a defense of the Ninety-Five Theses, but he did not give us his personal account of nailing them up. Still, only a few scholars have concluded this event never happened. See Erwin Iserloh, *The Theses Were Not Posted: Luther between Reform and Reformation* (Boston: Beacon, 1968).

2. The best accounts of Luther's path from the Ninety-Five Theses to his break with Rome are E. Gordon Rupp, *Luther's Progress to the Diet of Worms*, Cloister Library (New York: Harper & Row, 1964); David V. N. Bagchi, *Luther's Earliest Opponents: Catholic Controversialists, 1518–1525* (Minneapolis: Fortress, 1991).

Painting of Luther nailing the Ninety-Five Theses by Ferdinand Pauwels

parts of the world as well. England, Scotland, and Germany became heavily Protestant, while Spain, Italy, and eventually France rejected the Reformation. Cities in Italy and other parts of Europe experienced calls for reform only for a season before these calls were silenced. The fault lines between Protestant and Catholic lands, and even within cities that had equal numbers of both, eventually sparked a series of wars that lasted almost a century. These were hot-blooded and bloody days. The story of the next three chapters, when seen through various confessions, will be the complicated relationships among the various Reformation movements—not all of them friendly. These tensions eventually led to the denominations that define modern Protestantism.

Two caveats are in order. First, although the Reformation was momentous, we must not make it appear to be the only fruitful time of theological reflection in Christian history. We have seen in our previous chapters that creedal and confessional developments have occurred throughout church history. Nearly all Protestant churches embraced the ancient creeds, and they saw their confessions as extensions of those early documents. Only the Anabaptists made a habit of rejecting the ancient creeds—and for that reason, other Protestants rejected *them*. The Reformation, then, should not be considered unique when it comes to confessional development. The second caveat is that one of the values of exploring the Reformation confessions is to gain a sense of those issues that divided the Reformers. All Protestants embraced justification by faith, but they differed widely on issues such as the sacraments, ecclesiology, political involvement, and Christian living. We could easily tell the story of the great unity of Protestant theology, but our focus on Reformation confessions will instead draw out their theological differences.

Before we discuss the confessions written during the Reformation in the following chapters, and thus before we treat both the continuities and discontinuities of that movement, it will be helpful to gain a sense of the broader story, to consider at least some of the causes behind the rise of Protestantism. Thus, in this chapter we must lay a foundation by examining the origins of the Reformation itself.

Medieval Background on Grace and Works

The church had not, by Luther's day, defined justification by faith. For example, none of the early creeds had discussed justification directly. Both students and scholars have found this omission curious, since it seems to have been a rather big oversight. However, as we have argued throughout this book, the creedal impulse in the early church was not irrelevant to the question of salvation, but instead, salvation was always the central issue: God came down to save us, to do for us what we could not do for ourselves by taking on human flesh, securing victory through the cross.

What the creeds did not state was how salvation *affected* the believer. Ancient councils did in fact condemn the teachings of Pelagius on works-based righteousness, but such condemnations did not make it into the creeds themselves. Nevertheless, Christians, ancient and medieval, believed that faith in Christ irrevocably changed believers, ushering them out of darkness and into lives of grace and discipleship. But the question of the role of good works was always open for discussion. Due to this ambiguity, the church over the centuries tolerated a variety of forms of Christian living.

By the time Luther was born, however, a series of developments had crystallized Catholic views on justification and good works into what scholars often call the *majority opinion* in the late medieval period—although the Catholic Church did not rule officially on justification until the Council of Trent (1545–63). Not everyone accepted the majority opinion, and several who took exception to it seemed to foreshadow Luther's concerns about not stressing our good works.[3] But by 1500 the majority opinion was established in practice and supported by the papacy, so there was a large amount of pressure to conform to it.

In outline, the basic thrust of this majority medieval view of salvation went as follows. At birth, all children were born with original sin. As such,

---

3. See Heiko Oberman, *Forerunners of the Reformation: The Shape of Late Medieval Thought* (London: Lutterworth, 1967).

Medieval piety seen in Michelangelo's *Pieta*

they were unable to save themselves or please God, since their wills were bent toward sin. On this point, the medieval church was in harmony with the early church (especially with the writings of Augustine), and all medieval theologians affirmed that humans were incapable of saving themselves.[4] Sin was a problem we could not fix, so God must intervene. Or, as we have put it earlier in this book, we could not rise up to God, so he had to come down to us.

Over the course of the Middle Ages, it became typical to teach that original sin was dealt with in baptism: the soul was washed and received an infusion of grace.[5] This is normally called baptismal regeneration today. We should

4. The Augustinian view of original sin is often challenged by Orthodox theologians as not in step with the early church, especially on the point that humanity bears Adam's guilt. For these debates and a uniquely positive take on Augustine from an Orthodox theologian, see Seraphim Rose, *The Place of Blessed Augustine in the Orthodox Church*, Orthodox Theological Texts 3 (Platina, CA: St. Herman, 2007).

5. For background to lay life, see André Vauchez, *The Laity in the Middle Ages: Religious Beliefs and Devotional Practices*, ed. Daniel E. Bornstein, trans. Margery J. Schneider (Notre Dame, IN: University of Notre Dame Press, 1997).

note that in this view of baptism, the Holy Spirit came to all baptized persons, infant or adult. In a manner of speaking, those who were baptized played no active role in their reception of grace. The Spirit drew the soul to Christ, washing away original sin and allowing the person's will to cooperate with grace. Notice, too, that this infusion happened regardless of faith. In the medieval era, infants were baptized at seven days—long before they could understand what was happening. It is crucial to see that Catholics did not (and do not) teach that this infusion of grace is itself salvation; thus, this infusion of grace does not correspond to the Protestant understanding of conversion. Rather, baptism was seen as regenerating the child and providing entry for the infant into the Catholic Church. The church then shepherded the person's soul throughout his or her life, primarily through the administration of the seven sacraments.

In other words, the infusion of grace at baptism did not give eternal security. It was instead the start of a journey. Grace covered the guilt of sin, but there remained a punishment for sins that must be removed.[6] For the remainder of one's life, the Christian's journey involved confession of sins and performing good works. The goal of these works, again, was not to save oneself but to maintain the state of grace given in baptism. Just as a precious work of art might be ruined by neglect, so, too, could a Christian ruin his or her salvation through repetitive and unrepentant acts of sin.[7] On the other hand, for those who strove to embrace the sacraments, the grace of the church was said to renew them in the grace of their baptism. Christians, of course, still struggled with sin, but these sins were dealt with first by confession to a priest and then by acts of penance—including giving alms to the poor, saying ritual prayers, making pilgrimages, and performing other good works. If sins were left unconfessed or if there was penance still left to perform at death, then these were believed to be worked off in purgatory (often seen as the final penance). After this final purgation, the soul entered heaven, where one awaited the resurrection.

Protestants often claim that Catholicism teaches *salvation by works*—by which is meant a form of Pelagianism or works righteousness. These claims are not entirely wrong. Some expressions of medieval piety, such as extreme

---

6. This was a crucial distinction in medieval theology, not always understood today, especially by Protestants. In medieval teaching, temporal punishment remained even when guilt was removed. For a discussion of this, see Alister E. McGrath, *Reformation Thought: An Introduction*, 4th ed. (Oxford: Wiley-Blackwell, 2012), 115–40.

7. Two illustrations were common in the medieval period to make this point: a gold coin (infused grace) that was tarnished and destroyed, and a spark of faith (infused grace) that winked out when it was not maintained.

acts of asceticism, could approach the point of works righteousness. We noted in our previous chapter, for example, how the Fourth Lateran Council seemed to teach this very notion of works righteousness. The doctrine of penance also rested on the notion of punishment for sin, and at times there was too much attention to the punishment. Too much talk of punishment and reward often drowned out any teaching on grace. So in a few cases, the medieval practice of penance resembled Pelagianism, in which the grace of God merely empowered believers to achieve their own redemption.

Nevertheless, the medieval view of grace and works, as normally practiced, did not constitute works righteousness per se, at least not in the same sense that Pelagius was reputed to have taught.[8] Instead, the system implied the believer's cooperation with grace, leading to salvation. To put it another way, the medieval Catholic system taught that one *entered* by the grace of baptism, but *remained* by both grace and good works. Both halves of this assertion were rejected by nearly all Protestants, although Luther retained something close to baptismal regeneration. Much Protestant rhetoric insists that the Reformers rejected the Catholic faith largely because it taught salvation by works. But in actual Catholic teaching, at least the initial grace of salvation came in baptism, apart from any work or even faith in the infant. This idea of the infusion of grace rested, in part, on the teachings of Augustine, who claimed that grace must first come to the soul for renewal. The medieval church tied this Augustinian concept exclusively to baptism, and in this way the church claimed to have successfully avoided Pelagianism. Good works and penance were said to be a result of grace, even if they were required for Christians. The Catholic Church, therefore, often referred to the ongoing Christian life—penances, confessions, and purgatory included—as a *life of grace*. For medieval Christians, grace was freely given in baptism but also had to be utilized by Christians to perform good works.

The medieval language of penance and good works shaped the grammar of the Reformation. Luther, for example, claimed that the Catholic Church taught salvation by works. By this he meant that the teachings and practice of the medieval church *amounted to* salvation by works, even though he was aware that Catholics described this life as one of grace. For Luther, one could fall into the trap of teaching what amounted to salvation by works even if one were not overtly proclaiming works salvation. Luther and the Reformers contended that, although Catholics claimed that salvation rested on grace, the

---

8. Pelagianism rests on the notion that one must not only perform good works but also perform them by one's own strength of will. Virtually no Christians taught anything close to this after the condemnation of Pelagianism, and few besides Pelagius did in his day, if even he did so himself. For our discussion of Pelagius, see chap. 9.

practice of the church actually grounded Christian life in works of the law. This meant that the Reformation debate on justification was far more subtle than a simple dispute about grace versus works. The Protestant contention was that to *add* works to grace—to make them necessary for salvation—always resulted in a form of legalism. Luther, especially, insisted that even when one used the language of grace and forgiveness, there would always be the possibility of smuggling in works righteousness. We will write more on this in the next chapter.

For now, it is enough to notice the practice of the medieval church. Christians were said to have received grace in baptism. That grace, however, had to be maintained inwardly, through acts of charity and love. Indeed, as we will see in chapter 16, the Council of Trent ultimately asserted that we are justified by "faith working itself out in love."[9] Not a few Protestants today have read this and wondered why this was a problem for the Reformers. But Trent's language was meant to enshrine the medieval practice of faith with good works, not to offer a newer understanding of faith and works as twin gifts from God. For Catholic believers, sin must be handled through penance and the sacraments, and where the sinner lacked time or the means to perform such penance, purgatory would be the final stage of the journey before heaven. For those who neglected their baptism entirely, the end would be condemnation.

The Catholic Church by Luther's day, however, found that this tension between grace and works resulted in some confusion. For example, it was unclear what constituted *enough* works of love to give Christians assurance of their salvation. Could one perform penance merely out of duty, or did one have to be truly sorry for sin? Since the threat of purgatory loomed, at what point was one actually contrite instead of merely being afraid of punishment? Anyone with children knows the difference between a genuine apology and one said through gritted teeth!

These issues were compounded by the fact that the monastic life—whose influence extended far beyond monasticism in the ancient church—was said to be the ultimate life of penance. Those who entered the monastery often did so believing that their life of penance was superior to that of laypeople. Not a few Catholics assumed, therefore, that the life of a layperson was an inferior journey that placed one in danger of losing the grace of baptism. Even when medieval theologians attempted to lighten the burden of penance by stressing grace over works, the penalty always remained. Indeed, Luther

9. Norman P. Tanner, ed., *Decrees of the Ecumenical Councils*, vol. 2, *Trent to Vatican II* (Washington, DC: Georgetown University Press, 1990), 674. Also in *CCFCT* 2:830.

chose to enter a monastery for this very reason: he hoped that it would give him assurance. According to the teachings of the medieval church, he was not wrong in pursuing monastic life to maintain his salvation.

Luther's Road to Reformation

Luther's criticism of the Catholic Church was more than merely intellectual. As a monk, he felt the full weight of his guilt, and he ultimately decided that the system did not rest on the New Testament's teachings about grace and salvation. The explosion of the wider Reformation, as non-Lutherans formed their own Protestant churches, reveals that Luther was not the only one who saw this problem. If the medieval system had a single glaring weakness, it was the question of security: Did one need to perform a certain number of good works to maintain the grace of baptism? On this question, Luther's overwhelming consciousness of his own guilt became an example of what could go wrong if one took penance with deadly seriousness.

In the years leading up to the Reformation, Luther famously experienced a great deal of anxiety while serving as an Augustinian monk, first in Erfurt and then later in Wittenberg. He entered the monastery in July 1505, after completing his preparation for law school. That summer he traveled home to visit family and friends, but on the way back to Erfurt he was caught in a violent thunderstorm—a bad omen by medieval standards, since a sudden death was viewed as a judgment of God. Luther was scared enough that he vowed to St. Anne to become a monk.[10] His vow was more than a cry for safety. It was a cry of anguish about the state of his soul, and his response was appropriate for the late medieval era. He wondered whether he was taking his obedience to Christ seriously enough by living as a simple layman. The Catholic Church encouraged those who struggled with anxiety to consider the monastic life if they had the strength of will, since the assumption was that monks and nuns sacrificed an ordinary life to perform an incredible work of spiritual heroism. The life of a monk was focused on prayer, penance, and good works—just the thing for those who needed to pursue holiness.[11]

In the monastery, however, Luther continued to feel unchanged, spiritually cold. The ordinary monastic practices did not work for him. He confessed

10. On Luther's early life and his entering the monastery, see the very enjoyable recent biography by Lyndal Roper, *Martin Luther: Renegade and Prophet* (New York: Random House, 2016).

11. A complexity not appreciated today is the inability of some to get to confession. Those living in rural areas, or even those who worked beyond a short distance from a church, were often unable to confess regularly.

frequently, to the point of extremism, hoping in vain to take his penance seriously enough to satisfy his longing for assurance. On one occasion, he finished a lengthy confession and then remembered other sins on the way back to his cell, and so he dashed back to his confessor to continue the session.[12]

In the end, the breakthrough in Luther's life came because of the expansion of his professional career. Despite his troubles, Luther was an accomplished scholar and a budding leader in the monastic order.[13] In 1512, he earned his doctoral degree and soon began lecturing on the Bible. As his personal crisis of faith reached a boiling point, Luther underwent what he later called his "tower experience"—what scholars today call his reformation breakthrough.[14] We do not know when the breakthrough occurred (he had experienced it at least by 1515), but we do know that it involved a theological upheaval. Luther no longer saw works of penance—or any good works—as a path to eternal security. The grace that came by faith, Luther later explained, was itself the security one needed, since it was not *infused* into the Christian at baptism but counted as the believer's by *imputation*. This was overtly legal or forensic language, in which the believer was *declared* free of all guilt and punishment based only on the work of Christ. Nothing was infused into the soul, and so nothing needed to be maintained. Salvation belonged to the Christian not by cooperation, but merely as a gift. In fact, at heart, the contrast between Catholic and Protestant teaching on salvation can be epitomized in these two words: "infused" and "imputed."

Luther's Break with the Catholic Church

Armed with his new breakthrough, Luther did . . . nothing. At least, he did nothing that showed he wanted a reformation, and he certainly did not believe that his theology made him a heretic. We must not let our understanding of the later Luther—the fiery Protestant thundering from Wittenberg—cloud our judgment of his attitude at this point in his life. After his breakthrough, he simply believed that the changes were for the improvement of his own soul. But he also believed that he was still a good Catholic. How could this be?

12. Many myths and legends are told of these years, although we have less solid material than one might think. On this portion of Luther's life, see Franz Posset, *The Real Luther: A Friar at Erfurt and Wittenberg* (St. Louis: Concordia, 2011). Another good resource for separating fact from myth is Richard Rex, *The Making of Martin Luther* (Princeton: Princeton University Press, 2017).

13. Luther is sometimes misremembered as a bumpkin, when in fact he was well educated.

14. On this breakthrough, see Alister E. McGrath, *Luther's Theology of the Cross: Martin Luther's Theological Breakthrough* (Oxford: Wiley-Blackwell, 1991).

Like many who have experienced a profound change in their personal lives, Luther was relatively unaware of all the implications of his break-through. He may not have had the language to describe this change, and he does not seem to have shared his experience with many people. Indeed, were it not for the controversy over indulgences in 1517, there is no telling whether Luther ever would have broken with the Catholic Church. Instead, the things occupying his mind at this early point were the *abuses* involved with the sale of indulgences—a relatively new practice in the medieval church that further complicated the practice of penance. Theology professors were known for taking public stands against abuse. On the issue of the sale of indulgences, many in Europe—including many who remained Catholic after the Reformation began—found indulgence sales to be a sleazy and corrupt practice.[15]

The practice of penance in Luther's day was not fully defined by the church, but the church knew that there was a problem with anxiety—or at least a general fear of purgatory—among lay Catholics. After confession, penances would be assigned, but since the requirement was merely one confession a year, people who actually confessed according to this pattern might feel that the number of sins to confess—or penances to be performed—was overwhelming. Without penance, though, would come more time in purgatory. And for many, the years amassed for punishment in the afterlife seemed to grow and grow. Indulgences were the answer to this problem. The idea behind an indulgence was not that one would prepurchase the right to sin but that one would, by indulgence money, fund the full-time prayers and good works of priests and monks. The system, in a sense, was designed to be communal: those who prayed were supported by alms, and those who gave alms were supported by receiving a reduction of time in purgatory, based on the additional prayers of those who served the church.

We should be able to see the potential for abuse in the indulgence system. Even though technically one was giving alms, it was hard to avoid the impression that one was actually paying to get a reduction of time in purgatory—making assurance of salvation appear to be a transaction. Moreover, there were no re-ported cases of contrite persons receiving indulgences during this time without money. Put simply, a donation was not a donation if it was required, even if the intention was to encourage generous giving by laity. And finally, the opulence of the church at the time also gave the impression that the church was fleecing the flock. For anyone willing to manipulate the emotions of laypeople, the

---

15. One example is Erasmus, who wanted a simple and biblical faith while remaining Catho-lic. See Richard L. DeMolen, *The Spirituality of Erasmus of Rotterdam*, Bibliotheca Human-istica et Reformatica 40 (Nieuwkoop: De Graaf, 1987).

Johann Tetzel, seller of indulgences

sale of indulgences could be quite lucrative.[16]

The most egregious example of an indulgence abuser was Johann Tetzel (1465–1519), who so upset Luther that he sparked the writing of the Ninety-Five Theses. But the authorization of the sale, in fact, came from Pope Leo X and Archbishop Albrecht von Brandenburg. Leo had a vision to rebuild St. Peter's Basilica,[17] Albrecht owed a lot of money, and both were nearly broke. Leo's vision for a grander basilica was suspect in the eyes of many because it was based largely on the ideals of the Renaissance papacy—luxury and polish instead of frugality. Albrecht's motivations were even more suspect, since he owed a great deal of money after purchasing his archbishopric (a practice outlawed by the church, but nevertheless very common at this time and rarely punished).

Because both Leo and Albrecht needed money, their solution was to offer a jubilee sale of indulgences. The irony here is important, because the decree was given in 1513—almost the exact year of Luther's breakthrough. Of course, no one knew who Luther was at the time. Leo and Albrecht agreed to split the profits, and Tetzel and others were hired to conduct the sale. The way Tetzel carried out the sale certainly was one of the worst abuses in the Middle Ages. He preached ruthlessly about the pain that one would suffer in purgatory—twisting the knife to squeeze money out of his audience. He would shriek from the pulpit about loved ones sobbing from the torment they endured. And then the jingle would come, the offer of hope: "As soon as a

16. The sale of indulgences—but not indulgences themselves—was outlawed at the Council of Trent. On this, see chap. 16.

17. Note that the name of the basilica is St. Peter's, although that church is often popularly called the Vatican. Technically, the Vatican or Vatican City is its own country, not a part of Italy or Rome, even though it is located within Rome geographically. It issues currency and functions in many other ways as a nation. St. Peter's Basilica is in Vatican City, which means, ironically, that technically it is not in modern Rome!

coin in the coffer rings, a soul from purgatory springs." Local money was collected, and then he and his troupe would set off for another city.

It's a wonder Tetzel made it through multiple cities alive. This type of behavior was despised by many in the church who desired internal reform.[18] What provoked the Reformation, however, was the fact that the abusive sale of indulgences accentuated Luther's new conviction about the free grace of the gospel. In other words, Luther's *personal* breakthrough drove him to voice *public* concerns about the abuse of indulgence sales. The Ninety-Five Theses, then, were only a partial expression of the change that Luther had experienced, which explains why Luther was not altogether clear about what he wanted in the Ninety-Five Theses. The theses themselves showed several different tones of voice—on the one hand, Luther posturing as a defender of the pope and traditional practices; on the other hand, Luther condemning any attempt to gain security through penance or indulgences. A few of the theses continued even to support good works, but it was Luther's language condemning indulgences and good works that drew the attention of church leaders.

After the Ninety-Five Theses were translated into German, the Catholic Church chose to make an example of Luther. He was an unknown monk teaching at a new university in Wittenberg, so he seemed an easy target. Over the next two years, Luther was asked to defend himself publicly and privately, and these opportunities to defend himself became the spur that drove Luther to reveal his deeper conflict with the church.[19] Luther refused to recant, and so in 1520 he was excommunicated and handed over to the emperor Charles V to be tried as a heretic.[20] At his trial before the emperor, Luther concluded with perhaps his most famous statement: "Unless I am convinced by proofs from Scriptures or by plain and clear reasons and arguments, I cannot and will not recant anything, for to go against conscience is neither right nor safe. [Here I stand, I can do no other.] God help me. Amen."[21] For his obstinacy, Luther was condemned to die, although Charles abided by his word and allowed Luther to leave unharmed at this point.

18. During the same indulgence sale, for example, Zwingli threatened bodily harm to the hawker traveling through Swiss lands.

19. The slow journey to schism is told in Scott H. Hendrix, *Luther and the Papacy: Stages in a Reformation Conflict* (Philadelphia: Fortress, 1981).

20. The process of executing heretics always followed this pattern: the church first excommunicated, then handed over to the political establishment the role of enforcing capital punishment for heresy.

21. Scholars are uncertain whether the famous phrase "Here I stand, I can do no other" is authentic, since it was inserted into the story only later. On this issue, most believe that he did not use the phrase "Here I stand." See Heiko Oberman, *Luther: Man between God and the Devil*, trans. Eileen Walliser-Schwarzbart (New Haven: Yale University Press, 1989), 39.

Major cities of Lutheran Reformation in Germany

He lived the remainder of his life as an outlaw. Now, though, Luther had fully broken with the church, and he set himself to the long process of reformation.

The Other Reformations

Martin Luther is a unique figure in history. He almost embodies the struggle for the Reformation, and it is rare to find a personal story so entwined with history. Indeed, his struggle to come to grips with sin and grace and his heroism in front of Charles V were a microcosm of the struggle of all those who left the Catholic Church. Still, Luther was not the Protestant pope. For many, he was only the catalyst that inspired them to separate from Rome. Almost immediately, though, it became clear that not everyone who agreed with Luther's views on justification and papal corruption shared his view on the remedy for these problems. Two reformation movements sprang up immediately that remained independent of the Lutheran fold, while nevertheless fitting under the umbrella of Protestantism.[22]

22. In the early decades of the Reformation, the name "Protestant" was often a synonym for "Lutheran" and did not refer to the other reform movements. Only later did all reform movements come to share the name "Protestant."

The first was the movement of the Reformed communities. Just over a year after Luther's writing of the Ninety-Five Theses, the city of Zürich began its own reforms under the leadership of Zwingli. In many ways, Zürich and Wittenberg should have been united: both were part of the imperial domains, both German-speaking, and both led by strong leaders. The relationship between Luther and Zwingli quickly broke down, however, and the hope of any Protestant union died with Zwingli on the battlefield in 1531. We will have more to write on this in the next chapter.

The Reformed movement has, in English-speaking churches, often been dubbed Calvinism. This is a misnomer, since the movement began in 1518, when Calvin himself was only nine years old. But we should not see Zwingli as the true founder of the Reformed movement either, as if he were some counterpart to Luther. In the case of Lutheranism, it is true that Luther's teachings became the standard of nearly every Lutheran church ever since, and even confessions written for Lutherans always base their theology on Luther's. In the case of the Reformed movement, however, there was no single voice that dominated the entire movement, and without a single voice, there was no single city or confession that came to dominate Reformed churches either.

During the sixteenth century, the various Reformed leaders saw themselves as a brotherly band, linked by two distinctive features. The first was that they wanted to be on friendly terms with Lutherans. At least at first, Reformed communities saw their movement as an internal critique of Lutheranism. The Reformed movement did not see itself as fully in opposition to Lutheranism—as, say, the Anabaptist movement saw itself in opposition to much of Protestantism. Nevertheless, there was a strained relationship between Reformed and Lutheran communities. The worst relationship was always between Wittenberg and Zürich—first with Zwingli and, after his death, with his successor, Heinrich Bullinger. Zürichers almost never trusted Lutherans—or those who got too close to Lutherans or their ideas—but this suspicion was not shared by other Reformed leaders. Calvin and his mentor, Martin Bucer, for example, were almost always willing to make another attempt to bridge the Lutheran and Reformed sides.

The generally friendly posture toward Lutheranism was shown by the fact that no major public work by a Reformed theologian criticized Luther directly. There was a respectful public silence,[23] although we know from the letters of the Reformed leaders that they were deeply troubled by his views on the

---

23. Another way Reformed theologians critiqued Lutheranism was by avoiding squaring up against Luther himself and instead attacking another Lutheran. Calvin, for example, attacked several Lutheran teachings in the *Institutes*, and often men such as Osiander, but never Luther himself.

sacraments. In most Reformed confessions, then, there was a willful yet respectful attempt to distance Reformed thought from Lutheran confessions, yet an equally important desire to stress the same points as Luther on justification.

The second distinctive feature was the issues that the Reformed church rejected in Lutheran confessions: the language of eating the physical body and blood of Christ in the Lord's Supper and the question of the Third Use of the Law (discussed more in chaps. 14 and 15). The issue of the sacraments, in fact, was the single most important distinction between Lutheran and Reformed churches for most of Protestant history. This can appear strange to modern Christians, since few today openly debate the presence of Christ in the sacrament. But for Reformed and Lutherans this was a groundwork issue, and Luther himself made it clear that he would brook no nonsense when it came to anyone denying his view of the Lord's Supper. Regarding the Third Use of the Law, Lutheran confessions rejected the moral use of the law for holiness and sanctification, while nearly all Reformed confessions embraced this use.

The story of Anabaptists, however, involves a more serious rupture with both Lutheranism and Reformed churches. Indeed, for most of their history Anabaptist communities rejected the name "Protestant." As we will see in the next chapter, there is a challenge in defining Anabaptist communities, but for now it must be clear that Anabaptists were almost immediately aware of their differences with Luther, especially on issues where they believed Luther did not go far enough in throwing out Catholic practices. As a result, most Anabaptist confessions went to great lengths to explain those areas where they did not agree with Lutheranism.

Conclusions

The Reformation was a crisis in Europe that led not merely to a break with Rome, but to further schism as well. The point that we must understand now, before we turn to the Protestant confessions themselves, is the amount of diversity that existed *from the beginning* of the Reformation. It can be easy to assume that Protestantism was harmonious in its early years—that denominations and divisions were a later invention. But one of the earliest attempts to create a new confession—the Marburg Colloquy in 1529—ended in failure. Luther and Zwingli met face to face, and yet their desire for unity hit a brick wall.

The way to understand this feature is to realize the unique way Protestants approach theology and confessions. One way to see the instinct of the

Reformers is to note how they lead with justification by faith—that is, with the solution Luther discovered in the monastery, that Christ's work alone pays the guilt and punishment of all sins. It is striking how little Protestant traditions differ on this subject. However, the application of this truth required more than merely the message of salvation. How must Christians live in this faith, how must they worship? That problem, coupled with the assumption that the Catholic Church had corrupted biblical faith, meant that the answers for many other confessional issues—especially sacraments and liturgy—became contentious for Protestants as soon as the Reformation began. These subjects, as we will see in our next chapter, made up the bulk of early confessions.

14

Early Protestant Confessions

The leaders of the early Reformation created many confessions, more than were produced in any other period in church history until the rise of global confessions in the modern church. Given the sheer number of Protestant confessions, it is reasonable to expect that they would come in various shapes and sizes, from quick summaries (almost bullet points) to longer, more careful sets of articles that shaped a church community from top to bottom.[1] Individual theologians wrote some; others were written by an appointed group of theologians. Some confessions gave authority to enforce their standards to a political entity, while other confessions had no more authority than the pledge of the community to uphold the standards.

In this chapter we focus on the earliest years of the Reformation, from the explosive reforms under Martin Luther to the wider Reformation that spilled out into other parts of Europe. The period covered in this chapter—1520–35, from Luther's trial to just prior to the publication of the first edition of Calvin's *Institutes*—is brief. The rationale for treating such a brief period is twofold. First, Calvin is always considered part of the "second generation" of the Reformation, and more importantly, by the time Calvin published the first edition of his *Institutes*, the hope of any unity between Reformed and

---

1. We avoid the word "denomination" at this point, since that word was not used at the time of the Reformation, and many of the features that later defined a denomination in the modern sense (e.g., several varieties of the same tradition) were not yet present.

Lutheran churches had all but vanished.[2] The last serious attempt to bridge this confessional divide occurred in 1536 with the Wittenberg Concord (to be discussed later in this chapter), spearheaded by Martin Bucer, who later mentored Calvin after his early failure in Geneva.[3] The second reason for treating such a brief period in this chapter is that the first fifteen years of the Reformation saw the splitting of Lutheran, Reformed, and Anabaptist communities into different confessions. Thus, looking at these crucial early years as a unit is important to help us understand the later periods.

Protestant Confessional Categories

Confessions were most often designed as boundary markers—to keep out heretical wolves—though some were used to train children in the faith. In the early years of the Reformation, Protestants wrote most of their confessions to prove that they were not heretics, especially when they were being persecuted. A confessional apology, at times, was written by individual representatives of a movement, such as Balthasar Hubmaier's confession during his trial. Moreover, some communities such as Anglicans wrote one confession (or a small number of confessions) and stopped, while others such as Reformed churches had almost limitless energy to write confessions. Put simply, there was no single model regarding the format and purpose of Protestant confessions.

Saying that early Protestant confessions were not identical is not to say that they lacked harmony. Protestants differed on issues such as the sacraments, the uses of the law, and the nature of Christian society, but such differences did not mean that they created entirely different theological standards. By far the most exceptional were Anabaptist confessions, which were almost always written as a critique of the magisterial Reformation, and which at times even offered a somewhat different understanding of sanctification.[4] In general, though, confessions emphasized a shared identity outside the Catholic faith. While

2. On Calvin's role in context, especially his relationship to the first-generation Reformers, the best study is Bruce Gordon, *Calvin* (New Haven: Yale University Press, 2009).

3. On Bucer, see Martin Greschat, *Martin Bucer: A Reformer and His Times* (Louisville: Westminster John Knox, 2004); David Wright, *Martin Bucer: Reforming Church and Community* (Cambridge: Cambridge University Press, 2002). For an authoritative short biography, see David C. Steinmetz, *Reformers in the Wings: From Geiler von Kaysersberg to Theodore Beza*, 2nd ed. (Oxford: Oxford University Press, 2002), 85–92.

4. "Magisterial Reformation" is a phrase used by scholars to indicate those Protestant communities that united, some more than others, with political authority to enforce change. Anabaptists universally rejected this reliance on the magistrate, and thus they rejected the "magisterial Reformation" as well. The two best surveys that cover these movements and their connections to one another are Diarmaid MacCulloch, *The Reformation: A History* (New York: Penguin,

all Protestants affirmed many of the same points, they almost always stressed the distinctive issues that formed their individual movement's identity.

At this point, it will be helpful to categorize the various forms of Protestant confessions to be covered in this chapter and the subsequent ones. These categories are not necessarily meant to be rigid, but rather indicate the different needs that created each confession. In general, we can identify three categories:

1. *Confessions of Orthodoxy.* These confessions were most often written with the intention of demonstrating the orthodoxy of Protestantism, and in most cases they were written to Catholic rulers. The tone of these confessions often was irenic, as the authors focused on affirming creedal views of the Trinity, Christology, and other norms of the church. They often tended to mute overt criticism of the Catholic Church in order to avoid further controversy, instead focusing on major Protestant doctrines. At times, these confessions even downplayed the major issues of contention between Catholics and Protestants, without denying these differences. The goal of these confessions was to come to some agreement that might halt persecution of Protestants.

2. *Confessions of Community.* These confessions were written for specific churches or families. They were more critical of the Catholic Church, but they also tended to focus on things such as worship, liturgy, Christian living, and other day-to-day realities of being a Protestant community. As such, these confessions focused on laity or new pastors, usually done in a question-and-answer format. Anabaptists, for example, emphasized in their confessions the unique features of their community—especially the role of excommunication—over against magisterial Protestants. At times, these confessions were even written as catechisms, though their use was so widespread that they served as confessions.

3. *Confessions of Controversy.* These confessions attempted to resolve problems that arose, either internally or by rejecting the views of another Protestant community. Early Reformed confessions, for example, focused on creating unity together on the presence of Christ in the Lord's Supper—not because this was all that defined them, but because this set them over against Lutherans. The Formula of Concord, too, fixated on issues that divided Lutherans. These confessions, however, rarely attempted to address more than a single doctrine or set of doctrines.

2005); Carlos M. N. Eire, *Reformations: The Early Modern World, 1450–1650* (New Haven: Yale University Press, 2016).

These three categories are meant to help us see how confessions emerged in the Reformation. We will find that some confessions look strange, but that strangeness may come from our expecting only one type of confession (namely, a longer confession that covers most doctrines). It may be tempting to suggest that a confession failed because it did not address a certain topic, or it gave only passing comment to older, creedal formulas. But this would be fair only in those cases where a confession attempted to address all major doctrines. Thus, as we assess the contents of a confession, we must pay close attention to the reason why it was written.

The Earliest Protestant Confessions

The earliest confessions came from the three initial Protestant branches: Lutheran, Reformed, and Anabaptist. During the earliest years of the Reformation, the Reformers hardly had time to write any confessions. Most focused instead on the immediate needs of their churches, others on simply staying alive. But within a decade, in most areas—including Wittenberg—the Reformers realized the need for confessions, due to problems that began to destabilize their churches. Thus, the earliest confessions appeared in the late 1520s or early 1530s, and they were often written quickly to address an immediate concern.

From the start, the most coherent body of confessions came from the Lutheran camp. Luther played a central role in the creation of each of the early Lutheran confessions, so their message was always similar.[5] By contrast, Reformed confessions were written in two major cities in the Swiss regions, Zürich and Bern, and they were influenced by Huldrych Zwingli, but never determined by him exclusively.[6]

Zwingli wrote the first Protestant confession.[7] As we saw in the last chapter, Luther sparked the Reformation, but almost immediately it was clear that he would hold sway only over the churches in the empire. (Remember again that the Holy Roman Empire comprised little more than modern

---

5. In addition to CCFCT, see Charles P. Arand and Robert Kolb, *The Lutheran Confessions: History and Theology of The Book of Concord* (Minneapolis: Fortress, 2012).

6. After the first generation, Reformed confessions sprouted up in nearly every country touched by Protestantism. Scholars thus describe Reformed confessions as multivalent. For a good study of the various confessions, see Jan Rohls, *Reformed Confessions: Theology from Zurich to Barmen*, trans. John Hoffmeyer, Columbia Series in Reformed Theology (Louisville: Westminster John Knox, 1998).

7. On Zwingli's life and thought, see W. P. Stephens, *The Theology of Huldrych Zwingli* (Oxford: Clarendon, 1988); Ulrich Gäbler, *Huldrych Zwingli: His Life and Work*, trans. Ruth C. L. Gritsch (Philadelphia: Fortress, 1986).

Portrait of the Zürich Reformer
Huldrych Zwingli by Hans Asper

Germany, not the whole of Europe.) Zwingli arrived in Zürich in 1519 after years pursuing the life of a humanist. He had come to take up the position of "public pastor" (*Leutpriestertum*),[8] which made him responsible for the preaching at the Grossmünster, the largest and most important church in Zürich. Though only in his thirties, Zwingli had earned a reputation as a Reformer, having worked to stifle the sale of indulgences in Swiss cities at almost the same time Luther wrote the Ninety-Five Theses. Zwingli went even further than Luther, threatening violence on an indulgence salesman if he ever set foot in Zürich. In the sixteenth century, the Swiss were known as a warrior people, and one did not take such threats lightly.[9] The indulgence salesman quickly left.

Zwingli was established at Zürich on January 1, 1519, and he soon revealed his penchant for breaking with tradition. In his first series of sermons, he threw out the lectionary (a pattern in which preselected texts were used

8. There was controversy about this appointment, since it was revealed that Zwingli had had an affair in Glarus and Einsiedeln before coming to Zürich. He was fortunate, however, since the other candidate had an equally sordid past.

9. Students often note that the pope today is still protected by the Swiss Guard—a relationship that extends back to the sixteenth century.

each week—the lectionary is still used today in liturgical churches). Instead, Zwingli preached straight through the Gospel of Matthew.[10] His brand of preaching quickly became a draw for local crowds, and the message fittingly became more reformist, especially after Luther sparked his reformation in Wittenberg. Before long—and after a public event in which Zwingli and his friends broke Lent by eating sausages—the city council was willing to hear arguments for the Reformation.[11]

In his preaching, Zwingli focused primarily on the issue of idolatry in worship—a controversial issue then and now in Reformed circles, but one that already marked the difference between Zwingli and Luther.[12] Luther, for example, feared the problem of idolatry only insofar as certain practices (such as praying to saints for help) obscured the doctrine of justification by faith. He was more concerned to preach the Reformation message than to cleanse churches of statues, art, and relics.[13] In 1521, when zeal turned to mob violence, Luther sided against the mob's decision to destroy church property. "Preach the gospel," said Luther, "and the statues will eventually lose their appeal." Zwingli, in contrast, saw images and art as harmful to lay Christians and was more zealous to see an end to idolatry.[14] For Zwingli, leaving images and traditional worship in place did more than merely delay their inevitable removal once people grew tired of them. Images inspired further idolatry and clouded the judgment of Christians, and permitting them was a violation of the clear commandment of God.

The first confessional document of the Reformation, then, was a set of sixty-seven theses, written by Zwingli in 1523, and submitted to the Zürich council. The focus was almost entirely on worship, or more specifically on the authority of the Bible instead of tradition to shape worship. The council members agreed to hear the complaint, making it clear from the start that they were the final authority to decide the matter. A Catholic priest from a neighboring city at first agreed to come and argue against Zwingli, but when he arrived on January 27, 1523, and heard that the council would hear arguments only from the Bible, he refused to participate. Zwingli stood alone

10. A pattern referred to as *lectio continua*, or continuous preaching through a book.

11. Keeping the Lenten fast was mandated by public law. Zwingli's friends who ate meat were imprisoned, although Zwingli preached against their imprisonment, and they were soon released.

12. The best study on Zwingli's iconoclasm and the wider effects of this movement is Carlos M. N. Eire, *War against the Idols: The Reformation of Worship from Erasmus to Calvin* (Cambridge: Cambridge University Press, 1989).

13. See Charles Garside, *Zwingli and the Arts*, Yale Historical Publications 83 (New Haven: Yale University Press, 1966).

14. It should be noted that Zwingli and others were ambiguous about art *outside* worship.

Iconoclasm in Zürich as shown in the book *Panorama de la Renaissance* by Margaret Aston

before the city council in an event today known as the First Disputation of Zürich, and he argued his case for the Reformation.[15] After Zwingli finished, the city council wasted no time, and their decision was unanimous: Zürich would break with the Catholic Church.

The Sixty-Seven Articles emphasized two main points: worship could be based only on the Bible, and most practices authorized by the Catholic Church were repugnant to the gospel. The arguments for biblical worship were unique, since Zwingli did not allow for much freedom of choice on indifferent matters. Zwingli wanted most of the church's practices thrown out in favor of a simple liturgy.[16] The articles ended with the type of vigorous style Zwingli became known for: "Let no one undertake here to argue with sophistry or human foolishness, but come to the Scriptures to accept them as the judge."[17]

Zwingli opened his argument by stressing that the Scriptures were the only authority inspired by God (*theopneustos*), although he was ready to admit

15. On the First Disputation and its wider significance for the Reformation, see Heiko Oberman, *Masters of the Reformation: The Emergence of a New Intellectual Climate in Europe*, trans. Dennis Martin (Cambridge: Cambridge University Press, 1981), 187–239.

16. On Zwingli's approach to worship reform, see Philip Benedict, *Christ's Churches Purely Reformed: A Social History of Calvinism* (New Haven: Yale University Press, 2004), 19–31.

17. CCFCT 2:214. This section is not in James T. Dennison, ed., *Reformed Confessions of the 16th and 17th Centuries in English Translation*, 4 vols. (Grand Rapids: Reformation Heritage Books, 2008–10).

that even his own interpretation was open to criticism: "I am ready to be instructed and corrected, but only from . . . Scripture."[18] The argument from there proceeded in a way identical to the Lutheran message: Christ alone is the savior of humankind; his righteousness is all that is needed, not human works; and the church is not the magisterium in Rome but rather the body united under its head, Jesus Christ. This was summed up with a simple message of Protestantism: "For belief in the gospel constitutes our salvation, and unbelief, our damnation."[19]

Most of the remaining points focused on differences between Protestant and Catholic practice. Indulgences, the Mass, prayers to saints, medieval penance, celibacy, and others—all were cited as examples of going beyond the Bible. Zwingli's confession, however, was unique in its rationale for rejecting Catholic practice. At several key junctures Zwingli mentioned the issue of using creation to worship God: Zwingli shared Luther's hatred for these practices, but Zwingli's position was based more on the conviction that God was separate from creation. Indeed, for Zwingli, creation itself almost by its nature was incapable of communicating spiritual benefits. The problem was not merely one of sin but of using creation to worship the Creator. Indeed, the next thesis stated that confession to another human—"to a priest or to a neighbor"—was unhelpful beyond friendly counseling.[20] One must confess to God directly, not through another human. Zwingli added that the ordination of a priest did nothing more than install him to an office; no connection between God's work and the priest's must be allowed.

The tension between Zwingli and Luther became more obvious when the two met at Marburg in 1529 (discussed later in this chapter), but even now we should note the anxiety that Zwingli had about the claim that a connection between God and creation led to spiritual benefit. Zwingli had a zeal to maintain a consistent ontological separation between heaven and earth: the physical was of no benefit to the spiritual, and vice versa.[21] Zwingli, of course, did not consider the physical creation to be evil (despite possible fears that his ideas could lead to Gnosticism), but his concern was to keep these categories separate to avoid idolatry.

After his success, Zwingli's influence spread to other cities in the Swiss regions. Indeed, if he had not died in 1531, Zwingli might have become as influential a Reformer over Swiss churches as Luther was over Germany. Even in the 1520s, Zwingli's stance on worship and idolatry won him adherents in

18. Dennison, *Reformed Confessions*, 1:2. Also in CCFCT 2:209.
19. Dennison, *Reformed Confessions*, 1:4. Also in CCFCT 2:210.
20. Dennison, *Reformed Confessions*, 1:7. Also in CCFCT 2:213.
21. This issue is dealt with in Stephens, *Theology of Huldrych Zwingli*, in the final two chapters.

important cities such as Bern. Two pastors there—Berchtold Haller (1492–1536) and Franz Kolb (ca. 1465–1535)—drafted ten thesis statements based on a revision of Zwingli's articles. Like Zürich, Bern put the Reformation on trial before the city council, and like Zürich, the council sided in favor of reform. The disputation occurred in 1528 and was attended personally by Zwingli, along with Bucer, Heinrich Bullinger, and other leaders of the growing Swiss Reformed community.

The Ten Theses of Bern signaled some of the issues that increasingly shaped Swiss Reformed theology. The statement covered the basic issues of justification by faith and the authority of the Bible alone in matters of faith and practice. However, the confession also sided with Zwingli against Luther's views on both the Lord's Supper and images in worship. The stance was not in direct opposition to Luther, but it did not share Luther's view that the Lord's Supper became the physical body and blood of Christ. We will look at the debate over the Lord's Supper later in this chapter, but for now it should be noted that the Ten Theses stated clearly, "It cannot be proved from the Biblical writings that the body and blood of Christ is essentially and corporeally received in the bread of the Eucharist."[22] On the subject of images, the confession was not quite as categorical, stating not that the images should always be rejected, but since "*they are a danger*, they should be abolished."[23] Perhaps this left room for sanctuary art and decorations that were not used for veneration, but it was more likely meant merely to keep angry mobs from taking worship reform into their own hands.

For Luther, the first and greatest need was not a confession to define the Lutheran church but catechisms to educate lay Christians, but he was not quick to write even catechetical texts. Between 1517 and 1525 Luther focused mostly on explaining his own position on grace and works, and then, after his trial at Worms in 1520, on contending with those who opposed him. He published three of his most important works in a single year, 1520: *On the Freedom of the Christian*; *The Babylonian Captivity of the Church*; and *Address to the German Nobility*.[24] After the trial at Worms, Luther spent most his energy working on the translation of the Bible into German and offering

22. Arthur C. Cochrane, ed., *Reformed Confessions of the Sixteenth Century* (Louisville: Westminster John Knox, 2003), 49.

23. Dennison, *Reformed Confessions*, 1:42 (emphasis added). Also in CCFCT 2:217.

24. On these important years for Luther, see Scott H. Hendrix, *Luther and the Papacy: Stages in a Reformation Conflict* (Philadelphia: Fortress, 1981); also Hendrix's more recent work, *Martin Luther: Visionary Reformer* (New Haven: Yale University Press, 2015). Also excellent are James M. Kittelson, *Luther the Reformer: The Story of the Man and His Career* (Minneapolis: Fortress, 2003); Lyndal Roper, *Martin Luther: Renegade and Prophet* (New York: Random House, 2017).

advice to Christians who had joined his movement. Letters and other publications poured out of Wartburg and Wittenberg, but not yet a confession.

By 1525, Luther had two additional targets in his sights. The first was the Anabaptists, since some had used Luther's name to start the Peasants' War in 1525.[25] The other was Erasmus, the famous humanist, who had come under fire for providing fodder for his followers who had embraced Protestantism. Frustrated with these accusations, Erasmus leapt into the struggle in 1524 and wrote a book, titled *On Free Will*, against Luther's understanding of original sin. Erasmus took the traditional position of most Catholic theologians, arguing against the view that our will is bound and unable to respond to God. He argued that this view made repentance and good works impossible and ruined Christian living. This work forever cemented Erasmus as an internal Catholic Reformer, much to the regret of his followers who had embraced Protestantism. Luther, however, responded with vigor in *The Bondage of the Will* (1525), in which he defended his position on the inability of sinners to accept the gospel without the activity of the Spirit.[26]

By the end of the 1520s, then, Luther had already published many works that explained and defended his reformation. So it was not until the publication of the *Large Catechism* and the *Small Catechism* (1529)—two of Luther's most important texts, still in use by many Lutheran bodies today[27]—that anything like a confession appeared. The year before their publication, Luther had toured churches in Saxony and Meissen, assessing the quality of reform in these areas. Luther found the state of affairs deplorable, especially among lay Christians, and he was shocked that progress had stalled after a decade of work. In both catechisms, then, Luther focused on ordinary Christian experience, and thus the language of both books showed how Luther translated complex theological issues into the language of the people. The difference between the two confessions probably was their use: the *Small Catechism* was brief enough to print on one sheet (almost like a theological blueprint), while the *Large Catechism* could be printed to include illustrations.

The preamble to the *Small Catechism* gave instructions on how they should be used: "the preacher should take the utmost care to avoid changes or variations in the text and wording." The issue here was not conformity but consis-

---

25. Luther's involvement with this war is covered in Hendrix, *Martin Luther*, 156–58, 163–65.

26. Both texts, along with a helpful preface, can be found in E. Gordon Rupp and Philip S. Watson, eds., *Luther and Erasmus: Free Will and Salvation*, Library of Christian Classics (Louisville: Westminster John Knox, 1969).

27. There are many modern-reader versions (including devotional editions) of both catechisms—for example, Timothy J. Wengert and Mary Jane Haemig, eds., *The Small Catechism, 1529: The Annotated Luther Study Edition* (Minneapolis: Fortress, 2017).

tency, as Luther allowed for variations in the wording from version to version, as long as people stuck to their version. Luther stressed not only the substance of the faith but also that the confession was to be memorized, so that a person might use it "year after year."[28] No one was to be compelled to accept the confessions, he reminded his readers—"you are not to make a law of this, as the pope has done"—though he wanted pastors to teach laypersons "how to distinguish between right and wrong according to the standards." Both catechisms, then, were to be used as a unit: progressing from the *Small Catechism* to the *Large Catechism*, to gain "a richer and fuller understanding."[29]

It is enough to look at the *Small Catechism* to get a sense of Luther's message. The structure rested on three main sections for memorization: the Ten Commandments, the Apostles' Creed, and the Lord's Prayer. Each was to be recited, and then the layperson was taken through a question or questions on each point. There was a Lutheran emphasis on grace and works throughout both catechisms. For example, the questions on the Apostles' Creed broke the points up into creation, redemption, and sanctification, with clear Lutheran positions expressed about the freedom of the Christian through grace. After proceeding through these memorized answers, Luther then included a series of questions on disputed issues for those who had recently come from the Catholic Church: questions on baptism, confession and absolution, and practices of the Mass. The catechism concluded with instructions for day-to-day Christian living, from morning and evening prayer to how to say grace at table.

The Separation of Zwingli and Luther

As we have seen, Luther and Zwingli shared many of the same principles that united Protestants against Rome: justification by faith alone, rejection of Catholic practices, and the exclusive authority of the Bible in matters of doctrine. Both were German-speakers and part of the Holy Roman Empire (though many Swiss regions had gained a measure of independence in their own affairs). It seemed reasonable to those around Luther and Zwingli that a union of their reformations would secure the future of Protestantism.

Philip of Hesse was especially concerned with the issue of Protestant unity. Once he embraced the Reformation, he quickly began to marshal his forces with those of other sympathetic princes to provide protection and political muscle for Lutheranism. After Luther's trial and the disastrous Peasants'

---

28. Wengert and Haemig, *Small Catechism*, 213. Also in CCFCT 2:31.
29. Wengert and Haemig, *Small Catechism*, 214. Also in CCFCT 2:32.

War of 1525, though, it was difficult to maintain the claim that Protestant-ism meant no harm to Catholic lands. Philip, therefore, felt the need to bring other leaders of the Reformation into the orbit of Wittenberg. Before long, the reputation of Zwingli as leader of the Swiss movement drew Philip's at-tention, and he pressed hard for a meeting between Zwingli and Luther.[30]

The problem with the meeting was Luther's strong aversion to language about the Holy Spirit. We will discuss this problem in more detail when we look at the Anabaptists later, but for now suffice it to say that Luther saw "spiritualist" language as thin justification for supporting anarchy. Indeed, Luther even created a new word to smear spiritualists: "fanatics" (*Schwär-merei*). Luther wrote a treatise against this type of theology in his *Against the Fanatics* (1526), arguing that those who claimed to follow the Spirit did so merely to disguise their own foolish desires. To claim legitimacy through personal divine inspiration, then, was regarded as a dangerous theological position.

Luther's language made it difficult to see any harmony with Zwingli's teachings on the sacramental presence of Christ. For example, Zwingli claimed that Christ was present by the Holy Spirit, and not necessarily present with the elements themselves, since the Spirit is always with the believer. The point of the Lord's Supper, in Zwingli's view, was the memorial shared by Christians; hence this view is known as memorialism. It should be noted that Zwingli never allowed for private interpretation of the Bible—especially on issues such as political rebellion—and his focus on the Spirit was aimed at the sacraments only.[31] But his language of the Spirit ultimately proved to make any alliance with Luther impossible. Put simply, the language that Zwingli chose to use regarding the presence of the Spirit in the life of the believer made it *seem* as if he were one of those whom Luther labeled as fanatics.

Philip remained steadfast, though, in his desire to seek an alliance, and so in 1529 he brought both sides together at the Marburg Colloquy. Luther and Zwingli were not the only Reformers present; the meeting included Bucer, Johannes Agricola, and Philip Melanchthon. Luther and Zwingli, though, were the stars. Later stories of the colloquy were infamous for their drama. Luther remained adamant that the physical body of Christ was offered to the communicant in the bread and wine, although he rejected the Catholic explanation that the elements had been transubstantiated. Zwingli, in turn, remained committed to his memorialist position. Luther rested his argument

---

30. On the context of this meeting, see Benedict, *Christ's Churches Purely Reformed*, 32–48.
31. Indeed, Zwingli's language of political obedience was some of the strongest in the Ref-ormation. On this, see Quentin Skinner, *The Foundations of Modern Political Thought*, vol. 2, *The Age of Reformation* (Cambridge: Cambridge University Press, 1978), 76–78.

The Last Judgment by Michelangelo. Luther and Zwingli debated Christ's heavenly and earthly presence.

Public Domain / Wikimedia Commons

chiefly on a literal reading of Christ's words "This is my body," seeing any hesitation to embrace this language as flouting the plain reading of the Scriptures. Zwingli's response was that not all biblical language should be read this way—as, for example, the language of Christ as a door, a vine, or other tropes. According to one eyewitness, the debate reached a crescendo when Luther scrawled on the table the Latin version of Christ's words: *Hoc est corpus meum* ("This is my body").[32]

Deadlocked and unable to come to an agreement, the participants drafted a confession (if we can call it that) that they all signed. According to the articles, the Lutheran and Reformed churches agreed on fourteen major points.[33] These included the creedal affirmations of the Trinity and Christology; the ongoing

32. The accounts differ, with some saying that Luther wrote this in the moment, while others say that he had it already written beneath the tablecloth.

33. For the list of fourteen affirmed points, see Hermann Sasse, *This Is My Body: Luther's Contention for the Real Presence in the Sacrament of the Altar* (Minneapolis: Augsburg, 1959), 169–72. Also in CCFCT 2:793–95.

effects of original sin after baptism; justification by faith; that works after conversion were a gift of the Spirit; infant baptism; that secular magistrates were allowed by the Bible; and that confession of sin should be free from compulsion by the church. On the fifteenth point, covering the presence of Christ in the elements, both sides drafted their own statement. They could affirm their shared view that both the bread and wine must be used in the Communion service—rejecting the Catholic practice of giving only the bread to the laity—and that the Catholic practice of the Mass was idolatrous. They nevertheless admitted that "at present we are not agreed as to whether the true body and blood are bodily present in the bread and wine."[34]

While it may be tempting to view this fight as the result of ego and bluster, there was a deeper issue that divided Luther and Zwingli. The material cause was the issue of Christ's physical or spiritual presence in the Lord's Supper, but the formal issue behind this was their different understandings of Christology. The debate centered on two readings of the Chalcedonian Definition from the fifth century (which we discussed in chap. 5).

For Zwingli, Christ retained his physical body after the resurrection—and Christ's body was the first *human* body to be resurrected, making it necessary that his human nature remain separate from his divine nature, as it was a type of our future resurrection. Christ still bore scars, he ate fish with his disciples, and, more importantly, he now sat at the right hand of the Father. It was impossible for Zwingli to conceive of Christ's physical body coming alongside the elements of the Lord's Supper, and ultimately he believed that it was unnecessary to bring Christ's physical body to the Christian. Luther's position differed on this very point: he argued that while Christ retained his physical body, the single personhood of Christ meant that divine attributes were not separate from his human nature. Later Lutherans based this view of the sharing of divine and human attributes on the concept of the *communicatio idiomatum*, but for Luther it was nonsensical to believe that Christ's human nature must necessarily remain finite. If Jesus promised to be present in the Lord's Supper—and not merely spiritually present but physically present, according to Luther's interpretation—then his physical body could do so. For much of the history of Lutheran and Reformed polemics, the two natures of Christ became the staging ground for the ongoing struggle to define the presence of Christ in the Lord's Supper.

The failure of Marburg was not merely a failure to achieve Protestant unity. It also led to a near cessation of relations between Lutheran and Reformed churches. There were a few attempts at reconciliation made in the next

---

34. Sasse, *This Is My Body*, 172. Also in CCFCT 2:795.

generation of the Reformation, especially by Bucer (who attended Marburg), and there were moments when personal relations between Reformed and Lutheran leaders stoked a desire for ecumenism. But from Marburg on, the clear majority of Reformed churches—especially those under the influence of Zürich's leadership—felt that Luther had not based his view of the Lord's Supper on Scripture. For his part, Luther forever assumed that Zwingli was somehow a fanatic.

The Augsburg Confession

Luther's hostility toward the Zwinglian position was ironclad. He forever remained allergic to those who spoke of the sacrament in spiritual terms, and he was committed to defining his church by a clear doctrine of the physical eating of Christ's body and blood in the sacrament. As we will see, between 1530 and 1536 there were several attempts to repair the relationship, but in the end the split remained.

Philip of Hesse and the other Protestant political leaders of Germany, however, were concerned about a more immediate matter: defending Lutheranism against the charge of heresy, since those condemned for heresy were subject to capital punishment. Avoiding this charge would, of course, be nearly impossible as long as Luther continued to live as an outlaw. Any churches that took Luther's name, and any prince who supported Protestant reform, would bear the brand of heresy in the eyes of Rome.

Luther and his colleagues quickly redoubled their efforts to achieve both confessional accord and political stability. Toward the first goal, Luther, Melanchthon, and several others worked on two key confessions that forever shaped Lutheran orthodoxy. The first became known as the Schwabach Articles (1529), written at first as seventeen articles in the run-up to Marburg, but reused afterward to create a new confession. This was followed up by the Torgau Articles, created in the city of Torgau at the request of Elector John of Saxony. Both eventually became the backbone of one of the most important Lutheran confessions: the Augsburg Confession.[35]

For all his bristling at heresy, Charles V was a shrewd emperor when it came to the wider issues of politics. Indeed, Charles spent much of his reign beating back the armies of either the French or the Ottoman Turks. While struggling for control of its borders, the empire could not risk a civil war with Lutherans. Philip of Hesse and John of Saxony both lobbied for Charles to

---

35. For a confessional reading of the Augsburg Confession, see Leif Grane, *The Augsburg Confession: A Commentary*, trans. John H. Rasmussen (Minneapolis: Augsburg, 1987).

Cities of Schwabach, Torgau, and Augsburg in Germany

hear the Lutheran confession at the next imperial diet to be held in Augsburg.[36] After the draft of the Torgau Articles was completed, Charles summoned Melanchthon and others to Augsburg (Luther was excluded, since he was still an outlaw). On his way, Melanchthon edited the two previous confessions into a smoother, more consistent document. He sent the draft back to Luther for final inspection and approval. Luther loved the confession, although he admitted that he himself would not have had so calm a tone if he had written it.

The Augsburg Confession is perhaps unique among Lutheran confessions, in that the situation drove Melanchthon to play down elements of the Lutheran faith that could provoke Catholic anger.[37] Melanchthon also feared being too coy, so he refused to pretend that Lutheran reforms were merely cosmetic. None of the articles, therefore, took up the rhetoric of the early Reformation with accusations of papal corruption or tyranny. Melanchthon instead stuck to the issues and covered each in a methodical way, though not necessarily belaboring each issue. The article on justification by faith, for example, was only a few lines, summarizing that people could not save

36. A diet was something of a moving congress of the emperor and Germany's lesser princes. Most official business was handled at these summits.
37. There is a great deal of trouble constructing the original text precisely. For various editions and a note on the various manuscripts, see *CCFCT* 2:49–51.

themselves "by their own strength," only to move on to stress that there was a "new obedience," in that "[our churches] teach that this faith is bound to yield good fruits and that it ought to do good works commanded by God."[38] The issue of faith and works was expanded later in the confession, and it was stressed that works were a gift of God, but Melanchthon's editorial work ensured that this topic was not singled out for excessive attention.

What was most striking about the articles was the extent to which Melanchthon focused on ancient heresies, condemning each in turn. Regarding trinitarian heresies, the article on God made it clear that Lutherans rejected "Valentinians, Arians, Eunomians, Mohammedans, and others like them." The article on original sin—an issue that, as we have seen, was a basic difference between Lutherans and Catholics—was buttressed by a rejection of Pelagianism. To defend the Lutherans further, Melanchthon made sure to indicate that they rejected the teachings of Anabaptists.

The issue of the Lord's Supper, of course, was basic for Lutherans. Here, too, Melanchthon stressed the physical eating of Christ's body and blood: "Concerning the Lord's Supper, it is taught that the true body and blood of Christ are truly present under the form of bread and wine in the supper of our Lord and are distributed and received there."[39] This language, of course, was the same as what we saw at Marburg, although the article avoids any debate over the difference between transubstantiation and a view in which the physical body and blood of Christ are merely "under" the elements. Of course, Catholics would never accept the Lutheran view without an explicit statement of the doctrine of transubstantiation, but Melanchthon avoided that doctrine in the Augsburg Confession. He later went further and denied the basis for any criticism of the Lutheran understanding of the Eucharist: "Our people have been unjustly accused of having abolished the Mass. But it is obvious, without boasting, that the Mass is celebrated among us with greater devotion and earnestness than among our opponents."[40] This was one of the distinguishing features of the Augsburg Confession; it was almost inconceivable that other Protestant communities would ever claim common ground with *this* Catholic practice. The point of this passage, of course, was not to overlook differences with Catholic practice, nor was this merely a stunt to win Catholic favor. Nevertheless, the language was striking. The Lutheran commitment to eating Christ's body and blood physically, as well as the commitment to the reformation of abuses in the Mass, allowed Melanchthon to

38. Robert Kolb and Timothy J. Wengert, *The Book of Concord: The Confessions of the Evangelical Lutheran Church* (Minneapolis: Fortress, 2000), 41. Also in CCFCT 2:61.

39. Kolb and Wengert, *Book of Concord*, 44. Also in CCFCT 2:64.

40. Kolb and Wengert, *Book of Concord*, 68. Also in CCFCT 2:85.

Diet of Augsburg by Christian Beyer

make a case that Lutherans were not fanatics who rejected Catholic views on the Lord's Supper. On the issue of the sacraments, the Lutheran faith was from the beginning far more conservative (in the sense of being more like that of Catholicism) than that of other Protestant communities.

The Augsburg Confession was not only a crucial statement of Lutheran beliefs but also the first political victory won against the empire. The confession was read to the princes at Augsburg, and while Catholic leaders lodged a series of protests, Charles begrudgingly admitted the Lutheran confession was not entirely heterodox. Charles later overturned this decision, but in 1530 the Augsburg Confession appeared to secure the future of Lutheranism.

Following the failure at Marburg, the relationship between Wittenberg and Zürich was forever torn. To make matters worse, Zwingli lost his life in the Second Battle of Kappel in 1531, just over a year after the Marburg Colloquy and only months after the Diet of Augsburg. Zwingli's death threw into chaos the budding Reformed community in the Swiss regions, and were it not for the leadership of Heinrich Bullinger (1504–75), there might not have been established as coherent a Reformed voice as we saw later in the Reformation.

Bullinger's leadership will be covered in the next chapter, but for now, it should be recognized that because of their stance on the Eucharist, the Swiss Reformed communities were excluded from both imperial protection (since they could not accept the Augsburg Confession) and from any Protestant political league formed by Lutheran princes. From 1530 on, the Reformed communities had to try to increase their base of churches by spreading reform to other Swiss cities.

The Anabaptist Critique of the Reformation

We have seen in this chapter that there was no single confessional identity from the start of the Reformation. There certainly were issues that united Protestants—we must remember that at Marburg Luther and Zwingli agreed on nearly every doctrine. However, we have already taken note of several areas where early Protestants disagreed with one another, notably on the Eucharist.

Even in Wittenberg, but especially in other parts of Europe, there were Reformers who felt that the Reformation demanded more radical action. In early 1522, Wittenberg was overrun with rioting and religious zeal, as mobs tore down religious art and threatened those in authority. The city council was forced to ask Luther to return from hiding—where he had been since his trial in 1520—to set things back on a firm foundation. Luther was not pleased: when he returned, he found that the ringleader of the rebellions was Andreas von Karlstadt, one of the men who had accompanied Luther to several of his disputations before Worms. Before long, Karlstadt was banished from the city.[41]

For the next three years, until the Peasants' War of 1525, Luther made it clear that his reformation was primarily about doctrine, not social upheaval. He condemned all those who took up arms against their superiors. Luther later changed his mind and condoned political violence in 1531 when Lutheran territories were threatened, but for now he wanted no hint of radicalism associated with his name. He at times blamed magistrates for not seeking the welfare of their people, but on most issues involving the plight of the average man or woman, Luther was hesitant to step in.[42]

41. On Karlstadt, see Steinmetz, *Reformers in the Wings*, 123–30. Karlstadt had no real tradition, although he did hold to some future Protestant ideas. See Augustine Pater, *Karlstadt as the Father of the Baptist Movements: The Emergence of Lay Protestantism* (Toronto: University of Toronto Press, 1984).

42. It is too often stated that Luther always wanted Christians to separate the two kingdoms or that he was eager for Christians to remain out of these issues. On his evolving views, see Skinner, *Age of Reformation*, especially the first two chapters.

In Germany, however, not everyone agreed with this cautious stance. Indeed, from almost the beginning of Luther's reformation there arose communities dotted throughout Germany and the Swiss regions—later spilling into the Netherlands, France, England, and other countries—that advocated for radical reform. In almost every book on the Reformation (including this one), these groups are called Anabaptists (rebaptizers).[43] The problem with this label is twofold: (1) it was a name devised by their enemies to mock their view of adult baptism, and (2) those who came under this umbrella often did not fit any simple pattern, and they occasionally even condemned one another. Recent scholars have preferred to call these groups the Radical Reformation since they wanted more thorough reform than Luther, Zwingli, or anyone else was willing to give. The Radical Reformation could include groups with all kinds of theological views, since they sprang from no single figure or location but arose almost at once in several areas of Europe. What is most important to understand about Anabaptists is that they were unhappy with the pace or extent of the Reformation as it occurred in major cities such as Wittenberg and Zürich.[44]

One of the most well-represented (and infamous) wings of this radical movement was that which tended toward apocalypticism. The upheavals in Wittenberg were likely inspired by a type of prophetic anticipation of the return of Christ. Apocalyptic groups grew out of more or less traditional forms of mysticism—as, for example, the teachings of Hans Denck (ca. 1500–1527).

Denck was a teacher and a humanist from the southern part of Germany. After he embraced the Reformation, Denck was known for his knowledge of biblical languages—he produced a translation of the Old Testament prophets from Hebrew.[45] Denck was later influenced by the teachings of Karlstadt (who had left Wittenberg and now preferred the name "Brother Karlstadt"), as well as Thomas Müntzer, who supported a radical form of social rebellion. Denck appears to have grown cold to Müntzer's teachings on violence, preferring instead to explore the mystical teachings of German medieval writers such as Johannes Tauler.

In 1525, Denck came under scrutiny in the city of Nuremberg, where the city council was gripped with fear of radical Anabaptists and where Andreas

43. For an introduction to Anabaptist faith, see Hans-Jürgen Goertz, ed., *Profiles of Radical Reformers: Biographical Sketches from Thomas Müntzer to Paracelsus* (Scottdale, PA: Herald, 2008).

44. In addition to Mark U. Edwards, *Luther and the False Brethren* (Stanford, CA: Stanford University Press, 1975), see Willem Balke, *Calvin and the Anabaptist Radicals*, trans. William Heynen (Grand Rapids: Eerdmans, 1981).

45. CCFCT 2:665 points out that this is the first translation from Hebrew into German during the Reformation, preceding Luther's by four years.

Osiander served as a pastor. Osiander was a staunch supporter of Luther's reformation and held a strong view of political obedience. The city council and Osiander questioned Denck on his views, and when they were not satisfied, they demanded that he submit a confession of faith.

Denck's confession was distinctive for the early Reformation, since it was the work of one person—although it did capture some of the spirit found in other mystical or apocalyptic brands of Anabaptism. The confession was admittedly rambling, and at times it is hard to grasp Denck's point. But two features of Denck's confession are notable, since they became popular with some Protestant churches over time: (1) his stress on holy living, and (2) his focus on inward, Spirit-led illumination over against education or biblical study.

On the issue of obedience or holy living, Denck signaled his unique perspective when he defined the nature of faith as being merely "life"—that is, Christian living. Faith was not trust in the work of Christ, but rather the entirety of one's life before God: "Faith has no sin. Where there is no sin, there the righteousness of God dwells."[46] Denck was later known for his stress on the need for rigorous discipleship (*Nachfolge*), which he leveraged to undermine all traditional forms of worship and practice, both in Catholic and in new Protestant communities.[47] For Denck, the reliance on doctrines such as God's election or original sin, and the encouragement to seek the sacraments or to study the Bible, were merely ways to prevent Christians from approaching God directly and mystically. Denck, for example, rejected the need for outward Communion services of bread and wine, when the point was "to drink from the invisible chalice, the invisible wine, which God from the beginning has distilled through his Son."[48]

Denck took the additional step of including in his confession statements about his suspicion of the Bible or the scholarly study of biblical languages. The inward light "compels me without any of my will" to read the Bible, but this is only "for the sake of [its] testimony." He carries this logic further: while the Bible is a light shining in the darkness, it cannot do anything itself, "as it is written with human hands, spoken with human mouths, seen with human eyes, and heard with human ears."[49] One is tempted to describe Denck's

46. Clarence Bauman, *The Spiritual Legacy of Hans Denck: Interpretation and Translation of Key Texts*, Studies in Medieval and Reformation Thought 47 (Leiden: Brill, 1990), 59. Also in CCFCT 2:669.

47. On Denck's context and others who stressed the need for *Nachfolge*, see Bauman, *Spiritual Legacy of Hans Denck*, 31.

48. Bauman, *Spiritual Legacy of Hans Denck*, 65. Also in CCFCT 2:671.

49. Bauman, *Spiritual Legacy of Hans Denck*, 57. Also in CCFCT 2:668.

theology as intensified Zwinglianism in its rejection of the idea that spiritual benefit could come through any physical or human means. Of course, there was no direct connection to Zwingli or the Swiss Reformation, but Denck had the same instinct as Zwingli, intensified through mysticism, that any physical act was harmful to the spiritual life or at least unnecessary. Such radical teaching forced Denck to spend much of his life as a wandering mystic. He found lodging in various cities in southern Germany and in the Swiss cantons until he died from the plague in 1527.

The confession of Balthasar Hubmaier, although equally committed to more radical reform, provides a good contrast to that of Hans Denck. Hubmaier was born in 1480 near the city of Augsburg, and he went on to have a notable career in academia. He embraced the Reformation early and eventually made his way to Zürich, where he came to know Zwingli and even participated in efforts to continue the reform of the Zürich churches. Hubmaier, however, became disillusioned at the slow pace of reform in the city. A year later he rejected the Zwinglian reliance on political power and embraced the more radical positions of the Swiss Anabaptists. He wrote a book in defense of baptism based on faith in 1525, and he eventually found his way to the city of Waldshut. The Peasants' War was still running hot at this point, and the city was later retaken by Catholic forces. In the end, Hubmaier fled to the city of Nikolsburg in Moravia (the modern city of Mikulov in the Czech Republic).

Hubmaier wrote several confessions, but the most mature and reflective one was *A Christian Catechism* (1526),[50] written after he had settled in Nikolsburg. The city allowed Anabaptists to settle there (the eastern part of Europe often tolerated religious dissent during the Reformation), and so Hubmaier could work and minister without fear. The catechism, though, was rather similar to Zwingli's theology, with some obvious differences on baptism and good works. But the point that Hubmaier wished to stress throughout his confession was that the radical reforms that he and others embraced were not heretical. He based his opinions not only on the Bible but also on the orthodoxy of the creeds.

A Christian Catechism begins in a standard way by addressing issues in a question-and-answer format. The reader is led through a series of statements about God, mostly generic in nature—that he is "the highest good, almighty, all-wise, and all-merciful."[51] The sinner, Hubmaier writes, is in-

---

50. The original title is *Ein christennliche Leertafel*, or *A Christian Instruction Board*, referring to the small tablets children would use to learn.

51. H. Wayne Pipkin and John H. Yoder, *Balthasar Hubmaier: Theologian of Anabaptism* (Scottdale, PA: Herald, 1989), 346. Also in CCFCT 2:676.

capable of saving himself or herself, and so must recognize sin through the law. The catechism then takes the reader through a recitation of the Ten Commandments.

At this point, one significant difference can be noted on the issue of good works. In these early years all magisterial Protestant confessions stressed that works, while expected, were a gift of the Holy Spirit. These confessions from Lutheran and Reformed communities focused on justification and Catholic corruption and tended to stress good works only to avoid the charge of lawlessness or antinomianism.[52] However, Hubmaier, like Denck, placed a distinctive accent on the issue of good works. For example, Hubmaier answered the question "What is repentance?" by writing, "Accusing oneself of sin before God, asking him for forgiveness, and thenceforth never again committing it; that is the highest form of repentance, namely, to guard oneself from sin and to walk henceforth according to God's word."[53] The first two clauses could be found in any Protestant confession; the last sentence, however, could not. Luther had explicitly rejected the notion that Christian repentance issued in a form of Christian holiness. Original sin always remained, as Christians read of Paul's struggles in Romans 7 and his ability or inability to follow God's commands. Hubmaier's choice of a "higher form of repentance" would likely also have been an issue for Luther, who steadfastly warned against using justification by faith as if it led to self-righteousness.

A *Christian Catechism* rested on several traditional understandings of theology that Hubmaier had not abandoned. First, Hubmaier retains traditional medieval views of Mary—in particular, that she was immaculate (sinless) and remained a virgin. Hubmaier wants to stress the language of *Theotokos* (discussed in chap. 5) to indicate that Mary was the Mother of God. He also refers to the Apostles' Creed as the "articles of the Christian faith," rejecting the claim of other Anabaptist communities that creeds were human creations and unbiblical. Hubmaier does change the Apostles' Creed's affirmation of the "holy catholic church" by stating, "I believe and confess the holy universal church."[54] The language that he uses here is almost certainly not an error in memory but rather a refashioning of the doctrine of

---

52. "Antinomianism" was a word coined by Luther himself in 1539, referring to those who believed that Christians had no need for God's law after conversion—that is, they no longer needed to feel conviction of sin. Luther never allowed the law to be used in a positive sense for sanctification, yet he also rejected the notion that the law was no longer used to convict Christians. These issues still shape Lutheran dogmatic reflection. See, for example, Nicholas Hopman, "Luther's Antinomian Disputations and *lex aeterna*," *Lutheran Quarterly* 30, no. 2 (2016): 152–80.

53. Pipkin and Yoder, *Balthasar Hubmaier*, 346–47. Also in CCFCT 2:677.

54. Pipkin and Yoder, *Balthasar Hubmaier*, 350–51. Also in CCFCT 2:679.

the church toward a body of adult, confessing believers. Hubmaier's choice to render "catholic" as "universal" was also intended to avoid any accidental identification with Rome or the papacy.

Perhaps Hubmaier's most influential statements were on the subject of baptism—on which, as we have seen, he had already written a treatise. The heart of the confession leads the reader through a series of statements about not only why infant baptism should be rejected but also the purpose and practice of baptism in a church community. Baptism "is a commitment made to God publicly and orally before the congregation," he argues, "in which the baptized person renounces Satan and all his imaginations and works."[55] Hubmaier then makes the surprising claim that believer's baptism was the true teaching of the Council of Nicaea: "Therefore, as one cares about the forgiveness of his sins and the fellowship of the saints outside of which there is no salvation, just so much should one value water baptism, whereby one enters and is incorporated into the universal Christian church. This is the understanding and decision Christianly issued by the Nicene Council."[56]

On the issue of the church and its formation around believer's baptism, Hubmaier was a leading voice for the Anabaptist perspective. But his voice was unique, revealing a mixture of traditional and radical elements. Hubmaier throughout claimed not only creedal orthodoxy but also the seemingly paradoxical right to throw out doctrines of either Catholic or Protestant confessions as he saw fit. In this sense, Hubmaier reoriented the entire church "on the oral confession of faith that Jesus Christ is the Christ, the Son of the living God. The outward confession is what makes a church, and not faith alone."[57] Neither Luther nor Zwingli (nor any Protestant) would have been likely to claim that faith alone was the exclusive ground of the church; however, Hubmaier's ecclesiology was based not on mere faith, nor even on a mystical insight, as with Denck. Instead, Hubmaier stressed that one must make a public, oral confession to join the church.

Up to this point, we have looked at leading voices within the early Radical Reformation. These Anabaptist leaders based their understanding of the faith on quite different foundations—Denck on spiritual illumination, Hubmaier on a substantial, if somewhat conservative, reform of Protestant categories. We turn now to discuss the first—and perhaps most influential—united confession of Anabaptists during the Reformation: the Schleitheim Confession

---

55. Pipkin and Yoder, *Balthasar Hubmaier*, 350–51. Also in CCFCT 2:679. On this, see Eddie Mabry, *Balthasar Hubmaier's Doctrine of the Church* (Lanham, MD: University Press of America, 1994), 140–42.

56. Pipkin and Yoder, *Balthasar Hubmaier*, 351. Also in CCFCT 2:681.

57. Pipkin and Yoder, *Balthasar Hubmaier*, 352. Also in CCFCT 2:682.

(1527). The obvious difference between this confession and the ones we have just considered is that the Schleitheim Confession was the confession of several bodies, not the work of an individual. The unique feature of this confession, however, was that it was based strongly on Zwinglian principles (or at least wider Protestant teachings), especially its commitment to the Bible alone as the authority for doctrine.

The Schleitheim Confession arose from the ongoing anxiety surrounding the reforms in Zürich. Several followers of Zwingli had been impressed with his commitment to the Bible and his antipathy to idolatry. Conrad Grebel (1498–1526) and Felix Mantz (1498–1527), in particular, found comfort in Zwingli's strong biblicism.[58] However, like Luther, Zwingli may have led his followers on most issues, but few were willing to embrace his opinions on everything. The first contentious issue with Zwingli's teaching was that he continued to support infant baptism. Grebel and Mantz found this inconsistent with Zwingli's view that practices not commanded in the Bible were human inventions. Neither found clear support in the New Testament for infant baptism, and so they began to doubt Zwingli on this issue.

The formal break with Zwingli's teachings, however, occurred the year of the First Disputation of Zürich in 1523. Later that year, another disputation was held on the use of images in worship. Zwingli argued forcefully that images were not simply bad choices but also harmful and idolatrous. The council agreed but urged caution for the sake of public peace, not wanting riots to be the method by which the churches were cleansed. Zwingli reluctantly agreed to a slower timetable for removing the images, and Grebel and Mantz were furious. This was a clear case, they argued, of bowing before the political authority at the expense of God's command.

The link between these two issues was the way the subject of believer's baptism and political authority became central to the Swiss Anabaptist movement. Grebel and Mantz doubted Zwingli's integrity in worship, and this likely fostered in them the desire to break formally with Zwingli on the subject of baptism. In 1525, after the city commanded them to cease meeting in private and to bring unbaptized children forward for the sacrament within eight days, Grebel and Mantz rebaptized their friend George Blaurock in defiance of city law. The city council viewed this as open sedition, not merely an act of conscience. With rumors of the Peasants' War reaching Zürich, the city began a campaign of first banishment and then capital punishment—including the execution of Mantz in 1527.

58. See Harold S. Bender, *Conrad Grebel, c. 1498–1526: The Founder of the Swiss Brethren Sometimes Called Anabaptists* (Eugene, OR: Wipf & Stock, 1998).

As we saw with the Augsburg Confession (and this continued in other magisterial Protestant confessions), it was common for Lutherans and others to confess their rejection of Anabaptist teachings. What the Swiss radicals needed, then, was a confession that defended their movement from the accusations of both Protestants and Catholics. This need provided the occasion for the Schleitheim Confession. By 1527, the Swiss Brethren (as they called themselves) were led by Michael Sattler (ca. 1490–1527), a Benedictine monk who had embraced the Reformation and later came under the teachings of Grebel and Mantz, and was himself rebaptized in 1526. Sattler brought the community together in Schleitheim, a city on the far northern border of the Swiss regions in the canton of Schaffhausen. The community agreed on seven articles, likely drawn up by Sattler himself, that became the backbone of Swiss Anabaptist communities for generations.

The Schleitheim Confession was written in the tone of a New Testament epistle, opening with words that echo some of Paul's greetings to his churches. The confession then claims that the "manifold cunning of the devil" has beset their community, as others are seeking to destroy the true faith. The community is encouraged to "stand fast in the Lord,"[59] so that persecution does not weaken their faith. It then points to the fact that several of their brethren have abandoned the faith, likely due to fear. The confession then spells out the seven features that unite them: "baptism, ban, the breaking of bread, separation for abomination, shepherds in the congregation, the sword, the oath."[60]

At this point, we should note the limited number of topics discussed in the Schleitheim Confession. This should not be seen as evidence that the Swiss radicals cared only for these few topics but rather that these issues were views that distinguished them from their Protestant persecutors. Infant baptism, for example, is described as "the greatest and first abomination of the pope"—stronger language on the subject of baptism than had ever been seen previously. The subject of the ban was present in various Anabaptist communities, but here it is given definitive treatment: those who do not walk in holiness, after several warnings from the community, are to be cut off until they repent of their deeds.

As with the work of Denck and Hubmaier, the Schleitheim Confession stresses the importance of obedience after conversion and baptism. Article 4, for example, stresses the obedience of faith, stating that those who do not obey "are a great abomination before God." This is beyond anything Luther or Zwingli wrote, since it is more than just a doctrine that because of original

59. John H. Yoder, trans. and ed., *The Legacy of Michael Sattler* (Scottdale, PA: Herald, 1973), 29. Also in CCFCT 2:696.
60. Yoder, *Legacy of Michael Sattler*, 30. Also in CCFCT 2:697.

sin Christians continue to struggle with sin even after conversion. Lutheran and Reformed churches, of course, believed that gross sin—or openly flouting God's Word—should be met with discipline, even to the point of excommunication. But the Swiss Brethren insisted that the corruption of sin was not only something that must be extinguished but also something harmful to others in the church community. The categories were stark: "good or evil, believing and unbelieving, darkness and light."[61] This is not to suggest that the Schleitheim Confession advocated the possibility of pure holiness or perfectionism, but it did represent a departure from magisterial Protestants on the practice of spiritual discipline within the community.

For modern readers, often the most intriguing feature of the Schleitheim Confession is its rejection of political power and self-defense. Not all Anabaptists agreed on these points—indeed, Hubmaier took up the sword in defense of Waldshut in 1525. Most Anabaptist communities, to be sure, rejected the notion that political authorities should be involved in the church, but there were several ways this goal could be accomplished. Hubmaier and others simply wanted city councils to mind their own business. For the Swiss Anabaptists, in contrast, the Bible was clear not only on the subject of the opposition between church and state but also on the topic of violence in general. Therefore, they stated in clear terms that magistrates existed only for those who were sinners. For those in the community—baptized, obedient, and captive to God's will—there should be no need for political involvement of any kind. This included, they wrote, those who were Christians who wished to be magistrates or civil leaders. "Christ was to be made king, but he fled and did not discern the ordinance of his Father."[62] Christians should never serve in any political capacity, and the community itself should remain separate. Moreover, article 6 is equally clear that Christians are never to use any form of violence, not even self-defense. The article stresses that Christ himself bore persecution without violence (the framers offer no explanation of the cleansing of the temple) and also that he intervened at the stoning of the woman caught in adultery. Violence, the article stresses, is always and everywhere in opposition to the gospel.

The Anabaptist confessions of these early years revealed several characteristics that shaped most radical communities throughout the sixteenth century. First, Anabaptists exhibited even more differences of opinion among themselves than did Lutherans and Reformed, although they all shared the belief

---

61. Yoder, *Legacy of Michael Sattler*, 30. Also in CCFCT 2:698.
62. This statement is ambiguous about why Jesus rejected a crown. The wording seems to suggest that Jesus disobeyed the Father, but it likely refers merely to Christ emptying himself of the glory he was due.

that the magisterial Reformation had not gone far enough. Second, while the Schleitheim Confession is perhaps the most studied and best known of the Anabaptist confessions, at the time of its creation it was embraced by only one community in the Swiss cantons. Over time, however, the Schleitheim Confession grew in reputation, and while not all Anabaptist communities subscribed to its teachings, many did embrace similar (or identical) teachings on government, Christian holiness, and separation from non-Anabaptist communities.

Conclusions

In this chapter we have looked at those confessions written from Luther's break with Rome up to 1536. The earliest years of the Reformation revealed that the distinct confessional identities of the three main groups—Lutheran, Reformed, Anabaptist—did not take long to develop. Indeed, in almost every case there were theological commitments already in place in the 1520s that shaped the successful and unsuccessful attempts to write Protestant confessions. From the beginning, the Lutheran and Reformed camps did not agree on the nature of the Lord's Supper, while both rejected Anabaptist views of baptism, political authority, and other vital issues. This confessional separation gives the lie to the common view that the Reformation was initially harmonious and only later ruined by confessional inflexibility. Different commitments and different theological emphases meant that, while all Protestants embraced justification by faith and reforms based on the Bible, there was also a large measure of theological variety from the very beginning of the Reformation. In the next chapter we will continue to look at the fallout of these early struggles between different groups of Protestants.

15

New Generations
of Protestant Confessions

As we saw in the previous chapter, the magisterial movements of Lutheranism and the Reformed churches shaped the early Reformation, while the more radical movement of the Anabaptists broke away and formed new communities. We also looked at the issues that divided these three branches of Protestantism—the sacraments on the one hand, and the challenges raised against the Reformation by Anabaptists on the other—although all Protestants shared the view that churches must separate from Rome.

In this chapter we cover Protestant confessions written from around 1535 until roughly the 1560s. The Reformers who wrote these second-generation confessions now assumed that there was some theological division between the different Protestant groups. In this second phase of the Reformation, not only did Reformed, Lutheran, and Anabaptist confessions strive more and more to define their camp within the wider Reformation, but there were also confessions written in other cities and countries for the first time (e.g., in England). Our focus in this chapter, then, is how Protestant confessions continued to unify these early Protestant camps internally, expressing their central beliefs, and also how the Protestant faith began to fan out into these new regions.

A Final Confession by Luther

Catholic apologists always claimed that Protestantism was a religion of rebellion and anarchy. They maintained that justification without works was a gateway to citizens without obedience. In response, Martin Luther was immovable when it came to any discussion of political violence.[1] He advocated instead for a position of passive disobedience (refusing evil commands, but never engaging in violent resistance). Luther's position became more entrenched after the Peasants' War broke out in 1525, as some used Luther's protest as grounds for overthrowing the medieval establishment. Luther responded with one of his most vicious tracts: *Against the Murderous, Thieving Hordes of Peasants.* His rhetoric was inflammatory, calling for the rebellion to be put down with as much haste and ferocity as was necessary. The problem with Luther's position, however, was that he was himself an outlaw. Lutheran princes and pastors who affiliated with Luther could, at least in theory, be accused of sedition if the empire did not wish to go to the trouble of an excommunication trial. A connection with Luther implied guilt by association.

In the previous chapter we looked at the initial success of the Augsburg Confession (1530), as Charles V cautiously admitted that the Lutheran message was tolerable (although he fumed in private that he could not pull out the roots of heresy). Charles needed to keep the princes of Germany unified against threats from the Ottomans and France, and Melanchthon's careful wording in that confession made it possible to avoid war between Catholic and Protestant princes. There was also the issue of Luther himself—now a celebrity and hero to Protestants around Europe (even to those who disagreed with his theology), and even a symbol of German pride. Charles knew the story of Jan Hus, whose execution in 1415 had infuriated his compatriots and forever cemented the Hussite rebellion against pope and empire. Charles did not want to make a martyr of Luther.[2]

The Lutherans, however, were not foolish enough to think that Charles would always have the patience of Job. Thus, the Lutheran princes agitated for a new defensive league—later named the Schmalkaldic League, since it came together at the city of Schmalkalden in 1531. The formation of this league was inherently seditious, at least in principle, since it involved imperial princes and citizens uniting under a potential banner of war.

1. For Luther's views on rebellion, see Quentin Skinner, *The Foundations of Modern Political Thought,* vol. 2, *The Age of Reformation* (Cambridge: Cambridge University Press, 1978).
2. A good recent book on Charles V, especially on the issues of international politics, is William S. Maltby, *The Reign of Charles V,* European History in Perspective (London: Palgrave, 2004).

Martin Luther
by Hans Brosamer

The issue that perplexed them was, in fact, Lutheranism—or at least Luther's teachings on political nonresistance. We have seen that his early position was necessary to avoid anarchy, but now it ruined any chance of forming a league in defense of the Reformation. For his part, Luther recognized the threat of war and knew that the stakes were high: if Charles were to win, he would impose Catholicism in Lutheran lands. So in 1531 Luther changed his position to allow for defensive resistance led by princes in order to repel Catholic armies, although not for outright rebellion and certainly not rebellion by private Christians. Luther argued that if attacked, if Lutheran princes gave the order, it was allowable to take up arms against the empire.[3]

The other critical issue at this time was that Pope Paul III called a church council to meet in 1536 in Mantua. The Lutheran and Reformed churches

3. For more on this, see Ryan M. Reeves, *English Evangelicals and Tudor Obedience, c. 1527–1570*, Studies in the History of Christian Traditions 167 (Leiden: Brill, 2014), chap. 1. On Luther's change of mind, see Skinner, *Age of Reformation*, 206–38.

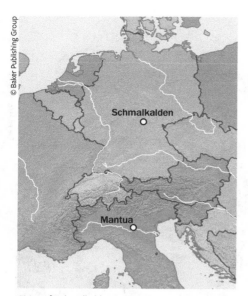

© Baker Publishing Group

Cities of Schmalkalden in Germany and Mantua in Italy

felt the need to offer some basis of a dispute, should they be invited. We will look later at the Reformed confession written as a response (the First Helvetic Confession), but for the formation of the Lutheran league, this was an important change of focus. Luther drew up the articles at the behest of John Frederick of Saxony, but while the articles were agreed to at Schmalkalden as part of the formation of the league, the Catholic council never materialized. The articles languished, and so in 1538 Luther published them in order to make public his mature views on all the important Reformation doctrines "if I should die before a council meets."[4] This was, in a sense, his confessional last will and testament.[5]

The Schmalkald Articles revealed Luther at his polemical best (or worst, from a Catholic point of view). The balanced language of the Augsburg Confession gave way to rhetoric like that of the early 1520s, as Luther no longer believed that there could be any positive outcome to a church council with Catholics. In his preface, Luther admits that he is exasperated by the constant need to defend the Reformation before his opponents: "I suppose I should reply to everything while I am still alive. But how can I stop all the mouths of the devil?"[6] One recent claim even stated that Lutherans had abandoned marriage entirely, and they now "live like cattle" together. Thus, Luther wanted one last confession, in the hope that it might somehow stop the mouths of his critics.

We can set aside the strong language of polemic, but there are several features of the Schmalkald Articles that deserve our attention. The articles are broken up into three main sections, and they open with a simple declaration that Lutherans affirm, like Catholics, the three central creeds: the Apostles'

4. Theodore G. Tappert, trans. and ed., *The Book of Concord: The Confessions of the Evangelical Lutheran Church* (Philadelphia: Fortress, 1959), 289. Also in CCFCT 2:122.

5. This is echoed in William R. Russell, *Luther's Theological Testament: The Schmalkald Articles* (Minneapolis: Fortress, 1995).

6. Tappert, *Book of Concord*, 289. Also in CCFCT 2:123.

Creed, the Nicene Creed, and the Athanasian Creed. Because they share these in common, "it is not necessary to treat them at greater length."[7]

The second section covers the "office and person and work of Christ," or the subject of redemption. This middle section rarely pulls any punches and is the most polemical section. The pope is stated to be the antichrist, and the Mass is "nothing else than a human work, even a work of evil scoundrels."[8] Still, this section has one of the more substantial declarations on justification, in that it writes that "faith alone justifies us." Not only do we rarely see such language from the Reformation, but we should also note how infrequently confessional (or other theological) texts mentioned it in this slogan form. Luther famously added the word "alone" to the text of Romans 3:28 ("one is justified by faith *alone*") when he translated it in the 1520s, but rarely did such a phrase thunder in the sources. Here Luther states it explicitly and adds, "Nothing in this article can be given up or compromised . . . on this article rests all that we teach and practice against the pope."[9]

Other than covering the typical issues of the Reformation—monasticism, celibacy, and the like—Luther states that the Mass would be the most important issue discussed at any council. The problem arose because, he admits, the Lutheran position is that the Mass is "nothing else than a human work, even a work of evil scoundrels . . . if the mass falls, the papacy falls with it."[10] Papal corruption was a critical issue to raise, but we should notice that Luther here says little of his position and only reports the issues that he holds against the Mass, mainly that it is supported by papal authority.

The third section is by far the most extensive treatment of the issues central to Lutheranism. It opens with a strong defense of the doctrine of original sin, which Luther says is "so deep a corruption that reason cannot understand it."[11] The doctrine of sin, he argues, is vital to understanding the gospel, as it contradicts the teachings of medieval theologians, who stated that the will remained free to do good works, though it was weakened apart from the sacraments. The law must come to teach sinners how wicked they truly were; and on this issue, Luther spells out one of the most important issues for later Lutheran and Reformed debates: the twofold use of the law that was becoming common in the Reformation. First, the law is useful "to restrain sins by threats and fear of punishment." We can remember the First Use of the Law by the analogy of a bridle: the law is used not for salvation but to restrain humanity

---

7. Tappert, *Book of Concord*, 292. Also in CCFCT 2:125.
8. Tappert, *Book of Concord*, 293. Also in CCFCT 2:127.
9. Tappert, *Book of Concord*, 292. Also in CCFCT 2:126.
10. Tappert, *Book of Concord*, 294. Also in CCFCT 2:127.
11. Tappert, *Book of Concord*, 302. Also in CCFCT 2:134.

Ancient scroll of Old Testament law. Luther articulated two uses of biblical law.

in its wickedness. In other words, this use of the law we might today describe as the political use of the law, whereby it is used to buttress civil action against murder, theft, and so forth. Few Christians today speak of biblical law in this light—or they oppose using the Bible in societies that separate religion from politics. In Luther's day, however, this First Use of the Law was affirmed by all Christians as a rationale for political action against evil.

Luther next goes on to focus on the Second (and weightier) Use of the Law for salvation. "However," he writes, "the chief function or power of the law is to make original sin manifest and show man to what utter depths his nature has fallen and how corrupt it has become." If the first use is a bridle, the second use can be understood as a mirror. Luther argues that the law was meant to expose our self-righteousness by holding up the perfect standard. Since we fall short of this standard, we despair in our works and cling to Christ's work in faith. This process of the law revealing sin, driving us to the cross, Luther explains, is located almost exclusively in the preached Word. This analogy of the mirror is important because it clarifies Luther's message: he was not opposed to the law per se, but he resisted using the law as a guide for Christian living or good works. Luther's point in this explanation is to claim that the law itself is holy, although it only reveals the ugliness in us.

Luther does not speak of a category called the Third Use of the Law, but this came into play shortly after his death and sparked debate well into the seventeenth century. The debate over the Third Use of the Law centered on the issue of how the law might be used *after* conversion: Was it to be used only as an instrument that *revealed our guilt* (Second Use of the Law), or could it ever be used in a positive sense to *guide the life of sanctification* (Third Use of the Law)? In other words, should the law be used only to reveal guilt and shame, or could it be appropriated into rules for living?

An analogy for the Third Use of the Law is a flashlight: the law spotlights the path that we should walk. The question was so crucial, in fact, that it received special treatment in the Formula of Concord (1577), which we will examine in chapter 17. But here it should be noted that Luther does not explicitly deal with the question, since the issue was not yet a controversy between Lutheran and Reformed theologians. Almost certainly, Luther would have rejected the notion of any positive, postconversion use of the law. Sanctification, he always stressed, came not from focusing on our righteousness but by grasping the work of Christ each day. Reformed theologians almost unanimously embraced the Third Use of the Law, and so another issue eventually came between them and the Lutherans.

The remainder of the Schmalkald Articles is much like what we have already seen from Luther. The importance of the confession, however, is that Luther wrote it just as his church was coming together as a military faction. The Schmalkaldic League fought mainly skirmish campaigns for several years to expand Lutheran territories and to gain the right to depose Catholic priests. When Luther died in 1546, however, with him died any hesitation from Charles V about ending Lutheranism. Charles was fortunate at this time, too, in that he no longer felt pressed on either side by Ottoman or French forces. He believed that the Schmalkaldic League had provoked war, and so he launched a series of campaigns (known today as the Schmalkaldic War) against the league between 1546 and 1547.[12] The Schmalkaldic League, technically, had superior forces and should at least have stood its ground. However, it lacked cohesion—due in large part to having too many voices jockeying for control—and so at the Battle of Mühlberg (1547) Charles conquered the Schmalkaldic League, removing any protection for Lutheran churches.

On May 15, 1548, Charles issued the decree known today as the Augsburg Interim, which was a piecemeal declaration, although it temporarily halted the spread of Lutheranism. By this point, Charles awaited the conclusion of the Council of Trent (to be discussed in the next chapter), before enacting stricter measures. The Augsburg Interim stipulated that all Lutheran churches must restore the seven sacraments, cease preaching on justification by faith,

12. On this war, see Philip Benedict, *Christ's Churches Purely Reformed: A Social History of Calvinism* (New Haven: Yale University Press, 2002).

and reinstate all former Catholic practices. As far as Charles was concerned, the Reformation was over.

With Luther gone, the obvious choice to take control was Philip Melanchthon. He had been Luther's right hand during the Reformation, and, by this stage, no other person had helped form Lutheranism more than Melanchthon. When he received the terms of the Augsburg Interim, however, Melanchthon chose a route that managed only to undermine his credibility with Lutheran pastors and theologians: he embraced the Augsburg Interim in a bid for peace. One can appreciate his flexibility, but Lutheran pastors at the time condemned what seemed a betrayal of the Reformation. Throughout Germany, hundreds of pastors chose prison over submission, and some lost property or family members to violence. As a result, Melanchthon's acceptance of the Augsburg Interim helped erode any support from Lutherans, allowing other theologians to rise to positions of strength. These issues resulted in the final Lutheran confessional standard, the Book of Concord, which we will look at in chapter 17.

The Spread of German Reformed Confessions

After Huldrych Zwingli's death, Heinrich Bullinger took over as the lead voice for Zürich. Zwingli had mentored him, and he was learned, patient, and committed to the same theological principles. Bullinger always remembered the struggles that Zürich endured after the failure to achieve unity with Lutheranism, and so he was suspicious of Reformers who continued to seek confessional unity with Wittenberg. Bullinger also strove to expand the horizon of the Reformed community beyond the Swiss cantons. One recent study has noted the astonishing number of letters that Bullinger sent to other Protestant leaders, as well as how frequently other cities asked Bullinger for his opinion on church matters. For the entirety of his career, Bullinger was a senior statesman for Protestantism.[13]

The need in Zürich was to silence those who saw their future only through the lens of the failures of the Marburg Colloquy. Several Swiss cities, for example, had already embraced the Reformed faith, with some even adhering to Zwingli's view of the Lord's Supper. Swiss cities, like modern Switzerland,

13. Bullinger has been neglected for too long by historians, though thankfully a lot of recent work has been published on him. See especially Bruce Gordon, *The Swiss Reformation* (Manchester, U.K.: Manchester University Press, 2002); Bruce Gordon and Emidio Campi, eds., *Architect of Reformation: An Introduction to Heinrich Bullinger, 1504–1575*, Texts and Studies in Reformation and Post-Reformation Thought (Grand Rapids: Baker Academic, 2004). For a basic but authoritative survey of his life, see David C. Steinmetz, *Reformers in the Wings: From Geiler von Kaysersberg to Theodore Beza* (Oxford: Oxford University Press, 2001), 93–99.

were shaped by different languages: Zürich, Bern, and others were German-speaking; Geneva and Neuchâtel were French-speaking. The city of Geneva and the surrounding Vaud canton were even under the authority of the Duke of Savoy (on the border of modern Italy and France). The Reformed confessions, therefore, were often based on two needs: on the one hand, they needed to continue the struggle to achieve recognition from the empire; on the other hand, they needed to unite themselves into a unified perspective—separate from Luther, yet still Protestant in message.

For example, when Charles V summoned the Diet of Augsburg and requested that the Lutherans submit a statement of their faith, the major Swiss cities worked feverishly to avoid being frozen out of any decision by Charles. If the Lutherans were granted protection, the Reformed churches wanted protection too. Their efforts produced the Tetrapolitan Confession—named for the four (*tetra*) cities that composed the assembly: Strasbourg, Konstanz, Memmingen, and Lindau. The confession was almost entirely the work of Martin Bucer (1491–1551), working in collaboration with Wolfgang Capito (1478–1541). Capito served as pastor in the important Swiss city of Basel, and there he had befriended Zwingli while also corresponding with Luther. Capito, therefore, was committed to working with both sides, though he favored the Reformed critique of Luther's view of the sacraments.

Bucer, however, spent his career working to unite the various sides of Protestantism.[14] His passion for unity was personal as much as temperamental, since it was Luther who had converted him. While serving as a Dominican monk, Bucer had attended the Heidelberg Disputation, where he witnessed Luther's agitation for reform. Within a year Bucer had arranged to have his vows annulled before fleeing to Strasbourg. Bucer, in other words, was both a defender of Reformed theology and forever indebted to Luther for his faith. He also believed that the two sides could eventually agree, given enough time and conversation. For this he was mistrusted and even scorned by leaders from both Lutheran and Reformed camps.

The central issue, of course, was the Eucharist. Bucer did not agree with Luther's commitment to the physical presence of Christ in the Lord's Supper, but unlike Zwingli, he was not committed to the idea that the bread and wine were only a memorial, which seemed to deny Christ's presence altogether. Indeed, the word "truly" would be ideal for understanding Bucer's position: Christ is *truly* present, *truly* offered, and *truly* there. This was not an attempt to play the middle but was instead based on Bucer's concerns about both

14. On Bucer, see Martin Greschat, *Martin Bucer: A Reformer and His Times* (Louisville: Westminster John Knox, 2004); David Wright, *Martin Bucer: Reforming Church and Community* (Cambridge: Cambridge University Press, 2002).

sides. He shared Luther's concern that the language of memorialism locked Christ away in heaven, separated from the sacraments; he also believed that the Zwinglian position would be better if it were strengthened to stress what *was* in, rather than what *was not* in, the Lord's Supper. Over the years, the churches of Strasbourg were frustrated by the Zwinglian position—at one point accusing Zwinglians of having a "Christless Supper"—but in these early days hope remained for Protestant unity. If they strengthened Reformed language on the sacraments, Bucer assumed that it would persuade those in Wittenberg.

The Tetrapolitan Confession, then, offered to the Diet of Augsburg a new Reformed articulation of the sacraments, although Bucer and Capito chose their words carefully. They first framed the struggle for the Reformation by noting that "since about ten years ago"—roughly since the Diet of Worms— "the doctrine of Christ began to be treated with somewhat more certainty and clearness."[15] Catholic teaching in the medieval church, since it focused on works, had confused the issue, so it was evident that the Reformers needed to stress the doctrine of justification without works during the early Reformation. Now the Reformed camp instead wished to underscore that "these things we shall not have men so to understand, as though we place salvation and righteousness in slothful thoughts in the mind, or in faith destitute of love, which they call faith without form."[16] The confession contended that their message was precisely the same as Augustine's teaching on "faith . . . efficacious though love," although they stressed that love itself is a gift of the Holy Spirit.

The confession focused next on practices that Protestants had thrown out of their churches: monasticism, mandatory fasting, and other patterns of life that implied the necessity of good works. They had also removed images from the church, because Catholics so abused them and they contravened the biblical teaching on worship. However, unlike Zwingli, the Tetrapolitan Confession did not see a sharp separation between spiritual and physical categories, because "the church lives here in the flesh, though not according to the flesh."[17] Perhaps the most striking feature of the confession, however, is its statement on the Lord's Supper that offered a closer relationship between physical and spiritual eating. It admits that "adversaries proclaim that our men change Christ's words [to mean] that nothing save mere bread and mere wine is administered in our suppers." In language that must have come from

15. James T. Dennison, ed., *Reformed Confessions of the 16th and 17th Centuries in English Translation*, 4 vols. (Grand Rapids: Reformation Heritage Books, 2008–10), 1:140–41. Also in CCFCT 2:221.

16. Dennison, *Reformed Confessions*, 1:143. Also in CCFCT 2:223.

17. Dennison, *Reformed Confessions*, 1:158. Also in CCFCT 2:236.

Bucer, the confession stresses instead that God "deigns to give his true body and true blood to be truly eaten and drunk."[18]

In the end, the Tetrapolitan Confession lasted only a year. It was never seriously considered (or even read) at Augsburg, and so it failed at its purpose immediately. To make matters worse, the language of the confession was rather dense—a feature of Bucer's writings in general—and at times the meaning was not clear.

Bucer and other Reformed leaders had more goals, however, and they continued to seek a stronger footing for Reformed theology. The number of Reformed confessions continued to swell, and in the early 1530s, two were particularly noteworthy: the First Confession of Basel (1534) and the First Helvetic Confession (1536). Today, these two confessions can create confusion—along with the more widely adopted Second Helvetic Confession—because all three are confessions from Basel, though two are titled the "first" confession and two include the word "Helvetic." But the Basel confession was written for needs different from the Helvetic confessions, and all three had different sets of authors. These three confessions were an important pivot for Reformed churches.

The First Confession of Basel was written by Oswald Myconius (1488–1552). He based his text on a shorter confession written by Johannes Oecolampadius, a leading early Reformer who had succumbed to the plague in 1531. The occasion for this confession was the slow pace of reform in the city of Basel, which had officially embraced the Reformation as early as 1524 but did not outlaw the Mass until 1529. Some in the city doubted whether the Reformation would last. Tensions in the city also erupted in one of the most violent riots of the Reformation, as an angry mob destroyed many of the images and statues in Basel's churches. Oecolampadius and Myconius were tireless in their efforts to restore order and further reform, and they were inspired by the work of Zwingli in Zürich. They feared Anabaptist fervor, and now that the city was willing to embrace the Reformation, they needed a simple confession to pass the city council. The confession was offered and accepted on January 21, 1534.

The First Confession of Basel has twelve basic affirmations, all relatively straightforward. One unique feature is the explicit connection of the doctrine of election to the doctrine of God—a standard feature of later Reformed scholastic theology, but not typical at this point, since most early Reformers discussed election only under the rubric of salvation. After an orthodox statement about the Trinity and God's creation of the world, the article states that God chose people to salvation before he created the world. Under this rubric,

18. Dennison, *Reformed Confessions*, 1:159. Also in *CCFCT* 2:237.

the act of God's election appeared to rest on creation itself, independent of the fall of humankind. In earlier confessions, by contrast, the topic was discussed under the subjects of the freedom of the will and original sin, which focused only on the question of how one came to faith. As we will see in chapter 17, these issues were raised again during the Reformed-versus-Arminian struggle in the seventeenth century.

Of course, as with many Reformed confessions around this time, the central focus is on the sacraments. The authors admit that the critical issue is a proper understanding of Christology, since it is the foundational doctrine for understanding the Lord's Supper. Like Zwingli, the confession states that Christ is "united with human nature in one person" but that "he ascended into heaven with body and soul where he sits at the right hand of God."[19] We should note that, by this point in the Reformation, the comment that Christ was seated at God's right hand was a bedrock assumption in Reformed churches. This language, of course, is not about heaven, or even about Christ's authority; it is a statement to identify that Christ is located *somewhere* (at the Father's right hand) and that somewhere has a *physical* space, making it impossible that his finite body can come to be physically in the Lord's Supper. The confession appeals to this doctrine twice, both in the context of the sacraments, and concludes, "Water remains truly water, so also does the bread and wine remain bread and wine in the Lord's supper, in which the true body and blood of Christ is portrayed and offered to us. . . . However, we do not enclose in the bread and wine of the Lord the natural, true, and essential body of Christ."[20]

The First Helvetic Confession was drawn up by Bullinger and Leo Jud after Pope Paul III had called for a church council. The context, then, was not an effort to begin the Reformation but to send an official statement of faith to the long-awaited Catholic council. The opportunity to give a single confession of the Reformed faith, however, proved tempting, and so on January 20, 1536, Bucer and Capito (as well as representatives from Bern) joined the meetings—making this the first attempt to unite the largest and most important cities of the Reformed movement into one confessional entity. Indeed, the opening statement of the confession described its framers as "churches banded together in a confederacy."[21]

The most crucial factors at the First Helvetic Confession meetings were the roles that Bucer and Capito played in the language of the confession— roles that eventually led to the confession's demise. Bucer, as we have seen,

---

19. Dennison, *Reformed Confessions*, 1:289–90. Also in *CCFCT* 2:275.
20. Dennison, *Reformed Confessions*, 1:291. Also in *CCFCT* 2:276.
21. *CCFCT* 2:282. The preamble is not included in Dennison, *Reformed Confessions*.

was concerned about the reputation of the Reformed faith. The Tetrapolitan Confession had done little to repair the reputation of Reformed churches among Lutherans, and so Bucer's presence was crucial. Eyewitness accounts after the session, in fact, admitted that both Bucer and Capito stressed the need for broader language about the orthodoxy of Reformed theology, as well as more exact language on the sacraments, so as not to give credence to the opinion that Charles should deal only with Lutherans.

The confession opens with a statement on both the authority and the interpretation of the Scriptures. The Bible's interpretation "ought to be sought out of itself, so that it is to be its own interpreter, guided by the rule of love and faith"—a rejection of the Anabaptist belief that the Spirit gives guidance when one is personally reading the Bible. The article goes on to affirm patristic writings as perhaps an even greater source than some admitted previously in Reformed circles: "From this interpretation [of faith and love], so far as the holy fathers have not departed from it, not only do we receive them as interpreters of the Scripture, but we honor them as chosen instruments of God."[22] The language is restrained, describing the fathers as mere instruments and not authorities in themselves, but it nevertheless casts Reformed theology as faithful to early creedal orthodoxy.

A few issues besides the sacraments are notable in the First Helvetic Confession. Perhaps the most striking addition—one that had not been mentioned in a Reformed confession previously—is the article on free will, which begins by affirming that humans as the image of God have a free will: "We ascribe freedom of choice to man because we find in ourselves that we do good and evil knowingly and deliberately." This concept is important to grasp if we are to understand later debates on free will between Calvinists and Arminians. When it came to basic free choice outside salvation, the Reformed camp always affirmed this as part of its teaching.[23] However, when looking at the central issue of free will—the question of our ability to choose God by our power— the framers of the confession (like all early Protestants) denied that we had such free will after the fall: "to be sure, we are able to do evil willingly, but we are not able to embrace and follow good (except as we are illuminated by the grace of Christ and moved by the Holy Spirit)."[24] The issue of free will,

22. Dennison, *Reformed Confessions*, 1:343–44. A slightly different English rendering is found in *CCFCT* 2:282.

23. This issue and its complexities are discussed in detail in Richard A. Muller, *Divine Will and Human Choice: Freedom, Contingency, and Necessity in Early Modern Reformed Thought* (Grand Rapids: Baker Academic, 2017).

24. Dennison, *Reformed Confessions*, 1:345. A slightly different English rendering is found in *CCFCT* 2:284.

in other words, depends on what one has in mind when one affirms or denies human freedom. If the question is about our choices day by day, especially our choice to sin, then the First Helvetic Confession confirms this freedom. When it comes to our choice to place our faith in Christ, however, the framers of the confession denied human capacity to do so and saw faith as a gift of regeneration given by the Holy Spirit. In chapter 17 we will see the importance that this issue had subsequently.

Naturally, the confession spends most of its space explaining the nature of the Lord's Supper (as well as baptism), focused as always on the nature of Christ's incarnation. The confession chose the most forceful language to date of any Reformed confession, stating that sacraments are "significant, holy signs of sublime, secret things."[25] The article affirms that the bread and wine are signs—just as Zwingli and Bullinger always stressed—but it goes on to say that "they are not bare signs, but they are composed of the signs and substance together." The choice to use the word "substance"—a key term in medieval teaching on the Eucharist—was meant to rule out a caricature of Zwingli's teaching on the sacraments. In a deft balancing act between Bucer and Bullinger, the framers conclude,

> In regard to the Lord's Supper we hold, therefore, that in it the Lord truly offers His body and His blood. . . . We do not believe that the body and blood of the Lord is naturally united with the bread and wine or that they are spatially enclosed within them, but that according to the institution of the Lord the bread and wine are highly significant, holy, true signs by which the true communion of His body and blood is administered and offered to believers.[26]

The confession then concludes with a plea that Reformed churches no longer be condemned for devaluing the sacraments.

The First Helvetic Confession was the most unified of the early Reformed confessions not only because so many Reformed leaders took part in drafting it but also because it signaled a new effort among some leaders to distance themselves from Zwingli. Bullinger later bristled at the notion that Zwingli's teachings were inferior, and he contended as well that he didn't knowingly sacrifice anything when Bucer and Capito requested this new language. So the First Helvetic Confession was plagued by the fact that Bucer seemed afterward to have been less than clear about his objectives. Bullinger had intended

---

25. CCFCT 2:288. This line from the confession is missing from Dennison, *Reformed Confessions*.

26. Arthur C. Cochrane, ed., *Reformed Confessions of the Sixteenth Century* (Louisville: Westminster John Knox, 2003), 108. Also in CCFCT 2:289.

only to explain the Zwinglian position, but some viewed the confession as a departure from Marburg. As a result, the relationship between Bucer and Bullinger was poisoned.

One more confession arose because of Bucer's efforts to unite Lutheran and Reformed sides: the Wittenberg Concord of 1536. As one scholar noted, Bullinger by this point joked that the Latin origin of Bucer's name must mean "to vacillate."[27] Following on the heels of the First Confession of Basel, Bucer and Capito attempted to write a confession with those in Wittenberg. Bucer felt optimistic after the result of Basel, but he may have felt that the issue just needed a Reformed voice to start the conversation. Surprisingly, he managed to get Luther and Melanchthon on board, and Melanchthon drafted a set of articles for their meeting. Both sides gave some ground. The Reformed party agreed not to use the offending Zwinglian word "memorial," though they minced no words about "the Zwinglian teachers" who strove "to introduce their error."[28] Luther as well briefly allowed that the presence of Christ was offered "with the bread and wine," and both sides rested the confession on the language that Christ's body and blood were "truly" offered.[29]

The Wittenberg Concord perhaps aspired to too much, especially when the unity between Lutherans and Reformed churches was only on paper. Bucer and Capito spoke for none of the Reformed churches the way Luther and Melanchthon could speak for the Lutherans. Once the confession was finished, the only party that appreciated it was the Lutheran faction. Some German Reformed cities rejected it, and nearly all Swiss churches scoffed at its language. An ironic twist was that Bucer's ministry in Strasbourg naturally led the city to embrace the Wittenberg Concord—although pastors in the city later began to interpret it in a Lutheran manner. By 1549, the situation was such that Bucer was no longer welcome there, and he accepted Thomas Cranmer's offer to teach in Cambridge. Bucer died there in 1555.

Rise of French Reformed Leaders

The legend of John Calvin (1509–64) has grown with the telling. Historians regularly find it necessary to remind students of Calvin's actual role in the

27. Wilhelm Pauck, *Melanchthon and Bucer*, Library of Christian Classics (Philadelphia: Westminster, 1969), 96.

28. Henry E. Jacobs, *The Book of Concord; or, The Symbolical Books of the Evangelical Lutheran Church* (Philadelphia: United Lutheran Publication House, 1911), 510. This portion of the confession is not in CCFCT.

29. Jacobs, *Book of Concord*, 511. Also in CCFCT 2:799–801.

John Calvin

Reformation, which was not as the founder of the Reformed faith, nor even the dominant influence on early Reformed churches, at least in his lifetime. Instead, Calvin was a second-generation Reformer, whose reputation was at first minimal in some Swiss regions, but he increased in stature by the end of his life. The publication and expansion of the *Institutes*, of course, made Calvin one of the most influential Reformers on future generations. However, today there is a host of dubious assumptions about Calvin and Calvinism, predominantly in the English-speaking world, and especially after the Reformed-versus-Arminian fights in the seventeenth century.

This is not to say that Calvin was unimportant, but that his importance was not as the sole founder of the Reformed movement. Instead, he was one of the many Reformed leaders to shape the future of their confessional identity. Indeed, perhaps the most pivotal role that Calvin played in his lifetime was his participation in talks to unite the Zwinglian Reformation to the other Reformed cities, first in the Swiss cantons and then in other parts of Europe.

The German Reformed com-
munities sprouted quickly and
since 1531 had spread to capture
new cities such as Basel and Bern.
The French-speaking Swiss cantons, however, had been marginalized during these years, due to the
barriers of language and culture
as well as the vagaries of local
political authority. In the early
1530s, this all began to change.
The Vaud canton managed to free
itself from the authority of the

© Baker Publishing Group

Cities of the Swiss Reformation

House of Savoy, opening the door to reform in these cities. Bern played a key
role in this and often initiated the reform efforts in nearby French churches.
Indeed, in 1536, Bern marched a small army to the city of Geneva and annexed
it. Some in the city were happy to unite with Bern, and some even hoped to
see reform.[30]

Bern needed French-speaking leaders to bring the Reformation to these
cities. To do so, the city relied on two men: Pierre Viret (1511–71) and William Farel (1489–1565).[31] Both had a reputation for being fierce in their
convictions—Viret was once almost stabbed to death by a Catholic priest—
and not a few times both were blamed for problems stemming from their
being too severe with city officials. Still, their German-speaking counterparts
in Bern were willing to tolerate these problems because Farel and Viret had
successfully brought the Reformation to both Neuchâtel and Lausanne in the
early 1530s. The relative isolation of Viret and Farel, though, explains why
they were eager to recruit the young John Calvin.

As the Reformation grew in these French-Swiss cities, there arose the need
to draft their own Protestant confession. Like Zürich, Basel, and Bern, they
needed this so that cities could ratify their conversion to Protestantism; so in
1536, the first of these confessions was drafted, the Lausanne Articles. The
meeting was led by Farel and Viret, though records tell us that Calvin attended
the session and argued for a few points. The publication of the first edition
of the *Institutes* that same year provided Calvin some measure of authority
in the sessions.

---

30. On this spread, see Benedict, *Christ's Churches Purely Reformed*, 49–108.
31. On Viret, see Robert Dean Linder, *The Political Ideas of Pierre Viret* (Geneva: Droz,
1964). On the relationship between Calvin and Farel, see Bruce Gordon, *Calvin* (New Haven:
Yale University Press, 2009), 63–81.

Calvin went on to see Farel again when the young Reformer stopped off in Geneva, and with enough arm-twisting (Farel threatened divine condemnation if Calvin were to abandon them and lead the French-Swiss Reformation alone), Farel convinced Calvin to stay. The relationship with city officials quickly soured, due in large part to Farel's and Calvin's insistence on using their own confessional standard. The problem was that Bern had annexed the city and already ordered Geneva—and Farel and Calvin—to abide by the Bernese confession. Historians have never fully understood why, but the two French Reformers decided to make a stand by drafting their own text. When city leaders balked, Calvin and Farel took the radical step of barring these men from Communion, effectively excommunicating them without a hearing. Calvin and Farel were given just a few days to leave the city or face arrest.

This painful moment in Calvin's life ultimately thrust him into the ongoing confessional struggle within the Reformed community. He made his way to Strasbourg, where Bucer nursed the wound to Calvin's pride and managed to smooth things over with Bern. This was not an easy task. The delicate issues in Geneva made it seem that Farel and Calvin had spoiled the Reformation before it had begun, but Bucer knew that the primary problem was that Farel and Calvin spurred one another into rash decisions. The two were now separated, and Calvin was given a home, sharing a garden with the Bucer household. Bucer even managed to find a wife for Calvin. When he returned to Geneva, Calvin was the same principled campaigner for reform, but he was not the brash man of his early years.

The proximity of Calvin to Bucer was crucial, since we have already noted the increasingly strained relationship between Bullinger and Bucer. While the two never publicly condemned each other, Bullinger grew wary of Bucer's efforts to build bridges with Lutherans. Although ecumenical in motive, these overtures revealed a flaw in Bucer's theology. Many now recognized Calvin's skill as a writer and defender of the Reformed perspective, especially since he had published the *Institutes*. But would Calvin be a figure like Bucer, or would he find common ground with Zürich?

The answer to this question came in the 1540s after Calvin had returned to Geneva and established himself there as the leading voice in the French-Swiss church. By 1549, it was clear that Zürich and Geneva would need to spearhead a statement of unity on the sacraments. The dark cloud hanging over the Zwinglian view was not bad enough to ruin their churches, but the Reformed faith needed to speak with one voice, especially now that other cities and countries were looking to the Swiss for theological leadership. Bullinger's views had also matured. He retained many of the essential points that Zwingli held on Christ's two natures, his sitting at the right hand of the Father, and the need for the presence of the Holy Spirit. But he had also found it wise to emphasize more the positive value of the sacraments, even to the point of asserting that Christ was truly there for our nourishment.

Calvin and Bullinger exchanged letters for some time until November 1548, when Bullinger sent a list of twenty-four articles that could form the basis of an agreement. Calvin then traveled with Farel to Zürich in May 1549—now with twenty articles that Calvin had recently used to argue his case in Bern. The final document, the Zürich Consensus, was a fascinating work of harmonization.[32] The agreement was ratified eventually in Lausanne, Basel, and Bern, an act that drew together for the first time the entire Swiss region into a united Reformed movement. Still, it should be noted that consensus confessions such as this succeeded when they allowed both sides to retain their unique views—and the Zürich Consensus did just this. Zürich still leaned more heavily toward Zwinglianism, while Calvin would always stress a view of real presence closer to that of Bucer. But the threat of theological war between the two—or an equally frosty relationship between Calvin and Bullinger—was now gone.

The Zürich Consensus offers first a new assessment of the sacraments, calling them the "appendixes to the gospel";[33] that is, they are not the focus of Christian devotion but its support. The framers stress that the real fruit of salvation comes by being united to Christ, but without the Zwinglian predilection to distinguish physical and spiritual benefits. The articles then go on to highlight the ongoing role of Christ as our High Priest, adding that he pours life into us by his Spirit and so unites us to his resurrection as to bring about all good works. This "spiritual communion," they argue, is primarily focused on our union with Christ.[34]

The agreement next describes the sacrament not merely as an oath (as Zwingli had), but as "marks and badges of Christian profession," which create a different effect by taking the focus away from the believer. The sacraments "incite us to thanksgiving and exercises of faith."[35] And then they add a delicately worded explanation of how this is to be understood: "For although they signify nothing that is not announced by the Word, yet it is a great benefit that there are cast before our eyes, as it were, living pictures which influence our senses in a deeper way, as if leading us up to the thing itself. . . . It is also a great

32. On the background of this meeting, see Emidio Campi and Ruedi Reich, eds., *Consensus Tigurinus (1549): Die Einigung zwischen Heinrich Bullinger und Johannes Calvin über das Abendmahl* (Zürich: TVZ, 2009). *Tigurinus* is the Latin name for the city of Zürich.

33. Dennison, *Reformed Confessions*, 1:539. Also in CCFCT 2:806.

34. Dennison, *Reformed Confessions*, 1:540. Also in CCFCT 2:806–7.

35. Dennison, *Reformed Confessions*, 1:540. Also in CCFCT 2:807.

benefit that what God has pronounced with his mouth, is confirmed and ratified as if by seals." This was a striking statement, retaining Bullinger's desire
to avoid confusing the bread and wine with the actual benefit of the Spirit,
while adding newer language that drew the two sides together. The suggestive
notion of the elements as "living pictures" or the ratification of something
sealed in us also balances Christ's real presence without making the elements
themselves the main focus. Article 22 then goes on to "reject therefore those
ridiculous interpreters who insist on what they call the precise literal sense of
the solemn words of the supper—This is my body, this is my blood."[36] This
statement meant that not only were the two sides united; they also found an
agreement so that the Lutherans were no longer the focus of their energy.

One final confession we should consider is the French Confession of 1559
(later ratified officially in 1571),[37] since it was the first Protestant statement
for the French Reformed churches. It was also the only lengthy confession on
the substance of the Reformation that John Calvin played a significant role in
drafting. The authors based the confession on an earlier document beseech-
ing the French king to halt persecution in that country. Persecution continued
nevertheless, but now that the French-Swiss had begun to expand their influence internationally, the French requested aid from Calvin and Theodore
Beza (1519–1605) in drafting a complete confession. The eight articles from
the original text were converted into thirty-five, and the result was one of the
most mature confessions of the first two generations of the Reformation, especially in its carefully balanced language and attention to detail. Calvin was
likely the hand behind the smooth style, since the text bears a resemblance
to his tight, humanist prose. The way each article builds on the previous one
and anticipates the next is exceptional. This type of arrangement had been
used in some confessions, but not always consistently. The maturity of the
French Confession does not mean that there are no questions raised from its
language; but this was a confession that was beginning to describe not just
a set of positions but a fully orbed theology with a confessional identity.

The framers of the French Confession were careful to affirm the Reformed
line on the sacraments, but in a fashion that was becoming the Genevan perspective on the subject—namely, they did not take the Zwinglian position,
but neither did they abhor it; they saw fruit in the work of Bucer to create a
bridge to Lutheranism, but they didn't insist on it. The confession opens with
a simple statement on the nature and attributes of God. Here the stress is laid
on the unity of God as a "sole and simple essence," rather than beginning

---

36. Dennison, *Reformed Confessions*, 1:544. Also in *CCFCT* 2:811.
37. Also known as the *Confession de foi* in some textbooks.

with a trinitarian formula of any kind. The second and third articles then address the issue of how we come to know this one God: through the order of creation (article 2) and finally through the sixty-six books of the Bible, which are listed by name (article 3). The confession also stresses that other authorities are inferior to the Scriptures, but it affirms the three official ancient creeds "because they are agreeable to the word of God."[38]

The confession then takes an unusual tactic in that it gets to trinitarian language only *after* these other matters are clarified. Perhaps because of this, some phrases suggest a less-than-traditional approach to trinitarian orthodoxy. As we saw in chapters 4 and 7, the early church primarily approached the subject of God by focusing on persons rather than essence. The French Confession places the stress first on the oneness of God, "this one and simple divine being." The confession continues:

> The Father . . . the first cause in order, and the beginning of all things: the Son, his wisdom and everlasting Word; the Holy Ghost, his virtue, power, and efficacy. The Son begotten of the Father from everlasting, the Holy Ghost from everlasting proceeding from the Father and the Son; the three persons not confused, but distinct, and yet not divided, but of one and the same essence, eternity, power, and equality.[39]

This language certainly is within the bounds of orthodoxy, and there is nothing here that overtly denies the Nicene Creed. But the confession is suggestive of the popular way in which Western and, by extension, Protestant theology has laid stress on the one essence before discussion of the three persons and has relegated any discussion of the persons to the role each person plays in salvation. The confession, therefore, refers to God in the next article as "three coworking persons" in the act of creation. The language of the Father as the "first cause" demonstrates the use of Aristotelian categories to describe God, which had been present in the early church and became increasingly common after the thirteenth century.

The most detailed and developed discussion in the French Confession, however, relates to the sacraments. As with other Reformed confessions, the treatment of the sacraments depends on an initial affirmation of Christology. In Jesus Christ, the framers write, "[Christ's] two natures are inseparably joined and united, and yet nevertheless in such a manner that each nature retains its distinct properties." In other words, there is a set of attributes that pertains to the different natures (e.g., omnipotence to the divine, hunger to the humanity),

38. Dennison, *Reformed Confessions*, 2:142. Also in CCFCT 2:376.
39. Dennison, *Reformed Confessions*, 2:143. Also in CCFCT 2:376.

but these are united first and primarily in the person of Christ. The confession stresses the need for a distinction without separating the two: "the human nature remained finite . . . and also Jesus Christ when he arose from the dead gave immortality unto his body, yet he never deprived it of the verity of its [human] nature."[40] From this basis, the confession argues a consistent line about both sacraments: they, too, must be distinguished between the physical and spiritual natures. And yet the confession can make bold claims that the Eucharist "feeds and nourishes us truly with flesh and blood" and is not merely "shadows and smoke."[41] Only after this strong affirmation does the confession clarify that "he is now in heaven, and will remain there til he comes to judge the world," and so it is "by the secret and incomprehensible virtue of his Spirit [that] he nourishes and quickens us with the substance of his body and blood."

> But we say this is done in a spiritual manner; nor do we hereby substitute in the place of effect and truth an idle fancy or conceit of our own, but rather because this mystery of our union with Christ is so high a thing, it surmounts all our senses . . . in short, because it is celestial, therefore, it cannot be apprehended but by faith.[42]

The confession thus incorporates some of the newer Reformed language about the Lord's Supper. In other words, its framers assert that a Zwinglian denial of the spiritual value of the bread and wine—although the French admitted that they *were* symbols—would be akin to denigrating the humanity of Christ in an effort to elevate his divinity. Rather, the French Confession stresses that we can speak of separation (bread and wine versus the presence of the Holy Spirit), but the language here affirms that we *do* take his flesh and body, and only then goes on to distinguish what the eating means.

The French Confession was an important step toward a more developed set of Reformed confessions, which we will look at in chapter 17. But the confession itself was relatively marginalized, due in large part to the resistance of the French crown to the Reformation. The confession was edited and affirmed at the National Synod at La Rochelle in 1571.

The Start of the English Reformation

If one were to search for the least likely country to embrace the Reformation, England would be at the top of the list. Almost immediately, Henry VIII responded

---

40. Dennison, *Reformed Confessions*, 2:146. Also in CCFCT 2:379.
41. Dennison, *Reformed Confessions*, 2:152. Also in CCFCT 2:384.
42. Dennison, *Reformed Confessions*, 2:152–53. Also in CCFCT 2:385.

to the Reformation with a mixture of anger and condemnation.[43] He had in his service two men who ensured that Lutheran seeds had no chance to grow: John Fisher (1469–1535) and Thomas More (1478–1535).[44] Fisher served from within the church, examining clergy and writing books against Luther's theology, while More served from the court for the same purpose. Both were learned men, known for their piety, and neither saw any value in the Protestant faith. The church corruptions so common in some European countries—sexual license and lavish spending—did not occur with much frequency in England. It was not easy, then, to point to overwhelming and obvious examples of the need for reform. Henry and his Catholic support- ers, therefore, were a bulwark against the encroachment of Lutheranism into England. Indeed, historians can count on one hand the number of people in England who sympathized with Protestant theology in the early years. If this would grow into Protestant England, it was at this stage only a mustard seed.

The problem that led to the formation of the English Protestant church was a dynastic crisis for Henry VIII. His family was the Tudor dynasty, which had taken the throne by force when Henry's father had defeated Richard III at the Battle of Bosworth Field in 1485. Henry VIII had been second in line for the throne—his older brother, Arthur, had died young in 1502, leaving behind his Spanish wife, Catherine of Aragon.[45] Spain was among the most powerful countries in Europe, and the new Tudor dynasty was not about to send Catherine home. So papal dispensations were secured, allowing Henry to marry Catherine. Such a marriage was forbidden in canon law, but for situations where hereditary monarchies were at stake, the pope normally accommodated, and did so in this case.

As Henry struggled against Lutheranism in England, he soon grew suspi- cious that something was wrong. By the mid-1520s, Catherine had suffered numerous miscarriages, provoking in Henry the fear that God was punishing him. In the end, he decided that the trouble lay in his marriage to Catherine— and he found Leviticus 18 to be a clear judgment against sexual relations with one's sister-in-law. Henry soon convinced himself that the pope should never have given a dispensation for the marriage. Indeed, historians have pointed

43. See, for example, Richard Rex, "The English Campaign against Luther in the 1520s," *Transactions of the Royal Historical Society*, 5th series, 39 (1989): 85–106.

44. On Fisher, see Richard Rex, *The Theology of John Fisher* (Cambridge: Cambridge University Press, 1991). On More, see Peter Ackroyd, *The Life of Thomas More* (New York: Doubleday, 1998).

45. The dynastic issues of the Tudors have inspired a number of books. The best, in our opinion, are Richard Rex, *The Tudors* (Stroud: Tempus, 2003); John Guy, *Tudor England* (Oxford: Oxford University Press, 1988); Susan Brigden, *New Worlds, Lost Worlds: The Rule of the Tudors, 1485–1603* (New York: Penguin, 2000).

out that, of all the options available, Henry chose the most difficult: the claim that the pope had no authority to dispense with the Levitical law.

Henry went on to marry a total of six wives, but this was not because of the king's libido. Nor was he merely stamping his foot to get his way. If Henry were to die without an heir, the Tudor house would likely fall, or at least England would plunge into civil war. Henry used every resource at his disposal to get an answer from Rome. After the pope used stall tactics and then refused to render a verdict in the matter, Henry was embarrassed enough to launch an attack on the church itself. To show an example to others, he also executed his two advisers in the fight against Protestantism— Fisher and More—since both opposed the annulment of his marriage to Catherine. Henry also had the entire English clergy accused of sedition (using an obscure fourteenth-century statute forbidding any petition to foreign authorities).[46] And, finally, he fell in love with Anne Boleyn—a woman known to identify with some Protestant teachings, and a shrewd woman who refused Henry's advances without a commitment to marriage. So in 1534, blameless only in his own mind, Henry VIII had himself declared head of the Church of England.

Despite his protest over Roman authority, Henry was overall a poor Protestant. True, several of his actions could have suggested he was inching toward evangelical faith. He attacked the monasteries in 1536, he outlawed many traditional practices, and he even allowed known evangelicals to serve under him. Thomas Cromwell (1485–1540) and Thomas Cranmer (1489–1556), both Protestant by the time of Henry's divorce, learned how to move Henry toward new ideas that favored evangelical opinion, such as the publication in 1549 of the first official English translation of the Bible (the King's Bible).[47] But no one ever managed to convince Henry of anything like justification by faith, married clergy, or removal of the veneration of saints. On these and other issues, Henry consistently supported traditional medieval views, though after 1534 he denied the very papal authority needed to justify these practices. As one contemporary argued, Henry VIII seemed in effect to be throwing a man from a tower and ordering him to stop halfway down.

46. This was the Statute of Praemunire, created to stop the nobility from usurping royal prerogative. It had nothing to do with the clergy, but it was leveraged in such a way that it treated the papacy itself as a foreign jurisdiction outside England. See the introduction in Linder, *Political Ideas of Pierre Viret.*

47. The King's Bible offered a unique blend of Henrician and evangelical reasons for publishing the Bible in English. On the one hand, it arose from the Protestant belief in the Bible alone, but Henry always believed the main focus of biblical learning was obedience to the crown.

Portrait of
Thomas Cranmer
by Gerlach Flicke

Public Domain / Wikimedia Commons

Others in England, such as Cranmer, had moved all the way down from the tower. In the early days of the Reformation, Cranmer would have sided with Henry VIII and the Catholic leaders, if more as a humanist than merely a conservative. But he was critical of the Reformation, finding Luther's message to be obviously heretical—and scholars have discovered his copy of a book by Luther, in the margins of which Cranmer scrawled his angry responses. By the time Henry's troubles with the pope began, however, Cranmer had moved irrevocably into the Protestant faith, far beyond Henry's attempts to remain Catholic without a pope. Swiss Reformer Simon Grynaeus visited from Basel in 1531, and he and Cranmer struck up a friendship. By this point, if not well before, Cranmer had sided with the Lutheran message of faith. The following year, while on official duty in Europe, Cranmer met Lutheran pastor and theologian Andreas Osiander (1498–1552), and he took the radical step of marrying his niece. In his mind, and now in his bed, Cranmer had thrown in with Luther.[48]

Once back in England, Cranmer chose the path of accommodation and patience rather than protest and martyrdom. This feature of his life made Cranmer one of the more curious figures of the Reformation: serving like Daniel in the court of a hostile king, who with the right strokes to his ego might be led to agree with reform measures, or, just as quickly, could order his adviser's execution.[49] The populace, too, was relatively unaccepting of even Henry's stance on papal authority, since there arose a serious rebellion known as the Pilgrimage of Grace (1536–37), which strove to restore everything about the traditional church, including obedience to Rome. Cranmer worked slowly and haltingly under Henry, though scholars are now aware that his hesitation was based not on conservative theology but on the need to survive.

This tense relationship between Henry and his court—some gritted their teeth against reform while others encouraged it—created the context for the first confession of the new Anglican church.[50] This was the Act of Ten Articles (1536), drafted by those in the court, though Henry had a heavy hand in editing the last version. The theology of this confession, however, was unique in the history of the Reformation (or ever since). The articles stitch together a variety of themes, both Catholic and Protestant, to create a mismatched identity. Some elements have an echo of Protestantism, such as the opening words that affirm the Scriptures and three primary creeds (Apostles, Nicene, and Athanasian) as the basis for all doctrine. Other articles, though, continue to support doctrines found in none of these ancient sources, since the pope had promulgated them later by his authority.

For example, the Act of Ten Articles allows for only three sacraments: baptism, Eucharist, and penance. Baptism is affirmed in a traditional sense as an action necessary for the infant. Still, in opposition to Luther, the next article states that baptism is regenerative and washes away original sin. Lutheran confessions, of course, mention that baptism is the source of faith— either then or later in the infant's life—but all Protestant confessions state categorically that original sin remains. The Eucharist, too, is said to be the

---

48. Osiander's life is covered in Steinmetz, *Reformers in the Wings*, 64–69.

49. A point described in detail in Diarmaid MacCulloch, *Thomas Cranmer: A Life*, rev. ed. (New Haven: Yale University Press, 2017), 41–135.

50. Scholars are rightly nervous about the name "Anglican," since it was not used in this way until the nineteenth century. At the time of the Reformation, the Latin phrase *Ecclesiae Anglicanae* referred not to a self-conscious Anglican identity but to the church that was in the country of England. Scholars, therefore, often refer to early Anglicans as "evangelicals," but we will use the more common word "Anglican" in this book. On this, see MacCulloch, *Thomas Cranmer*, 1–6.

physical body and blood of Christ, although there is neither an appeal to transubstantiation nor a Lutheran understanding of Christology, only a mere affirmation of this position. The third sacrament is the most peculiar, as it explicitly continues most of Catholic practice. Contrition, confession, and satisfaction—the Act of Ten Articles requires each of these practices in the English church. Since confession and penance were the material cause of Luther's reformation, it is hard to see in these articles any trajectory toward Protestantism.

The Act of Ten Articles was perhaps the greatest example of Henry's reformation. When he died in 1547, however, the stage was set for England to leap aggressively in a Protestant direction. For all of Henry's desire for traditional piety, he seems to have ignored the education of the heir he had worked so hard to produce, Edward VI. The boy king—as he became known—was educated by Protestant humanists, who saw to it that Edward would embrace the essentials of the Protestant message. Edward was only nine when crowned, making him a minor and unable to rule directly over England until the age of eighteen. As a result, evangelicals in court coordinated a victory in Henry's last hours, ensuring that the legislative board that would govern England for Edward would be composed entirely of Protestants, including Cranmer.

In 1547, then, England entered one of its most volatile phases during the Reformation. It would not be an overstatement to say that when Edward took the throne, England was still a Catholic nation, now run by a Protestant regime.[51] There was also the issue of what authority a governing board had when the king was still a minor. Henry had envisioned the board's role as only to keep the country running, but the governors of England saw an opportunity for reform, and they embraced it.

The reform efforts were centered especially on the subject of worship. Henry VIII had attacked the wealthiest monasteries, suspecting rightly that these were the central places that could resist the king and inspire Catholic loyalty among the people. Those who accepted the Royal Supremacy, however, remained until Edward's reign, and the evangelical leaders had them removed. All public places of Catholic worship—not churches, but places such as votaries and other shrines—were taken down. Cranmer also issued two editions of the Book of Common Prayer (in 1549 and 1555), the first designed to introduce Protestant worship to England, the second going further in its language. The new Anglican form of worship now had only two sacraments, a clear statement of justification by faith, and no liturgical language that might

51. On the complexities of the Edwardine reforms, see Diarmaid MacCulloch, *The Boy King: Edward VI and the Protestant Reformation* (Berkeley: University of California Press, 2002).

point Christians to either their own works or the veneration of the saints. In perhaps an indication of the public commitment to the Catholic faith, there were two riots by angry laity in 1549.

If the English church had a liturgy that expressed Protestantism, it also needed a confession. So, in June 1553, a royal mandate was issued that commanded use of the Forty-Two Articles in England. They were the work of Cranmer, and their message is overwhelmingly Protestant, although they take no noticeable side in the Lutheran or Reformed debate on the sacraments. Like many Protestant confessions, the articles begin by listing the commitment to creedal orthodoxy. The articles, therefore, affirm the Trinity and Christology. Next, they made it clear that the Bible alone is the source of doctrine, though in the next article they affirm the three creeds because their contents are confirmed in the Scriptures. Regarding other Catholic beliefs, the articles state that belief in purgatory, enforcing celibacy for priests, and basing church decisions on the authority of church councils are rejected by the Anglican faith.

The articles then cover the usual topics of Protestantism, affirming the ongoing nature of original sin, that justification is by faith, and that good works (before or after conversion) should not be the basis for assurance. On free will, the confession takes the same position as Lutheran and Reformed confessions, in denying free will to choose God by our efforts and by affirming that salvation is due to God's eternal election of sinners (predestination). One of the more striking views of the Forty-Two Articles is on the Lord's Supper, which it interprets in a Reformed way, similar to the views held by Bucer, Calvin, and others who were non-Zwinglian. The bread and wine are said to be "not only badges and tokens" but "certain sure witnesses, and effectual signs of grace." As we have argued in this chapter, this was a common second-generation Reformed position and not as close to Catholicism as the Lutheran position. There is no focus on the physical eating of Christ's body and blood, but rather the article states that God uses the Lord's Supper to "work invisibly in us."[52] To emphasize this view, the article adds that the bread and wine should never be gazed at or lifted up in such a way as to be regarded superstitiously.

The Forty-Two Articles were a crucial step for Anglicanism, but not during Edward VI's reign. The boy king died within a month of the royal mandate, and he was succeeded by his half-sister, Mary Tudor, a devout Catholic. Mary was the daughter of Catherine of Aragon—tossed aside by Henry, then re-

---

52. Dennison, *Reformed Confessions*, 2:8. CCFCT does not have the Forty-Two Articles in its volumes.

instated in the royal line behind Edward.[53] Mary viewed her mother's struggle to save her marriage to Henry and her death while Henry was married to Anne Boleyn as the fight of a martyr. Mary Tudor, therefore, quickly overturned the mandate for the Forty-Two Articles, leaving them to be reintroduced only later in the sixteenth century when Elizabeth I came to the throne.

It is important to understand where Anglicanism fit within the wider Reformation landscape. The major issue was deciding which phase of the English Reformation to biopsy, and which voice, which text, would become the leading example of Anglican identity. None of these questions were decided in the sixteenth century—if they are even decided today—but for each person leading the Edwardine reformation, the goal was always to embrace Protestantism without necessarily embracing the antagonism between Wittenberg and Zürich.[54] Far from seeking a midpoint between Catholic and evangelical, men such as Cranmer wished to stand as a middle way between Luther and Zwingli.[55]

Later Anabaptist Confessions

We round out this chapter by looking at a few Anabaptist confessions from the later Reformation. There are only a handful of texts from this period, due in large part to the persecution of Anabaptists throughout Europe. The radical communities that might have drafted confessions, therefore, were often fighting merely to survive. Many fled to safer lands, such as those in the eastern part of Europe. The Anabaptist confessions that we will consider come primarily from these regions.

As we have seen, the radical impulse that shaped all Anabaptist communities did not result in their sharing the same theological outlook. Some certainly were Protestant on almost every major issue, especially the issues of scriptural authority and justification by faith. Others, however, were more suspicious of traditional creedal orthodoxy because they believed that these creeds emerged only after the papacy had corrupted the church. If the church had come to

53. Mary's return to Catholicism seems to have lasted until her death in 1558. See Eamon Duffy, *Fires of Faith: Catholic England under Mary Tudor* (New Haven: Yale University Press, 2009).

54. A point argued effectively in Diarmaid MacCulloch, "The Myth of the English Reformation," *Journal of British Studies* 30 (1991): 1–19.

55. On the various theological influences in England, see Carl Trueman, *Luther's Legacy: Salvation and English Reformers, 1525–1556* (Oxford: Oxford University Press, 1994); Reeves, *English Evangelicals and Tudor Obedience*; Alec Ryrie, *The Gospel and Henry VIII: Evangelicals in the Early English Reformation*, Cambridge Studies in Early Modern British History (Cambridge: Cambridge University Press, 2003).

adopt erroneous views about baptism and political power, could it not have come to spurious views of Christology and the Trinity as well?

We can see this radical doubt about the ancient creeds in the teachings of Laelius Sozzini (1525–62), who was considered to be the founder of the heresy of Socinianism.[56] Sozzini, born in Siena and the son of a famous lawyer who played a role in Henry VIII's request for an annulment, eventually moved to the Swiss regions and immersed himself in the Reformed movement. The reputation he gained was mixed, as some found him a warm companion and others considered him a pest. Sozzini continually raised doubts about creedal orthodoxy. Although some still trusted him, Calvin and others had doubts about his opinions. A few years later, he sent Calvin several questions that seemed to indicate that he now openly doubted the Trinity and the Chalcedonian Definition. Bullinger, therefore, intervened and asked Sozzini to draft a personal confession on these issues. The result was Sozzini's Confession of Faith in 1555.

The text is concise and not based on any articles or declarations—at least not the kind found in most confessions. Sozzini's language, while confessing a desire for charity, is nevertheless laced with a degree of antagonism (perhaps driven by his frustration at having to write a confession in the first place). He opens the confession admitting that as a child he had learned the Apostles' Creed, and he acknowledges that it is ancient and used by all Christians. "But I have lately read others also," he continues, referring to the Nicene Creed, "and attribute all the honor I can and ought to." He then states that he recognizes "the terms Trinity, persons, hypostasis, consubstantiality, union, distinction, and others of the kind are not recent inventions, but have been in use for the last thirteen hundred years." The point, Sozzini asks, is whether these terms are necessary for all Christians as an issue of salvation, or whether they served a purpose only in the early church (only "necessary for the fathers").[57] He lists several heresies that he does not teach—belief in three separate gods, two distinct persons of Christ, Arianism—and he even denies by name the teachings of Servetus, who had been executed in Geneva for heresy in 1553.

56. "Sozzini" was the Italian form of his name, though he Latinized it (a popular practice in the Reformation era) to Socinus. On the Unitarian movement in Poland, see Stanislaw Kot, *Socinianism in Poland: The Social and Political Ideas of the Polish Antitrinitarians in the Sixteenth and Seventeenth Centuries*, trans. Earl Morse Wilbur (Boston: Starr King Press, 1957).

57. Edward M. Hulme, "Lelio Sozzini's Confession of Faith," in *Persecution and Liberty: Essays in Honor of George Lincoln Burr* (New York: Century, 1931), 216. Also in CCFCT 2:706. The original text can also be found in Antonio Rotondò, ed., *Lelio Sozzini: Opere* (Florence: L. S. Olschki, 1986), 98–100.

The central point for Sozzini is that he believed these controversies to be niceties of the Christian faith—important to theologians but not necessary for salvation. The theme throughout the confession is that Sozzini worries about the liberty to raise questions on doctrine. He also worries that punishment for not embracing doctrinal language found neither in the Bible nor in the Apostles' Creed is a step too far. One might say that Sozzini was radical about what constituted *enough* assent to doctrine for salvation. He saw the doctrine of the Trinity, Christology, and all other subjects derived from the ancient creeds as nonessential, so long as one held faith in Christ's work on the cross. He treats the Apostles' Creed as the earliest and only necessary creed:

> I will never suffer myself to be deprived of this holy freedom of inquiring from my elders and disputing modestly and submissively in order to enhance my knowledge of divine matters; for there are not a few passages in the Scripture, the interpretation and exposition of which, by the doctors even who are entitled to eternal honor, are by no means satisfactory.[58]

Sozzini eventually made his way to Poland, where religious liberty was protected. Although he had not, by 1555, broken with the Swiss Reformed movement, Sozzini and his nephew Faustus Sozzini (1539–1604) eventually did so. The two not only later rejected trinitarian and christological teachings from the creeds but also helped establish the community known as the Polish Brethren, who later gave rise to the Unitarian movement. The groups in the eastern part of Europe were committed to the imminent return of Christ. This apocalyptic stance increased their desire to foster moral purity, a commitment to the Bible alone (with no creeds), and the practice of immersion as a sign of public commitment to the community.

In 1574, the Polish Brethren drafted their Catechesis and Confession of Faith. The text was far more radical than the 1555 statement by Laelius Sozzini, although he and Faustus had influenced the author of the confession, Georg Schomann, who served in the Minor Church in Kraków. The community had split over not only the more radical antitrinitarianism of the Sozzini family but also the teachings of Jan Łaski (1499–1560).

The confession and catechism were hard for those outside the Polish Brethren circles to interpret. The text rarely speaks overtly in the language of a confession, and instead answers almost all questions with a series of biblical citations. Indeed, the most common question asked of the reader is either

---

58. Hulme, "Lelio Sozzini's Confession of Faith," 217 (translation modified). Also in *CCFCT* 2:707.

"Where is it said?" or "Where is instruction?" followed by a set of verses quoted at length. It is crucial to note, however, that important passages of the Bible either are not mentioned or are reinterpreted to fit within an antitrinitarian formula. John 1 is a sufficient example for us to see this point. Typically, this passage was and is read as evidence for trinitarian orthodoxy ("The Word was with God, and the Word was God"). However, in the Polish confession, the verse is reworked to mean that the Son is merely used by God as an instrument of salvation. There is, therefore, "the one God the Father" only "who is most high."[59] The Polish Brethren base their radical commitment to the Father alone on the Shema from Deuteronomy 6:4, "Hear, O Israel, the LORD our God is one." This passage opens the entire confession, and it is evident throughout each article that only the Father is to be considered truly God.

For example, when asked about Jesus as the Son of God, the next question states boldly, "He is a man, our mediator with God."[60] The text continues at length with scriptural proofs that Christ was a prophet, priest, and king, but it claims that nothing in the Bible points to his sharing divinity with the Father. Christ, then, could equally be described as Lord, though he was only a mediator, part of the created order. One question, for example, asks only, "Where is God said to have created this Jesus Lord and Christ?" The Brethren affirm their view with a long series of verses about Jesus being enthroned by God or glorified by God. The confession ultimately suggests that Christ is to be approached through "adoration and invocation," which harkens to the language the Catholic Church used to describe pious interaction with Mary and the saints.[61] Jesus, then, is our Master, but he is not God come in human flesh. The Holy Spirit is also explicitly denied worship or glory, and instead is described as "energy" or "power" of God.[62] Shifting focus, the remainder of the confession and catechism focuses on the moral life, discipline from the community for sin, and how to pray to God the Father (but never to Jesus), since the logic of the confession stresses that Christians must focus on "imitating his steps . . . that we may find rest for our souls."[63]

A notable contrast to the Polish confession was the Transylvanian Confession of Faith from 1579. The churches in Transylvania (present-day central Romania) were divided over matters similar to those in dispute in Poland,

---

59. English translation in Stanislas Lubieniecki, *History of the Polish Reformation: And Nine Related Documents*, trans. George Huntston Williams, Harvard Theological Studies 37 (Minneapolis: Fortress, 1995), 350. Also in CCFCT 2:711.

60. Lubieniecki, *History of the Polish Reformation*, 351. Also in CCFCT 2:713.

61. Lubieniecki, *History of the Polish Reformation*, 356. Also in CCFCT 2:719.

62. Lubieniecki, *History of the Polish Reformation*, 358. Also in CCFCT 2:722.

63. Lubieniecki, *History of the Polish Reformation*, 358. Also in CCFCT 2:721.

and even the king, John Sigismund, embraced a Unitarian position. The area was quick to embrace the Reformation, with cities divided equally in their adoption of Lutheranism or the Reformed position. Perhaps as a result, these cities maintained a position on religious freedom equal to that in Poland, although the role of the monarch in supporting Unitarianism had a strong appeal, especially among the upper classes. This confession, then, addresses the issue of Christ's divinity in a brief statement (only a page or two in a modern printing). The first article states that "the genuine sense of Holy Scripture" requires believers to refer to the Son as truly God. Echoing language of the early creeds, they admit that Jesus "is to be worshipped and adored."[64] The confession mentions nothing about the Holy Spirit, though this may derive from the fact that Christology was its sole focus. In other ways, though, the confession walks the same radical path as other Anabaptist statements: Scripture alone, not creeds or historical orthodoxy, is to govern all our speech. The authors, therefore, refuse to use any language of *hypostasis* or *persona*, or to speak positively of Nicaea, Constantinople, or any of the ancient councils. Instead, they base their christocentric belief (though not necessarily trinitarian belief) on their reading of the Bible alone.

Conclusions

In this chapter we have seen a few differences between second-generation Protestant confessions and the earlier confessions discussed in the previous chapter. The most notable change from the earlier to the later confessions was the increasing sense of identity within each tradition, as the various forms of Protestantism continued to chart their own path over time. There are few signs that Lutheran and Reformed churches were still seeking to unite confessionally by the second generation. Luther was in the twilight of his years, leaving his final statement before he passed in 1546. The Reformed churches no longer wanted Wittenberg's approval, but they were rapidly gaining ground in other parts of Europe. And finally, the Anabaptists had found an oasis in the eastern regions of Europe, and they no longer wrote as churches under the lash but as free citizens of Christ who wanted to govern themselves.

In spite of this increasing confessional identity, these later confessions give few hints of what had shaped them internally, either through controversy or theological development. Each group had been shaped into a tradition, but none had yet been tempered by trials into the form that it later showed. As

---

64. Text in George Huntston Williams, *The Radical Reformation*, 3rd ed. (Kirksville, MO: Sixteenth Century Journal Publishers, 1992), 1131. Also in CCFCT 2:747.

a result, much of what we might expect is absent in these second-generation confessions. The Reformed confessions say nothing about the covenant or the Sabbath, and only little about predestination. Lutheran confessions speak of grace and justification, but do not give voice to the controversies on the Third Use of the Law or the ubiquity of Christ. Anabaptist confessions sketch only a very simple summary of their unique community life. And in the Anglican communion there was only the scant Forty-Two Articles—and with the reign of Mary, these were cast out of England. Perhaps the best way to understand Protestant confessions during this phase is to say they were *maturing* but not yet *matured*.

In the next two chapters we will explore some of the reasons these four traditions began to reach maturity. In chapter 16 we will look at Catholic and Orthodox responses to the Reformation—responses that made the schism with Rome permanent and closed off even a relationship with the Orthodox Church. Chapter 17 will then look at the trials and successes in each Protestant tradition, as the various groups wrote more detailed and more substantive confessions that capped off the first era of Reformation confessions.

16

Catholic and Orthodox Responses
to Protestant Confessions

In the earliest years of the Reformation, it seemed as if Protestantism was going to sweep through all of Europe. Neither the pope's angry condemnation nor the naked threats by emperors made a difference. Of course, Protestantism began in only two backwater regions—the area surrounding Wittenberg and several Swiss cities—but it soon engulfed much of Germany, France, England, Scandinavia, and Eastern Europe, and Protestants were beginning to make inroads into Scotland and the Netherlands. After 1560, however, Protestant expansion slowed to a crawl. The Netherlands and Scotland finally came over to the Protestant faith, but France, Poland, much of Germany, and scattered cities throughout Europe began to return to Catholicism. Part of the reason for this turnaround was renewed energy within the Roman church. Catholic apologists slowly turned from writing doctrinal treatises against Protestants—almost always in Latin—to appealing to the populace to return home.[1] In addition, the Council of Trent (1545–63) met and officially sided against Protestantism on the core issues of the Reformation, ending any hope that Protestants would return to the church without abandoning their new positions on the disputed questions. Trent also gave new life to the practical side of Catholic faith, albeit life that did not develop

1. For more on this transition, see Carlos M. N. Eire, *Reformations: The Early Modern World, 1450–1650* (New Haven: Yale University Press, 2016), 372–77.

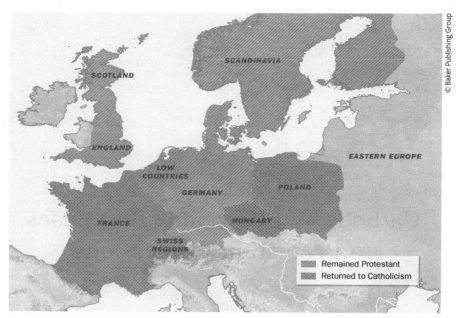

Protestantism and Catholicism in Europe

deeper roots until the next century.[2] Although the schism with Protestantism was painful, the Catholic Church responded to these changes with such stamina and strength that its conclusions defined modern Catholicism until Vatican II (1962–65).

The Orthodox Church was also aware of the schism in the West, and on at least three occasions Jeremiah II, the patriarch of Constantinople, offered his opinion on the new theology of Martin Luther. The response was far less hostile than any of the rhetoric of the Reformation—Catholic or Protestant—but Jeremiah nevertheless expressed grave concerns about Lutheran teachings. He stressed the Orthodox approach to the creeds and encouraged the Lutheran churches to consider coming under the authority of the East if they wished to experience true reform.

In this chapter we explore both of these responses to Protestant theology. The need to explore Trent is obvious, since the decrees of the council became

2. Historians once described Trent as ineffective because it did not bring about immediate change in the church. Recent work, however, has stressed the slow turn within Catholicism that led to its flowering in the seventeenth century. See John W. O'Malley, *Trent: What Happened at the Council* (Cambridge, MA: Belknap, 2013); O'Malley, *The Council of Trent: Myths, Misunderstandings, and Unintended Consequences*, Gregoriana 4 (Rome: Gregorian & Biblical Press, 2013).

official Catholic theology. These proclamations were an important development in Catholic history. In contrast, the response of the Orthodox Church to Protestant theology is rarely studied, but examining it helps us understand some of what made Protestant theology so radical. Jeremiah's response to the Augsburg Confession, although lacking the rhetorical heat seen in Catholic books, nevertheless revealed some of the same concerns.

Counter-Reformation and Eastern Reaction

Recent scholars have raised doubts about traditional descriptions of Catholic reform movements. Nearly all older textbooks called this phase of the story the "Counter-Reformation," a term that sounded austere and intimidating. There certainly is some truth in this nomenclature, as quite a bit of Catholic energy was spent *countering* the criticisms of Luther and others.[3] The Jesuits, for example, focused on the problem of reform, both positively in winning back cities to the Catholic faith and negatively in denouncing the errors of Protestantism. The Council of Trent, as we will see in this chapter, spent many of its sessions denouncing the doctrines that were central to the Reformation—so much so that it would be impossible to see Trent writing such decrees in any context besides that of the sixteenth century. By the second half of that century, Catholicism *was* reacting to the Reformation.[4]

Nevertheless, historians have grown uneasy with this portrayal of Catholic reform after the Reformation. The critique certainly is understandable: the description of the sixteenth century as a Counter-Reformation can seem bleak, and the tendency in many cases has been to focus on cases where Catholics merely rejected Protestant doctrine. That focus on the reactions of Catholics added a fair amount of Protestant bias to the story; indeed, it made the Catholic faith after Luther seem hostile and backward-looking, with little more to offer than rhetoric against its Protestant opponents. Even the Council of Trent was viewed as a series of sessions that reaffirmed the status quo. By contrast, recent scholars have pointed out that calls for reform were heard long before Luther and that the Council of Trent discussed internal reforms

3. Compare, for example, the earlier H. Outram Evennett, *The Spirit of the Counter-Reformation*, ed. John Bossy (Notre Dame, IN: University of Notre Dame Press, 1970); and the more recent R. Po-chia Hsia, *The World of Catholic Renewal, 1540–1770*, New Approaches to European History 12 (Cambridge: Cambridge University Press, 1999). Hsia's work by its very scope is more wide-ranging and charitable to the source material.

4. See, for example, Thomas Worcester, ed., *The Cambridge Companion to the Jesuits*, Cambridge Companions to Religion (Cambridge: Cambridge University Press, 2008), 1–31.

during each of its sessions.[5] Today, most scholars describe this as the Catholic Reformation—a name that highlights the connection to earlier Catholic reform movements without denying that there was an official response to the rise of Protestantism.[6]

The debate over scholarly terminology aside, we will nevertheless focus on the story of Catholic *reaction* to the Reformation, as well as *reactions* from the Eastern Orthodox Church. But we do not intend to go back to the older perspective enshrined in the term "Counter-Reformation." Our choice to focus on the reactions of Catholic and Eastern churches is, in fact, due to the opposite problem: we do not want to *isolate* Protestant confessions from their relationship to the other two branches of Christianity. The sheer number of Protestant confessions in the sixteenth and seventeenth centuries can obscure the fact that both Catholic and Eastern churches intentionally rejected the evangelical message. The Catholics focused on the doctrinal issues that divided them from Protestants, and their rejection of the Reformation was the most important step in shaping modern Catholicism. In the East, Jeremiah II was not only aware of the Reformation but was also asked to give his verdict on the Augsburg Confession (1530). Although his response was judiciously warm and charitable, Jeremiah still made clear that he was troubled by Protestant teachings.

The point of these stories is not that Catholics and Orthodox had problems with the Reformation. Instead, as we saw with the story of Christian creeds and heresies, the debate over essential doctrines was always helpful to clarify the grammar of the Christian faith. Looking at the response of two other branches of Christianity to Protestantism will similarly shed light on both Protestant confessions and the faith of Catholic and Orthodox churches, since the comparison reveals the touchstone issues that divided these traditions.

The Long Road to a Council

It is helpful to notice the heroic efforts of Protestants to defend their churches. The celebration of those who suffered martyrdom, for example, was epitomized in John Foxe's *Book of Martyrs*, published first in 1563 and expanded

5. A recent helpful survey that sees Trent in the context of late medieval councils is Nelson H. Minnich, *Councils of the Catholic Reformation: Pisa I (1409) to Trent (1545–63)* (Burlington, VT: Ashgate, 2008).

6. Notably in John W. O'Malley, *Trent and All That: Renaming Catholicism in the Early Modern Era* (Cambridge, MA: Harvard University Press, 2000).

The death and burning of the most constant Martyrs in Christ, D. Robert Barnes, Thomas Garret, and William Hierome in Smithfield, an. 1541.

A page from John Foxe's *Book of Martyrs*

into several large volumes by the 1580s.[7] Foxe's account of the suffering and death in Protestant churches had a profound impact on the historical memory of the Reformation, since it connected these miseries with the persecutions of the early church. Especially in England, although also in other parts of Europe, the power of the Reformation was seen in the light of those who died for the faith.

Nevertheless, it is easy to overlook how difficult it was to be a late medieval reformer. The Renaissance papacy was often dominated by sinners rather than saints.[8] The Roman curia during the Reformation was largely controlled by powerful families—most famously the Borgia and Medici—and the popes were often corrupt and unwilling to curb their lavish spending. Those who strove to reform the church internally, therefore, faced enormous opposition to change, and this resistance was made worse once Protestants began to challenge the authority of the church. Charles Borromeo, for example, was a

7. The official title was *Acts and Monuments*. On the history of this book, see Thomas Freeman and Elizabeth Evenden, *Religion and the Book in Early Modern England: The Making of John Foxe's "Book of Martyrs,"* Cambridge Studies in Early Modern British History (Cambridge: Cambridge University Press, 2014). A critical edition of the book is now available online at https://www.johnfoxe.org.

8. As described in Eamon Duffy, *Saints and Sinners: A History of the Popes*, 4th ed. (New Haven: Yale University Press, 2015), 177–95.

tireless reformer in Milan (the largest archdiocese in Italy at the time), where he served as archbishop from 1564 to 1584.[9] Once he took office, he began a campaign of reform by removing the lavish ornaments in local churches, visiting monasteries and churches to restore their obedience, and stressing the need for people to live as faithful Catholics. As a result, many found him to be a nuisance. On one occasion, a local priest attempted an assassination, and Borromeo was saved only because the bullet could not pierce his heavy vestments. Many similar stories could be told of the perils of Catholic reformers.[10]

Such internal resistance to change was therefore part of the reason why the pope hesitated to call a council. It was unpopular to focus on the problems of the church, and the Reformation made the situation only worse. The reformers within the Catholic Church not only appeared to deny the authority of Christ's vicar on earth but also lampooned Catholic excess and laziness in countless woodcuts and pamphlets that flew throughout Europe.[11] Even when Protestants supported the call for a council, they did not want the pope involved. Luther himself wished for a council to be held in the empire, but he wrote to the German nobility, asking them to ensure that the papacy was barred from influencing any decision.[12] Those loyal to the Catholic Church knew that if a council gave in to the cries for reform, things could get worse, since this would be an admission of guilt. Local reform leaders, such as Borromeo in Milan and Girolamo Savonarola in Florence, were unpopular even with those who were not targeted by their campaigns. According to many Catholics, the dignity of the church was at stake.

The other damper on the possibility of a council was the political turmoil in Europe. Any pope who called a council had to balance all sides if he wanted to avoid headaches. On the one hand, some feared that a council would come down heavily on Protestant teachings, forever closing the door to a reunion. Not a few princes in Europe, especially those with divided territories, feared a civil war if a council took heavy-handed measures. Catholics who were sympathetic to Protestant reforms feared too harsh a verdict from a council. On the other hand, the political tensions among European nations meant that a council had to be held in a neutral location, with no single nation in control, and the pope would need enough persistence to ensure a strong

9. The story of Borromeo's struggle is told in Eire, *Reformations*, 369–70.

10. For example, see the various stories in Jean Lacouture, *Jesuits: A Multibiography* (New York: Basic Books, 1997).

11. Their name in German, *Flugblätter*, means "flying leaves," although we normally translate this as "pamphlets."

12. This is a central argument in Luther's *Address to the Christian Nobility* (1520).

turnout of Catholic leaders. To top it off, the defeat of conciliarism in the Catholic Church was barely more than a century in the past. Conciliarism was a movement that had arisen in response to the disastrous fifteenth-century situation in which two popes, one in Rome and the other in Avignon, both claimed to be the rightful heir of St. Peter. Conciliarists believed that a council was superior to the pope, and everyone feared the return of such a (to them) radical idea if a council, not the pope, were the means to fix the problem of the Reformation. During most of the early Reformation, the pope would rather stay in Rome than summon a council—and with it, the ghosts of the conciliar movement that might undermine his own authority.

The Council of Trent

With all these headwinds blowing against a council, the pope who finally summoned one was an unlikely reformer. Pope Paul III (r. 1534–49) was born Alessandro Farnese, whose family had long dealings with the papacy.[13] Like many of the popes of his day, Paul III rose to his office through a series of family connections, the most lurid of which was that his sister Giulia had been mistress to Alexander VI (1431–1503), the controversial Borgia pope known for killing Savonarola, fathering several children with various women, and ultimately doubling the gossip that surrounded the curia.[14] For his part, Paul III was only slightly better. Before he was elevated to the rank of cardinal in his early twenties, he had spent time in the court of Lorenzo de' Medici, enjoying the extravagant lifestyle of a powerful noble. After several years of wanton behavior, however, he seems to have been inspired to renew his Catholic faith, and so he sent away his mistress and committed himself to the cause of reform.[15]

We know that Paul III was in favor of a council from the start of his papacy, although he was slow to implement this vision. He called for a council to meet first in Mantua in 1536—the source of several Protestant confessions[16]— though another war between France and the emperor Charles V sank the plans before the council opened. He was unmoved by the setback, however, and sought to approach reform through a special commission led by the reliable reformer Gasparo Contarini, a man sympathetic to reform who had sat at the

---

13. The same family produced Boniface VIII, whose late thirteenth-century bull *Unam Sanctam* was discussed in chap. 12.

14. Giulia's relationship with Alexander inspired the macabre joke that she was "the Bride of Christ."

15. On Paul III, see Duffy, *Saints and Sinners*, 196–207.

16. See our discussion in chap. 15.

Diet of Worms during Luther's trial.[17] The commission produced a surprising report, the *Concilium de emendanda ecclesia* (Council for the Correction of the Church), which placed the church's problems squarely at the feet of the papacy. The report was circulated among the members of the curia, although its harsh language provoked ill will toward the cause of reform, forcing Paul to ignore any attempt to implement the proposals.[18] Other efforts—such as the Regensburg Colloquy in 1541 that brought together Catholics and Protestants for discussion—made no progress.[19] But in 1545, almost a generation after the start of the Reformation, Paul finally summoned a council to meet in the city of Trent.

Despite the importance of the matter, the Council of Trent opened with lackluster support and poor attendance. Suspicion plagued the council almost from the beginning, since Catholic nations waited to see whether this council would fall apart as had the one in Mantua. When the council opened on December 13, only thirty-six people were present.[20] Once the session opened, however, others began to trickle into Trent, and several hundred attended the final session in 1562.

The first session spent most of its time scrutinizing the doctrines of the Reformation. Due in large part to Protestant claims about medieval doctrine, the delegates worked feverishly to explain the Catholic position, often going to great lengths to reaffirm medieval practice. This served an essential need, since the church had never ruled on justification by faith and the role of good works in the Christian life.[21] The articulation of other doctrines—such as original sin and the role of penance and purgatory—also needed further nuance. In a move that appeared conciliatory, the Lutherans were asked to attend the council, although this was not viewed as an opportunity for collaboration. The Protestants were offered safe travel and arrived in January, but simply to observe the proceedings. A month later, news arrived that Luther had died, and, strengthened by this news, the delegates to the council quickly issued a decree on the inerrancy of the Vulgate and the use of tradition. In this article, they emphasize that their purpose is "for the uprooting of heresies, for the

---

17. On Contarini, see Elisabeth G. Gleason, *Gasparo Contarini: Venice, Rome, and Reform* (Berkeley: University of California Press, 1993); Peter Matheson, *Cardinal Contarini at Regensburg* (Oxford: Clarendon, 1972).

18. Much of the turmoil was because none of the curia were represented on the committee. Contarini was well respected, but it was easy to target the report as needless complaining from those on the outside.

19. Contarini was also involved at Regensburg. See Matheson, *Cardinal Contarini at Regensburg*.

20. They were composed of one cardinal, thirty-one bishops, and four archbishops.

21. See chap. 13.

peace and unity of the church," and this opening statement set the tone for the remaining sessions.[22] The Lutherans left after only four months.

Overall, the first phase of Trent (1545–47) concluded with eight sessions, covering not only the Vulgate and tradition but also justification and the sacraments. Each of these points was at the center of the Reformation struggle, and the decrees leave no room for Protestant interpretation. Doctrine is to be determined not only by the Scriptures, nor even by unwritten traditions, but also by traditions "handed on as it were from the apostles themselves at the inspiration of the Holy Spirit."[23] Such language explicitly affirms that traditions arising even *after* the early church—including those of relatively recent origin—are themselves inspired. The practices of the church, no matter when they were established, must always be held as the witness of the Holy Spirit. Even Protestant communities such as the Lutheran and Anglican that valued the extrascriptural traditions of the early church did not go far enough in affirming the inspiration of the papal magisterium's decrees. All Roman practices established by the authority of the pope had to be embraced.

The second decree focuses on the role of the Vulgate in the Catholic Church. Protestants and humanists had lampooned the quality of Jerome's translation, but the council responded that the Vulgate was "the authentic text in public readings, debates, sermons, and explanations; and no one is to dare or presume on any pretext to reject it." No room is left for "personal judgment in matters of faith and customs," since the Catholic Church alone "is to pass judgment on the true meaning and interpretation of the Sacred Scriptures."[24] Those printers in Europe who printed Bibles that were not officially sanctioned or anonymous books of theology, or who "added notes and commentaries of anyone at all," were subject to penalty. The statement on the sacraments charts a similar path, since it rejects even conservative Protestant positions on Christ's presence—such as Luther's view of the physical presence of Christ in the Lord's Supper—since they do not affirm the language of transubstantiation as defined by the Fourth Lateran Council.[25]

Perhaps the two most important decrees of Trent during this phase were on original sin and justification by faith. As we argued in our previous two chapters, Protestant churches were united in their belief that original sin remained after regeneration. The believer experienced sanctification, Protestants agreed, but the corruption of sin was not eradicated, and therefore all good works must be

---

22. Norman P. Tanner, ed., *Decrees of the Ecumenical Councils*, vol. 2, *Trent to Vatican II* (Washington, DC: Georgetown University Press, 1990), 660. Also in CCFCT 2:821.
23. Tanner, *Decrees of the Ecumenical Councils*, 2:663. Also in CCFCT 2:822.
24. Tanner, *Decrees of the Ecumenical Councils*, 2:664. Also in CCFCT 2:823.
25. See chap. 12.

based on the work of the Holy Spirit. In this way, Protestant confessions always affirmed that justification was based only on Christ's work, without denying that our good works come by the gift of the Holy Spirit. What Protestants contended—especially in Lutheran confessions—was that any focus on good works necessarily resulted in confusion about our own righteousness. Trent noted this issue and affirmed that these issues had arisen as the central issue for Protestants, but "the council now wishes to call back those who are going astray."[26]

First and foremost, the council began by affirming many of the same points that Protestants endorsed. Like Protestant confessions, it condemns those who claim that Adam's sin did not plunge all of humanity into sin. The will is enslaved to sin, and there is nothing in us that can respond to God by human strength. This conforms to many of the teachings of Augustine on original sin. However, the council continues: "If anyone says that the guilt of original sin is not remitted through the grace of our lord Jesus Christ which is given at baptism . . . let him be anathema." This declaration upholds the medieval teaching on baptismal regeneration—namely, that the will is in bondage until baptism, at which time the infusion of grace renews the infant, allowing the Christian to respond to grace. The council admitted that some manner of original sin remains, but the delegates stressed that this was "left as a form of testing." Christians must offer "strong resistance" to sin so that "that person will be crowned who competes according to the rules."[27] The rules referenced are the entire system of confession and penance that Luther had challenged and that all Protestants agreed corrupted the biblical understanding of salvation.

The decree on original sin left little room for a Protestant concept of justification by faith. But the council wanted an even stronger statement, with no room for confusion, and so the delegates added a lengthy statement to explain the Catholic position on faith and works. The statement opens with a wider look at the work of Christ to secure salvation through the cross. It reaffirms that this work "cannot take place without the waters of rebirth or the desire for them." Grace comes first on the believer through the Holy Spirit, but "neither does the person do absolutely nothing in receiving the movement of grace, for he can also reject it." The Catholic Church therefore affirms that "the wicked are justified by God by his grace."[28] But the statement carries the argument further by including the assertion that sinners *must work* for their salvation, since there is a "preparation [that precedes] the actual justification, which consists not only in the forgiveness of sins but also in the sanctification

---

26. Tanner, *Decrees of the Ecumenical Councils*, 2:665–66. Also in CCFCT 2:824–25.
27. Tanner, *Decrees of the Ecumenical Councils*, 2:667. Also in CCFCT 2:826.
28. Tanner, *Decrees of the Ecumenical Councils*, 2:672. Also in CCFCT 2:828–29.

and renewal of the inward being by the willing acceptance of the grace and gifts whereby someone from being unjust becomes just."[29] Here justification and sanctification are purposefully linked so that they become a single unit, or essentially the same experience in the believer—the work of Christ has begun the process, but there must be cooperation with grace to receive justification. The virtues needed are "infused at the same time" as baptism, making them, paradoxically, both a divine gift and the result of human effort. The delegates then concluded by claiming that this definition was how they linked Paul's language of justification by faith with Augustine's language that we are justified by "faith working itself out in love."[30]

> But though it is necessary to believe that sins are not forgiven, nor have they ever been forgiven, save freely by the divine mercy on account of Christ. Nevertheless, it must not be said that anyone's sins are or have been forgiven simply because he has proud assurance and certainty that they have been forgiven, and relies soley on that. For this empty and ungodly assurance may exist among heretics and schismatics, as indeed it does in our day, and is preached most controversially against the Catholic Church.[31]

Trent's statement on original sin and justification by faith created a united theological stance against the Protestant confession of justification by faith alone. The language of "faith working itself out in love" is biblical (Gal. 5:6) and was acceptable to Protestants, and it even appeared in the Tetrapolitan Confession.[32] But Trent situated the concept of "working in love" differently than did any Protestant church, by viewing it through the lens of the penitential system of the Catholic Church. Despite the efforts of those on both sides to find common language, the council's ruling now made it impossible to see any possible path forward to reconciliation.

Jeremiah II and Augsburg

The Catholic Church was not the only branch of the church to respond to the Reformation. In the latter half of the sixteenth century, the Eastern Orthodox patriarch of Constantinople, Jeremiah II, was a reformer embroiled in his own

29. Tanner, *Decrees of the Ecumenical Councils*, 2:673. Also in CCFCT 2:829.

30. Tanner, *Decrees of the Ecumenical Councils*, 2:673. Also in CCFCT 2:830. Notice, of course, that Paul affirms "faith working itself out in love" in Gal. 5:6. But it was Augustine, not Paul, who linked that phrase directly to justification.

31. Tanner, *Decrees of the Ecumenical Councils*, 2:674. Also in CCFCT 2:830.

32. See chap. 15.

struggle with enemies—a struggle for which he was deposed and excommunicated in 1579.[33] Three years earlier, however, in the buildup to the writing of
the Lutheran Formula of Concord, Jeremiah sent a lengthy letter to the city
of Tübingen—the first of three such letters over several years. Jeremiah was
responding to the invitation of two Lutheran theologians, Martin Crusius
and Jakob Andreae, who had sent Melanchthon's Greek translation of the
Augsburg Confession, hoping to establish a relationship with the Orthodox.
The desire for such a relationship grew out of the frequent Lutheran claim that
their faith was nothing new, that it was consistent with the ancient church, and
by extension consistent with the contemporary East. The reply from Jeremiah
was a personal letter, but it was so heavily based on Orthodox principles and
an Orthodox reading of the creeds that it effectively amounted to a confession,
as we are using that word in this book. Today these letters are referred to as
the Three Replies. Here we will focus only on Jeremiah's first reply, since it
is the lengthiest and most substantive letter that he sent to Tübingen. As the
correspondence continued, by 1581 the patriarch felt hounded by questions,
and he begged the Lutherans to cease sending him letters.

The first letter begins in a cordial fashion, although Jeremiah feels free on
multiple occasions to tell the Lutherans where they do not agree with Orthodox
theology.[34] Jeremiah opens the letter by underscoring its purpose, which is "to
clear the issues in which we agree and those in which we disagree."[35] He begins
by noting that the Lutherans' understanding of Nicaea and Constantinople
is "correct," as well as their adherence to the Apostles' Creed. Jeremiah is not
willing to let the matter stand with a mere affirmation of the creeds, however,
and goes on to detail the Orthodox reflections on Nicaea. He writes that affirming the creeds as the "true philosophy according to Christ" is one thing,
but "in practice they are a higher ethic which teaches us and leads us to salvation." So, for example, he argues, "Humility is aroused by the descent of God
. . . modesty, by the incarnation," all of which find their basis in the creeds.[36]

Of the Lutheran doctrines that Jeremiah affirms, he mentions his approval
without hesitation, though usually mixed with criticism. He agrees that Communion should consist of both the bread and wine (unlike the Catholic practice of offering only the bread), although he insists that the Orthodox Church

---

33. A not uncommon occurrence when rival factions rose up in Constantinople. Jeremiah was
restored to his office the following year, only to be arrested, beaten, and deposed again in 1584.

34. Translation in George Mastrantonis, *Augsburg and Constantinople: The Correspondence between the Tübingen Theologians and Patriarch Jeremiah II of Constantinople on the
Augsburg Confession* (Brookline, MA: Holy Cross Orthodox Press, 1982).

35. Mastrantonis, *Augsburg and Constantinople*, 31. Also in CCFCT 1:395.

36. Mastrantonis, *Augsburg and Constantinople*, 35. Also in CCFCT 1:399.

affirms seven sacraments, not two.[37] He gives general praise that the Lutherans still hold to infant baptism—although he again corrects their view, since they do not apply the chrism immediately to the baptized child. He agrees that remorse and confession are all that is needed after sin, but he is bewildered at the Lutherans' "total rejection of the canonical satisfactions."[38] Those ordained to ministry, Jeremiah agrees, ought to be blameless and holy, but he worries that such talk will lead to the ancient heresy of Donatism.[39] He also notes that the Orthodox allow for married priests "who are unable to remain celibate" since "God has ordained marriage," but he stresses that the ancient ideal was for a celibate clergy.[40]

On other matters, Jeremiah is not as charitable. The subject that he finds of greatest concern is justification. Affirming the basic desire to foster faith and assurance in Christians, he nevertheless argues repeatedly that one must not be allergic to the discussion of good works. "Let us show our faith by works. He [God] does not ignore our deeds. Therefore, we should do good works according to our ability, and not plead the excuse of human weakness."[41] The interpretation of the Lutheran message implied in these comments may not have been entirely fair—or at least Jeremiah misunderstood the role original sin played in the Augsburg Confession—but certainly it undercut the Lutheran stance on the role of works in salvation. Jeremiah was far more open to encouraging good works, although he did not, like Trent, include works as part of the basis for justification. "The present life is a road which needs leading by the hand from above," and therefore, he stresses, "There is need for a struggle, and this struggle must be great and lawful."[42] He agrees in principle that this leading toward sanctification comes by God's work, yet he continues to find the Lutheran position incomprehensible. In the end, he judges the Augsburg Confession as only resting on one part of the Christian life:

> One must not always dwell on the basic elements, not merely lay a foundation, but one must also complete the rest of the building and even the roof, which is the perfecting of good deeds. If one forever dwells on the basic elements, or

37. He also has no problem chiding the Lutherans for stating their position "not in depth and not too clearly." See Mastrantonis, *Augsburg and Constantinople*, 54. Also in CCFCT 1:420.

38. Mastrantonis, *Augsburg and Constantinople*, 57. Also in CCFCT 1:422.

39. The Donatists were a separatist group in North Africa in the fourth and fifth centuries. The Donatist view that Jeremiah labeled heretical was the idea that serious sin on the part of a priest not only voided his ordination but also rendered any sacrament performed by that priest ineffective. This means, for example, that those ordained by a disgraced priest need to be reordained.

40. Mastrantonis, *Augsburg and Constantinople*, 91–92. Also in CCFCT 1:461.

41. Mastrantonis, *Augsburg and Constantinople*, 37. Also in CCFCT 1:401.

42. Mastrantonis, *Augsburg and Constantinople*, 39. Also in CCFCT 1:404.

about the foundation, there will be nothing more for him to do, neither will he complete the house, nor hold fast the foundation of wisdom, nor become wise. If, then, we love Christ as we ought to love him, we shall grow in virtue and will punish ourselves when we sin. We shall not fear hell, but we shall fear offending God.[43]

The value of good works and the pursuit of wisdom never featured heavily in the Lutheran doctrine of salvation—at least not in any capacity that might inspire self-righteousness. The Lutheran position on good works is perhaps best summarized in the Formula of Concord, which states that good works come "spontaneously" on the Christian, without any command or encouragement.[44] Jeremiah's critique of the Augsburg Confession, however, rests on his approval of those who pursue these virtues, and he saw no reason to avoid encouraging holiness in Christians. On the subject of encouraging good works, Jeremiah also found the Lutheran position to be out of step with the historic church.

Conclusions

In this chapter we have noted how both Catholic and Orthodox churches reacted to the theology of the Reformation. In the case of Jeremiah, we can hold his comments lightly, since he was responding only to the Augsburg Confession and he had no personal experience with Protestant churches. Still, his comments must be understood as a critique of the Reformation—not that he might not have agreed in principle with justification by faith, but that he refused to countenance silence about good works. Jeremiah never stressed the role of penance, and he did not allow for indulgences, but his confession meant that the Orthodox opinion of the Augsburg Confession, at least, was not favorable.

The Council of Trent, in contrast, issued a more thorough critique of the Reformation, dismantling the positions held by most Protestants and even closing the door to the Lutheran understanding of the sacraments. For nearly four hundred years, the Catholic Church held Protestants as heretical and schismatic—and Protestants likewise never again brooked any talk of unity with Rome.

Nevertheless, the severity of Trent's condemnation of Protestantism and the comparative mildness of Jeremiah's response to the Lutherans should not

43. Mastrantonis, *Augsburg and Constantinople*, 40–41. Also in CCFCT 1:405.
44. See our discussion in chap. 17.

blind us to the fact that, in many ways, Roman Catholicism and Protestant-ism were more alike than either was like Orthodoxy. Both Western groups worked from a juridical framework focusing on guilt and innocence/grace, and this framework elevated to the highest position the question of how and on what basis one was justified. Orthodoxy, in contrast, saw Christian life not as a legal state but as a journey, and justification was never regarded as the centerpiece of salvation.[45] Thus, Jeremiah's bewilderment at the Lutherans' pronouncements may actually have been the result more of an inability to comprehend Western categories for expressing salvation than of an ironclad disagreement about it. To use the language of this book, Jeremiah's grammar for understanding Christian life was somewhat different; he was speaking of salvation in a different theological language. Catholics and Protestants were at least speaking the same theological language, and therefore the differences between them were more obvious, the debates more heated.

45. For a discussion of this difference in perspective, see Donald Fairbairn, *Eastern Ortho-doxy through Western Eyes* (Louisville: Westminster John Knox, 2002), 1–6, 79–95.

17

Protestant Confessions
in the Late Reformation

It was midday on October 9, 1601, when a sword cleaved Niklaus Krell's head from his body. His crime was heresy, and although executions were common at the time of the Reformation, this was an unusual case: a Protestant cutting off the head of another Protestant.

Niklaus was a German, educated in Leipzig, and he had risen to be chancellor in the region of Saxony. These were Lutheran lands, and he was expected to support the official faith. But Nicklaus had been won over to the Reformed teachings on the Eucharist, and his office gave him control of major political appointments. This allowed him to advance Calvinists to positions of high rank, although it is unclear how he expected to get away with this. Elector Christian II (1583–1611) might have forgiven Niklaus for his personal convictions, but in leveraging his office to push Reformed theology Niklaus went too far. A lengthy trial ensued, but in the end, the Lutheran prince wished to silence Crypto-Calvinism, and Niklaus Krell became a martyr for his form of Protestantism as the executioner held up his severed head and bellowed to the crowds, "Beware of Calvinism!"[1]

1. It may very well have been the case that Niklaus had merely joined the Philippists (discussed later in this chapter), a group whose views were often slandered as Crypto-Calvinism. The experiences and theology of various communities who suffered martyrdom in the Reformation are told in Brad S. Gregory, *Salvation at Stake: Christian Martyrdom in Early Modern Europe*, Harvard Historical Studies 134 (Cambridge, MA: Harvard University Press, 1999). Krell's story

As we noted in chapter 1, the years from 1560 to 1650 are often seen as the high-water mark for Protestant confessionalism.[2] In one sense, this view is correct, if only because the length and depth of these confessions go beyond those drafted in the early Reformation. Not a few denominations today still hold these latter confessions as the full expression of their faith. But even considered on their own, their theological range was impressive—as was the story of their creation. Some were crafted over years, often by an army of theological advisers; others were written to clarify certain doctrines for future generations. So even though there are still confessions written today—and we will look at a number of them in our next chapter—few modern confessions attempt anything to rival the confessions that closed out the Reformation. If the early Reformers hungered for new confessions of faith, their heirs in the seventeenth century were overfed to the point of bursting.

We have argued in this book against too narrow a definition of a confession, and in doing so we have sought to avoid the popular notion that the Reformation was the only period that produced confessions. But we must add a word of caution here, since our view is not based on a cynical blindness to the importance of these last Reformation confessions. Protestant confessions were always contentious on important doctrines, so these latter confessions did not add a quarrelsome spirit to Protestant confessions, but rather made the rifts between churches permanent—and just on the eve of the wars of religion (ca. 1560–1648).[3] In other words, expanding our definition of what constitutes a confession should not force us to see all confessions as equally significant in shaping Protestant history. These later confessions often were much longer than earlier ones, and they were adopted as the expressions of faith not only of churches but even of nations. Thus their significance in many ways outstripped that of the earlier confessions.

This chapter focuses on these late Reformation confessions, although given their size and complexity, we will not plumb their depths (an act that would take a book of its own) but instead will focus on key themes that shaped

---

is told in Carlos M. N. Eire, *Reformations: The Early Modern World, 1450–1650* (New Haven: Yale University Press, 2016), 586–87.

2. As in John M. Headley, Hans J. Hillerbrand, and Anthony J. Paplas, eds., *Confessionalization in Europe, 1555–1700: Essays in Honor and Memory of Bodo Nischan* (Burlington, VT: Ashgate, 2004).

3. We will not discuss the wars in detail, but we must note the vague usage of the term "wars of religion." At times, this phrase refers to specific wars in a region (e.g., the French Wars of Religion), but more often historians use the term more generally to refer to all religiously motivated European wars in the Reformation and post-Reformation periods. On this, see Benjamin J. Kaplan, *Divided by Faith: Religious Conflict and the Practice of Toleration in Early Modern Europe* (Cambridge, MA: Belknap, 2007). On the various wars for the faith, see Richard S. Dunn, *The Age of Religious Wars, 1559–1715* (New York: Norton, 1979).

each tradition. One thing that we will explore in this chapter is how doubts about the Protestant message of predestination—or doubts about how the grammar of this doctrine was used—led to the creation of new Arminian confessions. By contrast, the Reformed and Lutheran traditions altered or intensified their theology in opposition to these same impulses. This was a major shift in Protestant confessions. From the start of the seventeenth century, voices across the Protestant world began to seek new ways to explore Christian living and holiness, and several began to do so by challenging the earlier Protestant teaching on predestination or election. These changes helped to produce new Protestant communities—especially Pietistic and Methodist ones—that sought to reorient theology around Christian experience.

Philip Melanchthon versus Lutheranism

Up until his death, Martin Luther was the exclusive voice defining Lutheranism.[4] He wrote or approved all of the earliest Lutheran confessions and catechisms, and those who wanted to be part of the tradition had to adjust themselves to Luther's views. Moreover, when people were expelled from the ranks of Lutheranism, the reason often was a personal battle with Luther.[5]

As a result, the first crisis in Lutheranism after its founder's death in 1546 was over the question of how faithful the movement should remain to Luther. The problem is exemplified in the person of Philip Melanchthon (1497–1560). In his early years, Melanchthon and Luther had been inseparable—a famous portrait of the Luther family included their young friend—and he had served as a sounding board for Luther.[6] It would be almost impossible to think of Lutheranism without his influence, mostly by his work on the Augsburg Confession and the *Treatise on the Power and Primacy of the Pope* (1537), both of which ironically became permanent confessions for German churches. By Luther's death, however, not a few Lutherans saw Melanchthon as little more than a turncoat against their Reformation.[7] Their rationale was that Melanchthon had begun to move

---

4. Confessional Lutheran scholars often make note of this. See Robert Kolb, *Luther's Heirs Define His Legacy: Studies on Lutheran Confessionalization* (Brookfield, VT: Ashgate Variorum, 1996).

5. The classic example is Andreas Karlstadt. See Amy Nelson Burnett, *Karlstadt and the Origins of the Eucharistic Controversy: A Study in the Circulation of Ideas*, Oxford Studies in Historical Theology (Oxford: Oxford University Press, 2011).

6. A good biography is Timothy J. Wengert, *Philip Melanchthon, Speaker of the Reformation: Wittenberg's Other Reformer* (Burlington, VT: Ashgate Variorum, 2010).

7. On this and the other factors that drove Lutherans to quarrel with Melanchthon, see Eric W. Gritsch, *A History of Lutheranism*, 2nd ed. (Minneapolis: Fortress, 2010), 76–81, 86–91.

Public Domain / Wikimedia Commons

Portrait of Philip Melanchthon
by Lucas Cranach the Elder

away from strict adherence to Luther's theology, notably on the role of good works after conversion and the presence of Christ in the Eucharist.[8] Each of these matters had provoked Luther to break fellowship with other Reformers. Melanchthon's "retreat" on both issues led not a few Lutherans to see him as a defector to Zwinglianism.

The most important of these issues was the role of good works after conversion. Luther's discussions of justification, of course, had always been intensified by the need to clarify the message against Catholic teachings. This explains his frequent use of polemic and hyperbole—and he never allowed Lutheran clergy to describe works as necessary, obligatory, or required. Indeed, this language is crucial for understanding Luther's message, since he himself always stressed that fruit *would be added* in the Christian life. His concern was that the human will, because of original sin, could not focus on works

8. There are several more issues than these two; however, even in their own literature these two become the supreme issues for both sides. See Philip Benedict, *Christ's Churches Purely Reformed: A Social History of Calvinism* (New Haven: Yale University Press, 2002), 9–76.

without fouling up justification. In particular, he rejected any attempt to discuss works when addressing the question of our faith in Christ's work.[9]

Even before Luther's death, Melanchthon came to see the matter differently. It seems that his ongoing study of the patristic period played a role, although we cannot rule out other factors.[10] Others were aware of this change in Melanchthon, but he never attempted to convince Luther of his views. But for Melanchthon, it seemed clear that the New Testament did encourage Christian obedience, even if that obedience was based on grace and gratitude. He found it reasonable, then, to reincorporate some of these elements into the Lutheran message, especially now that the early separation from Rome was over. It didn't take long for Lutheran theologians to spot the flaw. Even before Luther's death, theologians such as Matthias Flacius and Andreas Osiander attacked Melanchthon for his teaching.[11] Luther, due to his love for Melanchthon, was unwilling to hear the evidence. Until Luther died, Melanchthon was safe on this subject.

Almost immediately after Luther's death, however, Lutheranism erupted in controversy. The setting was the military campaign by the emperor Charles V to reconquer Lutheran lands for the Catholic faith. After the Diet of Worms, Charles had first been unable to capture Luther, then found himself occupied with wars abroad, and then had to rest on his laurels rather than go after the now popular hero of the German people. With Luther dead, Charles pounced. He won decisive victories over the Lutheran princes and imposed the Augsburg Interim—an edict that required Lutherans to halt their worship and return to the Mass, at least until negotiations for a full restoration to Rome were conducted. Of course, for anyone to comply with this order was a betrayal of the Reformation, and many Lutheran pastors were unwilling to knuckle under without a fight.[12] Melanchthon, however—perhaps from a sense of duty not to force Lutherans into martyrdom—sided with the Augsburg Interim.

9. A recent study on this has shown its parallels to medieval thinking. See Richard Rex, *The Making of Martin Luther* (Princeton: Princeton University Press, 2017).

10. Melanchthon's change on this issue is covered in Gregory B. Graybill, *Evangelical Free Will: Philipp Melanchthon's Doctrinal Journey on the Origins of Faith*, Oxford Theological Monographs (Oxford: Oxford University Press, 2010). A great deal of energy is devoted to assessing the sources that drove Melanchthon to this point; see, for example, E. P. Meijering, *Melanchthon and Patristic Thought: The Doctrine of Christ and Grace, the Trinity, and the Creation*, Studies in the History of Christian Thought 32 (Leiden: Brill, 1983).

11. On Flacius, see Oliver K. Olson, *Matthias Flacius and the Survival of Luther's Reform* (Leipzig: Harrassowitz Verlag, 2002). On Osiander's view of salvation, see Timothy J. Wengert, *Defending Faith: Responses to Andreas Osiander's Doctrine of Justification, 1551–1559* (Heidelberg: Mohr Siebeck, 2012).

12. An important feature in Luther's movement—and one that grounded Lutheran resistance to the Augsburg Interim—was his reform of the German liturgy. See especially Bryan D. Spinks,

Some agreed with Melanchthon's hard decision, but many felt that his support for the Augsburg Interim was the last straw. As a result, two factions emerged: the Philippists (those who supported Melanchthon and advocated a change in Lutheran theology) and the Gnesio-Lutherans[13] (those who wanted to abide by Luther's teachings).[14] Almost immediately, the fight grew bitter and hot-blooded, and by the 1560s, both began to intensify their theological positions. Philippists now called for changes in other Lutheran beliefs, while the Gnesio-Lutherans grew stauncher in their loyalty to Luther, seeing his works as the only faithful teaching from the Bible. This tension between the two Lutheran factions was the material cause of the most important Lutheran confessional text, the Book of Concord.

The Book of Concord

The struggles between Melanchthon and the Gnesio-Lutherans culminated in the final historical confession of that tradition, the Book of Concord. This was not actually a new confession but a bundle of earlier Lutheran confessions followed by one new text, called the Formula of Concord. (Not a few students struggle to keep the Book and the Formula distinct!) In terms of its weight in Lutheran history, the Book of Concord established the Gnesio position as the Lutheran faith, and so this confession was the lodestone that drew together the various churches within Germany. And as Lutherans began to come to the New World, they carried with them the Book of Concord as the bedrock of their faith.

Since it was published with Luther's confession, the Formula of Concord was careful not to speak beyond or against the original Lutheran message. The elector of Saxony had called for the work—perhaps to see an end to controversies, although the work happened to come on the fortieth anniversary of the Schmalkald Articles. The main architects of the Formula of Concord were Jakob Andreae (1528–90) and Martin Chemnitz (1522–86).[15] Both played a heavy role in shaping Lutheran identity after Luther, filling in where Melanchthon had

---

Luther's Liturgical Criteria and His Reform of the Canon of the Mass, Grove Liturgical Studies 30 (Bramcote, UK: Grove, 1982).

13. "Gnesio" derives from Greek *genesios*, which means "genuine" or "authentic."

14. It is probably unfair to allow Gnesio-Lutherans the claim that they *merely* followed Luther, since Lutheran scholasticism began to flourish at this time. For the complexities of this teaching, see Robert D. Preus, *The Theology of Post-Reformation Lutheranism*, 2 vols. (St. Louis: Concordia, 1972).

15. The background and other framers of the Book of Concord are discussed in Charles P. Arand, James A. Nestingen, and Robert Kolb, *The Lutheran Confessions: History and Theology of the Book of Concord* (Minneapolis: Fortress, 2012). See especially Theodore R. Jungkuntz,

left a void. Their goal was to craft the Formula of Concord as a confession that focused on recent debates over Luther's message. In fact, it would be accurate to say the Formula of Concord was simply a commentary on the earlier Lutheran confessions, the final polish to Lutheran confessional unity.[16]

The Formula of Concord is divided into two sections: the Epitome (a set of twelve declarations of faith) and the Solid Declaration (which clarifies and condemns views based on the twelve declarations). The first work was completed by Andreae, Chemnitz, and roughly fourteen other theologians between April and June 1576. This first work was called the Torgau Book, which the committee then circulated among Lutheran churches and universities.[17] Comments or suggestions were sent back, and a smaller team used them to create the final document, known as the Bergic Book, which was presented to the elector of Saxony in 1577.

Now assembled, and with political backing from Lutheran princes, the Book of Concord quickly became the central confessional document for Lutheranism. The Saxon leaders required existing Lutheran pastors to sign it, and between seventy-five hundred and eight thousand embraced the new Lutheran standards. Some pastors expressed fear of creating a false unity, at least if conformity was reached only by using political muscle. The main fear was that some honest critiques might be silenced. As a compromise, therefore, any pastors with misgivings about Concord were asked to send in their disagreements, and if their scruples were judged to be fair, then those pastors could keep their positions. Notably, the Lutheran communities in Sweden and Denmark refused to sign the document, thus creating a split between German and Scandinavian Lutheran churches.[18] Neither side wanted controversy, since the problem was largely cultural and political: the Scandinavian churches did not want to bow to the Germans. In time, however, this break led some in the Scandinavian churches to reject the Book of Concord on theological grounds, since the Formula of Concord itself added to Luther's existing confessions.

Formulators of the Formula of Concord: Four Architects of Lutheran Unity (St. Louis: Concordia, 1977).

16. Studies of its theology can be found in Lewis W. Spitz and Wenzel Lohff, eds., *Discord, Dialogue, and Concord: Studies in the Lutheran Reformation's Formula of Concord* (Minneapolis: Fortress, 1977).

17. The committee used two existing documents, the Swabian-Saxon Concord (by Andreae) and the Maulbron Formula from 1576.

18. For example, there has been debate on both sides as to whether Sweden rejected the Formula of Concord or simply created its own standard not out of step with the Formula. The important milestone for Sweden was not the Formula but the Synod of Uppsala in 1593. By and large, the churches of Sweden have not found the Formula to be binding or necessary, and they look instead only to the Augsburg Confession and Uppsala decision.

But for German Lutherans—and, by extension, the majority of Lutherans ever since—it was the Book of Concord, officially completed in 1580, that was the most widely embraced confessional standard.[19]

Prominent in the Formula of Concord was a fine-tuning of the Lutheran teaching on original sin and free will. Both issues had been central to Luther's theology, since original sin was the reason why Luther had denied free will. These issues will be discussed throughout this chapter, but for now, we should note that the question of "free will" in the Reformation was not what one would expect from the way many people use this term today. The modern notion of freedom, especially in the West, turns mostly on the question of the legal limits in society for speech and personal expression. In the time of the Reformation—in a world that still had the Inquisition, the consistory, and wooden pillories at the centers of towns—the notion of free political expression in the modern sense would have been incomprehensible.

When any Protestant confession—including the Formula of Concord— denied free will, its framers meant that we are unable, apart from grace, to contribute to our salvation. The issue in question was really about the *impact of sin on the will*, and so the sphere in which the question of free will was asked was the realm of Christian conversion. For the Reformers, humans are enslaved to sin after the fall—dead in our trespasses, according to Ephesians 2—and therefore are incapable on our own of submitting to God. So the question is not about the freedom to do *anything* or to choose *anything*, but about *spiritual freedom* to choose God. As the Formula of Concord framed the question, "Can man by his own powers, before he is reborn through the Holy Spirit, dispose and prepare himself for the grace of God?"[20] Luther had always said that this was impossible, because if we claim to choose God by our own power, we implicitly base salvation on our choice, which is the first step toward resting on human works.[21] Therefore, when Protestants claimed that there was no free will, they meant this not as a denial that we have choices

---

19. The other nine are the three ancient creeds (Apostles', Nicene, Athanasian), the Augsburg Confession, the Apology of the Augsburg Confession, the Small and Large Catechisms, the Schmalkald Articles, and the *Treatise on the Power and Primacy of the Pope*.

20. Theodore G. Tappert, trans. and ed., *The Book of Concord: The Confessions of the Evangelical Lutheran Church* (Philadelphia: Fortress, 1959), 469. Also in CCFCT 2:173. The Epitome goes on later to affirm that, once regenerated, "man's new will becomes an instrument and means of God the Holy Spirit" (CCFCT 2:175). There is a possible confusion of terms here, as free will is strongly condemned, and yet free will is restored at conversion, such that new Christians will never know a time when they do *not* have free will. This confusion returned in Reformed debates over Arminianism.

21. See Robert Kolb, *Bound Choice, Election, and the Wittenberg Theological Method: From Martin Luther to the Formula of Concord* (Grand Rapids: Eerdmans, 2005).

or as a claim that something outside ourselves prevents us from making one choice or another, but rather as a rejection of Catholic teaching on penance and good works.[22] If we understand the terms, then, we can understand why early Protestants found the denial of free will unobjectionable.

The Formula of Concord agreed with Luther and denied that humans have free will. But a problem had arisen in Lutheranism, as some misunderstood the scope of the denial of free will and began to teach fatalism—the view that God never uses *any means* of salvation. Fatalism goes beyond the doctrine of predestination, in other words, and subjugates all human activity to the naked choice of God. But the important point here is that no Protestant tradition—Lutheran, Reformed, or Anglican—taught fatalism, even though all denied free will. The difference is subtle but important. Luther's denial of free will in salvation did not mean that God therefore does not use human choice to accomplish his purposes. Indeed, God uses pastors to preach or share the gospel. Human effort and choice are the *secondary means* that God uses for his purposes.

The problem for some Lutherans was that Luther had published one of the strongest denials of free will in his *Bondage of the Will* (1525), and in sections of that treatise, Luther did indeed sound fatalistic, describing our response to God as merely passive or robotic.[23] At the very least, he used the term "free will" without a great deal of precision. Some of Luther's readers, then, had mistaken the point. By the end of his career, Luther became aware of the problem, and he provided an answer in his Genesis commentary: "I hear . . . vicious statements are being spread abroad concerning predestination or God's foreknowledge. For this is what they say: 'If I am predestined, I shall be saved, whether I do good or evil. If I am not predestined, I shall be condemned regardless of my works.'"[24]

Luther pounced on this teaching and ordered Christians not to dwell on these subjects, especially if they provoked fear of damnation. Luther also rejected any needless examination of predestination, and he wanted people to avoid speculation about God's decision in the lives of those who reject the faith. Predestination, he argued, should be used only to silence those who,

---

22. This is not to say that Catholic theology believed in *utter* free will to choose salvation.

23. It is important to note that Luther sounded this way largely because he wrote in hyperbole so often. Also, his main target was Erasmus, who rejected most of what Protestants taught on original sin. But not a few students have mistaken Luther for a "Calvinist"—a mistake that breaks both chronological and categorical rules.

24. Martin Luther, *Luther's Works*, vol. 5, *Lectures on Genesis 26–30*, ed. Jaroslav Pelikan (St. Louis: Concordia, 1967), 43–44.

after conversion, grew prideful about their decision to follow Christ. Otherwise, Luther said, the subject should be left in theology books.

The Formula of Concord expands on this and offers some helpful corrections for Lutherans. The text has a lengthy section on free will that clarifies the Lutheran position—one that affirms that God moved first on sinners, that salvation is by grace, and that even faith itself is given to us—while also silencing those who speculated on God's choice, the "mad dream of so-called Stoic philosophers and of Manichaeans."[25] It also stresses that salvation comes by secondary means, and the framers refused to see predestination as the grounds for doubting the power of preaching. It is true that "God changes stubborn and unwilling people into willing people," but the Formula of Concord hemmed this in, saying that "after the Holy Spirit has performed and accomplished this and the will of man has been changed," then we should expect to experience a willing desire for God, since "man's new will becomes an instrument and means of God the Holy Spirit."[26] For this reason, though it affirms predestination, Lutheran theology never developed this doctrine beyond the original intention in the early Reformation.

Perhaps the most critical adjustment in the Formula of Concord, however, was on the Third Use of the Law.[27] As is the case with free will, there are many today who mistake the Reformation concept of the law. In North America, especially, the work of Lutheran scholars such as Gerhard Forde[28] drew attention to this subject, famously defending the Lutheran rejection of the law, which he described as an attempt to encourage obedience. Some have assumed that Luther felt that the entire Christian life was free grace—guilt-free living without any correction of sin. But Luther not only rejected this notion; he also coined the term "antinomianism" (from a Greek phrase meaning "against the law") in a blistering attack on those who rejected the law.[29]

Instead, the Third Use of the Law was a debate over how Christians approached God's law *after conversion*. The issue was raised in the life of ministry: how to encourage Christian practice without suggesting that good works

25. Tappert, *Book of Concord*, 470. Also in CCFCT 2:174.
26. Tappert, *Book of Concord*, 472. Also in CCFCT 2:174.
27. See our initial discussion in chap. 14. For a good summary of the three uses and their meanings, see Michael Horton, *The Christian Faith: A Systematic Theology for Pilgrims on the Way* (Grand Rapids: Zondervan, 2011), 673–75.
28. His classic work is *On Being a Theologian of the Cross: Reflections on Luther's Heidelberg Disputation, 1518* (Grand Rapids: Eerdmans, 1997), which is not a history book per se, but instead sees Luther's story as each of our stories as well.
29. On this debate and Luther's attack on antinomianism, see Timothy J. Wengert, *Law and Gospel: Philip Melanchthon's Debate with John Agricola of Eisleben over* Poenitentia (Grand Rapids: Baker, 1997).

were necessary. Again, the Protestant message had always been that Christ saved believers apart from any obedience to the law. But the New Testament also gives commands, guidelines, and censures for Christians who fall into sin. The real challenge was how to preach the unmerited grace of God and also affirm that God places demands on Christians. As we discussed in chapter 14, the "uses of the law" was a set of categories that the Reformation employed to address this question.

Not surprisingly, Luther had a somewhat idiosyncratic position on the law.[30] For starters, he shared with other Protestants the view that the law—God's standard for perfect obedience—exposed sin and required Christians to trust only in Christ's obedience. In this sense, there could never be a positive use of the law that saw Christian effort as contributing to our salvation. So again, the question was about the law *after conversion*, since Christians resting on faith are told to bear fruit in their lives. Those who embraced the Third Use of the Law wanted to stress that obedience came by offering the law as a way of life, but only after one trusted Christ. By contrast, those who rejected the Third Use of the Law taught that churches could use the law only as a mirror to reveal sin—although Christians would perform good works without the law. The debate was really a practical problem for pastors: Could one use the law to encourage obedience or simply to stress the sinner's need for Christ?

A modern analogy may help us understand Luther's concern. Let's say a pastor notices on Sunday that half of the congregation forgot to bring a Bible. During the sermon, the pastor encourages members to bring their Bibles, and even promises to personally pay for a copy of the Bible for everyone in the congregation. The people need only to promise to read it and bring it with them to worship. Most churches would find this gesture at least charming, if not a powerful demonstration of Christian love. But under the terms of the Third Use of the Law, this pastor could be critiqued for preaching law. Why? Because of the *public encouragement* to bring Bibles—even if it is sound pastoral advice. Those who rejected the Third Use of the Law, in other words, feared that any command would provoke anxiety. In this case, the half who did not bring Bibles would be shamed, while all people with a Bible under their arm would be driven to pride, looking at their neighbors as a pitiful rabble, barely capable of true faith. All this from a simple admonishment! Luther always insisted that reliance on the law—even if done by Spirit-indwelled believers—was fundamentally reliance on self-righteousness, and self-righteousness was

---

30. The best study to begin with is Bernhard Lohse, *Martin Luther's Theology: Its Historical and Systematic Development*, trans. Roy A. Harrisville (Minneapolis: Fortress, 1999).

far more insidious than demanding penance. Luther was less concerned with the prodigal son, eating with swine and aware that he was an outcast, than he was with the smug older brother, living at home and following the rules.

Luther never used the term "Third Use of the Law," and there was enough ambiguity in some of his works to leave the door open to a positive assessment of the law. As a result, the problem was left to later Lutheranism to determine a verdict on the matter. But with Melanchthon's slow march away from Luther's theology, one of the main issues that he overturned was the Lutheran stance on the law. By the time the Formula of Concord was written, not a few Lutherans had their daggers drawn, ready to defend or reject the Third Use of the Law.

The Formula of Concord begins by noting that the controversy is serious, since those who misapply these terms are not simply wrong, but seriously jeopardize "the gospel [by returning to] a teaching on the law." On the one hand, they confess that although Christians are freed from the legal curse, "they are not on that account without the law."[31] They are concerned that too much rhetoric on the removal of the law would open the door to carnal Christians. They also make sure to stress the need to preach the law, not only at conversion but also throughout the Christian life, although they caution Christians against expecting holiness as long as they live in the flesh. After all of this nuance, the Formula of Concord then rejects any actual adherence to the Third Use of the Law: "Fruits of the Spirit, however, are those works which the Spirit of God, who dwells in the believers, works through the regenerated, and which the regenerated perform in so far as they are reborn and do them spontaneously, as if they knew of no command, threat, or reward."[32] The phrase "no command, threat, or reward" is indicative of Lutheran theology—and there is no more Lutheran adverb than "spontaneously." Good works will occur, but only if we cease from any attempt to force the law on believers.

Reformed Growth in Scotland

In chapter 15 we looked at one of the earliest confessions of faith to move beyond the Swiss and German cities of the early Reformed movement: the French Confession of 1559. This confession can be our starting point for our discussion of the growing Reformed churches throughout Europe. As one historian has shown, the Reformed faith in the latter half of the sixteenth

31. Tappert, *Book of Concord*, 480. Also in *CCFCT* 2:183.
32. Tappert, *Book of Concord*, 481. Also in *CCFCT* 2:184.

century was the most promiscuous movement of the initial Protestant Reformation, willing to accommodate to a variety of national contexts whenever possible. At times, those various contexts warranted confessions of their own.

Scotland had always been staunchly Catholic, and there is little evidence of much interest in Protestant theology. As a result, the road to Scottish Presbyterianism was not an easy path.[33] Not just the nation but also the crown had always been loyal to the pope, and Scotland had also found a dependable ally in France, another Catholic nation, because the two had shared a mutual hatred for the English since at least the Middle Ages. In fact, so committed to the Catholic faith was Scotland that its future reformer, John Knox (1513–72), spent the entirety of his early ministry as an Anglican priest under Edward VI. By 1555, however, he was determined to see his own country come into the Protestant faith—and if he had his druthers, it would be a church modeled on his short experience with John Calvin in Geneva.[34]

By 1560, many in the Scottish Parliament agreed with Knox. As was the case later in the Netherlands, in Scotland political leaders came to view the Protestant faith as the best choice for national independence.[35] Parliament could not move on its own authority, however, if a sitting monarch could interfere. But when the queen regent, Mary of Guise, died in 1560, Parliament plunged ahead with a policy of both Scottish independence and the creation of a new Protestant church. Both were believed to be essential for the future of Scotland. Parliament asked Knox—now returned after his exile in Frankfurt and Geneva—to draft a confession. He returned with one in four days, and the confession was authorized. With the rise of Mary Queen of Scots to the throne the following year, however, the confession did not receive royal approval until 1567, when she abdicated.

The confession opens with a lament about the state of religion in Scotland, and it even admits the framers "do not suppose that such malice can be cured merely by our confession."[36] The opening articles on God, creation, and original sin are plain in their language and conform to all previous Protestant

---

33. This story can be found in Alec Ryrie, *The Origins of the Scottish Reformation*, Politics, Culture and Society in Early Modern Britain (Manchester, U.K.: Manchester University Press, 2006).

34. On Knox, see Jane Dawson, *John Knox* (New Haven: Yale University Press, 2015).

35. This is not to deny that there were also spiritual reasons, but in a world before the separation of church and state, these factors were often united. There are, however, unique features to this reformation, as discussed in Margo Todd, *The Culture of Protestantism in Early Modern Scotland* (New Haven: Yale University Press, 2002).

36. George Henderson, ed., *The Scots Confession, 1560 (Confessio Scoticana), and Negative Confession, 1581 (Confessio Negativa)* (Edinburgh: Church of Scotland, Committee on Publications, 1937), 31. Also in *CCFCT* 2:389.

confessions. Article 4, however, hints at something new, as it casts redemption in what we today would call a covenantal structure—that is, a pattern of God calling, redeeming, and feeding his people throughout the Bible, thereby seeing Old and New Testaments as a continuum of God's redemptive purposes. The confession makes the same claim, stating that in the Old Testament "the promise was repeated and made clearer from time to time . . . from Adam to Noah, from Noah to Abraham, from Abraham to David, and so onwards to the incarnation of Christ Jesus."[37]

The remainder of the confession returns to standard Protestant stances on Scripture, election, faith, and good works. Indeed, the Scots Confession is notable for its plain and straightforward dealing with the subject, and we get a sense not only that the confession was written quickly but also that the luxury to create the country's first confession was not taken for granted. Knox's work is notably devoid of flourishes of language, of dwelling on pet peeves, and of stressing the church's antipathy to heresy. Instead, the Scots Confession is a simple yet candid description of the new Protestant faith.

Restless and Reformed in the Netherlands

Dutch Calvinists referred to the foundation of their church as the "Further Reformation" (*Nadere Reformatie*). During the early decades after Luther, there was an overwhelming variety of churches and confessions present in the Netherlands, and even the cities that became home to Protestantism did not always remain in the fold. Moreover, the country was politically under Catholic rule. The emperor, Charles V, held power in these regions. The Dutch had little affection for their Hapsburg emperor, however, and they struggled mightily to gain independence. By the latter half of the sixteenth century, just as in Scotland, the quest for reformation and the quest for Dutch independence became synonymous. This unfolding story culminated in 1648 with the Dutch Revolt, a civil war that led to the formation of the United Provinces of the Netherlands.[38] It also created the Dutch Calvinist church, a newcomer to the Reformed tradition that helped carry Calvinism around the globe.

At the start of the Reformation, Charles V wanted to pursue a policy of anti-Protestantism. Ironically, he exercised far more complete control in the Netherlands than in Germany, where the princes were a thorn in his side. Charles took out his frustrations on those who sided with Protestants,

---

37. Henderson, *Scots Confession*, 33. Also in CCFCT 2:391.

38. On this context, see Alastair Duke, *The Reformation and Revolt in the Low Countries* (New York: Bloomsbury Academic, 2003).

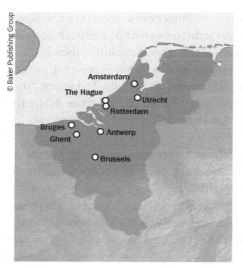

Cities of the Reformation in the Netherlands

instigating the pope to launch an inquisition, a move that led to much bloodshed and loss of Protestant leaders. For example, the English exile and Bible translator William Tyndale (1494–1536) was captured in Antwerp, put through a hasty trial, and executed. The Netherlands was full of people whose inclinations lay with Protestantism, so Charles was not slaying imaginary dragons. But the threat of bloodshed, while effective, often backfired on rulers, and Charles was increasingly seen as a rapacious overlord. Although the population of the Netherlands was barely two million, by 1566 as many as thirteen hundred people were executed for heresy—several times the number killed in other Protestant nations.[39]

Although the Netherlands became unreservedly Calvinist, ironically it had little connection to the Swiss Reformation. Calvin was nearly always focused on French-speaking areas, and even the most in-demand reformer, Heinrich Bullinger, had few contacts there. Indeed, of all the reform movements, the Netherlands was the closest to a grassroots movement. Church after church sprouted up in cities willing to tolerate Protestantism, and in cities without such tolerance, preachers dared to preach in open-air fields, just beyond the city walls.[40] But then in 1566—the Wonderyear—a new Reformed identity was crafted by a series of iconoclastic riots that destroyed many Catholic relics.[41]

In the thick of this story was Guido de Brès (ca. 1522–67), a former student of Calvin, now striving for reform in his native country. From a staunch Catholic family, Guido converted at a young age, and while we do not know the circumstances, many believe that his conversion came about by reading Protestant works that had been smuggled into the Netherlands. Much of what we know about him, however, comes from his involvement with the

---

39. Benedict, *Christ's Church Purely Reformed*, 175–77. Consider, for example, the attention that Bloody Mary receives for a "mere" three hundred executions during her reign.

40. This is an often-forgotten forerunner to later American open-field and big-tent preaching.

41. There were other factors in these riots that had nothing to do with Reformed theology. See Benedict, *Christ's Church Purely Reformed*, 185.

Belgic Confession of 1561.[42] This was the first confession written for this new movement toward Dutch Calvinism.

By the 1560s, Charles V had abdicated his throne and was succeeded by his son, Philip II. Like his father, Philip pursued an aggressive policy against Protestants,[43] although he increasingly lost ground in the Netherlands. By 1565, Guido was arrested for what might seem to us a trifling offense: singing the psalms with a congregation of Dutch Protestants. But in lands harboring rebellion against the Hapsburgs, the plain singing of the Bible was considered a rebellion.

Before his death, therefore, Guido worked to convince Philip of the integrity of the Reformation by writing a confession, although some have suggested that his real purpose was to bait Philip into open religious conflict in the Netherlands.[44] The result of his efforts was the Belgic Confession. He drafted the entire confession during his time as a pastor in the city of Tournai, and its tone does have a remarkably practical focus. Guido also had the luxury of consulting the other Reformed confessions. In preparation, we know, he used the French Confession of Faith,[45] although we cannot demonstrate word-for-word borrowings. He also used Calvin's *Institutes*—at least it is assumed so, since the opening structure follows a similar pattern.

Another Calvinist and former student of Calvin, Francisco Junius (1545–1602), was then asked to provide edits of the draft (all of them minor). Now that the completed draft was in hand, Junius wanted to test its quality by sending it to Geneva, which sent back its approval. This first edition was printed in 1561, and we are told that Guido hurled it over the castle walls in Tournai, hoping that someone would deliver it to Margaret of Parma (1522–86), the half-sister to Philip and governor of the Netherlands when he was away.

The Belgic Confession that we have today is not the same as what debuted in Tournai, although it is in principle still the work of Guido and Junius. It holds an important place in the story of the Netherlands, since those struggling in the Dutch Revolt came to be a symbol of their new national identity, not least because of Guido's martyrdom. Once the dust began to settle in the wars with Philip, several synods were called, and the original text was edited,

---

42. The name "Belgic" is a reference not to Belgium, which did not yet exist as a separate province, but to the entire region (*Gallia Belgica*). The standard work on the confession, covering much of its context, is Nicolaas H. Gootjes, *The Belgic Confession: Its History and Sources*, Texts and Studies in Reformation and Post-Reformation Thought (Grand Rapids: Baker Academic, 2007).

43. He was Bloody Mary's husband from 1554 until her death in 1558, so for at least five years they were a powerful duo in the protection of Catholic orthodoxy.

44. There is no reason, for example, to assume that Philip would even read the confession.

45. Discussed in chap 15.

approved, and distributed as the official version of the Belgic Confession. It did not reach its final form, however, until the Synod of Dordt adopted it as one of the official confessions of the Dutch Reformed Church in the early seventeenth century.

The Belgic Confession opens with an affirmation that God is the source of truth. It next asks how we can know this truth, and two answers are given: we know God by creation itself—what the Reformed tradition later referred to as "common grace,"[46] though other traditions call it "natural knowledge"—in that the beauty and the wonder of creation are displayed. This notion of knowing God by creation had not yet been expressed in a Protestant confession. Of course, just like later Protestant teaching on natural knowledge, the confession admits that this knowledge is incomplete and fleeting. Much of the early confession is then fixated on the doctrine of Scripture—the infallible source of all true knowledge of God. The Belgic Confession, in fact, had one of the lengthier discussions on the Bible at the time, even going so far as to list all the canonical books, setting them over against the Apocrypha.[47]

There were some features that, while Reformed, are less staunch on Calvinist doctrine. For example, election and predestination are given only a few lines, and details about God's role in the damnation of sinners is stated as only a fact that God is "just in leaving the others in their ruin and fall into which they plunged themselves."[48] However, it also cautions against speculating on these matters: "We do not wish to inquire with undue curiosity into what he does that surpasses human understanding."[49] A generation later, the Arminian controversies at Dordt, of course, provoked much more discussion of this issue.

Perhaps the most remarkable articles of the Belgic Confession are the ones that describe the daily obligations of church life. Almost certainly, we can attribute this feature to the fact that Guido and Junius were serving at the time as pastors of a beleaguered community. The Belgic Confession also has strong convictions on the doctrine of the church, since the "congregation is the gathering of those who are saved and there is no salvation apart from it, no one ought to withdraw from it, content to be by himself."[50] The church is to be marked by faithful members, committed to the discipline of the community, in gratitude to Christ for salvation. The confession also seeks to give

46. Common because it is common to everyone—that is, universal.
47. On the Apocrypha in the Reformation and post-Reformation, see Ryan M. Reeves and Charles Hill, *Know How We Got Our Bible* (Grand Rapids: Zondervan, 2018).
48. CCFCT 2:413.
49. CCFCT 2:412.
50. CCFCT 2:419.

marks of the true church, though here the material is remarkable because it insists that all the marks of the church center on a congregation demonstrating love. They know they are sinners, "fleeing from sin and pursuing righteousness," and they also love their neighbors without exception. But the Belgic Confession sees the marks of the church displayed not in pastoral acts such as preaching or sacraments, but principally by those who appeal to "the blood, suffering, death, and obedience of the Lord Jesus."[51] The next concern, however, is that readers could mistake this for anti-institutionalism, and so the Belgic Confession offers one of the first confessional statements on both church government and the selection of officers.

> We believe that ministers of the word of God, elders, and deacons, ought to be chosen to their offices by a legitimate election of the church . . . and in good order, as the word of God teaches. . . . As for the ministers of the word, they all have the same power and authority, no matter where they may be, since they are all servants of Jesus Christ, the only universal Bishop, and the only Head of the church.[52]

The confession even urges congregations to hold pastors "in special esteem, because of the work they do, and be at peace with them, without grumbling, quarreling, or fighting." We can assume that the framers' experience as pastors shaped articles such as these.

Heidelberg: An Ironic Achievement

One area in Germany continued to feel the tension between Lutheran and Reformed churches. It was known as the Palatinate, located on the western side of Germany along the Rhine, and though it was part of the Holy Roman Empire, it was supervised by one of the leading secular princes. Given its proximity to Swiss Reformed cities, the region often was at the crossroads of the early division between Luther and Huldrych Zwingli.[53] Heidelberg, the main city of this region, embodied these tensions. Heidelberg was where Luther had defended his Reformation views before his excommunication. Martin Bucer had attended the disputation and was won to the Reformation by Luther's arguments. Almost symbolically, although the Lutheran faith did secure the region, it never developed an outright hatred for Reformed teachings.

51. *CCFCT* 2:420.
52. *CCFCT* 2:421.
53. Discussed in chap. 14.

Zacharias Ursinus

The struggle between Philippists and Gnesio-Lutherans was part of the reason why the Heidelberg Catechism was needed.[54] The elector at the time was Frederick III, and he grew weary of the struggle, although he tended to find Melanchthon's revised version of Lutheranism a worthy effort. Tileman Hesshus (1527–88) had brought the fight to Heidelberg when he published several brash works on the Lutheran view of the physical presence of Christ in the Lord's Supper. The controversy became a public concern when Frederick sought Melanchthon's opinion. Hesshus had studied under Melanchthon, but now the two crossed swords, and Melanchthon was provoked to write against this teaching in his later work titled *Responsio* (1559). Hesshus lost his teaching position, which only doubled his resolve on the matter.

Fears also had grown in Frederick's mind that the youth were no longer zealous for the Reformation—at least it seemed to him that churches were struggling to find adequate pastors. A local pastor, Zacharias Ursinus (1534–83), had made headway in the region for the Reformed faith. He was born in Poland[55] but enrolled at the University of Wittenberg at fifteen, and he was a personal disciple of Melanchthon. He went on a tour of the Reformed centers of education, studying in Strasbourg, Lausanne, and eventually with Calvin in Geneva. If some found it impossible to keep Lutheran and Reformed theology in collaboration, Ursinus seemed to be unaware of the problem.

Ursinus was no wilting flower, however, and he did find the Gnesio-Lutherans a problem for church stability. So when Frederick called on him to draft a catechism for training youth, he also wanted to train new believers in the basics of Reformed theology. For this reason, the Heidelberg Catechism

---

54. The standard work on this is Lyle D. Bierma et al., *An Introduction to the Heidelberg Catechism: Sources, History, and Theology* (Grand Rapids: Baker Academic, 2005). This is augmented by Lyle D. Bierma, *The Theology of the Heidelberg Catechism: A Reformation Synthesis* (Louisville: Westminster John Knox, 2005).

55. His birth name was Baer (bear), although like many in that day he Latinized his name to Ursinus.

became, ironically, both the later Reformation's most irenic confession and an indirect condemnation of confessional Lutheranism.

These tensions within the Heidelberg Catechism are largely forgotten today in evangelical circles, mainly because Ursinus and the later editors created a warmer tone, mostly pastoral in focus, as the catechism walked young Christians through the basics of the faith. Of course, Luther and others had written catechisms with similar qualities, so we should not think that the Heidelberg Catechism was the only Protestant work of pastoral ministry. The most unique feature of the catechism is its design: 129 questions with answers, arranged to be taught each Sunday for the entire year. Each week's material is labeled as "Lord's Day" and is accompanied by the week in which it is to be rehearsed. For pastors, teachers, and parents, these decisions were an enormous benefit in Christian formation, since so much of the attention in the Reformation had previously been on reform among clergy.

Famously, the confession does not open with affirmations on subjects such as the Trinity. Rather, it asks a simple question: "What is your only hope, in life, and in death?" The prescribed answer is:

> That I belong—body and soul, in life and in death—not to myself but to my faithful Savior, Jesus Christ, who at the cost of his own blood has fully paid for all my sins and has completely freed me from the dominion of the devil; that he protects me so well that without the will of my Father in heaven not a hair can fall from my head; indeed, that everything must fit his purpose for my salvation.[56]

The catechism mingles the notions of comfort, protection, and reliance on Christ—all biblical themes, but not always present in confessions. We must be careful, however, not to see this as somehow a new course in Protestant confessions—as if the Heidelberg Catechism gleamed like a beacon of light, at last focused on real-world faith in a dark world of cold orthodoxy. This opening question, in other words, was not a response to Gnesio-Lutherans. The Heidelberg is a catechism, and such language is typical for the genre, and so it is comparable to Lutheran catechisms, as well as most other catechisms from this century.

Instead, we should focus on the fifty-two-week structure to understand why the Heidelberg Catechism opens with these words. The point of this opening, as we can see in the following articles, is to provide a pedagogical tool for learning the Bible. The second question then asks, "What do you need to know in order to live and die in the joy of this comfort?" Three answers are

---

56. CCFCT 2:429.

given: (1) that we are sinners, (2) how we receive salvation, and (3) how we respond in gratitude. Indeed, this three-part structure—misery, comfort, and gratitude—has nearly always been a synopsis of the Heidelberg Catechism.

What is perhaps the most unique part of the Heidelberg Catechism, then, is not the content of its message but the manner of its questioning in these sections. In addition to the opening question, the theme of comfort is included in several other places. Furthermore, the drafters of the catechism went to great lengths to anticipate questions that new Christians might ask. Questions routinely start with one truth, and then ask, "How do you understand this?" or "Why is this the case?"[57] The text even plays devil's advocate in places—those with children know that answers are often disputed—and it gives answers to the standard criticism of a doctrine. In all of this, the catechism makes a sincere attempt to provide theological material in a way suited for new Christians, not theologians brawling over tough but obscure doctrines.

Nevertheless, the Heidelberg Catechism is restrained in its criticism of Lutheranism—far more so than all earlier confessions that dealt with the sacraments. It denies that the body and blood of Christ are truly present but admits that "in accordance with the nature and usage of sacraments, it is called the body of Christ."[58] Thus, in a way that is not always appreciated, this catechism slowly sifts the issues between Lutheran and Reformed views of the sacraments. No pound of flesh was taken, and the rationale for Reformed positions lacked a polemical edge. The gentler language used in this catechism is uncommon, especially during this period of the Reformation.

The Five Points of Arminianism

If the Heidelberg Catechism is remembered for its generous tone, the Synod of Dordt met in a time of serious division, and it drafted its articles in the teeth of civil war. The fight was between Arminians and Calvinists—both eager to lead the new Dutch Protestant church. It defined a generation of theology in the Netherlands, and it still reigns as one of the most common disputes among evangelicals.[59] The fight later landed in England, took root, and flowered in the Anglican Church, and thus made its way to the New World and around the globe.

57. CCFCT 2:429, especially questions 2–6.
58. CCFCT 2:444.
59. A good survey is Alan P. F. Sell, *The Great Debate: Calvinism, Arminianism, and Salvation* (Grand Rapids: Baker, 1983).

Nevertheless, few stories of the Reformation have been as misunderstood as the rise of Arminianism. Not only is the story murky for modern Christians—not a few of our students think that Jacob Arminius and Calvin were contemporaries—but also the theological terms used in the seventeenth century were quite different in meaning from the way many use them today. One should not embark on a conversation about the Dutch Reformation without warning. Here be dragons.

We can begin by dispelling two myths. First, while today many would claim to be Arminian, this does not mean that they hold the same views as Arminius.[60] (This is true of Calvinism, too, and common enough in all movements that last centuries.) The original movement was largely suppressed during the Reformation and cast out of the new Dutch church, although it endured as a small community in the Netherlands known as the Remonstrance faith. In contrast, Arminianism as we know it today is largely the product of the teachings of John Wesley, who read and appreciated Arminius, but whose ideas came as much from the Greek church fathers as from Reformation-era debates.[61]

Second, despite the popular view, Dordt did not create the "Five Points of Calvinism," at least not as they are understood today.[62] The alleged connection of the acronym TULIP to the council is simply part of folk history.[63] Things only get dimmer when we hear the claim that the Dordt confession was a summary of the Reformed faith itself. The delegates at Dordt did not think that their articles were a *synopsis of* the Reformed faith but, instead, an *answer from* the Reformed faith to certain claims of Arminianism. Their canons were point-by-point replies to the five points of the Arminian faith, which were drafted almost a decade earlier.

The real story of the Synod of Dordt is far more important for what was occurring in Protestantism. As with the Formula of Concord, the issue of free

60. A point made recently in Keith D. Stanglin and Thomas H. McCall, *Jacob Arminius: Theologian of Grace* (Oxford: Oxford University Press, 2012). See especially the introduction.

61. Historians typically distinguish between Dutch Arminianism (i.e., Remonstrance) and Wesleyan Arminianism. Perhaps the best place to start is Roger E. Olson, *Arminian Theology: Myths and Realities* (Downers Grove, IL: IVP Academic, 2006).

62. The modern usage itself is not the problem, but reading this modern usage back into history is. For a good survey of TULIP in its modern form, see David N. Steele, Curtis C. Thomas, and S. Lance Quinn, *The Five Points of Calvinism: Defined, Defended, Documented* (Philipsburg, NJ: P&R, 2004).

63. Obviously, TULIP is an English acronym, so it could not have come from theologians writing in Latin and Dutch. One study has found the earliest use of TULIP was in the early twentieth century, so it was only relatively recently that students began to believe that this came from Dordt itself. See Kenneth Stewart, *Ten Myths about Calvinism: Recovering the Breadth of the Reformed Tradition* (Downers Grove, IL: InterVarsity, 2011), 75–98.

will and predestination was an underlying tension from the early Reformation. Dordt was not the first instance of this debate, nor was it necessarily the result of overly philosophical speculation. Indeed, since we saw this issue arise in the Formula of Concord, this was not the first time these questions were debated by Protestants. Dordt was, however, an intensification of the Reformed position.[64]

The debate arose from the question "How is God loving when he does not save everyone?" Properly speaking, then, the issue was not whether God is both loving and just—all Christians would affirm both—but the relationship between God's love and his power. Christian theology had always affirmed that God, as the Creator, is not bound by his creatures. But the fact remains that God, at some stage, *could* have intervened to prevent the fall. He could have made humans incapable of sin, or he could have intervened for Adam—or he could just not have created the angel who became Satan in the first place. At some point, all Christian theology affirms that God nevertheless created the world and allowed angels and human beings to fall into sin.

But, of course, Christians also affirm that God loves this world and is not to blame for our sin. In its simplest form, then, the problem is that Christian theology must deal with this tension: God allowed evil (but did not cause it) and yet he is not to blame for it (though he allowed it). In the end, there is no perfectly satisfying answer that does not fall back on this tension. Those seeking a simple solution to the problem of sin will look in vain, if they do so measuring God's decisions as they would human choices.[65]

All Protestant theologians, including Arminius, agreed with this starting point.[66] Where they differed was in the way they balanced the concepts and what terms they used to protect both truths. The friction between Arminians and Calvinists—the same tension experienced by Lutherans—arose whenever a term was misunderstood (or misapplied) in a way that did violence to one of these truths.

Reformed theologians, then, were not unique for their reflections on predestination. Where they stood alone was in their willingness to *explore* the

---

64. The development of Reformed orthodoxy is best described in Richard Muller's works. See, for example, *Calvin and the Reformed Tradition: On the Work of Christ and the Order of Salvation* (Grand Rapids: Baker Academic, 2012); Muller, *After Calvin: Studies in the Development of a Theological Tradition*, Oxford Studies in Historical Theology (Oxford: Oxford University Press, 2003).

65. These issues and terms were very complex in the Reformation, but for a good survey (and correction to modern assumptions), see Richard Muller, *Divine Will and Human Choice: Freedom, Contingency, and Necessity in Early Modern Reformed Thought* (Grand Rapids: Baker Academic, 2017). Muller also rightly takes issue with modern teaching on the subject.

66. The issues are, of course, complex. A good place to begin is Richard Muller, *God, Creation, and Providence in the Thought of Jacob Arminius* (Grand Rapids: Baker, 1991).

grammar of God's election—not shying away from dwelling on these matters as Lutherans generally did.[67] They also did not feel that it was inappropriate to say that God determined the fate of all humans, including the reprobate. Of course, they always made sure to stress that God loves the world and that he did not cause sin. Arminius, however, came to doubt Reformed theology on this point, since he found its willingness to discuss predestination tantamount to denying God's love.

Arminius was also energized in his critique with the emergence of the Dutch Republic. One of the earliest times he voiced concern about Reformed theology, however, was based in part on his reading of the Belgic Confession. The rapid adoption of the confession was part of the surging pride of the new Netherlands, and so the controversy over its theology drew the attention of political leaders. The connection went deeper, since in 1603 Arminius was appointed to the faculty at Leiden to fill the vacancy left by Junius, the man who had edited the Belgic Confession in the 1560s.[68] Like all theology faculties, Leiden's professors debated the issues, and Arminius won a few of the faculty to his side. Before long, given the political tension in the Netherlands, the problems spilled out from the lecture hall to envelop the entire Dutch Reformed Church.[69]

Arminius died in 1609, but by then he had won even more supporters, though still the minority in the Netherlands. Several months after his death, nearly fifty pastors and two of Leiden's professors met in The Hague to draft several issues that they had with Reformed theology, as well as suggestions for better terms. It was this original document—the Five Articles of Remonstrance—that launched the Netherlands into further controversy.

The Five Articles, in general, can be seen as expressing a single idea: God's love should no longer be discussed under the rubric of predestination. His love for this world should not simply qualify God's relationship to sinners, once election and reprobation were discussed. Instead, Arminianism held that if Christians were to be truly biblical, they needed to make love the start and end of the theology of salvation. Reformed theologians, of course, dismissed the critique, pointing to the fact that God's love featured heavily in

---

67. Perhaps the best example of this was William Perkins, who wrote two separate books on the doctrine of predestination, neither of them brief: *The Golden Chain* (1591) and *On the Order and Mode of Predestination* (1598). The first was in English, the second an academic work written in Latin. A good study of the twists and turns of this theology, albeit from the context of England, is R. T. Kendall, *Calvin and English Calvinism to 1649*, Oxford Theological Monographs (Oxford: Oxford University Press, 1980).

68. Technically, two vacancies fell open after the plague ravaged the area, but one was Junius's.

69. A fact that at least implies that these issues were not unique to the Netherlands.

their confessions. But for Arminianism, the reorientation around God's love drove the Five Articles in a new direction.

For most of the Five Articles, however, the differences were subtle. Those who are saved, the professors confessed, are simply those who "shall believe on the . . . Son"—a crisp sentence that leaves off election or reprobation and avoids any language about God determining our destiny. The next article goes further, affirming the view that Christ died for all, not simply the elect. The framers did not believe that Christ's death secured salvation, of course, as this would be a form of universalism. Instead, they affirm that Christ loved the world and died for all, but only Christians will be saved, since "no one in fact becomes a partaker of this forgiveness except believers."[70]

In the third article, the framers unexpectedly deny free will. But again, we need to remember that they were using the term "free will" as the early Reformation did, not as we do when we assert the modern idea of freedom. Article 3 states that we are incapable of placing our faith in Christ apart from the Holy Spirit. This in itself is not surprising, since this was a bedrock view for all Protestant teaching on salvation. Likewise, article 4 begins in a traditional fashion, stating that all good works and movements of the will come about because the Holy Spirit moves on the believer. In a surprising move, however, the framers continue by adding "what pertains to the operation of grace—this is not irresistible."[71] In other words, the Five Articles maintain the common Reformation view that we do not *choose* God by our own strength, but they claim that we can *refuse* God by our own strength, even if the Holy Spirit is at work in us. Calvinists later pounced on this, since this claim appears to contradict article 3, but here the Remonstrance group seemed to want to leave the issues in tension. Of course, the article does not speculate on how this works, stating only that some resist the Spirit in the New Testament (e.g., in Acts 5).

Article 5 addresses the question of our ongoing struggle with sin—what in Calvinism is called "perseverance of the saints." The same steps are again taken: the terms used by Reformed theology are reworked to absolve God of any responsibility for sin. The framers affirm both that God will carry his children to the end and that we must struggle against sin and not lose our salvation. Indeed, they stress that Christians "have been abundantly equipped by this power in order to fight against Satan, sin, the world, and their own

---

70. James T. Dennison, ed., *Reformed Confessions of the 16th and 17th Centuries in English Translation*, 4 vols. (Grand Rapids: Reformation Heritage Books, 2008–10), 4:43. Also in *CCFCT* 2:549.

71. Dennison, *Reformed Confessions* 4:43 (translation modified). Also in *CCFCT* 2:549.

The Synod of Dordt by François Schillemans

flesh."[72] The article does admit, however, that the Remonstrance leaders are uncertain about this, and they conclude, "[this] must be more accurately sought from the sacred Scriptures before we are able to teach others with full persuasion (πληροφορία) of our minds."[73]

Article 5, then, is perhaps the most crucial break with Lutheran and Reformed categories. For Luther and all early Protestants, the focus was

---

72. Dennison, *Reformed Confessions*, 4:43–44 (translation modified). Also in *CCFCT* 2:550.

73. Dennison, *Reformed Confessions*, 4:44. Also in *CCFCT* 2:550. In the New Testament the Greek word *plērophoria* is typically translated as "full assurance" or "full confidence" (e.g., Col. 2:2).

on how our faith is imperfect and weak, and how we are prone to wander. Their main opponent, of course, was the Catholic Church and its belief that one must work out salvation through penance, since Christians are infused with grace to struggle against sin. But the Catholic Church also affirmed that there was a requirement to exercise this strength in order to persevere, lest we fall away and lose the grace of our baptism. This Catholic background helps us to see why the Synod of Dordt repeatedly condemned the Remonstrance language as a form of Pelagianism, since the delegates at Dordt were using the same rhetoric used in the debates with Catholics. The fear for Reformed theologians was that the Remonstrance article 5 ties our salvation to our obedience—that our works are important or necessary to ensure our salvation. This article is perhaps the first evidence that we have of a new movement within Protestantism—one that no longer feared talk of good works or holiness. This development reached its apex in the teachings of John Wesley, who went so far as to call these efforts "Christian perfectionism," and it became the norm for the majority of modern evangelical churches in the New World.

Returning to the story of the Dutch Reformation: tensions grew worse. But in terms of numbers, there was no contest, since Calvinist influence in the Netherlands had grown by leaps and bounds. The earliest debates over Arminius's teaching, while at times hostile, never became a total war. The Remonstrance group submitted its articles to the new Dutch government in 1610, and the Calvinists interpreted this as a power play. Both sides then began theological battles that would last eight years. In the end, the Calvinists had the muscle to prevail, and they scored the final victory at the Synod of Dordt in 1618–19. Thirteen leaders of the Remonstrance camp were invited, but their participation was minimal.

Point by point, the synod critiqued the Remonstrance—which is why the document was known then simply as the Counter-Remonstrance. The canons go down each of the five articles and advocate for the now-established views within Reformed theology: predestination is both to salvation and reprobation, Christ's death therefore is efficacious only for his elect, our will is incapable either of choosing or refusing God by its own power, and those who are true believers are preserved by God's grace to the end of their lives. The synod reaffirms that these teachings do not make God the author of sin, but also that they do not mean anything less than God is love. Once the canons were completed, the government stepped in and ordered all pastors in the Netherlands to embrace the Reformed faith. Those who refused—about two hundred pastors—left in exile to Schleswig-Holstein in northern Germany.

England: New Voices but a Growing Dissonance

If England was a latecomer to the Protestant fold, it soon found that the slow ferment of the Anglican Church produced something that satisfied. Europe by then was embroiled in confessional differences, especially between Lutheran and Reformed churches, and these had grown into a root of bitterness—hence the story of Niklaus Krell with which we began this chapter.[74] In England, the benefit of the Thirty-Nine Articles was their broad adherence to the Protestant faith, but without the political edge. Anglican bishops increasingly viewed this as a way to avoid division. This was not what the reformation under Edward VI necessarily intended for the original Forty-Two Articles, but by the reign of Elizabeth, Anglicans found that they preferred their confession this way. As one historian put it, Anglicans made a virtue of a necessity.[75]

Not everyone in England agreed. The English Puritans faulted the church for failing to complete the Reformation, and they worried that half measures would lead to abuse and superstition. Under Elizabeth I, Puritan criticisms of the church grew bolder, and some now claimed that traditional elements of worship—such as the wearing of vestments—were the "dregs of popery."[76] Anglicans who favored a more ornate style of worship rejected these allegations, and they stressed that when the church used these elements, it did not intend them in a Catholic sense, to continue the medieval separation of the clergy from laity. Rather, the vestments were to ensure order (almost as we would today think of a uniform worn for certain professions). The Puritan faction disagreed, even to the point of suggesting that Anglicanism was only half Protestant. In the end, neither side kept cool heads when it came to public debate.

The struggle with Puritans was not necessarily against Reformed theology, but against the *Puritan expression* of this tradition.[77] The English allergy to Calvinism was an acquired complaint, coming largely during the seventeenth century. But just as Anglican leaders were struggling against Puritanism, new issues arose that forced them to draft a new confession. This was the Lambeth

---

74. Anabaptists, since they were nearly universally condemned, were not a significant influence until at least the seventeenth century. Also, at times the bitterness was driven by the need for political control rather than by theology.

75. Diarmaid MacCulloch, *All Things Made New: The Reformation and Its Legacy* (Oxford: Oxford University Press, 2016), 255.

76. Newcomers to the subject should see Francis J. Bremer, *Puritanism: A Very Short Introduction* (Oxford: Oxford University Press, 2009). From there, go on to John Coffey and Paul C. H. Lim, eds., *The Cambridge Companion to Puritanism*, Cambridge Companions to Religion (Cambridge: Cambridge University Press, 2008).

77. An argument that Ryan Reeves has made elsewhere. See Reeves, *English Evangelicals and Tudor Obedience, c. 1527–1570*, Studies in the History of Christian Traditions 167 (Leiden: Brill, 2013). Benedict makes a similar case in *Christ's Church Purely Reformed*.

Articles (1595), the text of which embodied the "Reformed but not Puritan" ethos, although it was never adopted officially within Anglicanism.

The problem underlying the Lambeth Articles, just as in other Protestant churches, was the subject of free will and predestination. In England, the issue arose at the University of Cambridge, since a number of students and teachers felt the need for clarity on these issues. To end the bickering, a session was called by John Whitgift, the archbishop of Canterbury, a man who spent much of his time resisting Puritan complaints, although he himself was Reformed. To address the issues at Cambridge, he called together a committee to draft an explanation that would affirm the doctrine of predestination. The text that they drafted opened with a clear statement that God not only elects some to salvation but also chooses others to reprobation.

The problems between Anglicans and Puritans continued into the reign of James I.[78] Puritans in England were optimistic about their chances to see reform at last, since James had not only ruled Scotland but had also never openly provoked controversies within the Scottish church. The moment was too important, and so, not waiting for James even to arrive in England, a party rode to meet him on the road, where they offered him the Millenary Petition—so named for the alleged thousand signatures that it carried. The petition urged James to continue to reform Anglicanism and included suggestions that the drafters felt deserved his attention. The honeymoon did not last long.

Wanting to meet with both parties together, James called the Hampton Court Conference (1604), where he was forced to sit like Solomon and hear the quarreling. As it turned out, James's primary purpose was to set the tone for his reign, letting both sides know that they could not control his hand. In the end, neither side truly won, although the Puritans took the biggest hit when James made it clear that he was not coming to England under a banner of change.[79] If England had lasted this long as a Protestant nation and if its church had bishops, vestments, and other elements in worship, then the Puritans would need to bend the knee and conform. He maintained an openness toward good ideas, however, and sometimes supported Puritan views. His balancing was part of the reason why the church was at peace for much of his reign.

This was not the case for his son Charles, a king whose misguided policies made a good argument for limited government. If James ruled as Jeroboam,

78. He also had the title James VI of Scotland, so he is often referred to strangely as James VI/I.

79. Too many accounts treat James as a quasi-Anglican the moment he arrived. In fact, what he wanted was to ensure stability during the transition. Too little attention is paid to the fact that James supported measures that the Puritans found favorable—most famously, the translation of the Authorized, or King James Version, Bible.

Charles wished to be Rehoboam—scourging with scorpions and breaking the backs of Puritans to conform to the Anglican establishment. His most effective tool was supporting those who shared his distaste for Puritan theology. Charles was aware of the controversies in the Netherlands, and he saw two opportunities to drive Puritans away for good. First, he thrust Arminian theologians into senior roles within the church, especially through the appointment of William Laud to the archbishopric of Canterbury. Second, he supported the development of a high Anglican approach to worship—elaborate not simply for order but to add medieval flourish to the Book of Common Prayer. On both counts, Charles was out of step with the policies of Elizabeth and James, who had simply wanted peace and conformity, not the ruination of Puritanism itself. But Charles resolved to rid England of the problem, and by his authority Arminianism landed like a dandelion nettle on English soil.

Charles then launched a disastrous policy in Scotland.[80] At some point in the 1630s, it dawned on Charles that part of the reason why the Puritans were pressing for reform was that Scottish Presbyterianism, also part of the king's dominion, had practiced a simplified form of worship since the years of John Knox. Charles wanted to rectify this, and so in the summer of 1637 he ordered Scottish churches to remove their form of worship and use instead the Book of Common Prayer. The first service at which this was attempted lasted only a few minutes before chaos broke out. The church was St. Giles Cathedral, located on Castle Rock at the city center of Edinburgh. A local woman, Jenny Geddes, attended service with her sitting stool (pews were a later invention), only to hear the opening words of the English liturgy. Furious, Geddes hurled her stool at the pastor, shouting, "False thief! Dare you say mass in my ear!"[81] She and other angry folks were hustled outside, where they threw rocks at the church windows, banged on the doors, and shouted obscenities during the remainder of the Anglican service. Charles had not reckoned with the determination of the Scots.

Scotland and England soon launched into the Bishops' Wars (1639–40). Almost from the start, the fighting did not go well for England, and so Charles was forced to summon Parliament to request more troops and money. Parliament was happy to convene, but the members immediately made it known that they, too, were angered by the king's policies. Once summoned, they quickly passed legislation that the king could not dismiss the Parliament

---

80. The Scottish role in the civil war was crucial but less often told in accounts of the English Civil War. On the Scottish revolt, see David Stevenson, *The Scottish Revolution, 1637–1644: The Triumph of the Covenanters* (Edinburgh: John Donald, 2003).

81. Quoted in David Fuller, *English Church and State: A Short Study of Erastianism* (Morrisville, NC: Lulu Press, 2016), 48.

again without their approval—thus beginning the Long Parliament (1642–53), where both houses sat in session for half a generation.[82] Not a few members of Parliament were Puritan or at least sympathetic to Puritanism, and so the struggle with Charles immediately began to look like a theological struggle for England. The Parliament's forces—or the New Model Army—soon came under the leadership of Oliver Cromwell. He was a shrewd military mind, and he is largely credited with securing the victory for Parliament. Charles was captured, put through a trial, and beheaded in 1649.

Throwing stools and civil war thus comprised the background to the Westminster Confession of Faith, the lengthiest confession written in the Reformation. The delegates, however, were initially appointed by Parliament only as a committee to study the Thirty-Nine Articles and make suggestions on their expansion. As part of the initial collaboration with Scotland, which banded with Parliament at the start of the war, several advisers were sent to participate. The hope was to create a consensus, reform the church, and establish its confession. By and large, it failed at these goals.

The failure was not through confessional bickering within the sessions. Rather, the committee was asked to achieve something that, by 1640, was impossible: unite English Protestants. We tend to see Puritans as a single brand of Reformed theology, but, in fact, they were a motley crew with a number of different views. There were others, such as the Quakers, who were not Puritan. Within Puritanism there were groups that tended to be more radical, more antiinstitutional, such as the Congregationalists. Others were perfectly happy with a state church, even an Anglican Church, as long as some reforms were made.

Those who were invited nevertheless came to Westminster Abbey and convened their sessions on July 1, 1643. The first session met in the Henry VII Chapel (in the far back of the abbey), but most of the sessions took place in the smaller Jerusalem Chamber, one of the private rooms of the dean of Westminster that was, in fact, the same room where the King James Bible committees had met. In sum, there were 121 theologians and thirty laymen, along with the Scottish advisers.

After so many years debating the subject of worship, the delegates made sure to correct the errors that they felt were present in the Anglican Church. This was the first work they undertook, in fact, and in 1645 they issued the

---

82. Those not wishing to read full accounts of the war can find relevant material in the introductions to studies on the Westminster Confession. See Chad Van Dixhoorn, *God's Ambassadors: The Westminster Assembly and the Reformation of the English Pulpit, 1643–1653* (Grand Rapids: Reformation Heritage Books, 2017). Still useful, though dated in several ways, is the modern printing of B. B. Warfield, *The Westminster Assembly and Its Work* (Lindenhurst, NY: Great Christian Books, 2015).

Directory of Public Worship to replace the Book of Common Prayer. Parliament had ordered a revision of the Thirty-Nine Articles, not a wholesale new confession. There was not a lot of controversy over this, since the Thirty-Nine Articles had never been a sore subject for the Puritans, beyond those who felt that they needed more detail. Before long, the delegates decided not to shoehorn their work on to the existing articles, but instead to start afresh and create a new confession. They completed this work in 1646 and submitted a draft to Parliament. Everyone was pleased with the work, although Parliament wanted one addition: biblical proofs for each section. Modern Christians have laughed at the thought that the Puritans somehow forgot to use the Bible until instructed to do so by Parliament, but, in fact, it was uncommon for printed confessions at the time to list their biblical support. Nevertheless, the assembly complied and sent back the final version of what we today call the Westminster Confession of Faith.[83]

Of all the confessions we have looked at so far, the Westminster Confession was the closest to a consensus expression of Reformed theology in England. Many of the doctrines that it lays out are ones we have seen before—such as the Reformed exposition on the spiritual presence of Christ in the Lord's Supper, and the affirmation of Dordt's language of reprobation. What we should notice, however, are the places where the Westminster Confession provides newer language—or more precise language—than had existed previously in Reformed theology. On the question of Scripture, most of its teachings are similar or identical to other Protestant confessions, although the delegates added two points that were unique. First, there is a section on how to approach difficult texts in the Bible, since "All things in Scripture are not alike plain." These difficult texts, the delegates stress, must be read in the light of other verses that are clearer. Second, they added the first confessional statement about the authority of the Scriptures in the original languages, as well as an opinion on their preservation by God: the Bible was "kept pure in all ages" in the Greek and Hebrew.[84] The delegates also stress that any debate over texts must go to the original languages and not to a translation, although they also insist that the Bible must be translated into vernacular languages.

The most influential addition was the section on the covenant.[85] After the opening chapters on the Bible, God, creation, and the fall, the assembly added a chapter on the biblical covenants, and with them the basic framework of salvation. It opens with a statement that God "hath been pleased to express"

83. They also completed two catechisms—the Longer Catechism and the Shorter Catechism—the longer one for pastors and the shorter one for lay Christians.

84. Dennison, *Reformed Confessions*, 4:236. Also in *CCFCT* 2:607.

85. Dennison, *Reformed Confessions*, 4:242–43. Also in *CCFCT* 2:615–16.

Painting of the Westminster Assembly by John Rogers Herbert

salvation by means of a covenant.[86] The delegates then list two distinct covenants: the "covenant of works" made with Adam, and the "covenant of grace" for all humans ever since the fall. Of course, these are theological terms and do not originate from any specific verse but comprise the delegates' interpretation of the biblical story. Adam was given his covenant as a test: he was to obey God and not eat of the fruit. The rebellion of Adam, therefore, plunged humanity into sin, making people covenant-breakers. God extended his grace, however, by issuing a new covenant structure, albeit a temporary one. Christ's coming in human flesh was to keep the covenant of works and obey the law. In this scheme, the Westminster Confession grounded the subjects of faith in Christ not on the experience of the believer but on the need to grasp hold of Christ as the substitutionary covenant-keeper.

Despite the confession's successes, the adoption of the Westminster Standards was a different story. Even if the assembly had achieved a deft balance of theology for all English people, and even if Parliament stamped it with the authority of government, many in England had seen changes like these before. In fact, the English had developed a measure of callousness to such changes—having been ripped from Catholicism under Henry, thrust back into its bosom under Mary, restored to a kind of Protestantism under Elizabeth, and now reformed in a Puritan fashion.[87]

86. Dennison, *Reformed Confessions*, 4:242–43. Also in CCFCT 2:615–16.
87. A point made in Norman Jones, *The English Reformation: Religion and Cultural Adaptation* (Oxford: Blackwell, 2002), chap. 1.

Moreover, the measures used by Parliament to enforce and encourage the standards overstretched their purpose. In 1643, for example, clergy began to be expelled, while others were reexamined.[88] It was also assumed that lay Christians would be examined as soon as possible, to determine the seriousness of their faith. These ideas originated in Parliament, but for many it seemed that the Westminster Assembly itself was treating the majority of England as non-Christian. Their opponents, in fact, accused them of abusing their new political power—an ironic reversal of the story after the previous century. As a result, most English churches refused to embrace the Westminster Standards. Two years after Parliament ordered all churches to comply, many did not even own a copy of the Directory for Worship.

Ultimately, the fate of Westminster turned on the fate of the English crown. The lord protector, Cromwell, had founded a republic in place of the monarchy. However, since this remained a world that entangled the issues of politics and religion, to have a Congregationalist holding power in England was enough to provoke Scotland to defect. In an ironic twist, the Scots offered the crown to Charles's son—crowned Charles II—and broke faith on its allegiance to Parliament. The younger Charles was happy to accept—after all, Scotland was not responsible for his father's execution. For Scotland, though, the signs in England clearly pointed to a more radical establishment, or rather a more radical attack by Congregationalists on national synods. The views held by these radical churches not only laid the ax to the root of Anglicanism but also soon found fault with Presbyterianism.

The restoration of Charles in Scotland was followed eventually by his return to England as well, an act that ended Puritan control of the church and forced some to resettle in the now-flourishing American colonies. The Puritans thus carried the Westminster Standards with them to the colonies, while back in England the slate was wiped clean and the Anglican Church reestablished.

Conclusions

In this chapter we have seen several developments within Protestant confessionalism. First, from the Book of Concord to the Westminster Standards, the confessions created by Protestants began to turn away from disputes on the sacraments to questions about salvation. Issues such as the Third Use of the Law and predestination centered on the question of divine and human choice in

88. See Van Dixhoorn, *God's Ambassadors*, 2–4.

salvation. It is notable that the Lutheran, Reformed, and Anglican traditions had to weather storms to maintain their early grammar of salvation. But some voices in Protestantism were clearly hoping to chip away at the question of good works. The exploration of these ideas, therefore, paved the way for the eighteenth century, when movements such as Pietism and Methodism stressed both justification by faith and the obligations of Christians to holiness.

As we will see in our next chapter, however, these major Protestant confessions also smoothed over the growing din of voices that rejected the state's control of the church. In the seventeenth century, churches became voluntary societies, responsible for their own confessions. As such, the modern world, even with the Enlightenment on the rise, did not quiet the Protestant impulse to create confessions—it only fractured it into a staggering number of denominations, communities, and churches.

PART 5

Confessions in the Modern World

(1650–Present)

18

The New Grammar
of Modern Confessions

One might have thought that the end of the Reformation period in the mid-seventeenth century would lead to a pause in the writing of confessions, since most people regarded the language of creeds and confessions to be durable enough to continue serving the Christian communities well. Indeed, many in the Protestant world regarded one particular Protestant confession or another as the final word on Christian teaching and could envision no possibility of ever needing to revise that statement. To return to a metaphor we have used in various parts of this book, the grammar of Christian theology seemed to many to be fixed. But as it turned out, such fixity was illusory, and in the modern world, under the influence of both Protestant pluralism and later Enlightenment intellectual ferment, a new grammar for theology began to emerge. This led to a renewed surge in confession writing, as the old, standard confessions gave way to new ones that tended to revise previous confessions or that addressed new problems. As two historians have suggested, the transition from Reformation to modern confessions was a shift from "we believe, teach, and confess" to "I believe; help my unbelief."[1]

In this chapter we briefly survey the changing landscape of modern church confessions. We will explore those confessions in the West that altered their traditions to meet new circumstances. As we will see, nearly every Protestant tradition in America at some point changed, updated, or modified its

1. CCFCT 3:3.

confessional standards. Even some churches whose forebears had loathed any confession besides the Bible began to write confessions for the first time. Moreover, by the twentieth century, confessions had sprouted up across the globe, and so we will examine what non-Western churches offered as they began to raise their confessional voices.

This chapter will show that the desire to write confessions has actually increased in the last few centuries. The Catholic and Orthodox churches have certainly issued new definitions of their faith, but Protestants especially have rapidly increased their efforts to write confessions. The primary reason was that the Protestant fragmentation that began early in the Reformation crystallized into various denominations, and new missionary efforts exported the various versions of Protestantism around the world. New communities or churches often created new confessions. We will also note those cases where Protestant denominations revised their confessions, often to the point of creating a new standard for their churches.

Old Confessions, New World

Later in this chapter we will see that there were many tensions in twentieth-century confessions. These tensions actually started centuries earlier in Puritan England and colonial America, and so our story needs to turn back to the beginnings of the modern world. One important factor was the proximity of numerous confessional churches to one another. These churches had lived separately in Europe, but once Protestants settled in the New World, they now lived together. As a result, American Christianity was a welter of traditions that included Moravians, Quakers, Baptists, Congregationalists, Presbyterians, Anglicans, German Lutherans, and eventually growing numbers of Catholics, French Huguenots, Dutch Calvinists, and many others. This was remarkably different from European church life.[2] As a result, each church had to reckon with the possibility that laity might convert to another Protestant tradition. Added to this threat was a steady increase in what historians call the "democratization" of the New World faith—the stripping of authority from pastors, elders, and bishops, and the rising voices and opinions of those in the pews.[3] Under such democratizing forces, the old bonds of confessional identity began to erode almost immediately.

2. A longer account of this trend is Mark A. Noll, *Old Religion in a New World: The History of North American Christianity* (Grand Rapids: Eerdmans, 2001).

3. See, for example, Nathan O. Hatch, *The Democratization of American Christianity* (New Haven: Yale University Press, 1991).

Several of these trends had been present in England during the Puritan regime. Although Puritanism achieved a measure of success with the Westminster Standards, there were many groups that disagreed with some portion of its teachings. These dissenting groups fell across a spectrum, but historians refer to most of them as either Independents or Congregationalists.[4] These churches were opposed to Anglicanism, yet they did not support every teaching in the Westminster Confession.[5]

In 1596, even before the Westminster Assembly, a small group known as the Brownists drafted A True Confession. This church was founded by Robert Browne (ca. 1550–1633), a Puritan who preferred a low-church version of Congregationalism to the established church vision of the Westminster Standards. Unhappy with their prospects in England, the Brownists made up the majority of those who left on the *Mayflower* in 1620.[6] (Until Americans began to call them Pilgrims, the initial settlers in the colonies were often called Brownists.) But A True Confession revealed that while many wished to be Reformed, not everyone in England held the same views. The most important difference was that the Brownists stripped elders of the full power of ordination and excommunication, placing these prerogatives instead in the hands of "the whole body together."[7] They affirmed the value of ordination but expressed concern that authority held by only a few was ripe for abuse.

After the Westminster Assembly, other confessions were drafted in opposition to aspects of mainline Puritanism. In 1644, the First London Baptist Confession was drafted by Particular Baptists (also called Reformed Baptists).[8] This was the first attempt by Baptists to express opposition to Puritan teachings on infant baptism, and it made sure in its preamble to deny any connection between its faith and Anabaptism. The framers insisted on their Reformed identity, but they disagreed with most of the Reformed tradition on infant baptism.

4. In their day, they were known as Dissenters. Identifying distinct groups is hard, so we can use these categories only in a qualified sense.

5. On this, see the relevant sections in John Coffey and Paul C. H. Lim, eds., *The Cambridge Companion to Puritanism*, Cambridge Companions to Religion (Cambridge: Cambridge University Press, 2008).

6. The context of this is described in Nathaniel Philbrick, *Mayflower: A Story of Courage, Community, and War* (New York: Penguin, 2007).

7. James T. Dennison, ed., *Reformed Confessions of the 16th and 17th Centuries in English Translation*, 4 vols. (Grand Rapids: Reformation Heritage Books, 2008–10), 3:756. (Dennis titles it "Second Confession of London-Amsterdam.") Also in CCFCT 2:40.

8. Their opponents were known as General Baptists, who embraced Arminian teachings. On this, see Thomas S. Kidd, *Baptists in America: A History* (Oxford: Oxford University Press, 2015).

The text was based on both the Brownist True Confession and portions of the Westminster Confession of Faith. The main purpose of the confession, however, was to offer a Baptist articulation of the sacrament of baptism— not only that it should "be dispensed only upon persons professing faith" but also that the mode of baptism should be "dipping or plunging the whole body under water."[9] What this confession neglected, however, was the Lord's Supper. In fact, the confession does not mention the Lord's Supper at all, making the First London Baptist Confession a monosacramental expression of the church. Other parts of the text needed editing also, and so a corrected and expanded version was released in 1689—the Second London Baptist Confession—which then was brought to the colonies and became the Philadelphia Confession of Faith (1742).[10]

Baptists were not the only community that revised or rejected some parts of the Westminster Confession. In 1658, a group of 120 pastors of Congregationalist churches gathered at Savoy Palace in London, where they revised and shortened the Westminster Confession into the Savoy Declaration. The main issue at Savoy was the role of synods and elders in governing the church. These pastors, too, stressed their commitment to the Reformed tradition, and the confession had a preface by eminent Puritan theologian John Owen (1616–83). But the Congregationalists who had fled to the New World also felt the need to make their polity clear, which they did in 1648 in the Cambridge Platform—the first confession written in the New World. We might describe this confession as an appendix to the Brownist True Confession, since it does not discuss doctrine and instead only addresses church polity and the selection of pastors. So while we can harmonize these confessions into a Reformed tradition, we should note that as early as 1650 there was no consensus on ecclesiology or the sacraments. Those churches that differed with Westminster, therefore, felt compelled to draft alternative confessions.

The main anti-Puritan confession from England was also Baptist. Arminian thought from the Netherlands found a home in England and became popular with some Anglican priests. It also became popular with some Baptists, who later named their churches either General Baptists or Primitive Baptists. In 1651, between the First and Second London Baptist Confessions, those who conformed to the Arminian faith produced The Faith and Practice of Thirty Congregations Gathered according to the Primitive Pattern. The confession is a series of seventy-five statements, most of them expressing Protestant views in general, though they focus on the Arminian view of free or resistible grace.

9. Kidd, Baptists in America, 59.
10. Today, most Baptists who adhere to this confession affirm the latter version.

These confessions show us a key development for Protestant confessions. Rather than seeing Puritanism as the end of Protestant confessionalism, we should see this period as the beginning of something new: the separation of Protestant traditions into new denominations. The relatively small number of Protestant confessions gave way to new Protestant groups that embraced only parts of these earlier confessions. Moreover, churches increasingly felt free to revise historic confessions for their own purposes. As a result, the American colonies quickly became a tangle of denominations, each with a confession of its own.

American Confessions Revised

Perhaps the latest time at which we can identify only a handful of Protestant traditions is in the colonial period of America. Before long, however, the solvent of the new American ethos began to loosen the grip of traditional church authority. Movements such as the Great Awakenings allowed the laity to hear preaching as they chose.[11] One of the first debates in colonial churches, in fact, was over how to view these revivals, either positively or negatively.[12] These pressures in time led to the creation of new confessional churches, many of which revised their standards to fit the new spirit of revivalism.

One area with higher than normal interest in revivals was the region spanning Kentucky and Tennessee. The Presbyterian churches in these states clashed over the question of revival and the Westminster Confession's teachings on predestination. The dispute ended in a schism in their ranks and ultimately in the formation of the Cumberland Presbyterian Church in the early 1800s. The new denomination produced a new confession, which was simply the Westminster Confession updated to remove "the idea of fatality."[13] The new confession labors to maintain many of the teachings on God's providence, but not a few of its changes mimic the Arminian critique of Reformed theology, some even going beyond the Remonstrance faith. For example, under the article on original sin, the framers confess only that humankind is "inclined to evil" yet still "free and responsible . . . without the illuminating influences

11. The First Great Awakening came in the 1730s and 1740s; the Second lasted from around 1790 to 1820. See Thomas S. Kidd, *The Great Awakening: The Roots of Evangelical Christianity in Colonial America* (New Haven: Yale University Press, 2009).

12. In Reformed churches, this was known as the Old School versus New School or New Light and Old Light debate. See Sean Michael Lucas, *For a Continuing Church: The Roots of the Presbyterian Church in America* (Philipsburg, NJ: P&R, 2015).

13. *Creed and Constitution of the Cumberland Presbyterian Church* (Nashville: Cumberland Presbyterian Publishing House, 1892). Also in *CCFCT* 3:223.

of the Holy Spirit." The call of God for sinners to have faith in Christ, like the Arminian faith, "is not irresistible, but is effectual in those only who . . . freely surrender themselves."[14]

That some Presbyterians embraced Arminianism did not sit well with most Reformed theologians, who feared what seeds had been planted in their churches. The problem for some was due to confusion over the experiential faith affirmed in the Westminster Confession, which had described the need to internalize salvation and know the fruit of the salvation. To clarify this issue, therefore, the Auburn Declaration (1837) was drafted, which urges that "we bear in mind that with the excitement of excessive revivals indiscretions are sometimes intermingled."[15] The Auburn Declaration then sets out sixteen errors in applying the Westminster Confession to revivalism—problems that its framers thought forced emotionalism onto Christians in a way that led to works righteousness.

The most influential voice in the First Great Awakening was, of course, John Wesley (1703–91), an evangelist who wanted his ministry to be embraced by the Anglican Church. When the bishops in England stonewalled attempts to allow bishops in the colonies—a vital need after so many conversions— Wesley chose instead to form his own denomination, the United Societies of Wesley.[16] The new church needed a confessional identity, and Wesley opted against a new one and instead revised the Thirty-Nine Articles. Theologians have long tried to notice differences between the two confessions—attempting to deduce Wesley's intentions for removing certain phrases of the Anglican confession—but the most important addition was a comment on the new United States. The Revolutionary War had made it awkward to affiliate with the English heritage, and Wesley offered a clear statement that "the said States are a sovereign and independent nation."[17] It was unclear how an af- firmation of American government qualified as a confessional standard, but Wesley seemed to want his churches never to mistake the English origins of Methodism for anti-Americanism.

Anglicanism did eventually establish a bishop in America, although that church took longer to grow deep roots because of its connection with En- gland. The Book of Common Prayer was updated in 1892 to what can now

14. CCFCT 3:230.

15. CCFCT 3:251.

16. Also known as the Methodist Episcopal Church—the Episcopal name noting the con- nection to Anglicanism.

17. Philip Schaff, ed., *The Creeds of Christendom, with a History and Critical Notes*, 3 vols., 6th ed. revised by David Schaff (1877; repr., Grand Rapids: Baker, 1998), 3:812. Also in CCFCT 3:207.

be described as the American version of the Anglican liturgy. One of the men responsible for these revisions was William Reed Huntington (1838–1909), an Episcopal[18] priest who in 1870 published an essay suggesting that a "Quadrilateral" should serve to refashion Anglican identity in the New World. The four standards of the proposal were (1) the Bible as the ultimate standard of the faith, (2) adherence to the Apostles' and Nicene Creeds, (3) two sacraments, and (4) a church structured around the episcopal system of the ancient church. The standard here has been noted for its anticonfessional posture, its minimalism, and its cutting back from even the Thirty-Nine Articles.[19] The Quadrilateral, however, became a rallying point for modern Anglicanism, and it was adopted by the General Convention in America in Chicago (1886) and by the Lambeth Conference meeting of Anglican bishops (1888), and it has ever since been known as the Chicago-Lambeth Quadrilateral.

Perhaps the most strident alteration to a confession, however, occurred with the formation of American Lutheranism.[20] In the early 1800s, Lutheranism divided over the legacy of Luther and his unique theology. In the 1830s, German immigrants and descendants in the state of Missouri—not far from the revival heartland of Kentucky—formed the Lutheran Church–Missouri Synod.[21] They were keen to remain faithful to their heritage, especially the Book of Concord. On nearly every theological subject, they stressed the long centuries when Lutherans had always rested on these confessional standards.

In almost direct opposition to Missouri Synod churches, the mainline American Lutheran Church drew up the Definitive Synodical Platform in 1855. This became the first Lutheran confession since the Formula of Concord, and, in fact, it overturned several key articles of the historic confessions. The opening remarks cite the fact that the German church had done likewise, and so this new confession shares its view that early Lutherans had reformed only "the greater part of the errors that had crept into the Romish church." Now the Definitive Synodical Platform sought to make further changes, the bulk of which pertained to worship and sacraments. The confession removes any suggestion of baptismal regeneration or superstitious practices related to the Mass or exorcisms. Perhaps the most radical changes, however, were central to Luther's own beliefs: the presence of Christ in the Lord's Supper

18. "Episcopal" is preferred over "Anglican" in North America and Australia, though the two are synonyms.

19. On the anticonfessional tone, see Robert J. Wright, ed., *Quadrilateral at One Hundred: Essays on the Centenary of the Chicago-Lambeth Quadrilateral, 1886/88–1986/88* (Cincinnati: Forward Movement Publications, 1988), viii–ix.

20. Or the General Synod of the Evangelical Lutheran Church.

21. Today they have roughly two million members, making them the eighth-largest denomination in North America.

and the necessity of good works. The framers protest that "our writers are falsely accused of prohibiting good works," and they give several pages of argument about the necessity of holy living.[22] On the presence of Christ in the Lord's Supper, they take the critique further, and noting that although Lutherans had taught that Christ is physically in the bread and wine, they claim instead, "for this view we find no authority in Scripture." They note that they are not alone on this point, since the desire to reform this teaching "was manifested in Melanchthon himself."[23]

Not all denominations in America had historically embraced confessions. In particular, those churches descending from Anabaptist communities found the need in the New World to write confessions for the first time. The Moravians thus wrote their Easter Litany (1749), and the Mennonite Church slowly adopted the Articles of Faith written by Cornelis Ris (first edition, 1766). Even the Shaker community, founded on rigid ascetical principles as it eagerly awaited the millennial restoration of Christ, drew up its Concise Statement of the Principles of the Only True Church (1790). The Shaker confession, in fact, says nothing about traditional doctrine, but affirms only that there are four dispensations in God's plan—the fourth and last culminating in their own church. Similarly, the Seventh-day Adventist Church added its confession in 1872, which describes its framers' position on the Sabbath and the end times.

One of the earliest groups to embrace a confession was the Quakers, who had settled largely in the state of Pennsylvania. Established during the English Civil War, the Quakers referred to themselves as the Religious Society of Friends.[24] Their confession—A Confession of Faith Containing XXIII Articles (1673)—describes "the anointing, which they received" as the inward manifestation of Christ.[25] It espouses some of the same views as Arminianism, proclaiming that grace and love are universal, but also stressing that God "enlighteneth every man."[26] Most striking is the affirmation that, after the resurrection, those "that have done good, [will go] unto the resurrection of life."[27]

---

22. CCFCT 3:312–13. The original version is *Definite Platform, Doctrinal and Disciplinarian, for Evangelical Lutheran District Synods: Construed in Accordance with the Principles of the General Synod*, 2nd ed. (Philadelphia: Miller & Burlock, 1856).

23. CCFCT 3:314.

24. Like many historic names—for example, "Puritan" and "Methodist"—the name "Quaker" was first used to mock the group that bore it, in this case because of the group's experiential form of worship.

25. CCFCT 3:137.

26. CCFCT 3:141.

27. CCFCT 3:148.

Churches in the twentieth century followed this same pattern, writing their own standards where they had possessed none previously. For example, the twentieth century was shaped profoundly by the Pentecostal movement. Emerging in the late 1800s, born from the Second Great Awakening, Pentecostalism first received national attention at the Azusa Street Revival (1906–15).[28] The Pentecostal form of worship was much like a Quaker service, though with a strong emphasis on speaking in tongues and miraculous healing. From these grassroots movements arose denominations such as the Assemblies of God, which was one of the earliest Pentecostal denominations. The Assemblies of God formed in 1914 and two years later drafted A Statement of Fundamental Truths—the first Pentecostal confession. The confession made sure that its churches knew that this was "not intended as a creed for the church, nor as a basis of fellowship among Christians." Still, its framers do claim that its theology "is held to be essential to a full gospel ministry."[29]

On most points of theology, the Assemblies of God confess their Protestant identity. They affirm the Trinity, original sin, and justification by faith.[30] They include, however, articles about distinctive Pentecostal beliefs on worship. In fact, A Statement of Fundamental Truths was the first confession to require "baptism in the Holy Ghost," which is "indicated by the initial sign of speaking in tongues." The framers affirm traditional practices of baptism and the Lord's Supper, but they add that miraculous healing "is provided for in the atonement, and is the privilege of all believers."[31] They end the confession by affirming the resurrection of the dead and restoration of creation, but they add a specific article that churches must affirm "the premillennial and imminent coming of the Lord."[32]

It might be expected that denominations in the New World simply carried over their confessions when they emigrated. However, in almost every denomination, there were additions to older confessions that addressed new situations or changes in belief, and in some instances, new confessions were written at the formation of new denominations. Indeed, the period from 1650 to 1900 did not see the end of confessions but a rapid increase of churches writing new confessions.

28. On Azusa Street, see Cecil M. Robeck, *The Azusa Street Mission and Revival: The Birth of the Global Pentecostal Movement* (Nashville: Thomas Nelson, 2017).

29. CCFCT 3:427.

30. They later affirm that the terms "Trinity" and "persons," while not in the Bible, "yet are words in harmony with Scripture." CCFCT 3:429.

31. CCFCT 3:428–29.

32. CCFCT 3:431.

The Catholic Faith and Ecumenism

For several centuries after the Council of Trent (1545–63), the Catholic Church took no positive steps toward other Christian traditions. The single issue that dominated the papacy from 1750 on, in fact, was the question of how to combat the rise of Enlightenment philosophies and the encroachment of political power into church matters. These issues were the central reason for Pope Pius IX's calling of the First Vatican Council (1869–70) to deal with rationalism and materialism. The pope had good reason to worry, since he had lost nearly all the territory known as the Papal States—the midsection of the Italian peninsula controlled by the pope since at least the eighth century. At this point he controlled only the city of Rome itself, and the papacy would soon lose even that (although in the early twentieth century it was given the small territory of Vatican City as an independent state). Within the church, there were also siren calls to embrace the new views of rational thinking and materialism—views clearly in opposition to Christian orthodoxy. For Pius, these problems were grounds for a more aggressive war.

In the run-up to Vatican I, Pius IX waged war on two fronts—philosophical and political—through two major promulgations. First, in 1854, he promulgated the bull *Ineffabilis Deus*, which made the belief that Mary was conceived free of sin official Catholic teaching.[33] Almost immediately, those in the Catholic Church who wanted an updated theology, more in step with rationalism, recoiled at this teaching. In response to this, Pius then issued his Syllabus of Errors in 1864. This document listed not only naturalism and "absolute rationalism"[34] as problems facing the church but even "moderate rationalism" and those who would say that "Protestantism is nothing else than a different form of the same Christian religion."[35] Even before Vatican I, therefore, Pius already embodied the sterner posture of Catholicism—one that allowed for unity only for those who submitted to the church.

Vatican I was called in the spirit of this protest against secularism, and this was the first council since Trent more than three hundred years earlier. Following the direction set by Pius, the council issued several rulings, the most important of which was The Dogmatic Constitution of the Church of Christ in 1870. The council saw its role as extending those heresies "condemned by the fathers of Trent."[36] The document walks through Catholic claims about

---

33. This is known as the Immaculate Conception today. Non-Catholics sometimes confuse this doctrine with the virginal conception of Jesus.

34. Under article 1 (see Schaff, *Creeds of Christendom*, 2:213–16). Also in *CCFCT* 3:325.

35. Schaff, *Creeds of Christendom*, 2:216. Also in *CCFCT* 3:326–27.

36. Schaff, *Creeds of Christendom*, 2:216. Also in *CCFCT* 3:343.

the authority of St. Peter and the way that authority was passed down until the modern papacy. The council then concludes with a final word on the "infallible teaching authority of the Roman pontiff."[37]

In the twentieth century, the Catholic Church turned away from merely rejecting modern theology—though it never liberalized—and pursued more ecumenically open relationships with other Christian traditions. The door to this was opened at the Second Vatican Council (1963–65), which Pope John XXIII called, he said, to let fresh air into the church. One of the most debated statements of Vatican II was *Lumen Gentium*, which seemed to offer a new path toward unity with Orthodox and Protestant churches. After defining the church as "one, holy, catholic, and apostolic," the document goes on to say that "this church, set up and organized in the world as a society, *subsists in* the Catholic Church . . . outside its structure many elements of sanctification and of truth are to be found."[38] One of the most debated religious issues in the twentieth century was how Catholics were to understand the words "subsists in," though many found it generous enough to open dialogue with non-Catholics for the first time.

One document that has become central to Catholic conversations with other traditions is Baptism, Eucharist, and Ministry—sometimes called the Lima Document or the BEM—which was drafted in 1982. One might say that optimism was high after Vatican II, only to leave Catholic leaders frustrated over debates that they felt needed further clarification. These three topics—the two sacraments and ordination—were those most cited as barriers to unity. Today, the BEM document continues to be used in talks between Catholic and Protestant churches.

So far, however, the willingness of the Catholic Church to dialogue with other traditions has yielded uneven results. One positive result, which we already noted in chapter 5, was a joint declaration implying that the Assyrian Church of the East—often called Nestorian in Western textbooks—in fact does not affirm the teachings of Nestorianism. After a series of talks with Catholic representatives, both churches circulated their Common Christological Declaration in 1994, which claims that the fifth-century division between the two churches was largely due to misunderstanding the terms. This declaration allowed a millennia-old schism to be at least partially healed and was based on the willingness of the pope to use different theological terms than

37. Schaff, *Creeds of Christendom*, 2:219. Also in CCFCT 3:356.

38. Norman P. Tanner, ed., *Decrees of the Ecumenical Councils*, vol. 2, *Trent to Vatican II* (Washington, DC: Georgetown University Press, 1990), 854 (emphasis added). Also in CCFCT 3:578. This is sometimes referred to as the *Subsistit In* controversy based on the Latin words behind "subsists in."

the church normally used for the sake of clarity in a certain situation. Similar conversations were held between Pope John Paul II and Bartholomew I, the ecumenical patriarch of Constantinople, leading to two documents both known as the Common Declaration (1994 and 1996). Neither attempted to bridge the divide between the churches, but both express an ongoing desire to see an end to the schism between them. It is likely that these continued talks will be part of the story of the twenty-first century.

Catholic agreements with Protestants, however, were both successful and unsuccessful. In 1994, for example, a group of evangelical and Catholic leaders met in the United States and drafted Evangelicals and Catholics Together (or ECT).[39] The document was based largely on the need to stress a shared worldview during the culture wars brought on by the Moral Majority, and so ECT does not discuss issues from the Reformation, especially justification by faith. This omission led to criticism of the entire approach taken by ECT. Similar criticisms were raised when the Lutheran World Federation and the Catholic Church issued the Joint Declaration on the Doctrine of Justification in 1999. The text paradoxically affirms accord on the doctrine of justification while at the same time stressing that the Council of Trent was not overruled. Indeed, it argues that the condemnations are still in effect and serious enough to serve as a warning to Christians.[40] This uncertain language raised the alarm in Lutheran circles, but the document has since been embraced by the World Methodist Council (in 2006) and recently by the World Communion of Reformed Churches (in 2017).

Perhaps the best way to understand the Catholic Church's stances in ecumenical talks is to recognize its need to affirm all prior decisions by the church, while also seeking to heal the schisms created in history. For this reason, any possible unity will always turn on the subject of prior confessional grammar, which will always be normative for the Catholic faith.

Global Confessions of Critique

One of the most important influences on the modern church has been globalization. We should remember that the church was very global in its first millennium, but for much of its second millennium, it was largely—though not completely—confined to Europe and then North America. Between 1850 and 2000, however, the church became largely a church of the Global South.

---

39. See Charles W. Colson and Richard John Neuhaus, eds., *Evangelicals and Catholics Together: Toward a Common Mission* (Dallas: Word, 1995).

40. The text can be found in *CCFCT* 3:878–88.

This was perhaps the single largest change in Christian history.[41] As the church grew in the south, it not only drafted new confessions, but these confessions often focused on issues not mentioned in earlier Protestant confessions, especially the concerns of suffering and poverty.

These new issues often led to confessional works that either offered a critique of Western oppression or searched their own confessional faith to answer a crisis. In the United States, for example, the African Orthodox Church was founded in 1921 as a response to the Jim Crow era. Its founders wanted to lay claim to their Christian identity, and they did so by rejecting the Protestant faith that had supported slavery in North America. The church's confession, therefore, sides with the Catholic faith on most issues save the recognition of the pope as head of the church. The framers affirm seven sacraments, "reverence of relics of the holy saints of God," and "the true doctrine of transubstantiation."[42] Methodist churches felt the same need for over a century. Black Christians who had converted during the Wesleyan revivals continued to endure racism, and they came to see their treatment as a betrayal of biblical principles. At revivals, all who received Christ were promised equality, but in the churches, things had never changed. In 1787, at St. George's in Philadelphia, black members were dragged off their knees during a time of prayer and told to leave. Weary of such treatment, Richard Allen and others formed the Free African Society, which became the African Methodist Episcopal (AME) denomination. In this case, however, creating an autonomous church did not mean creating a new confession; the AME denomination kept the Wesleyan revision of the Thirty-Nine Articles as its standard.

The most poignant confessional critiques came after the rise of liberation theology—a collection of ideas and teachings that called the church to address the severe poverty in South America. The Methodist Church of Brazil, for example, issued a call for "awareness of social responsibility" in its Social Creed of 1971.[43] The Methodist church in Korea issued a similar call for social justice in 1973 in its Theological Declaration, as did the Presbyterian church of Cuba in its Confession of Faith (1977).[44] In Honduras, the majority Catholic Church issued a Credo in Mass of the Marginalized People in 1980, confessing that God is "father to the poor, because all are of value in your eyes."[45]

41. On these shifts, see Todd M. Johnson and Cindy M. Wu, *Our Global Families: Christians Embracing Common Identity in a Changing World* (Grand Rapids: Baker Academic, 2015).

42. Arthur Cornelius Terry-Thompson, *The History of the African Orthodox Church* (New York: Beacon, 1956), 44. Also in *CCFCT* 3:436.

43. This was modeled after the American Methodist Social Creed of 1908.

44. Texts can be found in *CCFCT* 3:743, 761 (respectively).

45. Hans-Georg Link, ed., *Confessing Our Faith around the World*, vol. 3, *The Caribbean and Central America*, Faith and Order Paper 123 (Geneva: World Council of Churches, 1984), 45. Also in *CCFCT* 3:796.

Even the Catholic Church has experienced schisms, notably in the formation of the Philippine Independent Church, which split from Rome in 1902 and has since become the national church of the Philippines (although the Roman Catholic Church has continued in that country and far outnumbers the Philippine Independent Church). The reason for its rejection of Roman obedience was the pope's support of the Spanish occupation and oppression in the Philippines—a brutal regime that had ended only with the Philippine Revolution in the 1890s. In 1947, the church issued the Declaration of the Faith and Articles of Religion, confessing many traditional Catholic beliefs but coming to nearly Protestant views on some subjects. For example, the framers affirm the right of priests to marry and state that "salvation is obtained only through a vital faith in Jesus Christ." The confession also rejects the use of the Latin language in worship, affirming the need for vernacular Bibles. The framers nevertheless retain seven sacraments, veneration of the saints, and the view that the altar is where Jesus is present in the sacrament.[46]

One of the more painful confessions written during this time came from the Presbyterian Church of South Africa between 1979 and 1981, as the nation struggled to overcome the ravages of apartheid. That church issued a Declaration of Faith that calls for Christians to affirm that God created humanity "to live together as brothers and sisters in one family." The framers discuss the death and resurrection of Christ as achieving victory over division—"to break down every separating barrier and to unite all people into one body." They then call on everyone in church and society "to seek reconciliation and unity."[47]

Some of the confessions that offered critique managed to do so with a charitable spirit. For example, the Church of Toraja in Indonesia released its Confession in 1981, in which the framers attempted to explore their commitment to the Reformed tradition, while also rejecting what they found problematic in modern churches. They affirm the biblical canon and stress, as Protestant confessions had done, that the Bible alone is the standard for doctrine. But they add to this a strong counterclaim:

> Exegesis is the attempt of believers to understand the word of God, so that it can be applied in their situation here and now. . . . The Bible is a book of the history of God's saving activity, which calls mankind to believe. . . . The Bible

46. The text is found in CCFCT 3:526–31.
47. Lukas Vischer, ed., *Reformed Witness Today: A Collection of Confessions and Statements of Faith Issued by Reformed Churches* (Bern: Evangelische Arbeitsstelle Oekumene Schweiz, 1982), 27. Also in CCFCT 3:794.

is not a handbook of knowledge, and therefore it may not be contrasted with scientific principles.[48]

Other qualifications like this can be found throughout the *Confession*. The framers affirm substitutionary atonement, the three marks of the church, and a Reformed view of the sacraments, but they add to this the problem of "socioeconomic structures" in society, as well as "the inclination of man to misuse knowledge and technology for his own interests."[49]

The Barmen Declaration

The year 1934 saw the drafting of perhaps the best-known confession of the twentieth century, the Barmen Declaration.[50] The primary author was Karl Barth (1886–1968), likely the most influential theologian of the twentieth century (at least in European and American churches). Barth drafted the text in preparation for a meeting in Barmen, Germany, where pastors and theologians from a variety of confessional churches edited the text into its final form. That the statement involved the blending of Lutheran, Reformed, and other Protestant traditions pointed to a major new feature of modern confessions: the desire for ecumenical breadth. It is impossible to imagine the Barmen Declaration being written in earlier centuries. It proclaims that "we stand together" and "we are bound together" in a plain affirmation of a Protestant identity. The same traditions that once led people to shed one another's blood over their separate confessions were now tied together with the softer bonds of Protestant unity. But the churches at Barmen also professed their willingness "to remain faithful to our various Confessions."[51]

The origin of the Barmen Declaration was the rise of totalitarianism in Europe after World War I, which now seemed poised to launch a second war. For this reason, the confession attempted to give a prophetic call to all of Germany against "the ruling church party of the 'German Christians,'" which Barth claims had abandoned historic beliefs for the sake of "prevailing ideological and political convictions."[52] This was no mewling attempt

---

48. Vischer, *Reformed Witness Today*, 49. Also in CCFCT 3:800.

49. Vischer, *Reformed Witness Today*, 49–50. Also in CCFCT 3:805–6.

50. For a study of its origins, see Rolf Ahlers, *The Barmen Theological Declaration of 1934: The Archaeology of a Confessional Text*, Toronto Studies in Theology 24 (Lewiston, NY: Edwin Mellen, 1986).

51. Arthur C. Cochrane, ed., *Reformed Confessions of the Sixteenth Century* (Louisville: Westminster John Knox, 2003), 334. Also in CCFCT 3:506–7.

52. Cochrane, *Reformed Confessions*, 335. Also in CCFCT 3:506–7.

to admire the past and weep for the future; the Barmen Declaration was an assault on the modern notion that political life must encompass all aspects of human life. "We reject the false notion," the confession continues, that the state "could become the single and totalitarian order of human life, thus fulfilling the church's vocation."[53]

Surprisingly, the Barmen Declaration never gives a full, theological justification for its claims. Instead, it anchors its political voice to "the confessions of the Reformation," but leaves it open to each church to interpret this assertion within its own tradition. In other words, the paradox of Barmen (and other modern confessions) is that, in order to draw enough Protestants to the table, framers of a new confession had to give the confessional identity of each tradition a lower status than it had historically held. It was unlikely that those at Barmen could have achieved unity on the same doctrines over which their Reformation predecessors had been divided. To give one example, confessional Lutherans and Reformed still disagreed on the presence of Christ in the Eucharist. If the Barmen Declaration wanted to rest on Reformation confessions, its framers certainly did not want to repeat the divisions of the Marburg Colloquy.[54]

A new confession thus required a new approach to confessional identity. As a result, Barmen allows us to see the most important changes in the development of modern confessions: (1) they avoided issues that might create strife or division, and (2) they nearly always couched their texts in the language of the moment. Indeed, rare was the confession in the modern church that covered traditional debates on the Trinity, Christ, salvation, or the sacraments. Like the Barmen Declaration, these new confessions affirm a wider Protestant identity beyond that of a single tradition. Thus, one could say that the Barmen Declaration and others like it are *minimalist* confessions, refraining from language that divided, focusing on the task at hand. Often, such confessions rest on little more than creedal orthodoxy and the Reformation teachings on justification. Many say little or nothing about the sacraments. Almost all attempt to include as many views as possible, rather than exclude them.

The (Revised) Confessions of the Nations

At times, changes in confessions were not made in opposition to other groups of Christians, but instead were attempts to express the Christian faith in a new part of the world. In Korea, for example, the Methodist church issued

---

53. Cochrane, *Reformed Confessions*, 336. Also in CCFCT 3:508.
54. See our discussion in chap. 14.

its Doctrinal Statement in 1930, which speaks highly of the importance of "Mr. Wesley" and his interpretation of the New Testament. The Korean Methodist church, however, does not hesitate to affirm "that we should state the chief doctrines" of the Methodist confession. It provides eight articles, each only a sentence long, that are the core doctrines to be embraced by pastors—for example, the Trinity, forgiveness of sins, the Bible, church, and resurrection.

Interestingly, only a few global confessions resisted Western influence by translating the basic language of a confession into the idiom of different languages. Missionaries in East Africa, for example, found it appropriate to take basic creedal statements—even the Apostles' Creed itself—and tweak them for the Maasai (in modern Kenya and Tanzania). The text begins, "We believe in the one High God, who out of love created the beautiful world and everything good in it." Jesus is "a man in the flesh, a Jew by tribe, born poor in a little village, who left his home and was always on safari doing good," and he later died on the cross "but the hyenas did not touch him."[55] But such striking cultural accommodation was rare in global confessions. Instead, what occurred most often was that the lengthier confessions of Protestants (and in some cases Catholics) were pared down to be almost the same length as the Apostles' Creed. For example, the Evangelical Church of Togo released Our Faith in 1971, a confession that consists of four truths: God has a plan for this world, sin impedes this plan, Jesus came to accomplish God's plan of redemption, and the church community serves in the power of the Holy Spirit.[56]

In Ghana, there was a purposeful attempt to get beyond the Protestant division that had come to Ghana through the various missionaries who founded churches in the country. In 1965, Ghana commissioned a Union Committee, which issued The Faith of the Church as a path to achieve a unified Protestant church in that country. Those present at the discussions were Anglican, Methodist, Mennonite, and two denominations of Presbyterianism. The call for unity did not last, but the belief that the West imported such divisions was notably different from the way churches around the world saw Protestant traditions.

In South Africa, the same tensions played a role in the Reformed churches, although the impact of these confessions on the West has been mixed. The primary issue stemmed from the bleak history of apartheid, since the

55. Vincent J. Donovan, *Christianity Rediscovered*, 2nd ed. (Maryknoll, NY: Orbis, 1982), 200. Also in *CCFCT* 3:569.

56. Hans-Georg Link, ed., *Confessing Our Faith around the World*, vol. 2, *Africa, Asia, Australia, Europe, and North America*, Faith and Order Paper 120 (Geneva: World Council of Churches, 1983), 5. Also in *CCFCT* 3:737.

majority-white churches had either supported apartheid or turned a blind eye to the oppressive policies that grew out of it. These problems were felt most keenly in the Dutch Reformed churches, since the Dutch had played the largest role in shaping the policies of apartheid. By the twentieth century, each Reformed group had supported this legacy of racism and oppression. The problem in each denomination was that many opposed any admission of guilt and had a history of interpreting the Bible in a way that supported oppression. To combat these beliefs, nearly all of these denominations looked to create new confessions that could express the need for social change in their churches.

The tide began to turn in the 1960s, when the Dutch Reformed Mission Church in South Africa overturned its founding documents and, in 1962, began to receive members of all ethnic or social backgrounds. Changes in policy led to calls for new confessional statements to encourage further reconciliation with native South African Christians. As Jaroslav Pelikan and Valerie Hotchkiss point out, the churches were split over the New Testament command to obey political rulers (Rom. 13), which some understood as a call for the church to remain silent on social matters.[57] But after so many centuries of racism, the church desired to speak.

The first statement written as a confession came from the Broederkring, a group of lay and clergy leaders from several Reformed denominations called together to advance the cause of peace and unity within the South African church, as well as to oppose those who had dug in their heels against cultural change. The group issued a Theological Declaration in 1979. The text is more creedal than confessional. It has only four articles, using a trinitarian rubric to affirm social justice. Under the first article, which confesses belief in the "Father of Jesus Christ," it adds that God "struggles for his own righteousness with regard to God and fellow man. In this respect God chooses constantly for his own righteousness and consequently stands on the side of those who are victims of injustice." The confession then concludes,

> In our South African situation this means that we as part of the church of Christ in this world should unflinchingly persevere for establishing God's justice. The church may, in faithful allegiance to its Head, Jesus Christ, come into conflict with human authorities. If the church has to suffer in the process we know that this is part of the way of God's people through history and that the word of Christ remains in force, "I will never leave you or forsake you." (Heb. 13:5)[58]

57. CCFCT 3:793.
58. "Broederkring: Theological Declaration (1979)." http://kerkargief.co.za/doks/bely/DF_Broederkring.pdf.

This final article is important since it gives a clear statement about the context ("our South African situation") without assuming that such needs were shared by other nations. Still, the language was broad enough to ensure that the confession was not read as being relevant only to South Africa.

That same year another confession, the Declaration of Faith, was issued by the Life and Work Committee of the Presbyterian Church in South Africa, and this confession was adopted two years later by their General Assembly. It takes a similar approach, basing the need for justice on God's triune personhood. The Father is both creator and the one "who wants all people to live together as brothers and sisters in one family." The Son is the one who came not only to die and be raised for our sins but also "to break down every separating barrier of race, culture, or class, and to unite all people into one body." And finally, the Spirit is the pledge of Christ's return and serves "to warn that God judges both individual and the nation."[59]

In a sense, these South African confessions are actually quasi-creedal, because they are organized with an article about each of the persons of the Trinity. But unlike ancient creeds, these articles on the persons are tied together with statements about the implications of the Christian faith, at least about the implications of the faith for achieving unity in the fractured South African situation.

Of these confessions, the one that generated both high praise and sharp criticism was the Belhar Confession, first drafted in 1982 by the Dutch Reformed Mission Church (majority black), inspired largely by the leadership of Allan Boesak. It was then adopted formally in 1986 by the Dutch Reformed Church in Southern Africa (majority white). It has since been adopted by several Reformed and Presbyterian churches outside South Africa, such as the Reformed Church in America in 2010 and the Presbyterian Church (USA) in 2014. It became one of the foundational documents for merging several denominations into the Uniting Reformed Church in South Africa in 1994. The Belhar Confession, therefore, has been widely adopted by churches in both South Africa and North America, and this widespread use raised its profile beyond that of earlier South African confessions and has since inspired study and debate.

Like the earlier South African confessions, Belhar was based on a quasi-creedal formula, although its structure is less obviously trinitarian. It opens by stating, "We believe in the triune God, Father, Son and Holy Spirit, who gathers, protects and cares for the church through Word and Spirit."[60] Belhar then offers little else in terms of explicit creedal or confessional language.

59. Vischer, *Reformed Witness Today*, 27. Also in CCFCT 3:794.
60. "Confession of Belhar." https://www.rca.org/resources/confession-belhar.

Most notably, nothing is said about the work of Christ or redemption (though there is an oblique reference to "Word and Spirit" conquering the powers of sin and death and references to the work of reconciliation). There is not even a mention of older Protestant confessions that might undergird its new doctrines. Of course, the confession does not reject these doctrines or confessions, and even without direct references to them, Belhar conforms to the pattern of other modern confessions as *expansions* of older Protestant confessions. Thus, the second article describes the unity of the church as a group "called from the entire human family." From this foundation, it issues twenty affirmations and six doctrines to be rejected, all centered on social justice and unity.

Not surprisingly, the Belhar Confession favors social justice without qualification. Unity in the church is "both a gift and an obligation," and so it was "a binding force." Belhar also stresses that unity must be visible, not simply couched in the language of the invisible church. It then stresses that this unity cannot be coerced in Christians:

> This unity can be established only in freedom and not under constraint; that the variety of spiritual gifts, opportunities, backgrounds, convictions, as well as the various languages and cultures, are by virtue of the reconciliation in Christ, opportunities for mutual service and enrichment within the one visible people of God.[61]

Article 3 then carries the logic further, stating that reconciliation is necessary for all churches. Because sin and death are conquered, "therefore also irreconciliation and hatred, bitterness and enmity [are conquered]." It also states that evangelism and missions are thwarted in any nation where this is not an authentic part of Christian experience.

The fourth article of Belhar reaches back to the earlier Reformed confessions from South Africa, situating each of its proclamations in the being of God. The triune God "has revealed himself as the one who wishes to bring about justice," and "in a special way [to be] the God of the destitute, the poor and the wronged."[62] To make this point stronger, Belhar rehearses numerous biblical passages and phrases that reveal God's heart for the poor, such as that undefiled religion is "to visit orphans and widows in their affliction" (James 1:27). The article then concludes controversially:

> The church must therefore stand by people in any form of suffering and need, which implies, among other things, that the church must witness against and

61. "Confession of Belhar."
62. "Confession of Belhar."

strive against any form of injustice, so that justice may roll down like waters, and righteousness like an ever-flowing stream . . . namely against injustice and with the wronged; that in following Christ the church must witness against all the powerful and privileged who selfishly seek their own interests and thus control and harm others.[63]

Since later criticism of Belhar almost always focused on this passage, it is important to realize the debate was not over what it said, but what it did *not* say. After the first three articles, this fourth article expands the framers' vision, requiring not only unity and reconciliation in the church but also that the church stand against injustice in all public arenas. In addition to public issues, the church must side with people "in any form of suffering and need." Those who criticized this statement pointed out that no further guidelines are given to determine real need from the needs based on culture. (More on this in a moment.)

The doctrines rejected by Belhar, by contrast, focus on teachings that silence or delegitimize the work of reconciliation or social justice. It rejects anything "which absolutizes either natural diversity or the sinful separation of people in such a way that this absolutization hinders or breaks the visible and active unity of the church." It excoriates those who hold that Christians of the same confession "are in effect alienated from one another" though policies of racism or apartheid, that "sanctions in the name of the gospel or of the will of God the forced separation of people on the grounds of race and color and thereby in advance obstructs and weakens the ministry and experience of reconciliation in Christ."[64] In the end, all beliefs that reinforce or affirm injustice are contrary to the confession of Belhar.

When placed against the backdrop of other modern confessions, the Belhar Confession is unsurprising in the course it takes. It declines to affirm those doctrines already expressed in other confessions, giving only indirect mention of these beliefs, and expresses its articles as a coda to the wider Protestant symphony. The language of the Belhar Confession, however, also reveals why some have cast doubt on modern confessions. As we pointed out above, Belhar is a confession written in the language of a creed, but for all the positive statements against racism and injustice, and for its heroic stance against apartheid after centuries of oppression, the language is so broad that it could apply to *any* struggle for inclusion and unity. The Belhar Confession claims in the strongest of terms the need for unity, insisting that the very being of God demands unity and justice. But with no rationale for how to settle disputed issues, or any language that defines which issues are truly for

63. "Confession of Belhar."
64. "Confession of Belhar."

the sake of justice and which issues compromise biblical ethics, the Belhar Confession opened the door to confusion. For example, Boesak, perhaps the main influence behind Belhar, later claimed that the confession expected the church to embrace those from the LGBT community. The Reformed churches in South Africa sided against Boesak on this, claiming the matter of injustice was focused only on apartheid, racism, and systemic oppression. As a result, Boesak broke with the church.[65]

The Belhar Confession is a good example of the challenges faced by modern confessions. Modern confessions that created a sustainable message or that had a wide impact usually present articles that are both cautious and focused, making clear the framers' commitment to older Protestant confessions while also insisting on the need for a new confession. As we have seen in this book, Protestants from the beginning wrote confessions that were designed to address the needs of the moment. Modern confessions fit easily within this tradition. But local confessions, both in older or modern forms, always served the church best when they clarified the specific problems that were on the table. The Belhar Confession, for example, was not criticized for speaking against injustice but for making unclear what forms of injustice fell within the scope of biblical orthodoxy. Without at least some language to govern the discussion, it left itself open to widely divergent interpretations. In other words, for modern Protestant confessions to make a lasting impact, they need to be more overtly confessional rather than quasi-creedal.

Conclusions

In this chapter we have looked at a handful of the dozens of confessional texts from the modern church—indeed, for the sake of space, we could survey only a small portion of these writings. We have noted first that confessions in the West did not slow down after the Reformation. Just as churches fragmented into various denominations, it was only natural for these new churches to form their own identity using confessions. Even today, after the rise of the parachurch and nondenominational movements, we still see the same pattern—so much so that it would be difficult to find a Christian body that never drafts a confessional standard. If the Western churches have embraced individualism and autonomy—values created by the Enlightenment—then they have not ceased to be confessional, but instead have found themselves free to define themselves according to new confessions.

---

65. Boesak's career was not without controversy, which included conviction for fraud. Boesak later received a pardon.

Perhaps the most dramatic change to modern confessions came under the influence of the global church, which embraced confessions but curbed its message to a simplicity that was almost creedal. Not all in either Protestant or Catholic churches, we argued, were in opposition to the West. However, as the global church has raised its voice, there has also been a clear call from the Global South against those churches that either endorsed oppression or turned a blind eye to the suffering of fellow Christians.

Conclusion

This book started with a simple affirmation about our faith: Christianity begins not with a set of doctrines but with a name—the name of Christ our Lord. This Lord commanded us to baptize in the name of the Father, and of the Son, and of the Holy Spirit (Matt. 28:19). We confess who Christ is in relation to God, and we believe the fundamental truths about him—his incarnation, life, death, and resurrection. Thus, doctrines do not begin as abstract principles but instead start with a person, Christ—indeed, with three persons: the Father, his Son Jesus Christ, and the Holy Spirit, all revealed in Scripture.

From this simple starting point, the long and complex story of creeds and confessions has shown us that, throughout the centuries, Christians have consistently gathered to describe their faith. The creeds and confessions were short or long, simple or complex, but from them we see the efforts of their framers to find the terms both to *confess* the ones in whom we believe and to *express* the truths of Christian orthodoxy. We suggested that the process of confessing and expressing was the way the church developed the *grammar* of faith. The unfolding story was like our childhood: first we learned to speak, then to speak properly, and still later to articulate why this expression was proper and that one wasn't, via the rules of grammar. No parent scolds a toddler for clumsy speech or grammatical mistakes, but we expect more from adult conversationalists, and we believe that adults can express love and intimacy better by knowing how to use their words well. So this development of Christian grammar, leading to more exact and precise expressions, has led believers in history to *more intimacy* with Christ, not less. In the same way, our study of this development should lead *us* to more intimacy with Christ.

As we have watched the church learn its grammar, we have seen that the story often was not free of controversy. The Christians responsible for the creeds and confessions were sinners like the rest of us, and thus prone to less-than-ideal motives, conflicting interests, and unholy ambitions. This combustible mix of less-than-perfect attitudes often led to atrocious actions—bitterness, quarrels, even bloodshed and religious war. Admittedly, there have been times when the story has sounded dreadful. We admit that at times the story *was* dreadful.

But while conspiracies, accidental or even willful misunderstanding, misrepresentation of others' views, and even murder have been part of the story, perhaps they sometimes occupy too much of our attention. It is easy to cast the Council of Ephesus in 431 or the Marburg Colloquy in 1529 as stories of bullheaded theologians missing the point of Christ's love. And maybe these gatherings *were* run by bullheaded theologians—but maybe, too, something more important than we realize was going on there. Maybe the issues at stake were not trivial issues in Christian theology. Even if Nestorius and Cyril, or Martin Luther and Huldrych Zwingli, found the other view absurd, and even if their meetings were at times divisive, the fact remains that they were attempting to resolve the issue for the sake of bearing witness to Christ. Both sides recognized that we must say *something* about God. If they disagreed on the appropriate words to *describe* their faith, and even if we have to declare that one side or another was wrong or even *heretical* (as most of us do in the case of Nestorius, but few of us do in the case of Zwingli or Luther), the best way to bear such witness is to wrestle seriously with the language we use to describe our faith.

So without obscuring the failures of theologians, we have sought in our story to emphasize the common heritage that we share—the creeds first, and then the confessions that have shaped our various Christian traditions. We have suggested that the difference between creeds and confessions was more than their length or their age. We showed that creeds were, by definition, statements of allegiance to the persons of God. Building on the creeds, confessions served to define a given Christian community over against other communities—especially after the Reformation, with the emergence of various Protestant traditions. The story of creeds was, to a substantial degree, a united story, although fault lines emerged in the different ways the East and the West interpreted those creeds and the theology behind them. In contrast, the story of confessions was a fragmented story from the beginning. Today, though, that fragmentation is being partially undone as Christians pay serious attention not only to their own confessions but also to the confessions of other Christian traditions. So the church as a whole may now be moving past its confessional fracturing to a fuller appreciation of the creedal unity behind the confessions. The story of creeds and confessions is perhaps coming full circle.

This last point—the return to creedal unity—may be the most important result of the spread of Christian faith around the globe. Missionaries have found it impossible to impose confessional demands devised for a certain context on new communities of faith that dwell in utterly different circumstances. In sixteenth-century Europe and eighteenth-century America, the issues that dominated divergent confessions truly seemed to be of foremost importance. But in a global church struggling with persecution, injustice, poverty, secularization, and countless dehumanizing forces, it is hard to continue elevating the issues of distinctive identities above the common Christian loyalty to Jesus Christ confessed in the creeds. Creedal commonality has always been the basis for confessional distinctives, but it has long been easy to ignore this fact. Now, however, this fact is reemerging from the shadows into bright sunlight. Perhaps one of the most important things that the West continues to learn from global Christianity is that we can be one faith, one family—not in spite of our different confessions, but because we realize that our first bond of unity is in our common creed. With Christians throughout the world and at all points in history, we affirm, "We believe in one God the Father All Governing. . . . And in one Lord Jesus Christ, the only-begotten Son of God. . . . And in the Holy Spirit, the Lord and life-giver."[1]

---

1. From the Nicene Creed, in *Creeds of the Churches: A Reader in Christian Doctrine, from the Bible to the Present*, ed. John H. Leith, 3rd ed. (Atlanta: Westminster John Knox, 1982), 33. Also in CCFCT 1:163.

Index